# ENVIRONMENTAL LAW, THE ECONOMY AND SUSTAINABLE DEVELOPMENT

This book provides a comparative analysis of environmental regulation in multi-jurisdictional legal and political systems, focusing on the United States, the European Union, and the international community. Each of these systems must deal with environmental interdependencies that cross local borders, in some cases creating regional problems, such as acid deposition, ozone-type smog, and pollution of shared water bodies. Some transjurisdictional environmental problems are global, including stratospheric ozone depletion, climate change, and the loss of biodiversity. Other environmental problems, however, are localized in their effect on health and the environment: for example, municipal waste disposal, many forms of pollution and resource development, and drinking water quality. These varying jurisdictional and environmental circumstances pose the central question of how responsibility for addressing different environmental problems should be allocated among the different levels of decisionmaking and implementation in a multi-jurisdictional system.

RICHARD REVESZ is Professor of Law at New York University School of Law, PHILIPPE SANDS is Professor of International Law at the School of Oriental and African Studies, University of London and Global Professor of Law at New York University School of Law, and RICHARD STEWART is Emily Kempin Professor of Law at New York University School of Law.

# ENVIRONMENTAL LAW, THE ECONOMY AND SUSTAINABLE DEVELOPMENT

*The United States, the European Union and the International Community*

---

*Edited by*

RICHARD L. REVESZ

PHILIPPE SANDS

RICHARD B. STEWART

CAMBRIDGE
UNIVERSITY PRESS

PUBLISHED BY THE PRESS SYNDICATE OF THE UNIVERSITY OF CAMBRIDGE
The Pitt Building, Trumpington Street, Cambridge, United Kingdom

CAMBRIDGE UNIVERSITY PRESS
The Edinburgh Building, Cambridge CB2 2RU, UK www.cup.cam.ac.uk
40 West 24th Street, New York, NY 10011–4211, USA www.cup.org
10 Stamford Road, Oakleigh, Melbourne 3166, Australia
Ruiz de Alarcón 13, 28014 Madrid, Spain



First published 2000

Printed in the United Kingdom at the University Press, Cambridge

*Typeface* Minion 10.5/13.5 pt *System* QuarkXPress™ [SE]

*A catalogue record for this book is available from the British Library*

*Library of Congress Cataloguing in Publication data*

Environmental law, the economy, and sustainable development: the United States, the European Union, and the international community / Richard L. Revesz, Philippe Sands, Richard B. Stewart, editors.
p. cm.
ISBN 0 521 64270 1 (hb)
1. Environmental law – United States. 2. Environmental law – Europe. 3. Sustainable development – Law and legislation. 4. Environmental economics. I. Revesz, Richard L., 1958– II. Sands, Philippe, 1960– III. Stewart, Richard B.
K3585.E58 2000
344′.046–dc21 99-047718

ISBN 0 521 64270 1 hardback

# CONTENTS

## CONTRIBUTORS

SCOTT BARRETT is a Professor of Environmental Economics and International Political Economy and Director of the Energy, Environment, Science and Technology Program at the Paul H. Nitze School of Advanced International Studies, Johns Hopkins University.

STEPHEN BREYER is a Justice of the Supreme Court of the United States.

GRACIELA CHICHILNISKY is UNESCO Chair of Mathematics and Economics and Director of the Program on Information and Resources at Columbia University.

JOHN FEREJOHN is the Carolyn S. G. Munro Professor of Political Science at Stanford University and a senior fellow at the Hoover Institution.

GEOFFREY HEAL is the Paul Garrett Professor of Public Policy and Business Responsibility at Columbia Business School.

VEERLE HEYVAERT is Junior Research Fellow at the Law Department of the London School of Economics and Political Sciences.

JOHN HOUGHTON is Co-Chair of the Intergovernmental Panel on Climate Change.

ERNST-ULRICH PETERSMANN is a Professor of Law at the University of Geneva and a Visiting Professor of International Law at the Graduate Institute of International Studies at Geneva.

ECKARD REHBINDER is a Professor of Law at the University of Frankfurt and Chairman of the German Council of Environmental Advisors.

RICHARD REVESZ is a Professor of Law at New York University School of Law.

FRIEDER ROESSLER was formerly director of the Legal Affairs Division of the GATT and the WTO; he currently works as a consultant on WTO law in Geneva.

PHILIPPE SANDS is a Professor of International Law at the School of Oriental and African Studies, University of London, and Global Professor of Law at New York University School of Law.

RICHARD STEWART is the Emily Kempin Professor of Law at New York University School of Law.

ROGER VAN DEN BERGH is a Professor at Erasmus University Rotterdam.

# INTRODUCTION: ENVIRONMENTAL REGULATION IN MULTI-JURISDICTIONAL REGIMES

RICHARD B. STEWART

THIS BOOK provides a comparative analysis of environmental regulation in multi-jurisdictional legal and political systems, focusing on three important examples: the United States, the European Union, and the international community. These systems are, of course, quite different in many ways, political, institutional, legal, cultural, and economic. Yet they share certain fundamental structural similarities and must deal with similar problems in instituting measures to protect the environment while simultaneously promoting economic growth. This book develops a linked series of conceptual frameworks for understanding and evaluating the ways in which these three multi-jurisdictional systems are dealing with this challenge, drawing on the insights afforded by comparative analysis of their similarities and differences.

Each of these systems must deal with environmental interdependencies that transcend their constituent jurisdictions – states in the United States, the Member States in the European Union, and the nations of the international community. Pollution often crosses local borders, in some cases creating regional problems, such as acid deposition, ozone-type smog, and pollution of shared water bodies. Other transjurisdictional environmental problems are global, including stratospheric ozone depletion and climate change. Wastes are shipped across borders. There is a global stake in preservation of biodiversity, regardless of the jurisdiction where it is located. Yet, despite the maxim, held by certain ecologists and environmentalists, that everything is connected to everything else, some environmental problems, such as municipal waste disposal, many forms of pollution and resource development, and drinking water quality, remain localized in their effects on health and the environment.

These varying jurisdictional and environmental circumstances pose the central question of how responsibility for addressing different environmental problems should be allocated among the different levels of decision-making and implementation within a multi-jurisdictional system. They also pose distinctive questions as to the structure of institutions for decisionmaking and the regulatory instruments to be used in solving environmental problems. These issues are additionally complicated by the fact that environmental issues are inextricably bound with economic issues. The three legal and political systems examined herein are characterized by substantial but varying degrees of economic integration. The United States and the European Union were established with the purpose of developing integrated internal markets. The Bretton Woods institutions, as well as the GATT/WTO, have fostered a higher degree of economic integration at the global level. The wider markets and broader scope for competition and innovation resulting from market integration have contributed significantly to economic growth, although not without other consequences, whether environmental, social, or political. As experience abundantly demonstrates, economic growth can be the cause of serious environmental problems. Properly directed, economic forces might also help to solve those problems and promote ecologically sustainable development. In the international context, economic integration coexists with wide disparities in wealth and the level of economic development among different nations, disparities that are less pronounced but not entirely absent within the United States and the European Union. These disparities lead the poorer nations of the world – and poor communities within the US and the EU – to emphasize the development element in sustainable development, and create challenges as well as opportunities for the development of effective solutions to global environmental problems.

There can be little doubt that economic and environmental interdependencies, trade flows, and capital mobility have important implications for environmental regulation in multi-jurisdictional settings. Adoption of different environmental regulations of products in different jurisdictions can impede trade by increasing transaction costs and preventing realization of scale economies in the broader market. Industrial firms facing intensive competition on both a regional and a global scale are concerned that the costs imposed by stringent environmental regulation of production methods and processes by the jurisdictions in which their facilities are located will disadvantage them vis-à-vis competitors in other jurisdictions with less stringent regulation. Environmentalists in turn are concerned that industry will migrate to jurisdictions with laxer standards and that all jurisdictions will respond by competing in regulatory laxity in order to attract industry. Empirical studies cast considerable doubt on the existence or extent of competitive disadvantage or advantage associated with differences in environmental regulation. Nonetheless, the industry and environmentalist concern about a "race to the bottom" in regulation is an important political reality. These various considerations generate demands for adoption of harmonized environmental product and process regulation across jurisdictions, which in turn implies centralization of regulatory decision-making authority at a higher level. Alternatively, industry and environmental groups located in jurisdictions with more stringent standards may push for the adoption at the local level of countervailing duties on imports from jurisdictions with less stringent standards. This is but one example of the potential use of trade measures to advance environmental objectives, and the concomitant risk that trade restrictions advanced in the name of environmental protection could be deployed for protectionist purposes.

The interdependencies between environmental protection, trade, and investment also generate conflicts between developed countries and developing countries. For competitive economic as well as environmental reasons, developed countries have sought to promote adoption of more stringent environmental standards by developing countries, both through international agreements and, occasionally, the use of trade measures. These efforts have often provoked resentment and resistance from developing countries, who argue that it is their turn to develop and that the rich countries, who have already created many environmental problems in the course of their own development, should take lead responsibility for addressing them. On the other hand, economic instruments can also be used to harness market forces to advance environmental protection and bridge gaps between developed and developing countries by targeting private investment and technology transfer to promote ecologically friendly forms of growth in developing countries.

The contributions to this book, which were originally presented as papers at a colloquium on international and comparative environmental regulation at New York University's Villa La Pietra in Florence, provide legal, economic, and political–economic analyses of these and other issues, as presented by environmental regulation in the United States, the European Union, and the international community. The analysis is in part positive: how has environmental regulation evolved in relation to the challenges presented by environmental and economic interdependencies in multi-jurisdictional systems? The analysis is also normative: how can environmental and economic objectives be more effectively reconciled and promoted within such systems? The examination of these issues in the context of the three different systems provides rich opportunities for comparative analysis and insight.

Environmental law and regulation in the United States and Europe has matured to the point where cross-system comparisons and possible borrowings are highly fruitful. In the US, a highly legalistic command-and-control system may be approaching its limits. There is considerable interest in the use of the less adversarial regulatory approaches that are becoming prevalent in Europe, including environmental covenants and other forms of industry–government cooperation, and sectoral environmental planning and priority-setting. On the European side, the expansion in the EU's membership, concerns about a persistent democracy deficit in Community policymaking, gaps in effective implementation of Community legislation, and the general belt-tightening that is associated with the move to the Euro and harmonization of tax and fiscal policies call for a re-examination of current approaches, which have tended to emphasize detailed command-style legislation developed by the Commission. US practices, including comparative risk assessment, notice-and-comment rulemaking procedures, regulatory impact analysis, and use of tradeable permit systems, may come to be seen as relevant and helpful in the European context.

In both Europe and the United States there is concern with overcentralization of regulation and the need to provide greater flexibility and scope for innovation. Further, now that protection of the environment is explicitly recognized in law as an independent and central basis for Community legislation, there is no longer a legal need to attempt to justify Community environmental legislation as eliminating distortions to competition and promoting development of a common market. These developments have already provoked a re-examination in both systems of the justifications for centralized, uniform environmental regulation, and of whether they support the sweeping scope and intensive detail of regulations emanating from Brussels and Washington.

At the international level, as in the US and European contexts, issues of environmental protection, trade, investment, and competition are closely interrelated and shape both the positive and normative debate about level-of-jurisdiction issues and related issues of the most appropriate regulatory policies and tools. In the international community, however, there is only weak capacity for centralized environmental standard-setting and little capacity for centralized enforcement. In light of these circumstances, there are stronger arguments in the international context than in Europe or the US for allowing countries to impose environmentally based trade restrictions, unilateral or multilateral, to advance environmental objectives. Such measures may, at the same time, help to build momentum for stronger international institutions and measures for environmental protection. On the other hand, they may equally provoke conflict and discord.

Because differences in wealth, economic development, and political objectives and values among nations are far greater than within federal systems such as the US or than within the EU, and because there is no general system for economic redistribution in the international community, the distributional consequences of environmental policies should arguably play a far more salient role in the international context. Thus, in a politically integrated system of similar states, it might be desirable to adopt environmental policies to promote overall social welfare without undue concern about how the costs and benefits of such policies are distributed across different geographic subdivisions. Supra-jurisdictional governments regulate in many areas, and distributional consequences may well even out across programs. Thus, it may not be sensible to compromise the social welfare achievement of each program in order to achieve a better program-specific distribution. Even if such evening out of the aggregate distributional consequences of different programs does not occur, it is likely to be more desirable to redistribute through a system of taxes and subsidies than by compromising the efficiency of the various regulatory programs. The situation is different in the international community with its larger differences in wealth and economic development, considerable differences in political and social objectives, and lesser opportunities for redistribution.

Against the background of these general themes, the specific environmental regulatory issues addressed by the contributions may be grouped in the following clusters:

*First, at what level should decisionmaking responsibility for environmental regulation in a multi-jurisdictional system be located?* What issues should be addressed at the local level (state, member state, or nation) and which at the higher or more centralized level (US federal government, EU authorities, or international agreement)? Does the answer turn on the nature of the environmental problem in issue? Is the problem generated by products – for example, the health risks of genetically modified foods or air pollution from automobiles? Is the problem one of production and process methods – pollution from factories, the impact of fishing practices on endangered sea turtles, the destruction of tropical rain forests? To what extent does the problem involve pollution or wastes that cross jurisdictional boundaries? To what extent does the problem involve threats to rare or treasured ecosystems or natural resources or endangered species which may be of concern to persons outside the jurisdiction in which they are located? To what extent does the relation between market-based economic factors – investment and trade flows and competitiveness concerns – and environmental regulation affect the level-of-government issue? Do stringent environmental regulations cause significant competitive disadvantage for industry? Is there a real prospect of competition in environmental regulatory laxity among jurisdictions? To what extent should local jurisdictions be free to take initiatives unilaterally to impose more stringent regulatory requirements than their neighbors? Does it matter whether the regulation deals with products or with production and process methods? The contributions analyze how these issues have been resolved in the three different systems at issue, and also offer critiques of existing practices and proposals for change.

*A second cluster of issues revolves around the structure of decisionmaking institutions and the procedures for developing legal rules governing regulation of environmental risks.* The contributions address the respective roles of legislative bodies, administrative authorities, and courts and other dispute-resolution bodies in the development of environmental regulation in multi-jurisdictional systems. Related issues of transparency and accountability include the opportunities for non-governmental actors and interests to have access to information and an opportunity to participate in governmental decisionmaking processes. The contributions address differences and similarities as to how these questions are resolved in the US, the EU, and in the international community. Decisionmaking structures are in turn related to level-of-government issues. To the extent, for example, that harmonization of environmental regulation is desired, should it proceed by case-by-case judicial or other tribunal review of specific measures adopted by lower level jurisdictions that are challenged as incompatible with economic integration within the larger system – the method of so-called negative harmonization? This is the model of judicial review of state environmental health and safety regulation in the US under "negative commerce clause" jurisprudence; of review by the European Court of Justice of Member State regulations pursuant to Articles 30 and 36 of the Rome Treaty, and of review by the WTO Dispute Resolution Body of national trade measures for compatibility with GATT 1994, the Agreement on Sanitary and Phytosanitary Measures, and the Agreement on Technical Barriers to Trade. Alternatively, should differences in the environmental laws of different jurisdictions be addressed by legislative measures of "positive harmonization" – the adoption by Congress, the European Council (with the participation of the European Parliament), or by international treaties of mandatory measures to which all jurisdictions must adhere?

*A third set of issues concerns the selection of appropriate regulatory instruments for environmental protection.* The interdependencies between economic and environmental issues have confronted regulatory decision-makers with the challenge of meeting public demands for higher levels of environmental, health, and safety protection in an era in which there is increasing concern about regulatory costs and competitiveness and a trend towards privatization of many previously entrenched governmental functions. Yet, laissez-faire is not an acceptable solution to environmental problems because of the existence of pervasive market failures that lead to excessive pollution and environmental degradation. There has accordingly been increasing interest in and use of economic incentive systems and the creation of new forms of property rights to promote environmental protection in an economically more efficient manner. The contributions analyze a number of such innovative approaches, including the use of pollution taxes and tradable pollution rights; environmental covenants between industry and government; and the development of property rights in watershed protection services, genetic resources, and atmospheric quality, among others. The role of financial institutions in promoting these objectives is also examined. Further, the intersections between the choice of economic instruments on the one hand and level-of-government choices and decisionmaking institutions on the other are examined, as well as the potential contributions of financial instruments to harmonizing the interests of developed and developing countries and addressing global environmental problems such as climate change and stratospheric ozone depletion.

*A fourth cluster of issues involves the relation between trade measures and environmental protection.* Environmentally based trade measures, including import restrictions and tariffs such as border tax adjustments and countervailing duties, can be regarded as supplementary environmental regulatory instruments in the context of an economically integrated multi-jurisdictional system. A jurisdiction may adopt more stringent product standards than other jurisdictions and impose such standards on imports as well as domestically produced products. Even if applied in a nominally non-discriminatory fashion, is the purpose or effect of the measure to protect domestic industry? To what extent will the measure prevent realization of scale economies in the wider market? How should the environmental justification for a measure be weighed against its adverse economic impact on other jurisdictions, and what weight should be given to the importing jurisdiction's freedom to afford its citizens a higher level of environmental protection? How should disputes over such measures be resolved by higher level tribunals? To what extent should positive harmonization of product standards be undertaken, and how?

In addition, a jurisdiction may impose trade measures against product imports from other jurisdictions with laxer environmental process standards which do not affect the environmental performance of the product itself but only of the means by which it is produced. To what extent may such trade measures be justified in order to remedy asserted competitive disadvantages attributed to the differences in process standards? In order to deal with pollution or other adverse environmental consequences that have an impact on the importing country? The global commons? Does it matter whether such trade measures are adopted by a single or by a group of jurisdictions pursuant to agreement? Should disputes over such measures be resolved by a higher order tribunal, and, if so, how? Should they be addressed by some form of positive harmonization of process standards?

*A fifth set of issues deals with risk assessment and management.* The public demand for higher levels of environmental protection in the face of equally insistent concerns over competitiveness and excessive government interference requires not only the use of more efficient instruments of environmental protection but also careful assessments of the magnitude of different environmental risks and prioritization among them in order to target limited societal resources on the most significant and more readily resolved risks. Quantitative risk assessment has been more widely adopted in the United States than in Europe. It has played very little role in the international arena outside of the climate change context. Yet, despite the wide use of risk assessment, there has been increasingly sharp criticism of risk regulation in the US on grounds of inconsistency and faulty prioritization.

At the same time, there may be increasing pressures for more systematic risk assessment and prioritization in Europe. These issues are related to the structure of decisionmaking institutions. To what extent should risk assessment and prioritization be undertaken by experts, and to what extent should they be informed by political and public judgments which may be less informed in a technical sense but also may represent legitimate perspectives that the experts may slight?

Level-of-government issues are also implicated in the debates over risk assessment and management. To what extent should a subsidiary jurisdiction be free to pursue its own policies regarding risk assessment and management, even if this involves restrictions on imports of products from other jurisdictions? An example is the EU's ban, on grounds of protecting consumer health, on imports of meat from Canada and the United States from cattle that have received bovine growth hormones. The EU ban was attacked by the exporting jurisdictions before the WTO as lacking in scientific basis, which upheld their challenge. To what extent will higher level authorities have to engage in their own risk assessments in order to resolve such conflicts? How will they develop the institutional means of doing so?

A quite different and highly successful approach to risk assessment in the international context is the role played by the international scientific community in identifying and evaluating the effects on the stratospheric ozone layer of various ozone-depleting chemicals and the effects on climate change of anthropogenic emissions of greenhouse gases. The broad consensus reached by the international scientific community on these issues contributed importantly to the adoption of the Montreal Protocol and subsequent agreements to phase out or drastically limit the production and use of ozone-depleting chemicals and of the United Nations Framework Convention on Climate Change and the Kyoto Protocol to limit greenhouse gas emissions.

*Finally, methodological issues cross-cut the various contributions and their analysis of environmental regulation in multi-jurisdictional settings.* The use of economic analysis, in both positive and normative modes, is now a staple of legal and policy analysis of environmental regulation in the United States by academics, government authorities, and representatives of industry and environmental and consumer groups. These methodologies are gaining some ground in Europe and, even more slowly, in the international community. Many of the contributions to this volume draw on economic methodologies to analyze issues such as the appropriate level of government for regulatory decisionmaking and the performance of different types of environmental regulatory instruments. A number of contributors also use public choice analysis to examine the political and economic forces that shape government policy decisions. Other contributions employ more traditional legal and institutional analyses, yet reflect and acknowledge the increasing awareness of the significance of economic factors and instruments in environmental protection regulation. Overall, the contributions attest to the important role that economic methodology can play in our understanding of environmental regulatory issues and the potential for simultaneously promoting environmental and economic objectives. Noneconomic values and considerations, however, are not neglected. Some contributions, for example, contend that considerations of justice and equity require limitations on the use of economic instruments in environmental regulatory policy. Others affirm the importance of justice and equity considerations but contend that they can best be secured by wider use of economic understanding and economic instruments.

The remainder of this introduction summarizes and compares the analysis of these interrelated issues by the contributors to this book.

## The appropriate level of government for environmental regulatory decisionmaking

The seemingly inexorable trend in environmental regulation in the US and the EU has been towards greater centralization, notwithstanding strong criticisms in both systems that it produces excessively rigid, burdensome, costly, and environmentally dysfunctional measures. A similar trend can be discerned at the international level, as more and more environmental issues are addressed through international conventions, although the relative weakness of international institutions and the often sharp division of policy views between different countries, especially between developed and developing countries, has meant that operational centralization has not advanced to nearly the same degree as in the US and Europe.

Richard Revesz sharply challenges this trend. He asserts that preferences for environmental quality vary among jurisdictions and that both the costs and benefits of different levels of environmental regulation vary geographically because of such preference variations and local differences in environmental and economic conditions. In order to ensure that environmental regulation is appropriately tailored to these variables, Revesz embraces a presumption that regulation should be decided at a decentralized level. This presumption may be overcome if decentralization is shown to generate pathologies that can appropriately be cured by centralization and if the advantages in this regard of centralization outweigh its disadvantages. Revesz examines a number of asserted justifications for centralized regulation, and finds most of them lacking. Accordingly, he concludes that environmental regulation in many instances is excessively centralized. He develops this conclusion in the context of the United States, and then applies it to Europe and to the international setting.

Revesz concedes that scale economies may justify some centralized regulation of products, but strongly criticizes the current degree of centralization of process regulations. He first addresses the "race to the bottom" thesis that has frequently been invoked to justify uniform minimum regulation at the federal level in the United States. The thesis holds that decentralization will result in inadequate environmental protection because local jurisdictions will compete in regulatory laxity in an effort to attract industry. Revesz finds, on the basis of economic theory and economic models of decisions regarding regulation and investment, that the argument lacks analytic foundation. He concludes that to the extent such competition exists, it is likely to promote overall social welfare for reasons similar to those favoring competitive markets for goods and services. He further notes that if interstate competition in policies that affect business costs is socially pernicious, it cannot be eliminated by uniform centralized environmental regulation; state competition for industry will simply take another form, such as rivalry in lower business taxes.

Revesz further concedes that, in principle, centralized regulation might be justified in order to deal with interstate externalities such as pollution that spills over from one state to the other. Such spillovers can lead to decentralization failures because a state in which pollution originates will not have adequate incentives to control it because its industry will bear the brunt of the control costs while a portion of the benefits will accrue to residents of other states. Revesz finds, however, that centralized environmental regulation generally does a poor job of dealing with pollution spillovers, illustrating this conclusion with an analysis of the US Clean Air Act.

Next, Revesz considers the public choice arguments that environmental interests are underrepresented at the local level relative to the central level in multi-jurisdictional systems because of the difficulties of mobilizing unorganized interests in many local jurisdictions, and that central regulation is therefore justified in order to ensure adequately protective environmental regulation. Revesz finds this argument unconvincing, concluding that, because of collective action problems, impediments to effective organization of environmental interests are likely to be greater at the central than at the local level. He also concludes that current patterns of centralized regulation cannot be justified by invoking the right of all citizens to a basic minimum level of health protection.

This analysis, developed in the context of the United States, is then applied by Revesz to environmental regulation in Europe and the international community. He concludes that scale economies and market integration justify harmonization of product regulation by EC legislation, but that the current system of extensive EC process regulation is not justified by "race to the bottom" concerns, pollution spillovers, or the goal of equalizing the conditions of competition, a goal he finds both unpersuasive and unattainable. He reaches similar conclusions regarding harmonization of environmental process standards in the global context.

Roger van den Bergh, writing from a European perspective, agrees with Revesz's presumption of decentralization, his overall negative assessment of the rationales for centralized process standards, and his conclusion that the current extent of environmental regulation at the Community level cannot be justified. He believes that the "race to the bottom" thesis is not only inconsistent with economic theory but that it also lacks empirical support, pointing to studies which show that the costs of complying with environmental regulations are only a small fraction of total production costs and that the stringency or laxity of local environmental regulation does not appear to be a factor in most business decisions as to where to locate. Van den Bergh points out that the Commission has placed greater emphasis on market integration than on "race to the bottom" themes as a justification for regulatory legislation at the Community level, but concludes that integration cannot justify uniform centralized process standards. With respect to interstate externalities, van den Bergh suggests that they might be addressed by Coasian bargaining, resulting in bilateral or regional agreements among Member States in lieu of Community legislation. He cites the Rhine Action Plan as a successful example of this approach. Finally, van den Bergh offers public choice analysis as an additional reason for a presumption in favor of decentralized regulation in Europe. Decisionmaking in the European Union suffers from a well-known democracy deficit. He believes that this deficit contributes to a pattern of centralized regulation from Brussels that favors the interests of the Commission and provides little scope for subsidiarity, although he notes the possibility that the European Court of Justice might review Community legislation for consistency with the subsidiarity principle. Political distortions, van den Bergh believes, are best cured by competition among legislators, which is more likely to occur if decisionmaking is decentralized to the member state or regional level.

John Ferejohn does not share the presumption of decentralization advocated by Revesz and van den Bergh, and is inclined to favor centralization, despite its drawbacks. Ferejohn believes that decentralized regulation is likely to fail badly because of the presence of pervasive interjurisdictional spillovers. These include not only physical pollution spillovers, but also psychic spillovers generated by the concern that people in one jurisdiction have for environmental conditions in other jurisdictions in the same system.

## Trade and environment issues

The intersection of free trade rules and regimes and environmental regulation is an increasingly important and contentious aspect of environmental regulatory policy in multi-jurisdictional settings, one that is closely related to the level-of-government issues set forth above.

As noted by Frieder Roessler, the right of jurisdictions to protect their citizens against the harmful environmental, health, and safety effects of imported products is in principle acknowledged by free trade regimes such as the GATT/WTO, provided that national treatment, non-discrimination, and most-favored-nation principles are respected so that both domestically produced and imported products are subject to the same regulatory or tax measures. There is concern, however, that some product-based trade measures that nominally satisfy these requirements have in fact been designed or used in ways that impose disproportionate burdens on importers and protect domestic producers. Another concern, recognized by Revesz and van den Bergh, is that inconsistent product regulations adopted by different jurisdictions can prevent scale economies in production and distribution from being realized, increase transaction costs, and otherwise reduce the benefits of free trade. These considerations, they conclude, favor a degree of harmonization of product standards by authorities at a higher level.

As explained in the chapter by Stephen Breyer and Veerle Heyvaert, harmonization of product standards can be promoted through two different institutional mechanisms. Negative harmonization occurs when a tribunal or an administrative authority reviews particular trade measures against imports that are challenged by importers as contrary to the free trade regime, and invalidates those measures that are found to be discriminatory or involve adverse effects on exporters and on the trade regime that are not sufficiently justified by their environmental benefits. As previously noted, the form of harmonization is represented by decisions of the US courts, the European Court of Justice, and WTO dispute resolution tribunals reviewing measures adopted by local jurisdictions for consistency with the overarching free trade regime. The WTO Appellate Body decision in the Beef Hormones case, discussed by Breyer and Heyvaert and by Philippe Sands, is the most recent example of this technique at the global level. The principles adopted by the Appellate Body in that and similar cases provide a rich basis for comparative analysis with the principles applied by the United States Supreme Court and the European Court of Justice in analogous controversies. They will have important implications for future disputes, such as the brewing controversies between the EU and many developing countries on the one hand and the US and other agricultural exporters on the other over issues such as the safety of genetically modified crops and foods derived from them.

Positive harmonization of product standards occurs when a higher level of government adopts uniform standards that are binding, at least as minimum standards and in some cases as maximum standards as well, on lower level jurisdictions. Examples include US federal or EU product legislation and the adoption, linked with trade measures, of international product standards such as those in the Convention on Trade in Endangered Species and the Montreal Protocol. As Breyer and Heyvaert point out, positive harmonization may be preferred by powerful political actors because negative harmonization is typically piecemeal and incomplete and because such actors have greater control over the outcome of the legislative process than they do over adjudicatory outcomes. Positive harmonization is far more difficult to achieve at the international level, but it can be encouraged by validating national standards that are based on international standards, as the WTO SPS agreement does, and by placing the ultimate burden of justification on nations that impose trade restrictions on imports on the basis of domestic standards that are more restrictive than international standards, as the WTO Appellate Body did in the Beef Hormones case.

Process-based trade restriction or tariffs present quite different considerations from product-based measures. Such measures cannot be justified by reference to the adverse effects of the imported products on the importing state's citizens or environment. The processes by which the product was produced took place outside the jurisdiction of the importing nation. The traditional GATT position, reflected in the GATT Secretariat's 1992 Report on Trade and Environment and the GATT panels' Tuna–Dolphin decisions, is that all such extrajurisdictional measures are inconsistent with the free trade regime and therefore invalid. The validity of this conclusion turns in part on level-of-government issues discussed above. Some proponents of process-based trade restrictions contend that such measures are justified in order to equalize competition or avoid a "race to the bottom" in process standards. If one believes, with Revesz and van den Bergh, that these are not valid regulatory objectives, this justification for process-based trade measures disappears. Yet, Revesz and van den Bergh acknowledge that prevention of transjurisdictional spillovers such as pollution or biodiversity loss is a valid regulatory objective, and that jurisdictions in which such spillovers originate cannot be relied upon adequately to control such spillovers. The traditional free traders' response is that objectives such as prevention of spillovers should be achieved through multilateral agreements among all of the jurisdictions that are members of the free trade regime, rather than being unilaterally imposed by one jurisdiction or a subset of the whole. As Revesz points out, this may be a convincing retort in systems where it is not too difficult to adopt uniform process-based regulatory measures at a higher level, as in the US and the EU, but it is far less convincing in the global context, in which voluntary agreements among nations are difficult to achieve and implement effectively. This circumstance may justify greater latitude in the international context for imposition of process-based trade measures by one or a subset of jurisdictions to deal with transjurisdictional spillovers including impacts on common resources, such as the oceans and atmosphere, outside of national jurisdiction, provided that the same basic principles governing the validity of product-based measures, including non-discrimination and proportionality, are respected. This view, it should be noted, appears to have been endorsed by the WTO Appellate Body in the recent Shrimp–Turtle decision.

Roessler nonetheless takes strong exception to allowing States Parties to the GATT/WTO unilaterally to adopt process-based environmental trade measures to restrict imports. He rejects the argument that such measures are justified on the ground that they may be necessary in order to win domestic political support for domestic environmental measures, arguing that if such a rationale were accepted in principle, it could be used to justify all manner of protectionist measures in ways that could not be effectively reviewed by a higher level international authority, and would accordingly be used by nations in ways that would destabilize the system of reciprocal commitments and concessions established in the GATT/WTO. For similar reasons, Roessler rejects the claim that such measures are justified in order to offset competitive disadvantages due to different process standards. Such a rationale, he believes, is also inconsistent with the principles of comparative advantage that underlie the free trade regime and would violate most-favored-nation principles by allowing differentiation among imports from different nations based on local conditions in those countries. He argues that, to the extent that concerns over competitive disadvantage are valid, they can be addressed by domestic subsidies to industries, or by agreements among parties on countervailing import tariffs matched by reciprocal trade concessions to exporting nations, or by waivers granted pursuant to the GATT/WTO regime. Further, Roessler is opposed in general to cross-linkages of environmental and trade issues within the GATT/WTO framework, arguing that if Parties were free unilaterally to impose cross-linkages, such measures could not be limited to environmental issues but could be extended to many others, including labor standards, competition policy, foreign investment policy, immigration policy, and other policy areas. He argues that such developments would be profoundly destabilizing to the carefully designed structure of the GATT/WTO agreements, which severely limit cross-linkages among different agreements such as those regarding trade in goods and intellectual property.

Finally, Roessler agrees with the environmentalist critique that the current GATT/WTO dispute resolution process is insufficiently transparent. Roessler finds that confidentiality was understandable and appropriate in the past, when dispute resolution followed a negotiation model and its legitimacy was based on consensus among parties. Now that the dispute resolution process has shifted towards an adjudicatory model, transparency is a necessary element of its legitimation, although Roessler is worried that the result may be to increase the pressure and influence of protectionist interests.

Ernst-Ulrich Petersmann agrees that, in general, efficient environmental policies should be pursued at the domestic level, where production, distribution, consumption, and disposal occur, without the need for process-based trade barriers to advance environmental objectives. He also agrees that countries should not be able to use such trade measures to offset asserted competitive disadvantages due to differences in process standards. Petersmann asserts that these propositions are generally accepted by economists and by governments, and are reflected in GATT/WTO dispute resolution decisions invalidating such measures. Further, he agrees with Roessler about the need for transparency in the WTO dispute resolution process, although he is likewise worried that this may increase special interest influence.

Petersmann, however, disagrees with Roessler's view that all environmental trade linkages should be excluded from the WTO framework. In particular, he believes that the use of trade measures may be appropriate as a "stick" to deal with free-riding by other nations in addressing global environmental problems. Because EU-type integration cannot currently be achieved at the global level, use of trade measures under the WTO to promote integration of environmental policies for global problems is appropriate. Petersmann further believes that environmental taxes are a useful environmental policy instrument because they promote flexibility, cost-effectiveness, innovation, and transparency, and that border tax adjustments on imported products are a corollary of the domestic use of environmental taxes. The most difficult issue is whether border tax adjustments for process-based domestic environmental taxes are consistent with the GATT/WTO. Petersmann discusses a number of GATT/WTO provisions relevant to this question, and finds that they present considerable ambiguity. He further points out that the WTO Dispute Resolution Understanding provides that customary international law should be taken into account in interpreting and applying GATT/WTO law, and suggests that this may provide a means for finding process-based border tax adjustments to be consistent with international trade law.

Scott Barrett also agrees with Roessler that countries should not generally be able to use trade measures to win political support for domestic environmental measures. He argues, however, that they should be able to impose such measures to redress competitive disadvantages caused by other countries' low environmental standards where such standards are "unfair" because they are adopted in order to win competitive advantage, although he believes that such instances will be rare. Further, he argues that unilateral adoption of process-based trade measures, including measures that go beyond border tax adjustments, may be justified in order to deal with transjurisdictional spillovers such as stratospheric ozone depletion.

First, such measures may properly be adopted in order to offset the effects of the leakage of industrial investment from countries that adopt measures to deal with common environmental problems to countries that do not, thereby increasing the level of economic activity and pollution in the latter countries and transboundary pollution. Second, such measures may justifiably go further to deal with free-riding by the countries that have not adopted such measures, inducing them to do so. Such measures must, however, be "welfare enhancing and fair." He cites the trade measures Montreal Protocol as a successful example.

In his discussion of the Shrimp–Turtle decision by the WTO Appellate Body, Philippe Sands indicates that the law made through the WTO dispute resolution process may indeed be moving in the general direction that Petersmann and Barrett favor by recognizing that the GATT/WTO framework provides at least some room for environment/trade linkages of the sort opposed by Roessler. In that decision, the Appellate Body invalidated a US import ban on shrimp caught without use of devices required of US shrimp boats in order to protect endangered sea turtles from being harmed as a by-catch. The Appellate Body reasoning, however, did not follow the logic of the 1992 GATT Secretariat report and the Tuna–Dolphin panels, which had viewed process-based trade measures as *per se* GATT-illegal. Indeed, the Appellate Body indicated that process-based measures to protect turtles that swim in ocean waters within as well as without national jurisdictions could legitimately be the basis for non-discriminatory import restrictions. It nonetheless invalidated the US measure on the grounds that it arbitrarily required other nations to use protective measures identical to those of US domestic law, and that the US had not taken sufficient steps to secure multilateral agreement on turtle-protective measures. In this last regard, the Appellate Body is plainly seeking to encourage a multilateral over a unilateral approach to process-based trade measures; such an approach should alleviate some of the concerns voiced by Roessler.

## Instruments for environmental protection and sustainable resource management

A number of the contributions to this book focus on the selection of regulatory and legal instruments to achieve environmental protection objectives. In general, they advocate greater use of economic instruments and other alternatives to command-and-control regulation in order to achieve environmental goals at lower cost, promote resource efficiency and sustainable use, and steer private investment in the service of environmental protection. Their discussion of regulatory and legal instruments is also linked to the other themes in the book, including level-of-government issues, the linkage between trade measures and environmental objectives, and the relation between developed and developing countries in the deployment of international solutions to global environmental problems.

Richard Stewart advocates greater use of economic incentives systems (EIS), including taxes on pollution and other residuals and tradable quota systems, in lieu of the command-and-control measures that currently dominate environmental regulation both domestically and internationally. He views command environmental regulation as a form of central economic planning whose persistence is at odds with the worldwide recognition of the failures of state socialism and shifts by governments to market-based approaches in other areas of economic and social policy.

Stewart notes, as a fundamental distinction, that command regulation directly fixes the quantity of residuals that each source may emit, while EIS impose a price on residuals and allow each source the flexibility to choose its preferred level of residuals discharge, balancing the costs of reducing residuals against the price that must be paid on those residuals that remain. The most important potential advantage of the quantity-based command system is that it can control the location and the amount of residuals discharged by each source, and thereby prevent the occurrence of local pollution "hot spots" that may cause serious harm. In actual practice, however, command systems may not be entirely effective or efficient in achieving this objective. Also, EIS can be structured in ways to address "hot spot" problems, although such measures increase administrative complexity and diminish the economic advantages of EIS. Moreover, Stewart notes, many environmental problems, including global problems such as stratospheric ozone depletion and climate change due to global warming and regional problems such as ozone pollution and acid deposition, do not present significant hot spot problems. As applied to these types of problems, price-based EIS have important advantages over command systems: the flexibility and the incentives that they provide achieve limitations on overall residuals levels at much lower cost than under command central planning. EIS also stimulate continuing innovation in resource-efficient technologies. Stewart argues that EIS also have the advantage of economizing on governance by getting the government out of the business of making detailed economic and engineering decisions about the appropriate methods for achieving environmental objectives at myriads of individual sources, relying instead on the price system to decentralize such decisions to source managers. Also, he notes that environmental taxes or quota auctions have the advantage of generating revenues that can be used to improve the overall tax structure or be recycled to upgrade the environmental performance of industrial infrastructure.

Next, Stewart considers a number of distributional and ethical objections to use of EIS, including claims that they will lead to an unjust distribution of environmental risks, have a regressive distributional impact, improperly "commodify" environmental values, subvert the moral basis of obligations to prevent environmental harm, and convey an illicit "license to pollute" that will enable wealthier sources to buy their way out of their clean-up responsibilities. He concludes that on the whole these objections are either not persuasive or are not applicable when the use of EIS is limited to those environmental problems for which they are best suited.

Stewart next reviews the obstacles to broader use of EIS in environmental regulation, including the vested stakes of regulators, industry, and many environmental groups in the command status quo. Notwithstanding these obstacles, there has been a considerable increase in the use of EIS at the domestic level in the United States and Europe. For reasons that are not entirely clear, the United States has relied almost entirely on tradable quota systems, and Europe almost entirely on environmental taxes. He reviews the record of use of EIS, finding that some EIS programs have been quite successful while others have been limited by the persistence of command measures and other factors.

In conclusion, Stewart examines the use of EIS to address regional and global environmental problems, linking the choice of regulatory instrument to level-of-government issues. He argues that the advantages of EIS relative to command systems are greater in dealing with regional and global problems than with local problems because such problems are less likely to involve local hot spots, because cost savings are greater as a result of scale economies and the logic of comparative advantage in the wider market, and because EIS economize on government capacities, which are weaker at the international than at the domestic level. Taking global climate change as a case in point, he examines the role that could be played by command regulation, taxes, and tradable quotas in limiting greenhouse gas emissions. He concludes that EIS are superior to command regulation because they can achieve very large cost savings and spur innovation in environmentally sustainable technologies. He further concludes that a system of tradable greenhouse gas emissions quotas or credits is likely to be superior to a system of taxes because it will likely be better able to transfer capital, technology, and know-how to developing countries and thereby promote ecologically sustainable forms of development.

Eckard Rehbinder raises a number of questions about EIS. He is concerned that the flexibility that they afford could lead to excessive pollution and health risk in specific localities. He also believes that they would diminish the role of the courts in protecting individuals' environmental rights because government's role would be limited to setting the overall level of incentives by determining the aggregate amount of quotas or the level of environmental taxes, and it would no longer bear responsibility for control of individual sources. He raises additional questions about quota trading schemes, observing that in many US programs most trading has been internal within firms or plants rather than external. He suggests that this partial failure of trading may help explain the European preference for taxes, which, he observes, are increasingly used for incentive purposes. He also questions the justice of quota trading systems that give quotas to existing sources for free while requiring new sources to purchase quotas is just.

Rehbinder then discusses the use of environmental covenants or commitments in Germany and other European nations as another flexible alternative to traditional command regulation. As he explains, such commitments are generally negotiated between government and industry trade associations. The industry makes commitments to achieve certain overall residuals limitation objectives, such as limitations on greenhouse gas emissions, in lieu of otherwise applicable regulatory requirements. Industry gains greater flexibility, opportunity for cost savings, and a degree of longer-run predictability in environmental requirements. The public may gain because this technique may enhance compliance and produce environmental benefits more quickly than more cumbersome command alternatives. On the other hand, Rehbinder notes, the public is effectively excluded from the negotiations, and industry agreements may have anti-competitive effects. Also, a point that Rehbinder does not mention, the role of the courts in reviewing such arrangements and their local impacts is highly limited.

Finally, Rehbinder discusses the use of EIS at the global level, noting the provision in the Montreal Protocol for trading of ozone-depleting substance production quotas as a precedent. He believes that allocation of quotas among nations is a serious hindrance to the adoption of a global greenhouse gas emissions trading scheme, although it would seem that the same or similar problem is presented in securing international agreement on regulatory controls or tax rates. Rehbinder favors trading of emissions rights among states, without the participation of private entities, as a first step in the development of a global international emissions trading regime.

Graciela Chichilnisky believes that international greenhouse gas (GHG) emission quota trading could make important contributions to international equity as well as to preventing harmful climate change. She finds we are undergoing a global transition from a form of society based on industry and intensive exploitation of natural resources to one that is knowledge-based. She believes that international GHG trading can accelerate this environmentally beneficial shift by channeling investments in resource-efficient technologies from the developed to the developing countries. A critical question in this regard, also noted by Rehbinder, is the allocation of GHG quotas. Chichilnisky asserts that economic considerations can and should guide the allocation decision. Atmospheric quality is a pure public good, consumed equally by all citizens of the world. On utilitarian premises, welfare would be maximized by having the citizens of richer countries pay more for this shared good than citizens of poor countries. In this regard, she notes, as does Stewart, that although the monetary costs of GHG abatement are generally lower in developing than in developed countries, the social costs, in terms of foreclosed opportunities for alternative uses of resources, may well be higher. She believes that the most effective method of appropriately reducing the social costs to developing countries of participating in a global effort to abate GHG emissions is to allocate such countries an appropriately higher allotment of quotas under a GHG trading scheme, a step, she argues, that will promote global equity as well as efficiency.

Chichilnisky also proposes creation of an International Bank for Environment Settlements (IBES) that would use financial mechanisms to promote global environmental objectives. For example, the IBES could help initiate and supervise a global GHG trading system. It could reconcile the reluctance of developing countries to transfer GHG quotas on a long-term basis with the interests of industry in long-term quota security by "borrowing short and lending long," granting industry a long-term supply of quotas secured by a series of short-term quota purchases, backed up by options arrangements. An IBES could also provide developing countries with immediate capital by securitizing the expected revenues from a multi-year stream of quota sales. In these and other ways, the IBES could reconcile environmental protection and economic efficiency.

## Risk assessment and management

Stephen Breyer and Veerle Heyvaert examine institutional arrangements for environmental risk assessment and management in the US, the EU, and the global community. They are concerned both with horizontal issues regarding the distribution of competence among different governmental institutions at a given level of government, and also with the vertical level-of-government issues discussed by other contributors.

Breyer and Heyvaert first examine risk regulation in the US, drawing on Breyer's earlier work, *Breaking the Vicious Circle*. Environmental regulation of both products and processes is substantially centralized in Washington, D.C. There are, however, serious problems of horizontal fragmentation within the federal government, both at the legislative and administrative levels, which prevent the development of a systematic, integrated process for comparing different environmental risks in different media and settings, prioritizing those risks, and directing societal resources to reduce overall risks in the most cost-effective fashion. The US administrative system for risk regulation is further complicated by the elaborate system of formal decisionmaking processes and judicial review developed in the US in the effort to control administrative power and cure bureaucratic "democracy deficits" by promoting transparency and public participation and accountability.

The authors find that the US risk regulatory system is characterized by a linked set of pathologies, including bureaucratic tunnel vision that results in a single-minded pursuit of risk reduction far beyond the point where the costs of additional regulation exceed the marginal environmental benefits; a random process for setting regulatory agendas and priorities; and inconsistency among regulations, which vary enormously in the costs that they impose in order to achieve equivalent risk-reduction benefits. These problems are in turn attributed to the interactions among the structure of public risk perceptions, which are driven by psychological heuristics that cause distortions and serious errors in public estimations of risks; random and uncoordinated legislative reactions to different risk problems and public perceptions thereof; and technical regulatory uncertainties.

The cure that the authors propose for these pathologies is to give regulatory agencies greater and not less discretion and to establish more centralized and expert structures of administrative decisionmaking authority in order to strengthen the Weberian bureaucratic virtues of rationality and consistency. They suggest that a centralized agency should establish uniform procedures and standards for risk assessment, develop acceptable cost/benefit ranges (such as ranges of cost/life saved) for regulations, build sensible risk assessment models and techniques, and set an overall agenda for decisions by subordinate and more specialized US risk regulatory agencies such as the Environmental Protection Agency, the Occupational Health and Safety Administration, and the Nuclear Regulatory Commission.

Breyer and Heyvaert then use this framework to undertake a comparative assessment of risk regulation in the EU. They note that European political and administrative traditions at the national level result in government administrators having greater authority and insulation from other government organs and outside interests than in the United States. At the EU level, they discern a complex horizontal and vertical authority structure in which the dominant trends have been to shift many risk regulatory decisions from the Member States to Brussels in the name of harmonization and market integration, and to give substantial authority to the Commission in devising and overseeing the Member States' implementation of such regulations. They suggest that the review of Member State regulations for consistency with Community law might be given to the Commission, which has greater regulatory expertise than courts, noting that Congress sometimes gives authority to federal agencies to review the consistency of state regulations with federal law.

They note that in many cases both industry and environmentalists prefer uniform Community standards. They acknowledge, however, the emergence of decentralizing forces, which invoke principles of flexibility and subsidiarity and attack Community environmental regulation as excessively rigid and centralized.

Breyer and Heyvaert conjecture that, given the considerable centralization of risk regulatory authority in the Commission and the European traditions of relative bureaucratic insulation, one should expect better prioritized and more consistent risk regulation in the EU than is found in the United States. On the other hand, they note countervailing factors: the proliferation of specialized Community environmental health and safety agencies located in various Member States; the growing role of the

European Parliament and its sensitivity to public perceptions of risks like that of "mad cow" disease; the growing use in Community legislation of framework laws and other techniques that leave greater discretion to the Member States; and the EU's lack of budget powers to make public health expenditures when they would more effectively protect health than additional risk regulation.

The authors advance a number of potential institutional reforms to improve risk regulation in the EU. They propose that the EU consider adopting the US notice-and-comment process for administrative rulemaking as an alternative or supplement to the corporatist consultative process currently used by the Commission in developing and implementing legislation, although they note the danger of excessive formalization and delay. They also advocate that the Commission develop an overall risk assessment and management policy, akin to that they recommend for the US. Further, they suggest that US models for federalism impact statements and cost/benefit and cost/effectiveness analyses could usefully be adopted in the EU context.

Finally, Breyer and Heyvaert turn to the global level and the potential internationalization of risk regulation. They note that the GATT/WTO and other free trade regimes are in the process of evolving into a deeper form of integration, perhaps analogous to the path followed by the EU, and that such a development is likely to require the GATT/WTO to devote increasing attention to risk regulatory issues. They point out that a process of negative harmonization is already underway through decisions by GATT/WTO dispute resolution bodies that have invalidated a number of domestic trade measures as inconsistent with the free trade regime, and note the prominent role given to risk regulatory issues in the North American Free Trade Agreement. Further, they suggest that more thoroughgoing affirmative harmonization through international agreements could provide significant benefits by pooling resources and promoting greater cross-sectoral consistency – a point emphasized by Sands – but question the extent to which the current international system is capable of achieving this objective. Breyer and Heyvaert conclude that risk regulation in the US, EU and international contexts will continue to evolve and intersect in ways that will provide rich opportunities for comparative analysis and insight. The bovine growth hormone dispute between the EU, and the US and Canada, and the likelihood of further such disputes in the future, including disputes over food products from genetically modified crops, illustrates that different political systems will generate sharply opposed assessments of risk, and that such conflicts must increasingly be addressed at the international level.

Sir John Houghton discusses the role of the international scientific community in risk assessment through the Intergovernmental Panel on Climate Change (IPCC), established in 1988 on the model of the scientific and technical Assessment Panels of the Montreal Protocol. The three Working Groups of the IPCC have addressed the effects of increased anthropogenic GHG emissions on climate change, the impacts of climate change on the environment and human activity, and the economic aspects of these impacts and of measures to limit GHG emissions and adapt to climate change. In 1990, the IPCC reached the consensus conclusion that if no measures were taken to limit GHG emissions, human additions of GHG would likely cause a 1°C rise in global mean temperature by 2025 and a 3°C rise by 2100. This conclusion, and the credibility enjoyed by the IPCC, has played an important role in mobilizing international agreement on the United Nations Framework Convention on Climate Change and the Kyoto Protocol. Since 1990 the IPCC has conducted additional assessments that have contributed importantly to the understanding of climate change issues and the related policy process.

Houghton finds that several factors have contributed to the success of the IPCC. It has distinguished what is known with reasonable certainty and what is unknown or very uncertain. It has restricted itself to scientific assessments and avoided making judgments or giving advice on policy. The IPCC assessment process is open and transparent. It has used a worldwide peer review process to reach conclusions. It has involved governments, industry, and NGOs as well as scientific experts in the assessment process, giving them a sense of ownership of the conclusions reached. The success achieved by the IPCC process appears to provide a counter example to those who insist that it is impossible, both conceptually and operationally, to separate risk assessment and risk management.

Houghton suggests that the IPCC process could be used to address other international environmental problems, including loss of biodiversity, deforestation, and desertification. One might also ask whether the IPCC model could also help provide an answer to the institutional problems with risk assessment in the United States and the European Union, identified by Breyer and Heyvaert. Could it also be used to resolve international disputes over issues such as the safety of meat from cattle that have received bovine growth hormone or of foods produced from genetically engineered crops?

Is it possible that the very lack of strong international institutions for dealing with global environmental problems may create room for the successful development of a consensual scientific process? Such a process may be far more difficult to reconcile with strong regulatory structures like those found in the US or Europe. A consensual scientific process may also not be well adapted to the resolution of specific regulatory controversies presented through dispute resolution processes at the domestic level or through the WTO Dispute Resolution Understanding. Nonetheless, the potential promise of wider application of the IPCC model cannot be lightly dismissed.

## The international environmental legal framework for sustainable development

Philippe Sands provides an overview of the current and evolving legal and institutional arrangements for environmental protection and sustainable development. He notes at the outset a number of critical questions: How do we reconcile traditional notions of state sovereignty with ecological interdependence? How do we define the relation between international environmental law and institutions and other realms of international law and institutions, especially those dealing with economic matters? How do we define and implement the multi-faceted goals of environmentally sustainable development in light of the divergent interests and perspectives of different nations, including the developed and the developing countries? What should the role of the private sector be in these arrangements, and how can its role be incorporated in international legal arrangements that have traditionally focused on state actors?

Sands first identifies a number of key principles that have emerged in international environmental law: state sovereignty over natural resources and the obligation not to cause external environmental harm; good neighborliness and the duty to cooperate; sustainable development; the precautionary principle; and the polluter pays principle. He then summarizes the many international environmental conventions that have been adopted to address a wide range of environmental problems. He notes the emergence in these agreements of a number of important legal techniques including environmental impact assessment and other environmental information techniques; liability for environmental damage; and the expanded use of economic and fiscal measures, including arrangements to transfer resources from developed to developing countries to address global environmental problems.

Sands then discusses a number of critical current issues in international environmental law, many of which relate closely to themes addressed by other contributors. These include the approach taken towards environmental risk assessment in international law, contrasting the approach taken by the International Court of Justice in the Gabcíkovo dispute between Hungary and Slovakia over the construction of a barrage on the Danube with that taken by the WTO Appellate Body in the dispute over the EU's exclusion of imports from the United States and Canada of meat products from cattle that had received bovine growth hormones. Sands finds the approaches taken in the two cases to be inconsistent, and raises the question of how a more coherent and coordinated approach to risk assessment in the international context might be developed. This question links with the discussion by Breyer and Heyvaert of institutional competence in risk assessment in the international context.

A second critical international environmental law issue addressed by Sands is the subsidiarity principle and related level-of-government issues. Sands echoes Revesz and van den Bergh in thinking that higher level measures – here at the international level – are justified only when more decentralized approaches have failed and higher level approaches are superior. In this connection, he discusses the WTO Appellate Body's Shrimp–Turtle decision, which he views as promoting multilateral solutions to problems that can only be addressed successfully at such a level. Sands also suggests that in many instances transjurisdictional environmental problems are better addressed at a regional rather than at a global level of governance; he is plainly concerned with the ongoing proliferation of global environmental agreements that have not been effectively implemented.

This concern is linked in turn by Sands to a third critical issue, which is the need for international institutional reform, including reform of the law-making process, in the environmental field. Sands is concerned with the fragmentation of international environmental conventions and their administrative machinery, a concern which echoes the concerns of Breyer and Heyvaert regarding fragmented responsibility for risk regulation. Sands suggests that a lead international environmental organization – perhaps a greatly strengthened United Nations Environment Program – should be developed. A related issue is the need for better integration of environmental issues with international laws and institutions that are focused on other matters, especially economic matters. Sands argues that such integration can be promoted by according broader recognition to customary and other international environmental law in the interpretation and administration of regimes such as the WTO.

Other urgent environmental protection and sustainable development priorities identified by Sands include the closer and more systematic integration of non-state actors, including industry and NGOs, in international legal arrangements, and greater focus on effective implementation and enforcement of international environmental agreements, especially in developing countries. Sands believes that these objectives can be promoted by developing a stronger role for international organizations and NGOs, and by strengthening the capacities and expanding access to international dispute resolution tribunals.

Geoffrey Heal takes a quite different approach to sustainable development, focusing on the contributions that new systems of property and contract and the economic incentives which they provide can make to promoting sustainable use of natural resources. Initially, he notes that the various ecological services provided by natural resources and systems have tremendous economic value for human welfare, a value estimated in a range between $16 and $54 trillion annually, compared to a global gross national product of $18 trillion annually. Heal believes that in many cases these valuable services are being lost or impaired by shortsighted development policies and by mismatches between the costs of preserving ecological services and the benefits that they provide. On the latter point, he gives the example of rain forest preservation; the costs of preservation are borne by local populations, while the benefits are regional and global. Yet, there is no mechanism for charging the beneficiaries and using the proceeds to compensate local populations for preserving the resource. Heal believes that in many cases this problem can be resolved by adopting new property rights and contract regimes that harness market incentives in the service of resource protection.

Heal provides four examples of successful new property rights regimes. First, greenhouse gas emissions trading schemes provide incentives for forest preservation. Second, New York City is investing around $1 billion in upstate watershed preservation in order to protect the purity of its drinking water; such preservation is far less costly than the alternative of installing technologies to filter the water. Third, South African entrepreneurs have developed franchising arrangements under which local communities that preserve wild animal habitats receive a portion of the revenues paid by game hunters to hunt the animals supported by the habitat. Fourth, pharmaceutical companies have entered into bioprospecting arrangements with government authorities, under which the companies make payments to the authorities in exchange for preserving and granting the companies access to biologically rich rain forests containing species that may provide genetic templates for new drugs and other products.

Heal also discusses the issue of discounting future environmental benefits, arguing that the use in this context of market discount rates is inappropriate because they result in an unduly low value for longer-term ecological benefits. He argues that financial instruments can help solve the problem of shortsightedness by, for example, resolving liquidity constraints by securitizing the stream of future economic benefits provided by projects to protect and preserve ecological services. Securitization can provide needy developing countries with immediate capital to meet pressing social needs that might otherwise lead governments to pursue shortsighted, environmentally destructive development projects that offer a quick economic return.

## Methodological issues; the uses and limitations of economic analysis of environmental regulatory issues

A methodological issue which cross-cuts many of the contributions is the relevance, analytical utility, and normative authority of economic analysis in understanding and evaluating environmental regulatory issues. Environmental problems can be seen as instances of market failures, as noted by Stewart and Heal. This insight can inform the design of measures to redress environmental problems by targeting them at redressing market failure. A closely related issue arises from the circumstance that environmental regulation is designed to provide incentives for market actors as well as non-market actors to change their conduct in ways that will reduce environmental problems; economic analysis can be used to analyze the incentives provided by different types of regulation and their consequences, both positive and negative. Such analysis can help improve the design and performance of environmental regulation. Economic analysis may also assist in analyzing alternative institutional designs, including decisions about which level of government should be responsible for dealing with particular types of environmental problems. It can also illumine the impact of environmentally based trade measures on the performance of the international trade regime as well as on the achievement of environmental goals.

The insights developed from the application of economic analysis to these various subjects can be used to design legal and institutional arrangements to advance the normative goal of maximizing the overall economic welfare of society. Thus, both Revesz and Chichilnisky view the promotion of aggregate social welfare as the primary objective of environmental policy, and evaluate alternative institutional arrangements in terms of how well they promote that goal. As Stewart points out, however, one can also use the insights of economic analysis instrumentally in order to design measures as a means to promote goals based on justice and other moral and ethical values that are non-economic in character.

The many contributions in the book that rely on economic analysis to illumine economic regulatory issues use various methodological approaches. Revesz and Chichilnisky, for example, rely on formal economic models. Revesz relies on economic theory and on models of industry investment and location decisions in response to local environmental regulations to argue that competition among localities in environmental regulation will not lead to a "race to the bottom" that produces unduly lax regulation that will reduce overall societal welfare. Revesz supplements this analysis by reference to game theory, concluding that strategic interactions between jurisdictions competing for industrial investment could lead to suboptimally lax environmental regulation but could also lead to suboptimally stringent regulation. Chichilnisky relies on formal economic models in concluding that an international greenhouse emissions trading program that allocated quotas among nations in inverse proportion to their wealth would maximize global economic welfare.

Other contributors do not rely on formal economic models, but draw in a more eclectic fashion on economic theory and economic insights on matters such as market failures, incentive effects, cost-effectiveness, allocational consequences, discount rates, collective good and free-rider problems, scale economies, comparative advantage, and property rights regimes. They seek to use these insights to examine the consequences of different environmental regulatory arrangements and measures and to draw conclusions about the appropriate design of such measures. This approach is used by Petersmann and Barrett in order to examine environmentally based trade measures, Stewart to examine the performance of different economic regulatory instruments, Breyer and Heyvaert to examine risk assessment, and Heal to examine new ways to protect and preserve ecological services.

Some contributors also draw on empirical literature regarding economic issues. Van den Bergh, for example, relies on empirical studies showing that environmental regulatory compliance costs are a very small fraction of total production costs and that environmental regulation is not a significant factor in locational decisions by industry as evidence confirming the conclusion, reached by Revesz on the basis of economic theory and formal models, that decentralized environmental regulation will not lead to a welfare-diminishing "race to the bottom." Heal relies on the public responses to empirical surveys as evidence in support of his argument that market rates of time discount should not be used in evaluating the costs and benefits of projects that will produce long-term environmental benefits, such as prevention of damaging climate change.

Other contributors use public choice approaches to apply economic analysis to environmental regulatory politics and decisionmaking. Thus, van den Bergh believes that regulatory centralization may provide excessive scope for the exercise of bureaucratic self-interest; he favors decentralization in order to promote wider scope for legislative competition which, he believes, will reduce the agency problems associated with delegation of extensive powers to administrators. This prescription contradicts that advocated by Breyer and Heyvaert who have greater faith in expert competence than in more politically open processes of risk regulation, which tend to be driven by public and legislative perceptions and priorities. Ferejohn as well as van den Bergh fear alliance between environmental and industry interests that produce uniform central regulations that are harmful to overall societal welfare. Revesz uses collective action analysis to challenge the claim that centralized regulation is justified in order to offset the organizational disadvantages of environmental interests relative to production interests when regulatory decisions are decentralized.

A number of contributors also emphasize the relevance of non-economic values and objectives in the evaluation of environmental regulatory measures. Rehbinder, for example, questions the use of economic incentives systems on the ground that they could produce excessive local pollution levels that could infringe citizens' rights to a healthy environment. Revesz acknowledges that individuals have a right to a basic minimum level of health protection, but challenges the notion that such a right should be defined in terms of certain maximum permissible levels of exposure to specific residuals as opposed to being framed in more general terms taking into account basic living conditions and health care. Stewart acknowledges the relevance of various justice-based and ethical objections to the use of economic incentives for environmental protection, although he concludes overall that such objections should not stand in the way of the use of EIS that are properly constituted and applied. Chichilnisky, like Revesz, believes that distributional issues between rich and poor nations are extremely important in the design of measures to address global environmental issues such as climate changes, but concludes that a tradable quota system for greenhouse gases can be designed to promote simultaneously equity and efficiency.

This review of the methodological approaches in this volume points to several conclusions. There is increasingly widespread recognition of the relevance and value of economic analysis to understanding of environmental regulatory issues. This relevance is especially apparent in multi-jurisdictional settings, where environmental regulatory issues are closely connected with investment and trade flows within integrated and highly competitive markets. These linkages are keenly appreciated by scholars, such as Sands, who do not employ economic methodologies as such, as well as by those contributors who do use such methodologies. Among the latter, there is a wide range of approaches, from formal modeling or game theory, to more informal use of economic concepts and insights, to reliance on empirical work, to application of public choice theory. Students who use these various approaches are well aware of the non-economic dimensions of environmental regulatory issues, although the contributors to this volume generally do not view the welfare economic and non-economic dimensions of environmental policy as in fundamental conflict. Indeed, they tend to view them as mutually reinforcing, believing that well-crafted environmental regulatory institutions and instruments can advance both types of goals. Whether this view is unduly optimistic, especially given the challenges presented by multi-jurisdictional legal and political systems, must await the lessons of further experience. Nonetheless, there is no question that, for both environmental and economic reasons, environmental regulatory issues will increasingly be addressed through multi-jurisdictional structures of law and policy.

# Part I

## ENVIRONMENTAL REGULATION IN FEDERAL SYSTEMS

# 1

# FEDERALISM AND ENVIRONMENTAL REGULATION: AN OVERVIEW

RICHARD L. REVESZ

IN THE United States, vesting control over environmental regulation at the federal level is most commonly justified both in the legal academic literature and the legislative arena by reference to three distinct arguments. First, advocates of federal control argue that in its absence interstate competition would result in a "race to the bottom." Second, they maintain that federal regulation is necessary to prevent interstate externalities. Third, proponents of centralization raise the public choice claim that environmental interests will be systematically underrepresented at the state level relative to business interests.

This essay, which builds upon my prior works in the area,[1] has three

Prior versions of this essay were presented at the Conference on Law, Economics, and Sustainable Development in Florence, the Conference on Features of Federalism in Siena, and the Conference on Institutions Markets and Economic Performance in Utrecht; at the Distinguished Lecture Series sponsored by the US Environmental Protection Agency's Office of General Counsel, and at workshops at Resources for the Future and the Kennedy School of Government at Harvard University. My work has benefited greatly from the suggestions of the participants at these events. The generous financial support of the Filomen D'Agostino and Max E. Greenberg Research Fund at the New York University School of Law is gratefully acknowledged.

[1] Richard L. Revesz, "Rehabilitating Interstate Competition: Rethinking the 'Race to the Bottom' Rationale for Federal Environmental Regulation," 67 *NYU L. Rev.* 1210 (1992); Richard L. Revesz, "Federalism and Interstate Environmental Externalities," 144 *U. Pa. L. Rev.* 2341 (1996); Richard L. Revesz, "Federalism and Environmental Regulation: A Normative Critique," in John Ferejohn and Barry R. Weingast eds., *The New Federalism: Can the States be Trusted?* (Stanford, Calif.: Hoover Institution Press, 1997); Richard L. Revesz, "Federalism and Environmental Regulation: Lessons for the European Union and the International Community," 83 *Va. L. Rev.* 1331 (1997) ; Richard L. Revesz, "The Race to the Bottom and Federal Environmental Regulation: A Response to Critics," 82 *Minn. L. Rev.* 535 (1997). A different version of this article is being published in the inaugural volume of the *Yearbook of European Environmental Law.*

major purposes. First, it casts serious doubt on the validity of some of the arguments made in favor of centralizing environmental regulation. Second, it shows that, to a large extent, there has been a misallocation of responsibility over environmental regulation: the federal government has taken too aggressive a role with respect to matters best handled at the state level, but has been too constrained in its exercise of authority with respect to issues over which it enjoys a distinct comparative advantage. Third, it attempts to extract from the experience in the United States, lessons that might be of interest to the European Union and to the international trading regime.

The first section develops the arguments for a presumption for decentralization, which calls for vesting responsibility over environmental protection at the state rather than federal level, as a result of differences in preferences over environmental protection, as well as differences in the benefits and costs of such protection. This presumption can be rebutted if decentralization gives rise to some pathology that could be cured through federal regulation.

Subsequent sections examine the three most prominent justifications offered in the academic literature and in the legislative histories of the US environmental statutes for vesting responsibility over environmental regulation at the federal level. First, the "race to the bottom" rationale posits that states, in an effort to induce geographically mobile firms to locate within their jurisdictions, will offer them suboptimally lax environmental standards, so as to benefit from additional jobs and tax revenues. Second, the problem of interstate externalities arises because a state that sends pollution to another state obtains the labor and fiscal benefits of the economic activity that generates the pollution, but does not suffer the full costs of the activity. Thus, a suboptimally large amount of pollution will cross state lines. Third, a public choice claim posits that state political processes will systematically undervalue the benefits of environmental protection or overvalue its costs. I show that these three arguments do not justify the broad role over environmental regulation accorded to the federal government in the United States.

The next section attempts to define an appropriate federal role. It focuses on the types of federal regulation that may be desirable in light of (1) different types of interstate externalities (pollution externalities, benefits that accrue outside the jurisdiction in which the need for environmental protection arises, and existence or non-use values placed by out-of-state citizens on certain natural resources), (2) economies of scale, (3) benefits that might flow from uniformity in regulation, and (4) rights-based views concerning the protection of minimum levels of public health. It shows that these arguments justify a far narrower federal role than that embodied in the current environmental statutes.

The following section shows that much of the criticism to centralized regulation that flows from the preceding analysis of the institutional framework in the United States applies with equal force to the European Union. It also underscores the importance for the European Union of debates concerning the proper allocation of authority currently waged primarily on this side of the Atlantic.

The final section explains why the assessment of centralized intervention is different in the international community than in federal systems. It also provides a framework for analyzing the desirability of environmentally based trade restrictions in the international community.

## A presumption in favor of decentralization

My starting point is a rebuttable presumption in favor of decentralization.[2] This presumption rests on three independent grounds. First, the United States is a large and diverse country. It is therefore likely that different regions have different preferences for environmental protection. Environmental protection entails an important resource allocation question. We can generally purchase additional environmental protection at some price, paid in the currency of jobs, wages, shareholders' profits, tax revenues, and economic growth. Given the existence of the states as plausible regulatory units, the tradeoff reflecting the preferences of citizens of different regions should not be wholly disregarded in the regulatory process, absent strong reasons for doing so.

In the case of some social decisions, such reasons are present. The example of federal civil rights legislation, which trumped deeply held preferences of a large region of the country, is perhaps most prominent. But while I am sympathetic to the argument that the protection of a minimum level of public health ought to be viewed in quasi-constitutional terms and guaranteed throughout the country, as I explain below it would stretch this principle beyond its breaking point to say that it calls for the federalization of every decision having public health consequences.[3]

2 This section relies heavily on Revesz, "A Response to Critics," at 536–38.

3 See below, text accompanying notes 48–49.

Second, the benefits of environmental protection also vary throughout the country. For example, a stringent ambient standard may benefit many people in densely populated areas but only a few elsewhere. Similarly, a particular level of exposure to a contaminant may be more detrimental if it is combined with exposure to other contaminants with which it has synergistic effects.[4]

Third, the costs of meeting a given standard also differ across geographic regions. For example, a source may have a large detrimental impact on ambient air quality if it is directly upwind from a mountain or other topographical barrier. Similarly, a water polluter will have a far larger impact on water quality standards if it disposes its effluents in relatively small bodies of water. Climate might also play a role: certain emission or effluent standards may be easier (and cheaper) to meet in warmer weather.[5]

In principle, federal regulation could be attentive to these differences. Such a differentiated approach, however, would require a staggering amount of information. Clearly, the federal government does not have a comparative advantage at gathering such information. Thus, not surprisingly, federal regulation generally imposes uniform requirements throughout the country. Moreover, even when federal regulation imposes disuniform standards, the differences are not explainable by the factors discussed above.[6]

This presumption for decentralization should be overcome, however, if there is a systemic evil in letting states decide the level of environmental protection that will apply within their jurisdictions. In the following three sections I examine, respectively, the strength of the race-to-the-bottom, interstate externality, and public choice justifications for federal environmental protection.

[4] See James E. Krier, "On the Topology of Uniform Environmental Standards in a Federal System – and Why it Matters," 54 *Md. L. Rev.* 1226 (1995); James E. Krier, "The Irrational National Ambient Air Quality Standards: Macro- and Micro-Mistakes," 22 *UCLA L. Rev.* 323 (1974).

[5] See *Chemical Mfrs. Ass'n* v. *EPA*, 870 F.2d 177 (D.C. Cir. 1989), *cert. denied*, 495 U.S. 910 (1990); *Tanners' Council, Inc.* v. *Train*, 540 F.2d 1188 (4th Cir. 1976); *American Frozen Food Inst.* v. *Train*, 539 F.2d 107 (D.C. Cir. 1976); *Hooker Chem. & Plastics Corp.* v. *Train*, 537 F.2d 639 (2d Cir. 1975).

[6] For example, the Clean Air Act imposes disuniform ambient standards, determined by whether an area is covered by the Prevention of Significant Deterioration (PSD) or nonattainment programs. *See* 42 U.S.C. §§ 7473, 7502(c)(2), 7503(a)(1)(A) (1994). These differences turn on what ambient air quality standards regions had at a particular time, rather than differences in preferences, benefits, or costs.

## The race-to-the-bottom justification

The discussion proceeds in four parts.[7] First, it argues that interstate competition over environmental standards is, in essence, competition for the sale of a good. Second, it shows that the leading economic model of the effects of interstate competition on the choice of environmental standards demonstrates that interjurisdictional competition leads to the maximization of social welfare, rather than to a race to the bottom. Third, it argues that if game-theoretic interaction among the states leads to a departure from optimality, the result could be overregulation or underregulation; thus, even under this scenario there is no compelling justification for federal minimum standards, which are designed to correct only for underregulation. Fourth, it shows that even if states systematically enacted sub-optimally lax environmental standards, federal environmental regulation would not necessarily improve the situation.

### MARKET ANALOGY

Race-to-the-bottom advocates must clear an initial hurdle. If one believes that competition among sellers of, say, widgets is socially desirable, why is

[7] This section relies heavily on Revesz, "Rethinking the 'Race to the Bottom' Rationale"; Revesz, "A Normative Critique," at 99–107. For commentary generally supportive of my approach, see, e.g., David L. Shapiro, *Federalism: A Dialogue* (Evanston, Ill.: Northwestern University Press, 1995) David L. Shapiro, 42–43, 81–83; Krier, "Uniform Environmental Standards," at 1236–37; Richard B. Stewart, "Environmental Regulation and International Competitiveness," 102 *Yale L.J.* 2039, 2058–59 (1993); Richard B. Stewart, "International Trade and Environment: Lessons from the Federal Experience," 49 *Wash. & Lee L. Rev.* 1329, 1371 (1992); Stephen Williams, "Culpability, Restitution, and the Environment: The Vitality of Common Law Rules," 21 *Ecol. L.Q.* 559, 560–61 (1994).

Several articles have taken issue with my work on federalism and environmental regulation, particularly with my indictment of the race-to-the-bottom rationale for federal environmental regulation. See Kirsten H. Engel, "State Environmental Standard-Setting: Is there a 'Race' and is it 'to the Bottom'," 48 *Hastings L.J.* 271 (1997); Daniel C. Esty, "Revitalizing Environmental Federalism," 95 *Mich. L. Rev.* 570 (1996); Joshua D. Sarnoff, "The Continuing Imperative (but only from a National Perspective) for Federal Environmental Protection," 7 *Duke Env. & Pol'y F.* 225 (1997); Peter P. Swire, "The Race to Laxity and the Race to Undesirability: Explaining Failures in Competition Among Jurisdictions in Environmental Law," in *Yale L. & P. Rev./Yale J. Regulation, Constructing a New Federalism: Jurisdictional Competence and Competition* 67 (1996). My response appears in Revesz, "A Response to Critics".

competition among states, as sellers of a good – the right to locate within their jurisdictions – socially undesirable?

Indeed, states sell location rights because, even though they might not have the legal authority to prevent firms from locating within their borders, such firms must comply with the fiscal and regulatory regime of the state in which they wish to locate. The resulting costs to the firms can be analogized to the sale price of a traditional good. If federal regulation mandating a supra-competitive price for widgets is socially undesirable, why should it be socially desirable to have federal regulation mandating a supra-competitive price for location rights, in the form of more stringent environmental standards than those that would result from interstate competition?

It is easy to identify possible distinctions between a state as seller of location rights and sellers of widgets. These differences, however, do not provide support for race-to-the-bottom claims.

First, if individuals are mobile across jurisdictions, the costs that polluters impose on a state's residents will depend on who ends up being a resident of the state; the resulting supply curve is thus far more complex than that of a widget seller. In the context of environmental regulation, however, race-to-the-bottom claims have focused exclusively on the mobility of capital, thereby assuming, at least implicitly, that individuals are immobile. Moreover, it is not clear that individual mobility renders competition among states different from competition among widget sellers. Indeed, even if individuals move in search of the jurisdiction that has the level of environmental protection that they favor, [8] and if there is capital mobility, the choice of environmental standards can nonetheless be efficient.[9]

Second, while a seller of widgets is indifferent to the effect of the sale price on the welfare of the good's purchaser, a state ought to be concerned about the interests of the shareholders of the polluting firm who reside in the jurisdiction, both as individuals adversely affected by pollution and as owners of capital adversely affected by the costs of meeting regulatory

[8] *See* Charles M. Tiebout, "A Pure Theory of Local Expenditures," 64 *J. Pol. Econ.* 416 (1956); Truman F. Bewley, "A Critique Theory of Local Public Expenditures," 49 *Econometrica* 713 (1981).

[9] Wallace E. Oates and Robert M. Schwab, "Pricing Instruments for Environmental Protection: The Problems of Cross-Media Pollution, Interjurisdictional Competition and Interregional Effects" (November 1987) (unpublished manuscript on file with author, cited in Wallace E. Oates and Robert M. Schwab, "Economic Competition Among Jurisdictions: Efficiency Enhancing or Distortion Inducing?" 35 *J. Pub. Econ.* 333, 337 n. 7 (1988).

requirements. But this difference does not support race-to-the-bottom arguments. Indeed, if some of the regulated firm's shareholders did not reside in the regulating jurisdiction and if capital were immobile, a state could extract monopoly profits by setting suboptimally *stringent* standards, benefiting its in-state breathers at the expense of out-of-state shareholders. (If capital is mobile, competition eliminates this problem.) Nothing in this account provides support for the opposite proposition: that interstate competition leads to suboptimally lax standards.

Third, states are not subject to the discipline of the market. If a producer of widgets consistently sells at a price that does not cover its average costs, it will eventually have to declare bankruptcy. A state, in contrast, can continue in existence even if it recklessly compromises the health of its residents. This difference merely establishes that a state might undervalue environmental benefits. But such undervaluation can take place even if capital were not mobile: it is a public choice problem rather than a race-to-the-bottom problem.

Fourth, states do not sell "location rights" at a single-component price; they require that firms comply with a variety of regulatory standards and that they pay taxes. The resulting market is thus more complex than one involving the sale of a traditional good. For example, a jurisdiction that imposes a lax worker safety standard but a stringent pollution standard will be desirable for a labor-intensive, non-polluting firm, whereas a jurisdiction with stringent safety and lax pollution standards will be desirable for a capital-intensive, polluting firm. It is far from clear, however, why this additional complexity in the market would make interstate competition destructive. Instead, the example suggests a desirable sorting out of firms according to the preferences of individuals in the various jurisdictions.

In sum, while the analogy between interstate competition for industrial activity and markets for traditional goods is not perfect, it raises serious questions about race-to-the-bottom claims. At the very least, it should require race-to-the-bottom advocates to bear the burden of identifying relevant differences between the two markets, and explaining why they turn otherwise desirable competition into a race to the bottom.

## ECONOMIC MODELS

Quite to the contrary, and contrary to the prevailing assumption in the legal literature and in the legislative debates, the leading economic model of the effects of interstate competition on the choice of environmental standards shows that interjurisdictional competition leads to the maximization of social welfare, rather than to a race to the bottom.[10] Professors Wallace Oates and Robert Schwab posit jurisdictions that compete for mobile capital through the choice of taxes and environmental standards. A higher capital stock benefits residents in the form of higher wages, but hurts them as a result of the foregone tax revenues and lower environmental quality needed to attract the capital.[11]

In their model, individuals live and work in the same jurisdiction and there are no interjurisdictional pollution spillovers. Each jurisdiction produces the same single good, which is sold in a national market. The production of the good requires capital and labor, and leads to waste emissions. The various jurisdictions set a total permissible amount of emissions as well as a tax on each unit of capital. Capital is perfectly mobile across jurisdictions and seeks to maximize its after-tax earnings, but labor is immobile.[12] Each individual in the community, who is identical in both tastes and productive capacity, puts in a fixed period of work each week, and everyone is employed. Additional capital raises the productivity of workers, and therefore their wages.

Each jurisdiction makes two policy decisions: it sets a tax rate on capital and an environmental standard. Professors Oates and Schwab show that competitive jurisdictions will set a net tax rate on capital of zero (the rate that exactly covers the cost of public services provided to the capital, such as

[10] Oates and Schwab, "Economic Competition Among Jurisdictions."

[11] One commentator argues that interstate competition can lead to detrimental results owing to factors such as the excessive discounting of future damages, but provides no argument for why this determination would be performed better at the federal level. See John H. Cumberland, "Interregional Pollution Spillovers and Consistency of Environmental Policy," in H. Siebert et al. eds., *Regional Environmental Policy: The Economic Issues* (New York: New York University Press 1979) 255. For an argument to the contrary, see Wallace E. Oates and Robert M. Schwab, "The Theory of Regulatory Federalism: The Case of Environmental Management," in Wallace E. Oates ed., *The Economics of Environmental Regulation* (Cheltenham, UK and Brookfield, US: Edward Elgar, 1996) 319.

[12] In a companion, unpublished manuscript (see note 9 above), they argue that their conclusion that competition among states produces efficient outcomes holds even if individuals are mobile. If individuals are mobile, they will sort out, as in the Tiebout model, by reference to their preference for environmental protection. Individuals who are willing to trade off a great deal in wages for better environmental quality will move to jurisdictions that impose stringent controls on industry; individuals who attach less importance to environmental quality will go to dirtier areas.

police and fire protection). For positive net tax rates, the revenues are less than the loss in wages that results from the move of capital to other jurisdictions. In contrast, net subsidies would cost the jurisdiction more than the increase in wages that additional capital would generate.

In turn, competitive jurisdictions will set an environmental standard that is defined by equating the willingness to pay for an additional unit of environmental quality with the corresponding change in wages. Pollution beyond this level generates an increment to wage income that is less than the value of the damage to residents from the increased pollution; in contrast, less pollution creates a loss in wage income greater than the corresponding decrease in pollution damage.

Professors Oates and Schwab show that these choices of tax rates and environmental standards are socially optimal. With respect to tax rates, one condition for optimality is that the marginal product of capital – the increase in the output of the good produced by an additional unit of capital – must be the same across jurisdictions. Otherwise, it would be possible to increase aggregate output, and, consequently, aggregate social welfare, by moving capital from a jurisdiction where the marginal product of capital is low to one where it is high. Because capital is fully mobile, the market will establish a single rate of return on capital. This rate is equal to the marginal product of capital minus the tax on capital. The choice by competitive jurisdictions of a net tax of zero equalizes the marginal product of capital across jurisdictions and is therefore consistent with optimality.

With respect to environmental standards, competitive jurisdictions equate the marginal private cost of improving environmental quality (measured in terms of foregone consumption) with the marginal private benefit. For net tax rates of zero, the marginal private cost is, as noted above, the decrease in wage income produced by the marginal unit of environmental protection. This decrease is also the marginal social cost, since it represents society's foregone consumption. Thus, instead of producing a race to the bottom, competition leads to the optimal levels of environmental protection.

## NON-OPTIMALITY AS A RESULT OF GAME-THEORETIC INTERACTIONS

So far, the inquiry has not revealed support for the claim of systematic environmental underregulation in a regime without federal intervention. It is possible, however, that in particular instances, the game-theoretic interactions among the states would lead to underregulation absent federal intervention. In such cases, federal minimum standards would be desirable. But it is equally plausible that in other instances the reverse would be true: that the game-theoretic interactions between the states would lead to overregulation absent federal intervention. In such cases, federal regulation would be desirable as well, but federal *maximum* standards would be called for. Accordingly, there is no compelling race-to-the-bottom justification for across-the-board federal minimum standards, which are the cornerstone of federal environmental law.

As an example of such game-theoretic interactions, consider, in the Oates and Schwab model, a situation in which states decide to impose a positive net tax rate on capital, perhaps because they cannot finance the provision of public goods through a non-distortionary tax, such as a head tax. In such a situation, environmental standards will be suboptimally lax because the jurisdiction will continue to relax these standards beyond the optimal level in order to benefit from the additional net tax revenue that results from attracting additional capital.

A corollary, however, is that environmental standards will be suboptimally stringent if a jurisdiction, perhaps because of the visibility that attaches to attracting a major facility, chooses a tax rate on capital that is less than the cost of the public services that capital requires. Under this scenario, the optimal strategy for the jurisdiction is to strengthen the environmental standards beyond the optimal level so as to reduce the negative fiscal consequences.[13]

Similarly, recent studies relax the assumptions of constant returns to scale and perfect competition, which are a cornerstone of the Oates and Schwab model.[14] Instead, they consider the effects of state regulation on an industry that exhibits increasing returns to scale, a condition generally associated with imperfect competition. The conclusions of the model are

[13] There is no consensus in the academic literature on whether, on average, states and localities tax or subsidize capital. See Peter Mieszkowski and George R. Zodrow, "Taxation and the Tiebout Model: The Differential Effects of Head Taxes, Taxes on Land Rents, and Property Taxes," 27 *J. Econ. Lit.* 1098 (1989).

[14] See James R. Markusen, Edward R. Morey, and Nancy D. Olewiler, "Environmental Policy when Market Structures and Plant Locations are Endogenous," 24 *J. Env. Econ. & Mgmt.* 69 (1993); James R. Markusen, Edward R. Morey, and Nancy D. Olewiler, "Competition in Regional Environmental Policies when Plant Locations are Endogenous," 56 *J. Pub. Econ.* 55 (1995).

that, depending on the levels of firm-specific costs, plant-specific costs, and transportation costs, interstate competition can produce either suboptimally lax or suboptimally stringent levels of pollution.

Alternatively, if a firm has market power enabling it to affect prices, it will be able to extract a suboptimally lax standard. Conversely, if a state has market power, the reverse will be true. In summary, just as there are game-theoretic situations in which interstate competition produces environmental underregulation, there are other plausible scenarios under which the result is overregulation.

## Futility of federal regulation

But even if, left to their own devices, states systematically enacted suboptimally lax environmental standards, federal environmental regulation would not necessarily improve the situation. Race-to-the-bottom arguments appear to assume, at least implicitly, that jurisdictions compete over only one variable – in this case, environmental quality. Consider, instead, the problem in a context in which states compete over two variables – for example, environmental protection and worker safety. Assume that, in the absence of federal regulation, State 1 chooses a low level of environmental protection and a high level of worker safety. State 2 does the opposite: it chooses a high level of environmental protection and a low level of worker safety protection. Both states are in a competitive equilibrium, with industry not migrating from one to the other.

Suppose that federal regulation then imposes on both states a high level of environmental protection. The federal scheme does not add to the costs imposed upon industry in State 2, but it does in State 1. Thus, the federal regulation will upset the competitive equilibrium, and unless State 1 responds, industry will migrate from State 1 to State 2. The logical response of State 1 is to adopt less stringent worker safety standards. This response will mitigate the magnitude of the industrial migration that would otherwise have occurred.

Thus, if a race to the bottom exists, federal environmental standards can have adverse effects on other regulatory programs, in this case, worker safety. On this account, federal environmental regulation is desirable only if its benefits outweigh the costs that it imposes by shifting to other programs the pernicious effects of interstate competition.

More generally, the presence of such secondary effects implies that federal regulation would not be able to eliminate the negative effects of interstate competition, if such negative effects existed. Recall that the central tenet of race-to-the-bottom claims is that competition will lead to the reduction of social welfare; the assertion that states enact suboptimally lax environmental standards is simply a consequence of this more basic problem. In the face of federal environmental regulation, however, states will continue to compete for industry by adjusting the incentive structure of other state programs.

So, for example, if states cannot compete over environmental regulation, they will compete over worker safety standards. One might respond by saying that worker safety should also be (and is) the subject of federal regulation. But states would then compete over consumer protection laws or tort standards, and so on. And even if all regulatory functions were federalized, the competition would simply shift to the fiscal arena, where it would lead to the underprovision of public goods. Thus, the reduction in social welfare implicit in race-to-the-bottom arguments would not be eliminated.

The race-to-the-bottom rationale for federal environmental regulation is, therefore, radically underinclusive. It seeks to solve a problem that can be addressed only by wholly eliminating state autonomy. In essence, then, race-to-the-bottom arguments are frontal attacks on federalism. Unless one is prepared to federalize all regulatory and fiscal decisions it is far from clear that federal intervention in the environmental arena would mitigate the adverse social welfare consequences of a race to the bottom, if such a race existed.

## The interstate externality justification

The presence of interstate externalities provides a compelling argument for federal regulation under conditions in which Coasian bargaining is unlikely to occur.[15] A state that sends pollution to another state obtains the labor and fiscal benefits of the economic activity that generates the pollution, but does not suffer the full costs of the activity. Thus, a suboptimally large amount of pollution will cross state lines.

Several reasons might explain why transaction costs are sufficiently high to prevent the formation of interstate compacts. First, the baselines are not

[15] In contrast, if the transaction costs were sufficiently low to permit such bargaining, there would be no efficiency-based reason for federal regulation.

well defined in the current legal regime. Does an upwind state have the right to send pollution downwind unconstrained? Alternatively, does the downwind state have the right to enjoin all upwind pollution? Second, for different pollution problems, the range of affected states will vary, making less likely the emergence of conditions favoring cooperation. For example, in the case of air pollution, the states affected by a source at a particular location will depend to a large extent on the nature of the pollutant and the height of the stack. Third, the causation questions are not likely to be straightforward. Considerable scientific work needs to be undertaken in order to determine what sources of pollution are having an impact on the downwind state, and it makes little sense for these determinations to be replicated with respect to each compact.

The fact that interstate externalities provide a compelling justification for intervention, however, does not mean that all federal environmental regulation can be justified on these grounds. For environmental problems such as the control of drinking water quality, there are virtually no interstate pollution externalities; the effects are almost exclusively local. Even with respect to problems for which there are interstate externalities, such as air pollution, the rationale calls only for a response well targeted to the problem, such as a limit on the amount of pollution that can cross state lines, rather than the control of pollution that has only in-state consequences.

The analysis of the effectiveness of the environmental statutes in remedying interstate pollution spillovers proceeds by reference to the Clean Air Act – the statute designed to deal with the pollution that gives rise to the most serious problems of interstate externalities.[16] It examines the statute's ambient and emission standards, which are the core of the regulatory effort, as well as its acid rain provision and interstate spillover provisions, which are more directly targeted to the problem of interstate externalities. It shows that federal regulation has been both ineffective and potentially counterproductive.[17] The section ends with a discussion suggesting why marketable permit schemes might be a desirable solution to the problem of interstate externalities. These permits would be denominated in units of environmental degradation rather than, as is commonly the case, in units of emissions.

[16] This section relies heavily on Revesz, "Interstate Externalities"; Revesz, "A Normative Critique," at 107–20.

[17] Similar criticisms can be raised against the Clean Water Act, which is designed to combat an environmental problem for which the interstate pollution spillovers are also salient. See Revesz, "Interstate Externalities," at 2370 n.105.

## AMBIENT AND EMISSION STANDARDS

The core of the Clean Air Act consists of a series of federally prescribed ambient standards and emission standards. Ambient standards determine the maximum permissible concentration of particular pollutants in the ambient air, but do not directly constrain the behavior of individual polluters. Emission standards, in contrast, determine the maximum amount of a pollutant that can be discharged by an individual source.

The federal emission standards are not a good means by which to combat the problem of interstate externalities. These standards constrain the pollution from each source, but do not regulate the number of sources within any given state or the location of the sources.

Similarly, the various federal ambient air quality standards also are not well targeted to address the problem of interstate externalities, because they are both overinclusive and underinclusive. From the perspective of constraining interstate externalities at a desirable level, ambient standards are overinclusive because they require a state to restrict pollution that has only in-state consequences. Concern about interstate externalities can be addressed by limiting the amount of pollution that can cross interstate borders. Because some air pollution has only local effects, such externalities can be controlled even if the upwind state chooses to have poor environmental quality within its borders.

Conversely, the federal ambient air quality standards are also underinclusive from the perspective of controlling interstate externalities because a state could meet the applicable ambient standards but nonetheless export a great deal of pollution to downwind states because the sources in the state have tall stacks and are located near the interstate border. In fact, a state might meet its ambient standards precisely *because* it exports a great deal of its pollution.

The federal ambient and emissions standards could perhaps be justified as a second-best means by which to reduce the problem of uncontrolled interstate externalities. One might believe that by reducing pollution across the board they reduce interstate externalities proportionately.

Such a view, however, is incorrect as a matter of both theory and empirical observation. The amount of aggregate emissions is not the only variable that affects the level of interstate externalities. In particular, two other factors play important roles. The first is the height of the stack from which the pollution is emitted. The higher the stack, the lesser the impact close to the source and the greater the impact far from the source. Thus, absent a federal constraint, states have an incentive to encourage their sources to use tall stacks, as a way to externalize both the health and environmental effects of the pollution, as well as the regulatory costs of complying with the federal ambient standards.

Second, the level of interstate externalities is affected by the location of the sources. In the eastern part of the United States, where the problem of interstate pollution is most serious, the prevailing winds blow from west to east. Thus, states have an incentive to induce their sources to locate close to their downwind borders so that the bulk of the effects of the pollution is externalized. They can induce this result, for example, through the use of tax incentives or subsidies, or through permitting and zoning decisions.

The best evidence that states do indeed encourage sources to use tall stacks can be found in the provisions of the State Implementation Plans (SIPs) adopted by at least fifteen states in response to the enactment of the Clean Air Act in 1970. These SIPs allowed sources to meet the National Ambient Air Quality Standards (NAAQS) by using taller stacks rather than by reducing emissions.[18] In those SIPs, the permissible level of emissions was an increasing function of the height of the stack.[19] If the stack was sufficiently high, the effects would be felt only in the downwind states and would therefore have no impact on in-state ambient air quality levels. Through these measures, the states created strong incentives for their firms to externalize the effects of their sources of pollution.

It is true that states had an incentive to externalize pollution even before the enactment of the Clean Air Act in 1970 because, by encouraging tall stacks, states could make other states bear the adverse health effects of pollution. The 1970 provisions, however, created an additional incentive. By

[18] See Clean Air Act Oversight: Hearings Before the Subcomm. on Environmental Pollution, Sen. Comm. on Public Works, 93d Cong., 2d Sess. 330–31, 337, 357–59 (1974); Richard E. Ayres, "Enforcement of Air Pollution Controls on Stationary Sources Under the Clean Air Amendments of 1970," 4 *Ecol. L.Q.* 441, 452 and nn.28, 30 (1975).

[19] For example, the Georgia regulations that were struck down in *Natural Resources Defense Council* v. *EPA*, 489 F.2d 390, 403–11 (5th Cir. 1974), *rev'd on other grounds sub nom. Train* v. *Natural Resources Defense Council*, 421 U.S. 60 (1975), provided that, for sulfur dioxide, allowable emissions could be proportional to the cube of the stack height, for stacks under 300 feet, and proportional to the square of the stack height for stacks over 300 feet. See Georgia Rules and Regulations for Air Quality Control § 270–5–24–.02(2)(g) (1972). A similar formula applied to particulate emissions: § 270–5–24–.02(2)(m). Thus, a sufficiently high stack would eliminate the need for any emissions reduction.

encouraging the use of tall stacks, states could also externalize the regulatory impact of the standards, thereby availing themselves, for example, of the opportunity to attract additional sources without violating the NAAQS.

Taller stacks entail higher costs of construction and, possibly, operation. It is therefore conceivable that a state that did not view the externalization of health effects as sufficient by itself to outweigh imposing such costs on in-state firms would reach a different conclusion when tall stacks lead to the externalization of both health and regulatory impacts.

More generally, before 1970, the states had not developed extensive regulatory programs for controlling air pollution. The net benefits of taller stacks, if any, might not have been worth the institutional investment necessary to create a regulatory program to transmit incentives for such stacks. The Clean Air Act, by requiring states to prepare SIPs, gave them no choice but to create an institutional structure designed to regulate the emissions of industrial sources. With that structure in place, it became comparatively easier to encourage tall stacks.

In addition, the health benefits of reducing the impact of emissions on in-state ambient air quality levels are external to the firm emitting the pollution. Thus, a firm will take such effects into account only if required to do so by a regulator. In contrast, the regulatory benefits of reducing the impact on in-state ambient air quality levels can be captured directly by the firms, which, by using taller stacks, need to invest less to reduce their emissions.[20] While, before 1970, firms would have expended resources in tall stacks only if required to do so by a state regulatory agency, after 1970 they had an independent incentive for pursuing such a policy.

It is therefore not surprising that the use of tall stacks expanded considerably after 1970. For example, whereas in 1970 only two stacks in the United States were higher than 500 feet, by 1985 more than 180 stacks were higher than 500 feet and twenty-three were higher than 1,000 feet.[21] While the ability of states to externalize pollution in this manner is now less of a problem as a result of a system of regulation of stack height that followed

[20] The savings can be substantial. For example, a study in the early 1970s, when tall stack credits were most prevalent, showed that the costs of complying with regulatory requirements were between $60/kw and $130/kw for a new lime scrubber, as compared with between $4/kw and $10/kw for a tall stack. See Sen. Comm. on Public Works, at 210, 215.

[21] See Arnold W. Reitze, Jr., "A Century of Air Pollution Control Law: What's Worked; What's Failed; What Might Work," 21 *Env. L.* 1549, 1598 (1991); James R. Vestigo, "Acid Rain and Tall Stack Regulation Under the Clean Air Act," 15 *Env. L.* 711, 730 (1985).

the 1977 amendments to the Clean Air Act, tall stacks remain a means by which excessive pollution can be externalized.

In contrast to the experience with tall stack provisions, it is difficult to find direct evidence concerning whether states also provided incentives for sources to locate close to their downwind borders, because such incentives are unlikely to be reflected in regulatory documents. There is, however, literature suggesting that such incentives are present in the case of the siting of waste sites.[22] It would thus not be implausible to believe that states acted in the same manner with respect to air pollution facilities.

In summary, far from correcting the problem of interstate externalities, the Act's ambient and emission standards may well have exacerbated it.

## ACID RAIN PROVISIONS

The acid rain provisions of the 1990 amendments are often hailed as a means of reducing interstate externalities because acid rain is produced by pollution that travels long distances. However, these provisions apply only to the two pollutants that lead to the formation of acid rain: sulfur dioxide and nitrogen oxides. Further, they apply to only one type of facility: electric utilities. Moreover, these provisions are not structured to allocate emissions between upwind and downwind states in a desirable manner.[23]

With respect to nitrogen oxides, the provisions set emission standards for new and existing sources. As discussed above, emissions standards are not a well-targeted means for controlling interstate externalities.

With respect to sulfur dioxide, the acid rain provisions establish a system of grandfathered permits, under which existing emitters are assigned, for free, a number of permits equal to their historical emissions, subject to certain constraints. These permits are tradable in a single national market.

Although these constraints on the grandfathering of permits are likely to reduce the amount of acid rain, particularly after the year 2000, they make

[22] See, e.g., Daniel E. Ingberman, "Siting Noxious Facilities: Are Markets Efficient?" *J. Env. Econ. & Mgmt.* S–20, S–23 (1995); Bradford C. Mank, "Environmental Justice and Discriminatory Siting: Risk-Based Representation and Equitable Compensation," 56 *Ohio St. L.J.* 329, 421 (1995); Robert B. Wiygul and Sharon C. Harrington, "Environmental Justice in Rural Communities Part One: RCRA, Communities, and Environmental Justice," 96 *W. Va. L. Rev.* 405, 437–38 (1993–94); Rae Zimmerman, "Issues of Classification in Environmental Equity: How we Manage is How we Measure," 21 *Fordham Urb. L.J.* 633, 650 (1994).

[23] See 42 U.S.C. §§ 7651–7651*o* (1994).

no attempt to allocate emissions between upwind states and downwind states in an optimal way. The acid rain problem manifests itself primarily in the Northeast, but is caused primarily by emissions from the Midwest. Because the market is national, Midwestern sources can buy, without restriction, permits from the West and the Northeast. Such trades would have an undesirable impact on the Northeast. In fact, downwind states are attempting to prevent their sources from selling permits to upwind sources, though such measures may well be struck down on constitutional grounds.

## INTERSTATE SPILLOVER PROVISIONS

Sections 110(a)(2)(D) and 126(b), which date from the 1977 amendments, are the most comprehensive means for controlling interstate spillovers. These provisions prohibit a state from "contribut[ing] significantly to nonattainment in, or interfer[ing] with maintenance by," any other state with respect to the NAAQS, or "interfer[ing] with measures required by" any other state under the Prevention of Significant Deterioration (PSD) program.[24]

Unlike the federal ambient and emissions standards, the interstate spillover provisions are designed to prevent excessive pollution from crossing interstate borders. Unlike the tall stack and acid rain provisions, they are designed to deal with the problem comprehensively. Unfortunately, however, both in resolving various threshold issues and in interpreting substantive questions under the interstate spillover provisions, the administrative practice and case law have rendered these provisions virtually useless as a means of constraining interjurisdictional externalities.

The Environmental Protection Agency (EPA), through the resolution of various threshold issues, has blocked the prospects of downwind states complaining about excessive upwind pollution in important ways. First, it has maintained that it cannot predict such impacts more than 50 kilometers (about 30 miles) from the source of the pollution, and has summarily rejected the predictions made by downwind states on the basis of longer-range models.[25] Thus, sections 110(a)(2)(D) and 126(b) have been of no use to downwind states challenging pollution from sources not immediately contiguous to their borders.

[24] See 42 U.S.C. §§ 7410(a)(2)(d), 7426(b) (1994).

[25] See, e.g., *New York* v. *EPA*, 716 F.2d 440, 443–44 (7th Cir. 1983); *New York* v. *EPA*, 710 F.2d 1200, 1204 (6th Cir. 1983).

The second threshold issue relates to the treatment of pollutants that are transformed as they travel through the atmosphere. For example, increased sulfur dioxide emissions upwind have an effect downwind not only on ambient air quality levels of sulfur dioxide, but also on ambient air-quality levels of particulates. The EPA has consistently taken the position, which has been upheld by the courts, that the impact of transformed pollution need not be taken into account in evaluating whether the upwind pollution is excessive.[26] Thus, the phenomenon of acid rain, an important manifestation of the problem of interstate pollution, has been largely outside the reach of sections 110(a)(2)(D) and 126(b).

Third, the EPA has not set a national ambient air quality standard for sulfates,[27] even though a relative consensus developed within the scientific community in the 1980s concerning the adverse environmental effects of acid rain.[28] Nor has the EPA promulgated regulations to combat regional haze, [29] despite a statutory obligation under section 169A to do so by 1979. Had the EPA done so, it would have been required by sections 110(a)(2)(D) and 126(b) to take into account the impact of upwind emissions of sulfur dioxide on the downwind ambient air quality levels of sulfates as well as their impact on regional haze.[30]

The EPA's interpretation of the substantive standards of sections 110(a)(2)(D) and 126(b) has further contributed to render these provisions ineffective in controlling interstate externalities. It is useful in this regard to construct a three-category taxonomy defined by reference to whether the downwind state would meet the federal ambient standards if it did not have to face pollution transported from the upwind state and whether the downwind state actually meets the federal ambient standards despite the upwind pollution.

In the first category, the downwind state would meet the federal ambient

[26] See, e.g., *New York* v. *EPA*, 716 F.2d 440, 443 (7th Cir. 1983); *New York* v. *EPA*, 710 F.2d 1200, 1204 (6th Cir. 1983).

[27] See *Connecticut* v. *EPA*, 696 F.2d 147, 164–65 (2d Cir. 1982); Bruce A. Ackerman and William T. Hassler, *Clean Coal/Dirty Air* (New Haven: Yale University Press, 1981), 65–72.

[28] See J. Laurence Kulp, "Acid Rain: Causes, Effects, and Control," *Regulation*, at 41–43 (Winter 1990); Valerie Lee, "Interstate Sulfate Pollution: Proposed Amendments to the Clean Air Act," 5 *Harv. Env. L. Rev.* 71, 72–76 (1981).

[29] See, e.g., *New York* v. *EPA*, 852 F.2d 574, 578–79 (D.C. Cir. 1988), *cert. denied*, 489 U.S. 1065 (1989); *Vermont* v. *Thomas*, 850 F.2d 99, 103 (2d Cir. 1988).

[30] See, e.g., *New York* v. *EPA*, 852 F.2d 574, 578–79 (D.C. Cir. 1988), *cert. denied*, 489 U.S. 1065 (1989); *Vermont* v. *Thomas*, 850 F.2d 99, 104 (2d Cir. 1988); *New York* v. *EPA*, 716 F.2d 440, 443 (7th Cir. 1983); *New York* v. *EPA*, 710 F.2d 1200, 1204 (6th Cir. 1983).

Table 1.1 *Taxonomy of interstate spillovers*

| | Violation without upwind pollution | Violation with upwind pollution |
|---|---|---|
| Category I | No | No |
| Category II | Yes | Yes |
| Category III | No | Yes |

standards without the upwind pollution, and meets these standards despite the upwind pollution. In the second category, the downwind state would not meet the federal ambient standards even if there were no upwind pollution and, of course, does not meet the standards with the upwind pollution. In the third category, the downwind state would meet the federal ambient standards in the absence of upwind pollution, but does not meet these standards with the upwind pollution; here, the upwind pollution is the but-for cause of the violation of the federal ambient standards. This taxonomy is summarized in Table 1.1.

As to each of these categories, two questions are relevant. First, should the federal government play a role in controlling the upwind pollution? Second, assuming that such a role is appropriate, how should the federal government determine the permissible amount of upwind pollution that can enter the downwind state?

In Category I, absent a violation of the federal ambient standards – either the NAAQS or the PSD increments – the EPA has chosen to place no limits on the upwind pollution. In this situation, the upwind pollution will be unconstrained even if it leads to a violation of a state ambient standard in the downwind state that is stricter than the federal standard. Further, the upwind pollution will be unconstrained even if the downwind state has limited the emissions of its sources in order to preserve a margin for growth that will permit it to attract new industry. Finally, the upwind pollution will be unconstrained even if the downwind state has been unable to set a baseline under the PSD program, thereby constraining further environmental degradation, because no major source has applied for a permit.[31]

In Category II cases, where the upwind pollution exacerbates a violation

[31] See, e.g., *Air Pollution Control District* v. *EPA*, 739 F.2d 1071, 1085–88 (6th Cir. 1984); *Connecticut* v. *EPA*, 656 F.2d 902, 910 (2d Cir. 1981).

of a federal ambient standard in the downwind state, the EPA has never found upwind pollution to meet the "significant contribution" standard and has given little guidance on what factors distinguish a "significant" contribution from an "insignificant" one. In cases involving a single upwind source, the EPA concluded that contributions of 1.5 percent and of 3 percent were not excessive.[32] It reached these conclusions with no analysis, apparently basing its determination on the fact that those percentages do not seem particularly large. Nor did the EPA engage in any inquiry as to the cumulative impacts of upwind emissions. In light of the large number of sources that are likely to affect ambient air quality levels in the downwind state, this approach is quite unprotective of the interests of downwind states.

In Category III, the EPA has indicated that the plain meaning of the statutory phrase "prevent attainment" requires the Agency to deem excessive any upwind pollution that was the but-for cause of a violation of the federal ambient standards in the downwind state. In the only case in which the situation was presented, however, the Agency rejected the downwind claim, stating that it doubted the accuracy of the modeling analysis performed by the downwind state.[33]

In summary, three principal rules emerge from the administrative interpretations of sections 110(a)(2)(D) and 126(b), which have been uniformly upheld by the courts: upwind pollution is never constrained if the downwind state meets the federal ambient standards; upwind pollution that exacerbates a violation of the federal ambient standards in the downwind states is constrained only if the upwind source "significantly contributes" to the violation; and upwind pollution that is the but-for cause of the violation of federal ambient standards in the downwind state is always constrained.

The combination of these rules leads to illogical and, in practice, unprotective results. Consider first the Category I case of a downwind state that is not violating the NAAQS or the PSD increments. The amount by which the downwind state's ambient air quality levels are better than the federal ambient standards represents that state's margin for growth. If the downwind state is not able to attract new sources, because, for example, it is experiencing a temporary economic downturn, the rules allow an upwind state to consume the downwind state's margin for growth without constraint.

[32] See, e.g., *Connecticut* v. *EPA*, 696 F.2d 147, 165 (2d Cir. 1982); *Air Pollution Control District* v. *EPA*, 739 F.2d 1071, 1092–93 (6th Cir. 1984).

[33] See *New York* v. *EPA*, 852 F.2d 574, 580 (D.C. Cir. 1988), *cert. denied*, 489 U.S. 1065 (1989).

Indeed, the rules even allow an upwind state to consume the downwind state's margin for growth by amending its SIP to permit its existing sources to increase their emissions up to the point at which the federal ambient standards become constraining in the downwind state.[34] Once the air quality levels in the downwind state reach the level of the federal ambient standards (with the help of the upwind state), the downwind state will be unable to attract any sources without requiring emission reductions from its existing sources. At the extreme, a downwind state with no existing industrial base would be precluded from ever acquiring one.

In contrast, if the downwind state consumes its margin for growth first, either by attracting new sources or by amending its SIP to allow existing sources to pollute more, any increase in the pollution that the upwind state sends downwind would be deemed a violation of sections 110(a)(2)(D) and 126(b). An upwind state without an industrial base at the time that the downwind state reaches the federal ambient standards might be effectively precluded by this rule from attracting any polluting sources in the future if, as a result of the state's geography, any in-state emissions would be likely to migrate downwind.

Accordingly, the margin for growth in the downwind state would be allocated on a "first come–first served" basis. Such rules of capture are undesirable; they create incentives for both upwind and downwind states to use the downwind state's margin for growth at a faster rate than is economically desirable, and do not allocate this margin for growth to whichever state values it most highly.

The discussion so far has focused on a downwind state that intends to use its margin for growth for economic expansion. Instead, states might set state ambient standards that are more stringent than the federal standards because they attach more value to environmental protection. The federal environmental laws emphasize, as explicitly reflected in section 116 of the Clean Air Act, that federal standards are floors and not ceilings, and that, with exceptions not relevant to this discussion, states remain free to enact standards that are more stringent than the federal standards. Indeed, more stringent standards are undesirable only if they are an effort to externalize to other states the costs of pollution control.

Under the current administrative and judicial approach, however, more

[34] Of course, this strategy can be followed only if it does not lead to a violation of the federal ambient standards in the upwind state.

stringent state ambient standards can be used only to limit the emissions of in-state sources and cannot be invoked, under any circumstances, to constrain upwind emissions. Such a regime creates a disincentive for downwind states to have more stringent state ambient standards: downwind states bear all the costs of such standards (the costs of tougher emissions limitations for in-state sources), but the upwind states can appropriate the benefit by taking the additional opportunities created for the externalization of pollution.

The administrative and judicial approach to Category II situations, in which the upwind pollution aggravates a violation of the federal ambient standards, also is misguided. In Category II cases, the downwind state would be unable to constrain the upwind pollution unless the pollution was deemed a "significant contribution" to the violation. Under the nonattainment provisions of the Clean Air Act, however, the downwind state has an obligation to reduce its emissions until it meets the NAAQS. Thus, absent a "significant contribution" from upwind sources, the full burden of pollution reduction falls initially on the downwind sources, even if upwind reductions would be far less costly.

But once the downwind state made sufficient improvements so that it could meet the NAAQS were it not for the upwind pollution, the situation would change. The upwind pollution would then be the but-for cause of the violation of the NAAQS in the downwind state – a Category III problem. The upwind pollution would be enjoined as "prevent[ing] the attainment" of the NAAQS, even if the cost to the upwind state of doing so were wholly disproportionate to the cost to the downwind state of somewhat more stringent pollution controls. As already indicated, in cases in which all emissions from the upwind state have at least some impact downwind, such a rule would prevent any polluting activity in the upwind state. The downwind state, by reducing its emissions to the point at which it could meet the NAAQS in the absence of the upwind pollution, but no further, could effectively destroy the upwind state's industrial base.

In summary, of the three rules articulated by the EPA and the courts to address the problem of interstate spillovers, two are overly lenient. In contrast, the third is overly harsh, though, perhaps as a result of its harshness, the EPA has failed to apply it to any specific case.

Perhaps the best illustration of the inefficacy of the Clean Air Act's interstate pollution provisions is provided by a dispute in which Kentucky complained about excessive emissions from an electric utility just across the border in Indiana. The Indiana utility was emitting 6 pounds of sulfur dioxide per million BTU of heat input – a level that reflected no pollution controls at all. In contrast, the electric utility in Kentucky had spent $138 million installing scrubbers in order to meet a standard of 1.2 pounds per million BTU. Moreover, the Indiana utility consumed almost half of the permissible pollution levels in parts of Kentucky. Nonetheless, despite the compelling nature of the facts, the downwind state lost its challenge.[35]

## THE PROMISE OF MARKETABLE PERMIT SCHEMES

The preceding section identified an important structural problem raised by procedures such as those of sections 110(a)(2)(D) and 126(b) of the US Clean Air Act, which rely on administrative and judicial determinations of the permissible amounts of interstate externalities. This problem arises because requiring existing sources to reduce their emissions is generally more costly than imposing the same standards on new sources. Thus, from the perspective of maximizing aggregate social welfare over time, the periodic strengthening of the emissions reductions requirements to accommodate economic growth is likely to be more costly than "reserving" a margin for such growth by imposing more stringent requirements at the outset. This problem is present both when the federal ambient standards in the downwind state are constraining and when the downwind state has ambient air quality levels that are better than the federal ambient standards.

The problem would be far less serious if the effects of emissions were confined to a single state, which could, as part of its planning process, determine where in the jurisdiction to "reserve" the margin for growth. With interjurisdictional effects, however, the situation is more complex because neither an interstate nor a federal planning process is likely to work well to determine how to allocate the additional burden needed to "reserve" a margin for growth.

Recall that this inquiry involves predicting where new firms will choose to locate, what the costs of emission reduction will be, and what impact these emissions will have on ambient air quality levels. These factors will determine, when a firm proposes to locate in a given place, how the burden of ensuring compliance with the applicable federal or state ambient standards will be allocated among that firm, other firms in the same state, and

[35] See *Air Pollution Control District* v. *EPA*, 739 F.2d 1071, 1092–93 (6th Cir. 1984).

firms in other states. The purpose of this allocation, once again, is to maximize social welfare in light not only of the current pattern of emissions (the static inquiry), but also in light of future development (the dynamic inquiry).

In at least some ways, marketable permit schemes are better suited for addressing this issue than administrative or judicial inquiries. Most importantly, under such schemes it is not necessary for a federal decisionmaker to determine whether the likely growth will come to the upwind or the downwind state.

Instead, either the downwind state or the upwind state could acquire permits in the marketplace, thereby "reserving" for itself a margin for growth. Then, when the economic expansion materialized, the state that held the permits could either sell them to the firms proposing to build plants, or, as an inducement to locate in the state, simply give the permits to those firms.[36] Firms that were planning to build plants in the future could also buy permits directly in the marketplace.[37] Moreover, as with other commodities, futures markets would develop.

The marketable permits described here would be in units of environmental degradation in the downwind state, rather than in units of emissions. Under marketable permit schemes in units of environmental degradation, a source must purchase permits at each location at which its emissions will have an impact on ambient air quality levels. Thus, any upwind and downwind sources that affect ambient air quality levels at some location in the downwind state will have to purchase permits to degrade ambient air quality at that location.

Because it is obviously impractical for a source to buy permits at each of the infinite number of points at which such impacts occur, some geographic aggregation is necessary for the scheme to be administrable. Nonetheless, marketable permit schemes in units of environmental degradation, unlike marketable permit schemes in units of emissions, require that a source purchase permits in more than one market.

[36] Under the Clean Air Act's nonattainment provisions, it is not uncommon for states to provide the offsets as an inducement to attract new plants. See *National Comm'n on Air Quality, To Breathe Clean Air* (Washington, D.C., 1981) 136–37.

[37] This discussion does not address how the initial allocation of the permits would be conducted. For discussion of this issue in connection with the markets for acid rain, see Paul L. Joskow and Richard Schmalensee, "The Political Economy of Market-based Environmental Policy: The US Acid Rain Program," 41 *J.L. & Econ.* 37 (1998).

Under marketable permit schemes in units of environmental degradation, the permissible number of emissions for each source is a function of how the source's emissions affect ambient air quality levels at all the points at which it is required to purchase permits. For example, if eight units of emissions cause one unit of environmental degradation at a particular point away from the source, a permit for one unit of environmental degradation at this point would allow eight units of emissions at the source. These equivalencies would be predicted through mathematical modeling, and, for each pollutant, would depend on factors such as wind patterns and topography.

In contrast to marketable permit schemes in units of environmental degradation, marketable permit schemes in units of emissions are not well suited for the task at issue here. They cannot allocate, between upwind and downwind sources, respectively, the pollution control burdens that will lead to the attainment of the relevant ambient standards in the manner that maximizes social welfare. First, if the downwind and upwind state are in a single market for emissions trading, any one-to-one trades would be allowed, even if such trades compromised aggregate social welfare by transferring emissions from a location at which their impact is less serious to a location at which this impact is more serious. Second, marketable permit schemes in units of emissions cannot ensure compliance with particular ambient standards because if, as a result of the pattern of trades, a sufficiently large number of permits is transferred to a particular geographic area, the applicable ambient standards will be violated at the hot spots at which these emissions have their maximum impact.

Permits in units of environmental degradation solve this problem.[38] The number of permits in such units is defined by reference to the ambient standards that need to be met. Thus, hot spots cannot occur.

Marketable permit schemes in units of environmental degradation would minimize the cost of meeting any set of ambient standards. Under such schemes, at the point at which no further trades would be beneficial to the parties, for any two sources, say Source 1 and Source 2, the ratio of the marginal cost of emissions reduction for Source 1 to the marginal cost of emissions reduction for Source 2 would equal the ratio of the impact on

[38] For discussion of such markets, see David Montgomery, "Markets in Licenses and Efficient Pollution Control Programs," 5 *J. Econ. Theory* 395 (1972); Thomas Tietenberg, "Transferable Discharge Permits and the Control of Stationary Source Air Pollution: A Survey and Synthesis," 56 *Land Econ.* 391 (1980).

ambient air quality at every point at which the source purchased permits, of an additional unit of emissions from Source 1 to the impact of an additional unit of emissions from Source 2. Otherwise these sources would benefit from a trade.

The analysis presented here underscores an argument for the use of marketable permit schemes in units of environmental degradation that is independent of the goal of cost minimization. Such schemes solve a coordination problem between upwind and downwind states that poses difficulties for other allocative mechanisms, like reliance on administrative or judicial determinations of permissible spillovers in light of the possibility of future economic growth. Traditionally, the comparison between centralized regulation and marketable permit schemes focuses on how the central planner is unlikely to have sufficient information about matters such as the costs of emissions reduction to devise allocations that maximize social welfare. This problem is exacerbated here because if each state were an independent central planner, non-market mechanisms for coordinating the actions of these states would be exceedingly cumbersome.

This discussion seeks neither to design a fully specified marketable permit scheme nor to argue that, in light of all relevant considerations, such schemes are the preferred policy tool. Rather, the exposition seeks to explain why marketable permit schemes can remedy the serious problems of coordination that otherwise would arise.

One obvious objection to marketable permit schemes in units of environmental degradation, however, is worth addressing briefly. Critics are likely to argue that such schemes are exceedingly difficult to administer. In particular, in order for the markets to work, one needs accurate information about the manner in which emissions at each source translate into ambient air quality impacts at each location at which these emissions affect ambient air quality levels.

In fact, however, the same procedures are currently used to determine compliance with the federal ambient standards. Indeed, the EPA determines whether areas violate these standards primarily through the use of computer modeling, rather than by direct measurement.[39] These models are mathematical matrices that translate emissions at the various sources

[39] See, e.g., *Connecticut* v. *EPA*, 696 F.2d 147, 157–58 (2d Cir. 1982) (Connecticut II); *Cleveland Elec. Illuminating Co.* v. *EPA*, 572 F.2d 1150 (6th Cir.), *cert. denied*, 439 U.S. 910 (1978); 40 C.F.R. § 51.115 (1995).

into contributions to the degradation of ambient air quality levels at different distances from the sources. Thus, the technical inquiry undertaken to determine compliance with the federal ambient standards under the command-and-control regulatory system currently in effect is identical to the one that would need to be undertaken in order to administer a marketable permit scheme in units of environmental degradation.

## The public choice justification

As indicated above, I have not yet tackled in any comprehensive way the public choice analysis of issues concerning federalism and environmental regulation. I have taken a somewhat skeptical view, however, of the assertion, largely undefended in the legal literature, that federal regulation is necessary to correct for the systematic underprotection of environmental quality at the state level.[40]

First, it is not enough to say that state political processes undervalue the benefits of environmental regulation, or overvalue the corresponding costs. Federal regulation is justifiable only if the outcome at the federal level is socially more desirable, either because there is less underregulation or because any overregulation leads to smaller social welfare losses.

Second, given the standard public choice argument for federal environmental regulation, it is not clear why the problems observed at the state level would not be replicated at the federal level. The logic of collective action would suggest that the large number of citizen-breathers, each with a relatively small stake in the outcome of a particular standard-setting proceeding, will be overwhelmed in the political process by concentrated industrial interests with a large stake in the outcome. But this problem could occur at the federal level as well as at the state level.

In fact, the logic of collective action might suggest the underrepresentation of environmental groups would be more serious at the federal level. The costs of organizing on a larger scale magnifies the free-rider problems faced by environmental groups. Moreover, because environmental concerns vary throughout the country, there will be a loss in the homogeneity of the environmental interests when they are aggregated at the federal level, thereby further complicating the organizational problems. For example, environmentalists in Massachusetts may care primarily about air quality

40 This section relies heavily on Revesz, "A Response to Critics," at 542–43, 558–61.

whereas environmentalists in Colorado may rank the environmental implications of water allocation as most important. Other things being equal, state-based environmental groups seeking, respectively, better air quality in Massachusetts and a more environmentally sensitive allocation of water in Colorado are therefore likely to be more effective than a national environmental group seeking, at the federal level, better environmental quality with respect to both of these attributes.

In contrast, the situation is likely to be different for industry groups. For many environmental problems, an important portion of the regulated community consists of firms with nationwide operations. For such firms, operating at the federal level poses no additional free-rider problems or loss of homogeneity.

It is possible, however, that the additional organizational problems faced by environmental groups at the federal level are outweighed by benefits arising from the fact that the clash of interest groups takes place before a single legislature, a single administrative agency, and, in part, as a result of the exclusive venue of the D.C. Circuit over important environmental statutes, in a single court.[41] One can imagine models under which public choice problems are, indeed, ameliorated at the federal level – a task that none of my critics has taken on. The problem, though, is that such models are unlikely to provide a good account of reality.

For example, if one assumed that beyond a certain threshold, additional resources do not increase a group's probability of being successful in the political process, and if this threshold at the federal level is sufficiently lower than the sum of the corresponding thresholds at the state levels, it may be that environmental groups would not be at a disadvantage at the federal level even if they were at a disadvantage in the states. In this case, the economies of scale of operating at the federal level more than outweigh the increased free-rider problems.

The assumptions behind such a model, however, are not particularly plausible. The threshold concept might properly describe certain costs associated with effective participation in the regulatory process. For example, with respect to the regulation of a particular carcinogen, each group might need to hire a scientist to review the regulator's risk assessment. It may well be the case that a certain minimum will secure the services

[41] See Richard L. Revesz, "Environmental Regulation, Ideology, and the D.C. Circuit," 83 *Va. L. Rev.* 1717 (1997).

of a competent scientist and that devoting additional resources to the problem would be of little, if any, use. Thus, for costs of this type, the marginal benefit of additional expenditures is zero, or close to zero, regardless of the other party's expenditures.

The structure of other costs, however, is likely to be quite different. For example, with respect to access to the legislative process, the standard public choice account is that the highest bidder prevails.[42] Thus, the benefit that a party receives from its expenditures is a function of the expenditures of the other party. Unless the costs of this type are quite small, the economies of scale of operating at the federal level are unlikely to outweigh the additional free-rider problems.

Finally, if the relevant public choice interactions are characterized as involving the diffuse interests of breathers or other environmental beneficiaries on one side and the concentrated interests of industrial firms on the other side, the debate over which forum is relatively better for the environmentalist interests is not of great practical importance. What is important, instead, is that both fora are bad for these interests as a result of the diffuse nature of their interests. As a result, given this characterization of this problem, it is difficult to explain, in public choice terms, why there would be any environmental regulation at all.[43]

For this reason, the most plausible public choice explanations for environmental regulation posit that regulated firms obtain benefits from such regulation in the form of rents and barriers to entry, or that certain regions in the United States can obtain from the regulatory process advantages relative to other regions. An extensive public choice literature suggests that the impetus for environmental regulation sometimes comes, implicitly or explicitly, from the regulated firms themselves, which can obtain rents and barriers to entry that give them an advantage over their competitors.[44] At other times, the advocates are particular regions of the country, which hope to obtain a comparative advantage with respect to other regions.[45]

[42] See Sam Peltzman, "Toward a More General Theory of Regulation," 19 *J.L. & Econ.* 211 (1976); George J. Stigler, "The Theory of Economic Regulation," 2 *Bell. J. Econ.* 3 (1971).

[43] Professor Swire acknowledges this difficulty with his argument: "In light of the straightforward public choice analysis presented here, the puzzle remains how environmental protection ever succeeds in the political process." "The Race to Laxity," at 109.

[44] See Nathaniel O. Keohane, Richard L. Revesz, and Robert N. Stavins, "The Choice of Regulatory Instruments in Environmental Policy," 22 *Harv. Env. L. Rev.* 313, 348–51 (1998).

[45] See B. Peter Pashigian, "Environmental Regulation: Whose Self-Interests are Being Protected?" 23 *Econ. Inquiry* 551 (1985).

When the relevant interactions are seen in this manner, the case for federal regulation on public choice grounds is considerably weakened. A more definitive conclusion, however, must await further sustained analysis.

## Towards desirable federal intervention

The preceding discussion shows why the three principal justifications for federal intervention are unlikely to justify an absolute displacement of state authority.[46] Nonetheless, there is an important role for federal intervention to correct various pathologies that otherwise would result.

1 *Interstate externalities:* The preceding discussion has focused on pollution externalities, principally air pollution that crosses state lines, and has shown why the existence of such externalities provides a compelling reason for federal regulation. Other externalities that merit federal regulation arise with respect to different environmental problems. For example, to the extent that certain endangered species are located in a particular state, the costs of protection are largely concentrated in that state. The benefits of preservation, however, accrue nationally, or, for that matter, globally.

   Similarly, out-of-state citizens place value on the existence of certain natural resources – even resources that they never plan to use. Such existence, or non-use, values provide a powerful justification for federal control over exceptional natural resources such as national parks.

2 *Economies of scale:* Advocates of federal regulation often maintain, though without much empirical support, that centralization has strong economies of scale advantages. The economies of scale argument is most plausible in the early stages of the regulatory process, particularly with respect to the determination of the adverse effects of particular pollutants through risk assessment. Indeed, there is little reason for this determination to be replicated by each state. In this area, however, the federal government appears to have substantially underinvested.

   The force of the rationale, however, is far less compelling at the standard-setting phase. At this stage, not only are the savings from eliminating duplication of efforts likely to be much lower, but centralization will have serious social costs as a result of the difficulty of setting standards

46 This section relies heavily on Revesz, "A Normative Critique," at 121–25; Revesz, "A Response to Critics," at 543–45.

that are responsive to the preferences and physical conditions of different regions.[47]

3 *Uniformity:* As previously discussed, federal environmental standards are generally minimum standards. The states remain free to impose more stringent standards if they wish. Some standards that apply to pesticides and mobile sources such as automobiles, [48] however, are both floors and ceilings: they pre-empt both more stringent and less stringent state standards. Uniformity of this sort can be desirable for products with important economies of scale in production. In such cases, disparate regulation would break up the national market for the product and be costly in terms of foregone economies of scale.

The benefits of uniformity, however, are less compelling in the case of process standards, which govern the environmental consequences of the manner in which goods are produced rather than the consequences of the products themselves. Indeed, unlike the case of dissimilar product standards, there can be a well-functioning common market regardless of the process standards governing the manufacture of the products traded in the market.

4 *Protection of minimum levels of public health:* There is a powerful notion, informed in part by constitutional considerations, that a federal polity should ensure all its citizens a minimum level of environmental protection. At some level, this justification is compelling: a minimum level of health ought to count as a basic human right, in the same manner as minimum levels of education, housing, or access to employment. There are two major problems, however, with justifying federal environmental regulation in this manner. First, federal environmental regulation seeks to limit the risk of exposure to particular pollutants or from particular sources, rather than limiting aggregate levels of environmental risk. As a result, such regulation is both overinclusive (it regulates more than that which has a claim to quasi-constitutional legitimacy) and underinclusive (it makes no effort to determine aggregate exposure levels; therefore some individuals may in fact be below the minimum). Second, because environmental risks are only one component of health risks, it is difficult to understand why the federal government should have such a pre-eminent role in environmental regulation when it does relatively little

[47] See pp. 39–40 above.

[48] See 7 U.S.C. § 136v(b) (1994) (pesticides); 42 U.S.C. § 7416 (1994) (mobile sources).

with respect to the provision of general health care. In fact, investments in preventive measures such as immunizations or prenatal care would have a far larger impact on health than investments in environmental regulation. Thus, the justification for federal regulation based on the need to guarantee a minimum level of health calls for a radically different form of regulation than that currently in effect: one that focuses on aggregate environmental health risks and the interactions between environmental health risks and other health risks.[49]

## Lessons for the European Union

The legal issues concerning centralized environmental regulation are framed somewhat differently in the European Union than in the United States.[50] Two differences are particularly salient: the justifications for centralized intervention and the legal status of the debates over the proper allocation of authority. This section focuses solely on these two legal differences and does not attempt to address political, institutional, or historical differences.

The presence of interjurisdictional externalities has played a role in justifying centralized intervention in the European Union, as it has in the United States.[51] By relying predominantly on ambient standards and emission standards as the primary tools of environmental policy, the European Union's efforts to control interstate externalities are subject to the same criticisms as the federal environmental statutes in the United States.

49 Some federal role with respect to environmental regulation might also be justified by the federal government's responsibility to implement obligations flowing from international treaties.

50 This section relies heavily on Revesz, "Lessons for the European Union and the International Community," at 1338–41.

51 See, e.g., Roger van den Bergh, Michael Faure, and Jurgen Lefevere, "The Subsidiarity Principle in European Environmental Law: An Economic Analysis," in Erling Eide and Roger van den Bergh eds., *Law and Economics of the Environment* (Oslo; Juridisk Forlag, 1996), 121; Richard B. Stewart, "Environmental Law in the United States and the European Community: Spillovers, Cooperation, Rivalry, Institutions," 1992 *U. Chi. L.F.* 41, 45; Matthew L. Schemmel and Bas de Regt, "The European Court of Justice and the Environmental Protection Policy of the European Community," 17 *B.C. Int. & Comp. L. Rev.* 53, 80 (1994); Marcel M. T. A. Brus et al., "Balancing National and European Competence in Environmental Law," 9 *Conn. J. Int. L.* 633 (1994); Koen Lenaerts, "The Principle of Subsidiarity and the Environment in the European Union: Keeping the Balance of Federalism," 17 *Fordham Int. L.J.* 846, 880–81 (1994).

The other prominent justification offered in the European context for centralized regulation is that harmonization of environmental laws promotes the establishment of a common market; [52] this justification has not been nearly as prominent in federalism debates in the United States.

The harmonization rationale has some force in the case of product standards. A product cannot trade freely throughout a common market if states within the market can exclude it on environmental or health and safety grounds. Indeed, before the Single European Act in 1987 and the Maastricht Treaty in 1992 explicitly recognized environmental and health and safety protection as Community goals, the harmonization rationale embodied in Article 100 provided the basis for an extensive body of regulation in these areas.[53]

Harmonization arguments, however, have also been invoked to justify the vesting of centralized responsibility over process standards, such as environmental ambient and emissions standards. There are several serious problems with extending the argument in this manner.

First, as long as product standards are harmonized, there can be a well-functioning common market regardless of the stringency of the process standards governing the products' manufacture. Thus, more accurately, the argument must call for the harmonization of the products' production

[52] See, e.g., Auke Haagsma, "The European Community's Environmental Policy: A Case Study in Federalism," 12 *Fordham Int. L.J.* 311, 355 (1989); Owen Lomas, "Environmental Protection, Economic Conflict and the European Community," 33 *McGill L.J.* 506, 511 (1988); George Close, "Harmonisation of Laws: Use or Abuse of the Powers Under the EEC Treaty?" 3 *Eur. L. Rev.* 461, 470 (1978).

[53] The European Union (then known as the European Economic Community) was established by the Treaty of Rome in 1957. Treaty Establishing the European Economic Community, 25 March 1957, 298 U.N.T.S. 11 (hereinafter EEC Treaty). This treaty did not contain any specific rules dealing with environmental protection. Environmental regulation between 1957 and 1986 was based either on Article 100, which authorizes the issuance of directives "for the approximation of such provisions laid down by law, regulation or administrative action in Member States as directly affect the establishment or functioning of the common market," or on the residual powers granted by Article 235 ("If action by the Community should prove necessary to attain, in the course of the operation of the common market, one of the objectives of the Community and this Treaty has not provided the necessary powers . . ."). Thus, centralized involvement had to be justified by reference to the benefits of harmonization. The Treaty of Rome was amended by the Single European Act in 1986, OJ L 169/1 (1987), and by the Treaty on European Union (the Maastricht Treaty) in 1992. Treaty Establishing the European Community, 7 February 1992, OJ C 224/1 (1992), [1992] *C.M.L.R.* 573 (hereinafter EC Treaty). Now, Articles 100a and 130r through 130t provide the European Union with explicit authority to promulgate environmental standards.

costs, so as to deny a comparative advantage to states with lax environmental standards.

The second problem, however, is that the costs of complying with environmental regulation, or, for that matter, the costs of complying with any regulation, are only one component of the total costs of production. Other components include a state's investments in infrastructure, health care, and education, as well as its wages, labor productivity, and access to raw materials. These factors, which can have a significant effect on production costs, are unlikely to be (or are incapable of being) the subject of the European Union's harmonization efforts. Thus, rather than eliminating cost differences, the harmonization of environmental standards has the effect of conferring a competitive advantage on states with lower non-harmonizable components of costs.

Third, the harmonization argument cannot be used, as it has been in the European Union, to justify both uniform ambient standards and uniform emissions standards. A centralized regulatory regime consisting only of uniform ambient standards, which permits the states to allocate the pollution control burden among existing and new sources in any way they see fit, would confer a competitive advantage on the states with the smaller industrial base. Indeed, states with lower pollution output could offer their sources less stringent emissions standards without violating the ambient standards. The addition of centralized emissions standards moderates this comparative advantage but does not wholly eliminate it. Highly industrialized states, where the centralized ambient standards constrain further growth, would be unable to attract new sources without imposing additional costs on existing sources.

In light of these weaknesses, it is not surprising that recent European scholarship has sought to recharacterize the quest for harmonization in race-to-the-bottom terms. Commentators have argued, as have race-to-the-bottom advocates in the United States, that the goal of centralized intervention is to protect states from the pressure to impose suboptimally lax environmental standards as a means of attracting jobs and tax revenues.[54] But, obviously, the weaknesses of the race-to-the-bottom rationale for centralized environmental regulation are not confined to the United States.[55]

[54] See Ludwig Krämer, *E.C. Treaty and Environmental Law* (2d edn. London: Sweet & Maxwell, 1995), 62; Lenaerts, "Principle of Subsidiarity," at 881; van den Bergh, Faure and Lefevere, "Subsidiarity Principle in European Environmental Law"; *see also* Stewart, "Environmental Law in the US and the EC," at 45.

[55] See above, pp. 41–48.

In addition, the legal status of the debates concerning the strength of the rationales for centralized environmental regulation are also different in the European Union and the United States. In the United States, the choice between federal and state regulation (except when state regulation is coupled with trade restrictions) is, for the most part, a matter of policy. The constitutional constraints are extremely weak, even after the Supreme Court's decisions in *New York* v. *United States*,[56] *United States* v. *Lopez*,[57] and *Printz* v. *United States*.[58]

In the European Union, in contrast, the subsidiarity principle adopted in the Maastricht Treaty in 1992 permits action at the federal level "only and insofar as the objectives of the proposed action cannot be sufficiently achieved by the Member States and can therefore, by reason of the scale or effects of the proposed action, be better achieved by the Community."[59] Thus, in the European Union, the subsidiarity principle constitutionalizes the inquiry concerning the level of government at which responsibility for environmental regulation should be allocated. Although commentators are divided about the likely role of the European Court of Justice in enforcing the subsidiarity principle, some believe that the principle is fully justiciable.[60] The unsettled state of the doctrine lends particular significance to the strength of the various rationales for federal intervention. As a result,

[56] 505 U.S. 144 (1992) (holding that Congress may not require states to enact or administer a federal program).

[57] 115 S. Ct. 1624 (1995) (holding, for the first time in over fifty years, that Congress exceeded its authority under the Commerce Clause).

[58] 117 S. Ct. 2365 (1997) (holding that Congress may not compel state officers to execute federal laws).

[59] See EC Treaty, Art. 3b. A similar principle had applied exclusively to environmental regulation, between 1986 and 1992, under Article 130r(4) of the Single European Act in 1986. See Art. 130r(4) (as in effect in 1986).

For discussion of the application of the subsidiarity principle to environmental law, see Laurens J. Brinkhorst, "Subsidiarity and EC Environmental Policy," 8 *Eur. Env. L. Rev.* 20 (1993); Lenaerts, "Principle of Subsidiarity"; van den Bergh, Faure, and Lefevere, "Subsidiarity Principle in European Environmental Law"; Wouter P. J. Wils, "Subsidiarity and EC Environmental Policy: Taking People's Concerns Seriously," 6 *J. Env. L.* 85 (1994).

[60] Commentators are divided about the role of the European Court of Justice in subsidiarity inquiries. See, e.g., Lenaerts, "Principle of Subsidiarity," at 894 (Court could merely require reasons for federal action); A. G. Toth, "A Legal Analysis of Subsidiarity," in David O'Keefe ed., *Legal Issues of the Maastricht Treaty* (London and New York: Chancery Law Pub., *c.* 1994), 37, 48 (subsidiarity principle raises political questions); Josephine Steiner, "Subsidiarity under the Maastricht Treaty," in O'Keefe, *Legal Issues of the Maastricht Treaty,* at 49, 58 (subsidiarity principle is fully justiciable).

the debates concerning the proper allocation of authority over environmental regulation currently being waged primarily in the United States may well acquire an even greater salience in the European Union.

## Lessons for the international community

The issues concerning the desirability of centralized intervention are different, in two important respects, in the international community than in federal systems.[61] First, in the international community, there is only weak capacity for centralized environmental standard-setting and virtually no capacity for centralized environmental enforcement. Second, the differences in wealth and economic development are far more salient in the international community than in federal systems.

As a result of the lack of a viable system of environmental standard-setting and enforcement, there are stronger arguments in the international community than in federal systems for allowing countries to impose environmentally based trade restrictions. Even where centralized regulation might be preferable, for example as a result of interjurisdictional externalities, state regulation coupled with trade restrictions might be the best available outcome if centralized regulation is not feasible, or if it is not feasible in an enforceable manner.

The different treatment of process standards in federal systems and in the international community is therefore not surprising. In both the United States and the European Union, state-imposed trade restrictions have been coupled with product standards but not with process standards.[62] Instead, environmental regulation with respect to processes has been the domain of the federal government. There is little justification for allowing a state to impose a process standard designed to change the environmental behavior of another state when a centralized authority can do so directly.

In contrast, process standards have been coupled with trade restrictions in the international community – the United States' restrictions on the import of certain tuna products at issue in the Tuna–Dolphin case are probably the best-known example.[63] Even though the Secretariat of the General

[61] This section relies heavily on Revesz, "Lessons for the European Union and the International Community," at 1332–35, 1341–45.

[62] See Stewart, "Lessons from the Federal Experience," at 1342.

[63] See United States: Restrictions on Imports of Tuna, GATT, Basic Instruments and Selected Documents (BISD), 39th Supp., at 155 (1993).

Agreement on Tariffs and Trade (GATT), the WTO's predecessor, took a skeptical view with respect to the permissibility of such measures, [64] the issue continues to draw the body's attention.[65] The recent Shrimp–Turtle decision may herald a more favorable reception on the part of the WTO to the enforcement of process standards by means of trade restrictions.[66] In any event, in the coming years, this issue will be the subject of intense scrutiny in the context of the WTO's Committee on Trade and the Environment.

The second important difference between the systems of the United States and the European Union on the one hand and the international community on the other arises as a result of the more extreme differences in wealth and levels of economic development in the international community. This factor, coupled with the lack of a viable, widespread system for economic redistribution in the international community, implies that the distributional consequences of each policy ought to play a far more salient role in evaluating its relative desirability.

For example, in a federal system of relatively homogenous states, it might

[64] See GATT Secretariat, Trade and Environment, GATT/1529 at 10 (3 February 1992), in *World Trade Materials*, January 1992, at 37, 50 ("In principle, it is not possible under GATT's rules to make access to one's own market dependent on the domestic environmental policies or practices of the exporting country.").

[65] See WTO Secretariat, Report of the WTO Committee on Trade and Environment, PRESS/TE 014 at 2–10, 39–42 (14 November 1996).

[66] See United States: Import Restrictions of Certain Shrimp and Shrimp Products, 1998 WL 720123 (WTO) (report of the Appellate Body). In this case, the Appellate Body held that restrictions by the United States on the import of shrimp harvested in a manner detrimental to sea turtles (an endangered species) fell within the scope of Article XX(g), which permits the enforcement of measures "relating to the conservation of exhaustible natural resources." Nonetheless, the Appellate Body concluded that the restrictions were applied in a manner that constituted "arbitrary and unjustifiable discrimination," and thus violated the requirements of the "chapeau" of Article XX. *Ibid.* at 55.

Despite ruling against the restrictions imposed by the United States, the Appellate Body's Report contains language that ought to give hope to advocates of the enforcement of process standards by means of trade restrictions:

> In reaching these conclusions, we wish to underscore what we have not decided in this appeal. We have not decided that the protection and preservation of the environment is of no significance to the Members of the WTO. Clearly, it is. We have not decided that sovereign nations that are members of the WTO cannot adopt effective measures to protect endangered species, such as turtles. Clearly, they can and should. And we have not decided that sovereign states should not act together bilaterally, plurilaterally or multilaterally, either within the WTO or in other international fora, to protect endangered species or to otherwise protect the environment. Clearly, they should and do.

*Ibid.* at 55.

be desirable to adopt policies that lead to the maximization of social welfare without undue concern about how the costs and benefits of such policies are distributed across different geographic subdivisions. Indeed, federal governments regulate in many areas, and the distributional consequences may well even out across programs. Thus, it may not be sensible to compromise the social welfare properties of each program in order to achieve a better program-specific distribution. Moreover, even if such evening out of the aggregate distributional consequences does not occur, it is likely to be more desirable to redistribute through a system of taxes and subsidies than by compromising the efficiency of the various regulatory programs. The situation is different in the international community with its larger differences in wealth and economic development, and lesser opportunities for redistribution.

A full analysis of when process standards coupled with trade restrictions ought to be permissible in the international community obviously cannot be undertaken here. The following taxonomy, however, seeks to provide a useful way to begin to analyze the relevant issues.

The first element of this taxonomy is defined by reference to the geographic scope of the physical effects of the pollution that gives rise to the trade restriction. Six situations are relevant:

1 purely domestic effects in the exporting country;
2 physical spillovers into the importing country;
3 physical spillovers into third countries;
4 impairment of existence values in the importing country;
5 impairment of existence values in third countries; and
6 effects on the global commons.

In the first situation, if the effects of the pollution are confined to the exporting country, trade restrictions are hardest to justify. Producers in the importing country may be upset that one factor of production is cheap in the exporting country, but restrictions imposed for this reason are unlikely to be welfare enhancing. Moreover, given that the costs of production have many non-harmonizable components, such as wages, labor productivity, infrastructure, and educational systems, it is not clear why a single factor should be singled out for special treatment.[67]

[67] But see text accompanying notes 72–74 below (discussing legislative proposal and views of Vice President Gore).

A sufficiently egregious disregard for human health can be thought of as akin to the violation of a basic human right, and therefore sanctionable.[68] (The use of child labor might be seen as an example of such a violation.) Many environmental disparities between exporting and importing countries, however, do not give rise to problems of this magnitude.

In the second situation – the case of physical spillovers – trade restrictions might be the only way for the importing country to protect itself. In the United States, the permissibility of such restrictions is sometimes determined by comparing the welfare gains in the importing state with the corresponding welfare losses in the exporting state.[69] In the international community, however, the distributional concerns discussed above complicate the inquiry.

In the third situation – where the physical spillovers affect third countries – the importing country's trade restriction might nonetheless increase the global social welfare. Because the importing country is not affected by the pollution, however, one might be concerned that the asserted environmental reason for the restriction is a mere subterfuge, masking a protectionist motivation.

With respect to the fourth and fifth situations, there is no analytical reason for treating existence values, also known sometimes as non-use values, differently from physical spillovers. Citizens of the importing country might suffer a real loss in utility from learning about the destruction of a valuable natural resource abroad, even if they never planned to visit it. The claims of citizens of wealthy countries for trade measures to protect their existence values might not seem particularly sympathetic if the costs fall on citizens of far poorer countries, whose very livelihood might be at stake. Moreover, the controversy surrounding the use of the contingent valuation methodology, which is used to value existence values, makes problematic any attempt to weigh the interests of the various jurisdictions.[70] As a result, trade measures motivated by the impairment of existence values are likely to be viewed as less legitimate than trade measures motivated by physical spillovers.

Finally, with respect to the global commons, in some cases trade measures

[68] See text accompanying notes 48–49 above.

[69] See Revesz, "Interstate Externalities," at 2405–08.

[70] For an overview of the issues, see Paul R. Portney, "The Contingent Valuation Debate: Why Economists Should Care," 8 *J. Econ. Persp.* (Fall 1994), at 3.

Table 1.2 *Comparison of the stringency of environmental standards in countries A (exporting) and B (importing)*

| | B | | |
|---|---|---|---|
| A | Laxer than optimal | Optimal | More stringent than optimal |
| Laxer than optimal | a | b | c |
| Optimal | d | e | f |
| More stringent than optimal | g | h | i |

will be expressly permitted by international treaties.[71] Such treaties, however, often take a long time to negotiate (and an even longer time to result in the imposition of specific obligations). In the interim, unilateral trade measures may well be the best available way to protect the global commons.

The second element of the classification system is defined by reference to how the environmental standards in the exporting and importing countries compare with those that would maximize social welfare in the respective jurisdictions. The relevant categories are set forth in Table 1.2.

To illustrate this table by means of an example, consider the following circumstances which are consistent with situation *g*. *A*'s actual standard is 10 parts per million (ppm) of a pollutant, whereas its optimal standard is 12 ppm; thus, *A*'s actual standard is more stringent than its optimal standard. In turn, *B*'s actual standard is 8 ppm (more stringent than *A*'s actual standard) but its optimal standard is 6 ppm (thus, *B*'s standard is less stringent than its optimal standard).

In the event that *B*'s environmental standards are more stringent than *A*'s, should *B*'s use of trade measures be appropriate merely because its standards are more stringent than *A*'s? Such an approach was embodied in the proposed International Pollution Deterrence Act,[72] which would have authorized the imposition of countervailing duties equal to the amount that the foreign firm would have to expend in order to comply with the US standards.[73] Similarly, Vice President Gore wrote, while he was still a Senator: "Just as government subsidies of a particular industry are sometimes

[71] For a summary, see Richard L. Revesz, *Foundations of Environmental Law and Policy* (New York: Oxford University Press, 1997), 305.

[72] S. 984, 102d Cong. (1991).

[73] *Ibid.* at 3–4.

considered unfair under the trade laws, weak and ineffectual enforcement of pollution control measures should also be included in the definition of unfair trading practices."[74]

The problem with this approach is that it would authorize the erection of trade barriers even when the disparity in the environmental standards is justified by differences in the preferences for environmental protection, differences in the costs of pollution control, and differences in the extent to which pollution produces adverse health and environmental effects in the two countries.

Alternatively, should trade measures taken by *B* be appropriate only in situations *a*, *b*, and *c*, in which *A*'s standards are laxer than optimal? Such an approach would recognize the reasons why it is desirable for different countries to have different levels of environmental protection.

Or, should *B* be barred from using trade measures in situations *a*, *d*, and *g* because its own standards are laxer than optimal, even though *A*'s are laxer still? Such an approach would create incentives for *B* to adopt socially desirable standards.

In situations *c*, *f*, and *i*, where *B*'s standards are more stringent than optimal, should *B* be permitted to use trade measures only if its optimal standards are more stringent than *A*'s standards? An affirmative answer might be predicated on the undesirability of allowing *B* to penalize other countries as a result of its own public choice problems that lead it to adopt suboptimally stringent standards.

## Conclusion

The allocation of authority between the federal government and the states ought to look very different from how it does now. The federal government currently performs many functions that would better be discharged at the state level and fails effectively to perform some functions for which federal intervention is desirable.

The theoretical support for the federal government's extensive role with respect to environmental regulation is largely provided by the race-to-the-bottom, interstate externality, and public choice justifications for federal intervention. This essay explains why the arguments adduced in favor of the race-to-the bottom and public choice rationales are flawed. It also shows

[74] Al Gore, *Earth in the Balance* (Boston: Houghton Mifflin Co., 1992), 343.

that, while the presence of interstate externalities provides a compelling justification for federal intervention, to a large extent the federal environmental statutes have been ineffective and possibly even counterproductive at controlling such externalities.

The essay also shows, however, that a greater degree of federal attention would be desirable with respect to two areas. First, more effective regulatory structures are needed to deal with the problem of interstate externalities. Such a goal could be accomplished either through a well-designed adjudicatory system, relying on command-and-control regulation, or through the implementation of a marketable permit scheme in which trades take place in units of environmental degradation. Second, the current system of medium-by-medium, pollutant-by-pollutant, source-by-source regulation does little to ensure that all citizens of a federal polity enjoy an acceptable level of environmental quality.

The experience of the United States with respect to these issues is instructive for the design of policies to guide the European Union and the international trade regime. In the European Union, excessive federal intervention has been justified by reference to a misplaced and possibly futile effort to equalize production costs. With respect to international trade, close attention needs to be paid to the ways in which the international community is different from both the United States and the European Union, particularly in its weak capacity for centralized environmental standard-setting and its greater differences in wealth and levels of economic development.

# 2

# ECONOMIC CRITERIA FOR APPLYING THE SUBSIDIARITY PRINCIPLE IN EUROPEAN ENVIRONMENTAL LAW

ROGER VAN DEN BERGH

## Introduction

PROFESSOR REVESZ discusses three prominent rationales for vesting responsibility for environmental regulation at the federal level: the asserted danger of a "race-to-the-bottom," the problem of interstate externalities, and the public choice claim that state environmental regulation will be too lax. These three arguments are also relevant in the European context and may play a crucial role in the interpretation of the subsidiarity principle, as formulated in Article 3 B(2) of the EC Treaty. Following this principle, the Community shall take action "*only if and in so far as* [italics added] the objectives of the proposed action cannot be sufficiently achieved by the Member States and can therefore, by reason of the scale or effects of the proposed action, be better achieved by the Community." By stressing the need to take the effects of the proposed action into account the EC Treaty itself rejects a pure legal formalistic approach and invites economic analysis. An assessment of the subsidiarity principle that is consistent with economic principles must take into account the implications for social welfare of a diffusion of powers between different levels of government. In a first-best world environmental standards are decentralized: they are adapted to varying preferences of the population and they take regional diversity (i.e. differing costs and benefits across geographic regions) into account. However, in such a first-best world there are no externalities across jurisdictions. Each state bears the full costs of its own environmental regulation. In the real world the choice of the appropriate level of decisionmaking is much more difficult. On the one hand, varying preferences among citizens, differences in geographic, ecological, and industrial conditions, and the benefits of competition between legal orders as a learning process are reasons that might justify decentralization. On the other hand, the need to internalize externalities caused by transboundary pollution, the risk of destructive competition on the market for environmental legislation, the removal of trade barriers, and the achievement of scale economies in the regulatory process might justify centralization.

This comment first addresses the justifications which are usually advanced in the European Community to support centralized decision-making in environmental matters. It shows that the justification for federal intervention[1] is somewhat different in the European Community from that in the United States. The goal of establishing a common market, which has been a major justification for Community action in the early decades of EC environmental policy and still remains of considerable importance today, is not nearly as prominent in the federalism debate in the United States. Next, the three major justifications for federal intervention in environmental matters, namely the race-to-the-bottom rationale, the interstate externalities argument and the public choice justification, are addressed in sequence. With respect to each of these justifications, some additional arguments questioning the current broad scope of European environmental regulation are presented. This comment thus supports Professor Revesz's conclusion that a well-designed federal environmental law would look very different from how it does now. Also European environmental law performs functions that would better be discharged at the Member States' level and fails to address problems that can only be adequately solved at the federal level.

## Justifications for European Community environmental policy

The subsidiarity principle has put a heavy burden on the European Commission to justify Community intervention. It seems useful to look at the arguments which the Commission has advanced in the past[2] to support

1 To facilitate comparisons with the United States the term "federal" is used, even though the European Union, at its present state of integration, can hardly be called a federal state. Sometimes the term "quasi-federal" is used to make clear that the economic and political integration process is not yet complete.

2 Environmental policy was the first of the Community policies for which the subsidiarity principle was explicitly introduced in the Treaty. Specific provisions which empower the Community to take measures to protect the environment were included in the Treaty by

its initiatives. EC environmental rules tend to have different reasons for their adoption. Grounds of justification for Community action with respect to the environment can be found in the recitals of the environmental directives. Four reasons can be identified:

the need to solve the problem of transboundary environmental pollution;[3]
the need to create equal conditions of competition within the EC;[4]
the need to achieve free movement of goods;[5]
the protection of the "European environmental and cultural heritage" and human health.[6]

Footnote 2 (*cont.*)
the Single European Act, which entered into force on 1 July 1987. At the same time it was made clear that the Community should only exercise its powers if the Community's environmental objectives could be better attained at Community level than at the level of the individual Member States (Art. 130r(4) EEC Treaty). Before the Single European Act entered into force, environmental legislation could be based only upon Article 100 of the EEC Treaty (harmonization of laws to achieve market integration) or Article 235 of the EEC Treaty (attainment of the objectives of the Community for which the Treaty has not provided the necessary powers). At that time, by extensive interpretation of Article 2 of the Treaty, environmental protection was already considered an objective of the Community. In the Treaty on the European Union (Maastricht) the term "environment" is for the first time referred to in the key Articles 2 and 3 of the Treaty, which set out the objectives and activities of the Community (including "sustainable growth respecting the environment"). The subsidiarity principle has become a general principle of law by reference to which the legality of Community acts should be reviewed.

3 Examples include: Directive 76/464, Discharge of dangerous substances into the aquatic environment, OJ L 129/23 (1976); Directive 79/409, Conservation of wild birds, OJ L 103/1 (1979); Directive 82/501, Major accident hazards, OJ L 230/1 (1982); Directive 84/631, Transfrontier shipment of hazardous waste, OJ L 326/31(1984); Directive 91/676, Protection of waters against pollution by nitrates from agricultural sources, OJ L 375/1 (1991).

4 Examples include: Directive 75/440, Quality of surface waters intended for the abstraction of drinking water in the Member States, OJ L 194/26 (1975); Directive 76/464, Discharges of dangerous substances into the aquatic environment, OJ L 129/23 (1976); Directive 78/176, Waste from the titanium dioxide industry, OJ L 54/49 (1978); Directive 82/501, Major accident hazards, OJ L 230/1 (1982); Directive 86/609, Protection of animals used for experimental and other scientific purposes, OJ L 358/1 (1986).

5 Examples include the Directive concerning packaging and labeling of dangerous substances (Directive 67/548, OJ L 196 (1967)) and the Directives on noise levels and pollutant emissions of motor vehicles (Directive 70/157, OJ L 42 (1970)) and Directive 70/220, OJ L 76 (1970)).

6 Examples include: Directive 76/160, Quality of bathing water, OJ L 31/1 (1976); Directive 79/409, Conservation of wild birds, OJ L 103/1 (1979); Directive 80/778, Quality of water for human consumption, OJ L 229/11 (1980); Regulation 3529/86, Protection of forests against atmospheric pollution, OJ L 326/2 (1986); Directive 92/43, Conservation of natural habitats and of wild flora and fauna, OJ L 206/7 (1992).

These reasons are somewhat different from the dominant motivation of federal environmental initiatives in the United States to correct inadequate state regulation resulting from economic rivalry and inability to realize scale economies. In comparing US and EC environmental law it should always be kept in mind that federal environmental policies in the US arose after far-reaching economic and political integration had already occurred.[7] In the EC, by contrast, environmental law originated as a by-product of the Community's initiatives aiming at free movement of goods. The first environmental directive "avant la lettre" concerning the packaging and labeling of dangerous substances sought to pull down barriers to trade resulting from different labeling requirements.[8] Until 1 July 1987, the date on which the changes to the EEC Treaty brought about by the Single European Act came into force, the Community did not have specific powers aimed at the protection of the environment. Most environmental measures were based on Article 100 of the EEC Treaty, which could be used where differences in national environmental legislation had a detrimental effect on the achievement of the common market.[9]

Even today, in spite of the substantial progress that has been made in achieving an internal market, Community policies remain linked with the process of political and economic integration. Since integration is viewed by many as synonymous with uniformity, it is difficult to achieve diversity in environmental standards. As a consequence of internal market-oriented environmental standards, inefficiencies will ensue if location-specific circumstances and regional diversity are not taken into account. This in turn may lead to serious problems at the level of implementation of the directives, when Member States consider the standards set by the EC Directives as too stringent given geographic differences (for example, stringent ambient standards in scarcely populated areas).

[7] E. Rehbinder and R. Stewart, *Environmental Protection Policy* (Berlin, 1985), 320–22. Generally differences between American and European "federal law" can be explained by the different degree of market integration. Another example is competition policy: the less tolerant attitude towards vertical restrictions can be explained by the European Commission's fear that territorial and customer restrictions may impede market integration. For a critique of this EC policy, see R. van den Bergh, "Modern Industrial Organisation versus Old-Fashioned European Competition Law," 17 *European Competition L. R.* 75 (1996), with further references.

[8] Directive 67/548, OJ L 196 (1967).

[9] Additionally, environmental measures could also be based upon Article 235 of the EEC Treaty.

## The race-to-the-bottom rationale

Given the predominance of the market integration goal, the concern about destructive competition seems to play a more important role in the American debate than in European discussions. It is, however, possible to reformulate the argument about unequal competitive conditions in economic terms referring to the race-to-the-bottom rationale. The argument that competitive distortions may occur rests on the following premises. First, to distort competition environmental legislation must increase the costs of the production process. Second, compliance with strict environmental standards must make a firm less competitive. Third, the fear of losing a substantial part of their market shares must incite the harmed companies to move towards countries with more lenient environmental regulations. According to legal commentators these conditions seem to be satisfied. For example, Jans argues that emission standards, regulating the maximum permitted level of emissions of a given environmentally harmful substance, affect the investments companies have to make and their competitive positions. A Member State wishing to adopt more stringent emission limit values than is usual in other Member States would be put at a competitive disadvantage.[10] European environmental lawyers thus tend to see different environmental standards as detrimental to the functioning of the internal market and therefore generally favor centralization.

Professor Revesz rightly criticizes the race-to-the-bottom argument in the field of environmental policy. He shows that there is no support in the theoretical literature for the claim that there will be a race to the bottom over environmental standards. Environmental lawyers might reply that economic models cannot be relied upon to reach policy conclusions, because of the underlying unrealistic assumptions. This criticism may be upheld with respect to the Tiebout[11] and Fischel[12] models, because they disregard one of the cornerstones of race-to-the-bottom arguments: that jurisdictions will relax their environmental standards to suboptimal levels in order to provide attractive jobs for their residents. This is not the case

[10] J. H. Jans, *European Environmental Law* (The Hague, Kluwer Law International, 1994), 41.

[11] C. Tiebout, "A Pure Theory of Local Expenditures," 64 *J. Pol. Econ.* 416 (1956).

[12] W. A. Fischel, "Fiscal and Environmental Considerations in the Location of Firms in Suburban Communities," in E. Mills and W. E. Oates eds., *Fiscal Zoning and Land Use Controls* (Lexington, Mass.: Lexington Books, 1975), 119.

with the leading Oates and Schwab model,[13] the assumptions of which come very close to the race-to-the-bottom scenario, as it is presented (albeit in imprecise terms) in the legal literature. In the latter model different localities compete for capital through reductions in their tax rates and local environmental standards. The authors conclude that an efficient outcome will be reached, because the localities are trading environmental quality for additions to real output. In addition, game-theoretic analyses show that interstate competition can produce either suboptimally lax or suboptimally stringent environmental regulations. In sum, the theoretical literature calls for caution in the political debate on destructive competition.

Professor Revesz's criticisms of the race-to-the-bottom argument relate mainly to the fact that it is theoretically flawed and that it should, therefore, not play a prominent role in policymaking. Skepticism about race-to-the-bottom claims is further warranted as long as there is no (or very little) empirical evidence supporting such claims. The argument made by Professor Revesz may be substantially strengthened by the results of empirical work which analyzed the effects of environmental regulation on competitiveness. Empirical research has demonstrated that pollution control costs are only a minor fraction of the value of the total sales of manufacturing industries. With respect to American industries, Repetto cites figures between 1 and 2 percent of product prices; only in very few subsectors do they rise above 3 percent of the value of sales.[14] OECD data suggest that in environmentally friendly European countries (such as Germany) the costs of environmental regulatory programs are comparable to those imposed on US firms, whereas they are lower in polluter countries (e.g. France).[15] This allows the conclusion that compared to other competitive factors pollution control costs in European countries are unlikely to be noticeable, let alone decisive. The fear that compliance with environmental regulations makes a firm less competitive thus seems exaggerated.

There is also relatively little empirical evidence to support the hypothesis that environmental regulations have an influence on location decisions. It seems unlikely that firms will relocate existing plants and incur the costs of

13 W. E. Oates and R. M. Schwab, "Economic Competition among Jurisdictions: Efficiency Enhancing or Distortion Inducing?," 35 *J. Pub. Econ.* 333 (1988).

14 M. Repetto, *Trade and Sustainable Development,* 1 (UNEP Environment and Trade Series, 1994), at 21–22.

15 *OECD Environmental Data Compendium 1991* (Paris: OECD, *c.* 1991); *Pollution Abatement and Control Expenditures in OECD Countries* (Paris: OECD, 1993).

acquiring a new site, building a new facility, and recruiting and training new workers, only to save pollution control costs totaling less than 2 percent of the value of sales.[16] At most, differences in the stringency of environmental regulations may have an impact on the location of new plants. Empirical studies do not provide much support for the belief that differences in regulatory stringency or environmental control costs are useful in explaining patterns of international trade and investment, or changes in the location of production. The results from US studies indicate that there is little direct evidence of a relationship between stringency of environmental regulations and plant location decisions in the American common market. Jaffe, Peterson, Portney, and Stavins recently published an overview of the research results.[17] An analysis not taking the stringency of environmental regulations into account showed that low taxes, the availability of public services, and the existing level of manufacturing activity have positive effects on the decision where to locate, whereas unionization of the labor force has a strongly negative effect. In analyses that included measures of environmental stringency the hypothesis that industries will move to states with the most lenient environmental standards was refuted. It was found that state government air and water pollution control expenditures, average costs of compliance, and allowable particulate emissions all had small but insignificant effects on plant location decisions. In a study of the automobile industry no significant effects of regional differences in environmental regulations on the choice of location could be detected. The empirical evidence supporting race-to-the-bottom claims is very limited. A significant, but small, negative impact of state environmental regulations on the start-up rate of small businesses was detected. Similarly the locations of new branch plants of large multi-plant companies in pollution-intensive industries were found to be somewhat sensitive to differences in pollution regulations. It may be concluded that, empirically, destructive competition is unlikely to be a problem in the United States (and plausibly also in Europe). Movements of companies because of differences in environmental legislation will rather benefit developing countries.

It may be added that the race-to-the-bottom argument has also been challenged by a revisionist view, which holds that environmental regula-

[16] Repetto, "Trade and Sustainable Development,", at 22.

[17] A. B. Jaffe, S. R. Peterson, P. R. Portney, and R. N. Stavins, "Environmental Regulation and the Competitiveness of US Manufacturing: What Does the Evidence Tell Us?" 33 *J. Econ. Lit.* 132 (1995).

tions decrease the overall cost of doing business and thus make firms more competitive. The latter view is generally associated with Michael Porter, who argues that differences in legal systems have an important, albeit partial, influence on national competitive advantages. A clean environment has positive impacts on productivity (healthy workers work better) and regulation may also stimulate innovation. Porter emphasizes that a number of industrial sectors subject to the most stringent domestic environmental regulations have become more competitive internationally: chemicals, plastics, and paints.[18] Also in the EC there is some evidence, albeit anecdotal, that compliance with strict environmental standards does not automatically imply that firms doing so will become less competitive. There is a market for environmentally friendly products and compliance with strict environmental standards stimulating innovations has opened up new markets.[19]

It may be concluded that the race-to-the-bottom arguments lack both a sound theoretical and an empirical basis. For the sake of completeness, it may be added (as Professor Revesz equally points out) that environmental regulation would not necessarily be an appropriate response to the asserted problem of destructive competition. In the EC the argument that disparities in legislation will cause unequal competitive conditions is used to justify emission standards and process standards. These Community interventions are often presented as legislation creating a "level playing field" for industry in Europe. The problem with the centralization plan, however, is that it equalizes *pollution,* not costs.[20] The costs of complying with environmental regulations are only one component of the total costs of production. The goal of creating a level playing field will not be reached, since some countries will keep an advantage in terms of age of plants, energy sources, access to raw materials, atmospheric conditions, wages, labor productivity, etc. Countries which perform well on the non-harmonized components of costs will thus keep a competitive advantage. Decisions to relocate within the EC may be the consequence of differences in costs (taxes, labor costs) which cannot be harmonized. As Professor Revesz rightly concludes, the

[18] M. Porter, *The Competitive Advantage of Nations* (New York: Free Press, 1990).

[19] For examples, see R. van den Bergh, M. Faure, and J. Lefevere, "The Subsidiarity Principle in European Environmental Law," in E. Eide and R. van den Bergh, eds., *Law and Economics of the Environment* (Oslo, 1996), 121 at 138.

[20] M. A. Cohen, "Commentary," in Eide and van den Bergh, eds., *Law and Economics of the Environment,* 167 at 169.

ultimate answer to the race-to-the-bottom problem is to eliminate the possibility of competition over any of these costs. Such a comprehensive Community intervention would equal an outright rejection of the subsidiarity principle.

### The interstate externalities argument

Although the need to internalize transboundary externalities may be a powerful argument to justify federal environmental regulations, there is no reason *a priori* to centralize regulatory decisionmaking simply because there is a transboundary pollution problem. The Coase Theorem provides a useful starting point to the understanding of the problem.[21] If a country's pollution affects another country the first attempt to solve the problem should be to specify property rights properly. If property rights are well specified, information is perfect, and transactions costs are negligible, an efficient solution will result without any further intervention by a federal authority. Although there are fifteen Member States and the costs of negotiation and enforcement must not be neglected, there may, in some instances, be opportunities for Coasian-type bargains between jurisdictions.[22] Before deciding that decisions ought to be taken centrally, a comparative institutions approach seems to be warranted. A comparison between standard-setting at the Community level and agreements between the Member States involved is needed to make a case for managing the joint environmental resources directly from Brussels. In this respect it should be noted that the European Community could also limit itself to organizing the negotiations between the Member States and seeing to it that the agreements are enforced.

An example of agreements between Member States aiming at solving transboundary pollution is the Rhine Action Plan, which was agreed upon by France, Germany, Luxembourg, the Netherlands, Switzerland,[23] and the EC, after the fire in a chemical warehouse owned by the firm Sandoz in Basle, Switzerland. The Rhine Action Plan has substantially decreased pollution from industrial sources, but has been less successful in reducing pollution from agriculture and towns. In spite of the progress made, the Rhine

[21] R. Coase, "The Problem of Social Cost," 3 *J. L. & Econ.* 1 (1960).

[22] Many externalities will not affect all fifteen Member States, but only a limited number of them.

[23] We make abstraction from the fact that the Rhine Action Plan involves a non-EC country.

Action Plan may be criticized for not relying on precise cost-benefit analyses and for not having paid sufficient attention to pollution from agriculture and towns.[24] There are, however, reasons to doubt that action at the EC level would have been more successful. European farmers, who have succeeded in capturing a major part of the European budget, are a powerful pressure group in Brussels. Moreover, in public opinion industries, not households, are usually seen as the polluters who should pay.

The European Community itself seems to be aware of the possible advantages of bilateral or multilateral agreements between Member States. For example, the air quality directives provide for an obligation to hold consultations in the event of transfrontier pollution. The European Court of Justice has decided that this obligation must be laid down by the Member States in mandatory legislation.[25] It must, of course, be added that to stimulate Coasian bargains, it does not suffice to make negotiations compulsory. The first attempt to solve the problem of transboundary pollution should be to specify property rights properly. Quality standards defined in very general terms, such as the "guide values" of the air quality directives, and minimum harmonization, which leaves scope for more stringent standards imposed by Member States, do not clearly define property rights, so that efficient solutions through negotiations cannot be reached.

With respect to the need for centralized standard-setting, another caveat should be made. In the European Community many directives have been issued which deal with relatively localized pollution. Economic theory teaches that the jurisdiction must be of sufficient size to internalize the great bulk of the pollution. When there are no significant transboundary effects, Member States (or even regions and metropolitan areas within a Member State) should retain their legislative powers. There are a number of pollutants for which "local" control may well represent the appropriate level for environmental management. Examples include noise and municipal waste. If, by contrast, the spillovers across boundaries are likely to be large, decentralized decisionmaking will not produce satisfactory outcomes. Some pollutants travel over substantial distances (acid rain) and some environmental problems require worldwide action (depletion of the ozone layer; greenhouse effect resulting from carbon dioxide emissions). Between these

[24] Centre for Economic Policy Research, *Making Sense of Subsidiarity: How Much Centralization for Europe?* (London, 1993), 142–43.

[25] Case C-186/91 *Commission* v. *Belgium* [1993] ECR I–851.

extremes, the magnitude of the interstate externalities varies. For example, there seems to be more scope for state-specific standards relating to water quality than for decentralized decisionmaking to combat air pollution. Given these differences in the extent of transboundary effects, it is remarkable that EC environmental law covers both local and Community-wide pollution, without always making the relevant distinctions between regional and interstate pollution. Directives have been enacted with respect to noise levels,[26] municipal waste,[27] and the quality of drinking water.[28] In these cases the interstate externalities seem either absent or at least less severe than in other fields, such as air pollution.

To understand (and possibly justify) these parts of European environmental law, reasons other than the internalization of pollution externalities must be taken into account. If the internalization of interstate pollution externalities were the only reason for Community intervention, many directives would violate the subsidiarity principle. However, centralization may be warranted to reach other goals, both economic (such as the achievement of scale economies) and non-economic (equity). Insofar as the spillovers across boundaries are the only concern, the size of the jurisdiction should not be larger than needed to internalize the externalities adequately. If centralization is defended on the basis of other reasons, these arguments should be judged on their own merits. The market integration goal may support the extensive Community legislation on noise levels, ranging from motor vehicles to compressors and power generators.[29] These directives implement total harmonization and thus favor the free movement of goods. The conservation of natural habitats and of wild fauna and flora may be justified under the rationale relating to the protection of the Community's natural heritage. In the latter case the externalities involved are of a different kind. Out-of-state citizens may highly value natural resources or suffer emotional losses from the extinction of endangered species (psychic spillovers).[30]

Even if centralization is justified, another equally important question

[26] Examples include: Directive 70/157, Motor vehicle exhaust systems, OJ L 42/16 (1970); Directive 78/1015, Motorcycles, OJ L 349/21 (1978); Directive 84/533, Compressors, OJ L 300/123 (1984).

[27] Directive 91/271, Urban waste water, OJ L 135/50 (1991).

[28] Directive 80/778, Water for human consumption, OJ L 229/11 (1980).

[29] See Jans, *European Environmental Law*, at 320, with further references.

[30] W. P. J. Wils, "Subsidiarity and EC Environmental Policy: Taking People's Concerns Seriously," *J. E. Env. Law* 85 (1994).

remains: what form should the federal rules take in order to cure the economic problem at issue adequately? Professor Revesz expresses serious doubts with respect to the adequacy of the American federal legislation on air pollution as an instrument to internalize interstate externalities. These criticisms are also relevant in the European context. Community legislation on air pollution establishes minimum air quality standards and maximum emission standards for certain harmful substances; it also aims at reducing the emissions of pollutants from cars and other motor vehicles. The central feature of the air quality directives[31] is an obligation to observe certain air quality limit values, which are defined as concentrations of pollution that must not be exceeded throughout the territory of the Member States. Measures limiting emissions from industrial plants can be found in directives on large combustion plants,[32] municipal waste incineration plants,[33] and hazardous waste incineration plants.[34] At the heart of the large combustion plants directive are emission limit values for sulfur dioxide, oxides of nitrogen, and dust. To prevent air pollution caused by vehicles, Member States must see to it that emissions meet the standards laid down in the directive.[35] Given these rules, the same criticisms as those relating to American environmental law seem to apply. The emission standards do not regulate the number of sources within any given state or the location of the source and, therefore, are not a good means to combat the problem of interstate externalities. The air quality standards are overinclusive because they require a state to restrict pollution that has only in-state consequences and underinclusive because they do not prevent states from exporting pollution to downwind states by locating sources near the interstate border. Overcoming the current inefficiencies may be more difficult in Europe than in America. A major obstacle to adopting efficient rules is one of the fundamental principles of European environment policy.[36] According to the

[31] Directive 80/779, Sulfur dioxide and suspended particulates, OJ L 229/30 (1980); Directive 82/884, Lead, OJ L 378/15 (1982); Directive 85/203, Nitrogen dioxide, OJ L 87/1 (1985).

[32] Directive 88/609, OJ L 336/1 (1988).

[33] Directives 89/369, OJ L 136/32 (1989) and 89/429, OJ L 203/50 (1989).

[34] Directive 94/67, OJ L 365/34 (1994).

[35] Directive 70/220, OJ L 76/1 (1970), lastly amended by Directive 94/12, OJ L 100 (1994).

[36] According to Article 130R(2) these principles are: the high level of protection principle, the precautionary principle, the prevention principle, the source principle, the polluter pays principle, the integration principle, and the safeguard clause. For a discussion of these principles, see Jans, *European Environmental Law*, at 19–32.

"source principle" environmental damage should preferably be prevented at source. This principle implies a preference for emission standards rather than environmental quality standards. Solving the problem of interstate externalities by using marketable permits in units of environmental degradation in the downwind state rather than in units of emissions may be incompatible with the "source principle". Politically sensitive principles of environmental law may thus cause substantial inefficiencies.[37]

## The public choice justification

Professor Revesz takes a skeptical view of the assertion, to be found in the American legal literature, that federal regulation is needed to correct the systematic underprotection of environmental quality at the state level. In the last part of this comment, the opinion is advanced that public choice arguments may better explain the need for competition between regulators, rather than giving support to federal environmental regulation. In the European context, concerns about a persistent democracy deficit in Community decisionmaking abound, but little has been done to redress the institutional balance in the Community. Hence, decentralization may be warranted to minimize the risk of political distortions in the European Community.

Public choice analysis starts from the important insight that politicians pursue their own goals, which may deviate from the preferences of the citizens. The resulting deviations of government policy and individual preferences may be called political distortions.[38] To eliminate economic distortions harmonization is called for. Political distortions, by contrast, require competition between legislators to bring their decisions better in line with the preferences of the citizens. The smaller the political distortions, the more democratic is a political system. They may be particularly severe in the European Union as it stands today. One of the main concerns is the lack of democratic accountability of the institutions. The

[37] Inefficiencies may also be the consequence of the application of the "high level of protection" principle if the diversity of situations in the various regions of the Community is not sufficiently taken into account and may equally follow from the "precautionary principle" which requires environmental regulation even before scientific evidence has been made available which incontrovertibly shows the causal connection between a certain activity and the harm.

[38] The term is taken from B. S. Frey and R. Eichenberger, "To Harmonize or to Compete? That's not the Question," 60 *J. Pub. Econ.*, 335–49, at 347 (1996).

Commission is not elected at all, the Commissioners being political appointments. Although the Council of Ministers is usually constituted of members of the national parliaments, those members tend not to have been elected for the purpose of serving as a member of the Council of Ministers. Any control is therefore indirect and only over the individual members rather than the Council as a body. Moreover, the deliberations of the Council are not public, which further limits the scope for democratic control. Another concern is the use of many non-elected bodies in the decisionmaking process, which fulfill an advisory role (for example, the Economic and Social Committee and the Committee of the Regions). The only directly elected body, the Parliament, has traditionally been the weakest of the institutions involved in the decisionmaking process, even though the Parliament's position has been improved by the Treaty of Maastricht and, more recently, by the Treaty of Amsterdam (which has not yet been ratified by the Member States). The control of Parliament over the Commission has been increased and the co-decision procedure has been generalized. These changes have increased democratic legitimacy to some extent, but important features of a truly democratic order are still missing.

The lack of democratic legitimacy is also clearly felt when it comes to decisions concerning environmental matters. The powers given to the European legislator to enact environmental regulations may be used by the European bureaucrats to increase their power and prestige by expanding the budget, personnel, and functions of the central government.[39] Even though the members of the Commission are appointed by the national governments, they must, in the performance of their duties, "neither seek nor take instructions from any government or from any other body" (Article 157(2) of the EC Treaty). Consequently, Commissioners should act in what they perceive to be "European interests," which remarkably tend to parallel their own interests. EU bureaucrats typically argue that centralized decisionmaking is required for the functioning of the European internal market. In their opinion, the achievement of market integration should be regarded as an exclusive competence of the European Community. This view severely limits the scope of the subsidiarity principle. Hence, to reduce the risk of political distortions responsibility over environmental protection should be vested at the state rather than at the federal level.

[39] See R. Vaubel, "The Political Economy of Centralization and the European Community," 3 *Journal des Economistes et des Etudes Humaines* 13 (1992).

A final remark seems appropriate. Increasing the power of environmental groups will not necessarily lead to more efficient regulation. Environmental groups do not have an interest in efficient environmental standards. The "Greens" face great difficulties in accepting a price for nature. To them every new piece of environmental legislation which raises the average standard of environmental protection is "profit." Hence, environmentalists will not aim at an optimal level of pollution reduction, taking into account both the benefits that accrue from such reduction and the costs of pollution control. They share with producers an interest in restricting the output below the optimum and may form with them a coalition to lobby for standards (command-and-control regulation) which may serve as entry barriers to deter competition. Interest groups and bureaucrats all favor standards,[40] although economists generally consider command-and-control legislation less efficient than economic instruments. The process of standard-setting tends to provide an important opportunity to expand the budget and size of governmental organization. The knowledge of experts is required and an administration is needed to set the standards and to monitor whether the firms comply with the regulation. Very often the only experts who can judge work inside the firms or inside the bureaucracy. Budget maximization may thus explain the great number of inefficient rules in the area of environmental policy (and in other policies as well).

## Conclusion

Professor Revesz has written a thoughtful and interesting chapter, which has improved our understanding of the reasons for centralized decision-making in the field of environmental law and the forms it should take. These insights are particularly relevant for the interpretation of the subsidiarity principle in the EC Treaty. At present European bureaucrats applaud the subsidiarity principle but do not always respect it. Economic theory teaches that decentralization is the first-best solution and that centralization should be limited to those cases where imperfections in markets for legislation impede efficient outcomes. The race-to-the-bottom argument does not provide a sound justification for centralization, neither theoreti-

[40] A. Körber, "Standards and Taxes in Environmental Law from a Public Choice Perspective," in B. Bouckaert and G. De Geest, eds., *Essays in Law and Economics II: Contract Law, Regulation, and Reflections on Law and Economics* (Antwerp: Maklu, *c.* 1995), 161.

cally nor empirically. The need to internalize interstate externalities is a more powerful argument in favor of centralization, but the argument should not be overstated. In EC law the principle of free movement of goods is relaxed by a "rule of reason" and in the field of EC competition policy a *de minimis* rule applies. Why then should EC environmental law be applicable to pollution, whose effects are largely restricted to the territory of individual countries or even locations in one Member State of the Community? If interstate externalities are not significant, other arguments are needed to make a convincing case for centralization. Moreover, to avoid inefficiencies the "federal" authority should take account of regional diversity and be protected from regulatory capture.

# 3

# THE POLITICAL ECONOMY OF POLLUTION CONTROL IN A FEDERAL SYSTEM

JOHN FEREJOHN

## Introduction

PROFESSOR REVESZ has shown that the problem that federalism poses for environmental regulation arises from the fact that pollution produces interjurisdictional externalities and not from jurisdictional competition. Without externalities, Revesz has shown that competition among jurisdictions is generally welfare enhancing and attempts of the central government to impose more stringent environmental standards will only induce the jurisdictions to react by competing on some other margin. When interjurisdictional externalities exist, however, states will typically have an incentive to push the costs of industrial activity off onto their neighbors by making suboptimal locational and abatement decisions, and this may justify federal regulations.

Secondly, Revesz shows that existing administrative and court practices under the Clean Air Act in the United States are inappropriate in inducing jurisdictions to internalize the costs of their polluting decisions. Indeed, he shows that, if anything, federal regulations have probably induced regulatory pathologies that have made interjurisdictional opportunism even worse than it had been. The result is that the pattern of environmental regulations is almost certainly quite perverse from a social welfare perspective. The pattern of court and agency decisions has increased the incentives for states and their industrial denizens to locate polluting plants at downwind borders and build excessively tall smokestacks, making inappropriate capital investment decisions and the like.

Thirdly, Revesz argues that the lessons of US environmental regulatory policies are a valuable source of cautionary tales for the European

Community and for the international community more generally. The nearly complete absence of central regulatory capacity in the international arena implies that environmental regulation must be carried on at the national or subnational level, even where interjurisdictional externalities are substantial. This fact has produced circumstances in which European states have employed trade policy instruments (either unilaterally or on a multilateral basis) as a method of attaining environmental objectives. The use of trade restrictions in this area has produced a number of policies that are difficult to justify. Particularly worrying is the use of trade restrictions against products that are produced using processes of which the importing country disapproves.

Each of Revesz's arguments is persuasively presented and I find them each quite convincing, at least within the setting in which they are argued. But, if one were to pose the main issue of the paper – is federalism an obstacle to effective environmental regulation? – I think the answer is probably "yes," whereas Revesz thinks the answer is "no." This is not to say that, all things considered, we should always, either in the United States or elsewhere, make environmental policy at central level – that is a question that involves much more extensive work on the structure and frequency of environmental spillovers and on comparative governmental performance. But, it is to point out instead that the regulatory policymaking by provincial units makes the problem of internalizing spillovers economically and politically difficult.

## Is there a "race to the bottom"?

I understand a "race to the bottom" to have two separable characteristics: it must be a "race" in the sense that an equilibrium with interjurisdictional competition is different from the equilibria without such competition – as in Revesz's "island" jurisdiction – and the equilibrium with such competition must be worse than that without such competition. By way of illustration, consider the case of a redistributive policy. Assume there are two provinces with identical (and uneven) income distributions between two classes (the rich and the poor), that there are more poor people than rich people in both jurisdictions, and that policy is set by majority rule within each jurisdiction. Assume that each jurisdiction is deciding on a uniform tax rate, where the proceeds from such a tax will simply be redistributed equally within the jurisdiction. If we consider the case of an island jurisdiction, an equilibrium outcome need only satisfy the majority rule constraint so that because the median voter is poor, the equilibrium tax rate is one and the resulting distribution of wealth is even. Obviously, as long as all the proceeds of the tax are redistributed this equilibrium is efficient.

With interjurisdictional competition, however, an equilibrium policy must not only satisfy the majority rule constraint but it must be one in which no-one wishes to relocate between jurisdictions. In this case it is clear that the complete expropriation of wealth cannot be sustained in equilibrium. To see this, notice that in any equilibrium both the tax rates and the ratio of the number of rich people to poor in each jurisdiction must be the same, otherwise there would be a population readjustment. Rich people would move to the jurisdiction with the lowest taxes. But if the (equal) tax rates are positive, each jurisdiction has an incentive to lower its rate to attract more wealth. Thus, the only equilibrium is where all tax rates are equal to zero.

In this simple example, the outcome with jurisdictional competition is different from that without such competition and both are Pareto optimal. The only difference between the situations is distributional. On Revesz's criterion we would say that there is no race to the bottom or, perhaps, that there is a race but it is not to the bottom. But this description seems to miss the obvious fact that these two equilibria are vastly different from one another in a way that people might actually care about. To say this is, in one sense, to say no more than that the efficiency criterion is a very blunt tool for policy analysis and that to find that an equilibrium is efficient is not necessarily to endorse it.

Now suppose that individuals care about the wealth distribution, so that utility is linear in post-tax wealth and some distributive statistic, but that the jurisdictions are sufficiently large that no-one's locational decision has a discernible effect on the wealth distribution. In this case a locational decision has an external effect on everyone through its effect on the distributive statistic, but this effect will not be reflected in equilibrium with interjurisdictional competition. Because there are distributional preferences there is a race and it is to the bottom. The point that the redistributional model brings out is that the notion of competition producing bad effects seems to rest intrinsically on there being interjurisdictional externalities of some sort so that decentralized competition fails to reach the Pareto frontier.

Within the model that Revesz actually analyzes – one where there are no interjurisdictional externalities – race-to-the-bottom phenomena can only arise if some units are behaving suboptimally. He cites the model of Oates and Schwab in which the race-to-the-bottom phenomenon can arise if subunits impose a positive tax on capital – in which case the jurisdictions will lower the tax on pollution in order to attract additional revenue-producing firms. Revesz suggests that the proper response in such a case is to correct the suboptimal choice in question and not have the central government place restraints on the competitive behavior of the jurisdictions. He argues that if the central government were to try to restrict environmental competition to attract polluting firms, competition would only emerge on some other margin, perhaps triggering more regulation of the provinces by the central government. Such a course of action would, Revesz claims, undermine federalism altogether by removing the autonomy of the subunits.

This line of reasoning seems plausible, argued abstractly, if the cause of the suboptimal choice is a simple irrationality or a miscalculation (as he characterizes it) but perhaps less so if the suboptimality is due to some restraint on subunit behavior – such as the infeasibility of lump sum taxes. But what if the irrationality is a feature of the internal (democratic) choice processes of the jurisdiction in question? Is it obvious that the appropriate response, all things considered, is for the central government to intervene to correct this irrationality?

Moreover, it is important to remember that this argument takes place within a model within which there are no externalities. Does this model actually apply to domains in which people would think that there may be race-to-the-bottom phenomena? I am not yet convinced. Here the issue seems to be how to characterize "externalities." Revesz implies, through his choice of examples if by no other means, that the externalities that are important are what might be called "material externalities:" garbage or pollutants flow across borders and have direct material effects on health or production. Without denying the importance of managing such flows, it seems true nevertheless that many environmental externalities are not of this form. We care about the air quality in Alaska in ways that are not accounted for by a material model (this resembles the concerns that many have over the distribution of wealth). If this is true, the appropriate environmental policy in Alaska must take account of the preferences of nonresidents as well as those held by residents. This seems to be a central feature of much conflict over environmental policy in federal states. In any case, in the presence of externalities of this kind (just as with any kind of externality), interjurisdictional competitive equilibria will not generally be efficient and taxes on pollution will generally be too low. Whether federalism is an obstacle to appropriate environmental regulation in the presence of these issues depends on how pervasive issues of this sort are.

## Political economy of environmental policy

Revesz's description of the provisions of the Clean Air Act (CAA) and subsequent amendments provides a devastating indictment of the Act as drafted and, even more so, as interpreted and administered. He shows that the original Act encouraged states to export their pollution by getting their firms to build suboptimally tall smokestacks and to locate them near their downwind borders. The recent attempts to alleviate acid rain problems by creating a national system of marketable emission permits induced firms to behave in ways that have little bearing on the problem. Moreover, the spill-over regulations led states to compete with each other to encourage premature siting of polluting firms in both upwind and downwind states in an effort to occupy all available space under the air quality standards. While states may have had some of these incentives (to export environmental "bads") without the CAA, the enactment of the CAA has arguably made interjurisdictional externalities worse than they would have been otherwise. Subsequent amendments, while they may have attenuated these problems slightly (as in the case of smokestack regulation), have not fundamentally improved things.

Granting Revesz's point we may ask how this situation came about. Why was the 1970 CAA written in such a way as to produce these perverse incentives and why did subsequent amendments not really improve matters? Was it mere ignorance of the effects of the various regulations that accounts for their structure or are there political forces that work to maintain these regulations in something like their present form? Moreover, however the various provisions of the CAA were drafted, what accounts for the peculiar pattern of agency and judicial interpretations that these provisions have received over the years? Without some understanding of the answers to these questions – of the forces producing the status quo – it seems unlikely that genuinely usable policy advice can be produced.

While Revesz does not attempt to formulate a political explanation he does present enough information for us to speculate loosely about what kind of an explanation might be plausible. From the fact that subsequent amendments in 1977 and 1990 have not substantially alleviated problems that were quite obvious by then, and from the fact that quite perverse agency and court interpretations have been sustained for such a long period, I think we may safely reject the hypothesis that lack of knowledge is the primary cause of the CAA's regulatory structure and look to political forces instead.[1] What kinds of political forces? I suggest looking at Congress, interest groups, agencies, courts, and the states.

From the standpoints of Congress and interest groups the debates over the 1970 Act and subsequent amendments were ripe opportunities for both symbolic and material politics and my guess would be that both kinds of forces were at work in each of these legislative events. As the acid rain problem developed elected officials from the Northeast, as well as environmental lobbyists, found it to be very important to be able to claim that the legislation would deal with the problem. However, while these groups fought hard to establish broad principles, they were more willing to compromise when it came to specific provisions. The Ackerman and Hassler[2] book provides a special example of a compromise of this sort – wherein environmentalists and eastern coal producers were able to agree to require (ineffective) scrubbers and tall smokestacks rather than substituting cheaper low sulfur western coal – but other examples are very easy to find. The result was very surprising: a legislative Act whose symbolic purposes are not closely related to its specific regulatory provisions.

If we turn to the agencies and the courts, the picture that Revesz paints is one in which Republican administrations, who are unsympathetic to the CAA's purposes and skeptical about the effects of regulatory policies, have given extremely narrow and rigid readings to the language of the CAA. Over the same period the courts have adopted a policy of deference to agency interpretation that has effectively neutered the SIP approval process as a procedure for rational environmental policy formation. Hostile Presidents and deferential courts have, on this account, taken an already defective CAA and made it worse.

Finally, in the case of the states, Revesz shows that, on average anyhow, they have tended to respond to the incentives that the CAA gave them. They have in fact encouraged firms to make suboptimal capital investment and

1 Actually, in the case of smokestack regulation informational issues may have played a central role since, as far as I know, there are still many engineers who endorse the old proposition that the "solution to pollution is dilution."

2 Bruce A. Ackerman and William T. Hassler, *Clean Coal/Dirty Air* (New Haven: Yale University Press, 1981).

locational decisions – building tall stacks and locating near downwind borders. Moreover, though he does not say so, the states and their representatives in Congress also seem to have political incentives to continue lobbying for more perverse policy, both at the symbolic and at the material level. In addition, as Revesz recognizes, many of the opportunistic incentives that have motivated the states were in place before the enactment of the CAA and repealing the Act probably would not remove them. But Revesz takes the continuation of these poor incentives as an indictment of federal regulation. One could understand them, instead, as evidence that the CAA did not really change the incentives for interjurisdictional opportunism. It merely exacerbated perverse incentives that were already in place – and these incentives arose from the existence of state boundaries that created interjurisdictional spillovers.

## Environmental policy with jurisdictional competition

The hard fact that Revesz reminds us of is that environmental policy is especially difficult to manage in a federal regime. The presence of externalities means that market equilibria will generally be nonoptimal in either federal or nonfederal jurisdictions, but federal states will have a harder time making the appropriate market corrections because decisionmakers in the provinces will tend not to pay enough attention to "outsiders." Moreover, the political incentives in a federal system make finding solutions to interjurisdictional spillovers even more intractable.

In other policy areas, the courts have employed the dormant commerce clause doctrine to limit the capacity of states to push costs onto outsiders. But judicial policing of the states seems not to be as successful here and the explanation for the failure seems traceable to partisan politics. Whether or not the Supreme Court itself is responding to such forces, its policy of deference to agency interpretation, while perhaps defensible on some views of democratic government, has the effect of making environmental regulations more rigid and perhaps less durable than they would otherwise be.

## Conclusion

As far as I can see there are two good reasons for managing environmental policy at the center of a federal regime. One is that interjurisdictional spillovers are in fact both ubiquitous and endogenous. Not only do smoke and water flow freely across boundaries but subnational units have every reason to increase these flows if they are the ones making environmental policy. Secondly, even ignoring material spillovers, we care about what other jurisdictions do to their environments and these cares seem to me to be increasing as people become more aware of what is going on elsewhere in the world. These "moral" externalities play an increasing part in explaining and justifying federal regulation in the United States and in international treaties as well. It seems to me that, using Revesz's examples, these concerns are increasingly common in the case of "process" issues. We care that products are produced using child or slave labor, that fish are caught in ways that kill mammals, etc., and we press our lawmakers to interfere with producers using such processes. Similarly, we also care about policy outcomes in ways that are not captured by efficiency criteria. Thus, in the example I gave above, concerns about income distribution would be a reason to conduct tax policy at the federal level.

Revesz is right to say, however, that there are powerful reasons to resist the impulse to centralize environmental policymaking. The central government may have difficulty in devising and administering flexible policies that respond to local tastes and circumstances. The institutional pathologies of large governments may also be worse than those of smaller ones – I think the jury is still out on this issue. But whether these institutional concerns overwhelm the growing importance of interjurisdictional spillovers – due either to exogenous technical forces of economic and population growth or to endogenous incentives of subnational jurisdictions to beggar their neighbors – is a judgment call and one that I think increasingly favors pushing environmental regulation to the national level.

# Part II

## ENVIRONMENTAL REGULATION AND INTERNATIONAL TRADE

# 4

# ENVIRONMENTAL PROTECTION AND THE GLOBAL TRADE ORDER

FRIEDER ROESSLER

## Introduction

TRADE ISSUES are rarely discussed in isolation from other policy issues. The conference that led to the adoption of the Havana Charter for an International Trade Organization was the United Nations Conference on Trade *and Employment.* The Charter assigned to the stillborn Organization the task of resolving the most pressing economic problems of the late 1940s. It was to work towards full employment and the removal of balance of payments disequilibria of its Members, take action against inflationary or deflationary pressures, and promote fair labor standards.[1] Its Members would have been committed to cooperating in the fields of economic development and reconstruction.[2] And the Organization was to be the forum for negotiating agreements on technology transfer, foreign investment, double taxation, and restrictive business practices, as well as commodity agreements.[3]

The central theme of international economic diplomacy in the 1960s and 1970s was the economic development of the third world, and the GATT's legal regime was gradually adapted between 1965 and 1980 to serve as an instrument of development policy: the principle of non-reciprocity in trade negotiations between developed and developing countries was recognized; developed countries were permitted to accord tariff preferences to developing countries; and developing countries were accorded the right to

The constructive comments of Alice Enders on an earlier draft of this chapter are gratefully acknowledged.

[1] Charter for an International Trade Organization, Chapters II and III.

[2] *Ibid.*, Chapter III.

[3] *Ibid.*, Chapters III and V.

exchange preferences among themselves in the name of collective autonomy.[4]

The voluntary nature of the preferences accorded to the developing countries induced some developed countries to link the granting of preferences to other policy issues. For instance, in order to obtain preferences from the United States, a developing country must not, *inter alia*, expropriate or otherwise seize control of property owned by a United States citizen, including patents, trademarks, and copyrights; repudiate an agreement with a United Stares citizen; impose taxes or other exactions with respect to property of a United States citizen, the effect of which is to expropriate that property; refuse to cooperate with the United States to prevent narcotic drugs from entering the United States unlawfully; aid or abet any individual or group which has committed an act of international terrorism; deny its workers internationally recognized rights, including acceptable minimum wages; refrain from enforcing arbitral awards; nor be a member of the Organization of Petroleum Exporting Countries.[5]

The 1986–94 Uruguay Round ended with the Agreement Establishing the World Trade Organization (WTO Agreement), which is the legal umbrella combining agreements on trade with agreements in the areas of services and intellectual property rights. The commitments in these disparate areas, which had hitherto led separate lives in separate institutions, are linked through an integrated dispute settlement mechanism under which, subject to certain constraints, a failure to observe obligations in one area may be responded to by a suspension of obligations in another.[6] When the Uruguay Round came to a close at a ministerial meeting in Marrakesh in April 1994, most speakers proposed that the newly established WTO take up further non-trade issues, in particular environmental policies, internationally recognized labor standards, competition policy, company law, foreign investment, immigration policies, monetary matters, including debt, and development, political stability, and alleviation of poverty.[7] The Ministers agreed to take up only one of these proposals: they decided that a

[4] See the decision of the Contracting Parties to the GATT on *Differential and More Favorable Treatment, Reciprocity and Fuller Participation of Developing Countries*, adopted on 28 November 1979.

[5] Trade Act of 1974, Subchapter V.

[6] Article 22 of the Understanding on Rules and Procedures Governing the Settlement of Disputes ("DSU").

[7] GATT document MTN.TNC/45(MIN), 12.

WTO Committee on Trade and the Environment should be created to continue the work of the GATT in the field of the environment.[8]

The decision to discuss environmental protection in the framework of the global trade order together with the plethora of proposals to take up other non-trade issues in the WTO raises a number of fundamental issues for the new institution. To what extent do the obligations under the WTO agreements prevent the pursuit of legitimate policy goals in other areas? Should WTO Members be allowed to offset the economic impact of differences between their domestic policies and those of others? To what extent can the operation of regimes established in disparate policy areas be made legally interdependent by including them in a single treaty with an integrated enforcement mechanism? What criteria should be used to determine whether trade objectives should be made subsidiary to non-trade policy goals? Do the WTO's decisionmaking procedures ensure that the WTO trade policy commitments are not interpreted or applied in a manner imposing constraints on the pursuit of legitimate policy objectives outside the sphere of trade?

This chapter explores the systemic, legal, and institutional consequences of linking trade and non-trade issues in the framework of the WTO, taking the proposed linkages between environment and trade as an example. It analyzes the four following arguments made by environmental organizations to justify the integration of environmental policy objectives in the global trade order:

1 The obligations under the WTO agreements prevent the attainment of legitimate domestic environmental policy goals and environmental policies should therefore be exempted from WTO obligations.
2 The principle of open markets of the WTO leads to a race to the bottom, forcing all WTO Members to lower their environmental standards to the level of the WTO Member with the lowest standards, and WTO Members should therefore be allowed to offset through trade controls the economic impact of differences in environmental standards.
3 The WTO prevents the use of trade sanctions to force WTO Members to raise their environmental standards, and the rights of market access under the WTO should therefore be linked to commitments to raise environmental standards.

[8] Decision on *Trade and Environment*, adopted by Ministers at the meeting of the Trade Negotiations Committee in Marrakesh on 14 April 1994.

4 The WTO lacks transparency and should open its decisionmaking to scrutiny by environmental organizations.

## Exempting domestic environmental policies from WTO obligations

An economic policy goal can usually be achieved with a variety of policy instruments. According to the theory of optimal intervention, the various instruments can be ranked according to the efficiency with which they attain the goal. The optimal instrument is the one that attains the policy goal with the least amount of undesired side-effect, usually the one that attacks the identified policy problem directly at its source. One of the conclusions that can be drawn from the theory of optimal intervention is that a measure discriminating between goods or services according to their origin or destination is rarely an optimal measure to attain any domestic policy goal; domestic policy goals require a domestic policy instrument.[9] There is consequently in principle no conflict between WTO law and the efficient pursuit of a domestic environmental policy objective.

In the negotiations on the General Agreement on Trade in Services (GATS), one delegation proposed that a clause permitting measures to protect the environment be included in the provision listing public policy exceptions to the obligations under the GATS. The delegation was asked under what circumstances deviations from the non-discrimination rules of the GATS were necessary to protect the environment. The delegation was unable to give a reply convincing the others, and the final version of the provision was therefore adopted without any reference to the environment.[10]

Why then do environmental organizations consider the WTO as a threat to domestic environmental legislation and why did they oppose its creation on that ground? Lori Wallach, a lawyer working for "Public Citizen", a Washington-based non-profit organization, said in a conversation with the author that many environmental and other public interest bills would simply not be adopted by Congress without elements that are contrary to WTO law. The constraints imposed by WTO law therefore effectively

[9] For a detailed discussion of the relationship between the principles of the GATT and the theory of optimal intervention see Frieder Roessler, "The Constitutional Function of the Multilateral Trade Order," in Meinhard Hilf and Ernst-Ulrich Petersmann eds., *National Constitutions and International Economic Law* (Deventer and Boston: Kluwer Law and Taxation Publishers, 1993), 53–62.

[10] See Article XIV of the GATS.

prevent the attainment of higher environmental standards, and the rulings of WTO panels put into jeopardy existing domestic laws furthering legitimate domestic policy objectives even when there is, politically, no prospect of a WTO-consistent solution.

The following examples illustrate the constraints imposed by WTO law on the formation of domestic political coalitions favoring environmental legislation. Suppose a new clean air standard is to be introduced for gasoline. This, by itself, can of course be done without any legal constraints under WTO law. However, the domestic political constraints can be such that the new standard would be endorsed by a parliamentary majority only if domestic gasoline is exempted from the standard for five years or, to put the issue in political economy terms, if the cost of reducing pollution is initially borne only by non-voting producers abroad. That discrimination would be inconsistent with the GATT's national treatment provisions of Article III and would most likely not be justifiable under the GATT's public policy exceptions of Article XX. The five-year exemption violating the GATT would thus not be *technically necessary to implement* a higher environmental standard (it would in fact reduce the new standard's environmental impact), but would be *politically necessary to adopt* the higher standard.

Another example is the phase-out mechanism included in the Montreal Protocol. Under that mechanism the consumption of ozone-depleting chemicals is reduced by lowering the production and importation of such chemicals. The decline in the domestic supply of these chemicals combined with import controls generates rents for the domestic producers during the phase-out period and the scheme therefore won their support. The phase-out of the chemicals could have been achieved through internal measures consistent with the national treatment principle, for instance a system of sales licenses. However, such a system would have imposed only burdens on the producers of the chemicals and would probably not have won their support. The import controls were thus not needed to protect the *ozone layer* but to gain the support of the *producers of ozone-depleting chemicals.*[11]

This raises the question of whether the principle of domestic political necessity could be incorporated into the legal system of the WTO. A rule

[11] See Alice Enders and Amelia Porges, "Conventional Success and Successful Conventions: The Montreal Protocol," in Kym Anderson and Richard Blackhurst eds., *The Greening of Trade Policy* (Harvester Wheatsheaf, 1991).

which states that the introduction of a discriminatory trade measure is justified if a legitimate domestic policy goal would not otherwise have been politically attainable does not mark a line between international trade interests and domestic policy constraints. It would establish a license for unprincipled policymaking and therefore submit completely the rights of market access under the WTO agreements to the vagaries of the domestic political process of the WTO Members. A viable trade order could not be based on such a rule. Moreover it seems unlikely that nations would accept, or even seriously propose, a rule that would entail a need for scrutiny of their domestic political constraints by an independent international tribunal and that would contain no justifiable principle on the basis of which the outcome of that scrutiny could be predicted.

The domestic policy constraints of WTO Members are reflected in the WTO procedures for the negotiation and renegotiation of market access commitments. The market access commitments under the WTO agreements are made by product (GATT), sector (GATS), and procurement entity (Agreement on Government Procurement). Reciprocity is achieved not through equal but through equivalent commitments and the schedules commitments of the different WTO Members therefore vary significantly. Moreover, the WTO Members are entitled to renegotiate their commitments. Both during the process of negotiating the commitments and after their acceptance, WTO Members thus have the possibility to modulate their trade obligations in accordance with their domestic political constraints. However, this modulation results from a negotiation and therefore maintains the balance of rights and obligations among Members. Reciprocity is an essential feature of the global trade order. If a unilateral right to withdraw market access commitments to take into account domestic political constraints in environmental policymaking were to be introduced, market access commitments that could be affected by this right would therefore no longer be exchanged.

## Permitting WTO Members to offset differences in environmental regulations

The border adjustment rules of the GATT and the GATS permit a WTO Member to apply to imported products and services the measures that it applies to domestic *products and services,* not however the measures that it imposes on its *producers or service suppliers.* For instance, a tax on the sale of electricity may be imposed equally on imported and domestic electricity, but a domestic prohibition to produce electricity with coal may not be extended to imported electricity.[12] This basic principle underlying the world trade order was challenged for the first time in the history of the GATT in the proceedings of the panel which examined the widely discussed Mexican complaint against the United States embargo of imports of tuna originating in countries that do not observe fishing techniques protecting dolphins. In these proceedings the United States argued that its tuna import embargo was part of an internal measure subject to Article III that was applied equally to imported and domestic products and consequently consistent with this provision.[13] The panel *rejected* this contention, finding that Article III

> calls for a comparison of the treatment of imported tuna *as a product* with that of domestic tuna *as a product*. Regulations governing the taking of dolphins incidental to the taking of tuna could not possibly affect tuna as a product. Article III:4 therefore obliges the United States to accord treatment to Mexican tuna no less favourable than that accorded to United States tuna, whether or not the incidental taking of dolphins by Mexican vessels corresponds to that of United States vessels.[14]

The principle, reaffirmed by this panel, that WTO Members may apply to imported products only those measures that they apply to their own products, not however those that they apply to their producers, has been severely criticized by environmentalists. One of the bases of this criticism has been that the inability of a WTO Member to offset through trade measures the economic consequences of the differences between its environmental policies and those of other WTO Members leads to a "race to the bottom". This concern is reflected in the following statement by Ralph Nader before the US Senate Finance Committee on the results of the Uruguay Round:

> US corporations long ago learned how to pit states against each other in "a race to the bottom" – to provide the most permissive corporate charters, lower wages, pollution standards, and taxes. Often it is the federal government's role to require states to meet higher federal standards . . . There is no overarching "lift up" jurisdiction on the world stage . . . The Uruguay Round is crafted to enable corporations to play this game at the global level, to pit

12 See the 1972 report of the Working Party on Border Tax Adjustments in: GATT, Basic Instruments and Selected Documents (BISD), 18th Suppl. 97.

13 BISD, 39th Suppl., 165.

14 *Ibid.*, p. 195. The panel report was not adopted because Mexico withdrew its complaint.

> country against country in a race to see who can set the lowest wage levels, the lowest environmental standards, the lowest consumer safety standards. Notice this downward bias – nations do not violate the GATT rules by pursuing too weak consumer, labor . . . and environmental standards . . . Any . . . demand that corporations pay their fair share of taxes, provide a decent standard of living to their employees or limit their pollution of the air, water and land will be met with the refrain, "You can't burden us like that. If you do, we won't be able to compete. We'll have to close down and move to a country that offers us a more hospitable business climate."[15]

This raises the question of whether a new general rule could be introduced into the WTO legal system that would permit WTO Members to apply import taxes and restrictions designed to offset the competitive advantages that differences in environmental and other regulations accord to producers abroad.[16] The answer is clearly no. With such a rule, the law of the WTO would provide legal security only for the products and services traded between pairs of countries with identical domestic production regulations. This would be contrary to the principle of comparative advantage according to which nations are to exploit their differences, differences that are often reflected in their regulations.[17] Moreover, the WTO principle that most-favored-nation treatment must be accorded *unconditionally,* [18] that is

[15] Statement of Ralph Nader before the Senate Finance Committee on the Uruguay Round Agreements of the General Agreement on Tariffs and Trade, 16 March 1994 (mimeograph).

[16] There is at present no provision in the WTO Agreement that permits trade restrictions specifically designed to offset differences in domestic policies. WTO Members may impose countervailing duties on products that benefit from a domestic production. However, a countervailing duty may be imposed even if the importing Contracting Party also accords a subsidy. Two WTO Members granting the same fiscal advantages to their steel industries may impose (and frequently impose in practice) countervailing duties on the steel products exported to each other. The countervailing duty provisions of the WTO are therefore not provisions permitting measures designed to offset policy divergences; they are provisions permitting the protection of import-competing industries contingent upon the protection of an exporting industry in another country. This observation can also be made in respect of the provision of the GATT that exempts measures related to the products of prison labor from the obligations under the GATT (Article XX(e)). It is true that the domestic policies of another WTO Member trigger in this case the right to impose import controls, but that right may be exercised independently of the prison labor regulations of the Contracting Party imposing the import control. A Contracting Party could consequently permit the sale of products produced in domestic prisons while restricting the sale of those made in foreign prisons.

[17] See Jagdish Bhagwati, "The Demands to Reduce Domestic Diversity among Trading Nations," in Jagdish Bhagwati and Robert Hudec eds., *Fair Trade and Harmonization: Prerequisites for Free Trade?* (MIT Press, 1996), vol. I: *Economic Analysis*, 9–40.

[18] See Article I of the GATT and Article II of the GATS.

independently of the policies of the country of origin, would be lost, and with it the peace-engendering impact of that principle. With a general rule that permits WTO Members to eliminate the external effects of the differences between them, the WTO legal system could therefore no longer fulfill its basic functions.

This does not exclude individual negotiated solutions. There are at present two instruments available under the law of the WTO to which WTO Members could resort if they perceive the need to protect a domestic industry to prevent a race to the bottom. The first would be to accord a production subsidy to the industry disadvantaged as a result of an environmental standard higher than that imposed on competing producers abroad. Production subsidies are in principle permitted under the WTO Agreement. If the subsidy impairs a tariff concession, injures a domestic industry of another WTO Member or otherwise causes serious prejudice to another WTO Member, the Member according the subsidy may have to renegotiate the impaired tariff concession, bear the consequences of countervailing duties or remove the adverse effects of the subsidy, for instance through an export tax. However, these constraints apply only to subsidies that are specific to an enterprise or industry or group of enterprises or industries, not to more generally available subsidies, and, within limits, subsidies with specified objectives, among them "the adaptation of existing facilities to new environmental requirements."[19]

The second legal option is the imposition of a tariff. The WTO Agreement permits import and export tariffs provided the tariff does not exceed the maximum tariff rate bound as a result of negotiations under the GATT.[20] Tariff bindings may be withdrawn after negotiations with the WTO Members with whom the tariff binding was originally negotiated or who have a principal supplying interest.[21] It is thus possible to impose trade barriers in the form of tariffs to protect an industry from foreign competition, but as a rule only after any negotiated market access right adversely affected by the tariff increase has been renegotiated.

[19] Articles 1, 2, 7 and 8 of the WTO Agreement on Subsidies and Countervailing Measures.

[20] Article II:1(a) of the GATT. While all WTO Members have bound import tariffs, there is at present no export tariff binding. Article I, Section 9, of the United States Constitution provides that: "No Tax or Duty shall be laid on Articles exported from any State". Export duties, while permitted under the GATT, are therefore not a legal option available to the United States.

[21] Article XXVIII of the GATT.

The WTO Agreement consequently permits WTO Members to take a domestic regulatory measure raising the cost of production in combination with subsidies or tariffs that maintain the competitive position of the domestic producers that have to bear these costs. The domestic industry and the environment can be protected at the same time. However, to the extent that the assistance accorded adversely affects the interests of other Members, in particular their negotiated market access rights, procedures designed to remove the adverse effects of the subsidy and to re-establish the negotiated balance of concessions must be observed. Proposals to create under the WTO Agreement the right to offset the economic consequences of differences in environmental regulations are therefore in fact proposals to eliminate the rights that WTO Members have when a Member exercises the already existing right to assist a domestic industry threatened by such differences.

## International bargaining across trade and environmental issues

There are many proposals to use the market access opportunities created by the obligations assumed under the WTO agreements as bargaining chips to induce other countries to change their environmental policies. Steve Charnovitz wrote:

> How can an agreement on minimum standards be achieved among a hundred countries with different values and resources? One approach is to devise a clever mix of carrots and sticks from a diverse enough issue garden to allow a cross-fertilization of concerns. The goal is not only to obtain an agreement, but also to maintain its stability. The carrots are the basic tool. Because countries face different economic trade-offs . . . an assistance mechanism can be developed to enable gainers to compensate losers and rich nations to "bribe" poor ones. This assistance could be in the form of financial aid or technology transfer . . . , or it could be trade concessions.[22]

The use of trade measures as carrots or sticks in international negotiations would generally be incompatible with the WTO agreements because of the unconditional nature of their most-favored-nation clauses.[23] To make this policy option legally available, the WTO Agreement would need to be changed or replaced by a new agreement with different rights and obli-

[22] Steve Charnovitz, "Environmental Harmonization and Trade Policy," in Durwood Zaelke, Paul Orbuch and Robert F. Housman eds., *Trade and the Environment: Law, Economics, and Policy* (Washington, D.C.: Island Press, c1993), 282.

[23] See Article I of the GATT and Article II of the GATS.

gations. The procedural obstacles to such a change or replacement are significant. Under the WTO Agreement, a waiver from obligations may only be granted with the consent of three-quarters of the WTO Members and only for a limited period of time. New environmental policy obligations cannot be created by majority decision under the WTO Agreement because amendments that change the rights and obligations of the WTO Members take effect (upon their acceptance by two-thirds of the Members) only for the Members that have accepted them.[24] The provisions incorporating the principle of unconditional most-favored-nation treatment can only be amended with the consent of all WTO Members.[25] All new environmental policy obligations would thus have to be agreed among the WTO Members and the benefits of market access could not be withheld from those WTO Members that have not accepted these obligations. This limits the possibilities to use, within the legal framework of the WTO, the threat of a withdrawal of market access rights as an incentive to induce other Members to accept new commitments on their environmental policies.

In the Uruguay Round, the obstacles to issue linkages created by the GATT's unconditional most-favored-nation clause have been overcome through the concept of the "single undertaking." The Uruguay Round covered fifteen negotiating areas. The commitments assumed under the GATT and in each of these areas have been incorporated into a single legal instrument – the WTO Agreement – which must be accepted in its totality.[26] The integrated dispute settlement system, under which failures to observe commitments in one area could result in retaliatory action in another, is to hold the negotiated package of commitments together. Trade and domestic policy issues thus have been successfully linked in the Uruguay Round because the negotiators decided to create a new legal system that replaced the GATT rather than attempting to amend the GATT or supplement it with new agreements. It was this approach that permitted bargaining across issue areas that have so far led separate lives in separate institutions, such as trade and intellectual property rights. Also in the future, major changes in the obligations of the WTO Members could be achieved only with great difficulty through a process of changing the rules of the multilateral trade order or of supplementing them with additional agreements. To realize the

[24] Articles IX and X:3 of the WTO Agreement.
[25] Article X:2 of the WTO Agreement.
[26] Article XIV of the WTO Agreement.

main objectives of environmentalists, the replacement of the WTO Agreement with a new agreement would most likely be necessary.

While the linking of trade and environmental issues in a future WTO negotiation would therefore be technically feasible, there would be numerous political, legal, and institutional obstacles to its realization. A replacement of the WTO Agreement is procedurally difficult and time-consuming and can therefore realistically be envisaged only in the context of a new negotiating round with a scope comparable to that of the Uruguay Round. The linkages proposed by environmentalists could therefore not be realized until an agreement has been reached on numerous other issues. The timing and success of negotiations on essential environmental matters would consequently be made dependent on political developments in unrelated areas. Moreover, in reciprocity negotiations a nation will not obtain in return for its market access commitments an equivalent market access commitment *and* commitments on environmental policies; it will obtain only one or the other and will therefore have to decide which of the two objectives to pursue. To propose that a multilateral negotiation cover market access issues *and* a raising of environmental standards is therefore to propose that nations with high environmental standards pursue their trade interests *or* their environmental interests.

In the introduction to this chapter, about two dozen worthwhile policy objectives have been identified which have been linked by governments at one time or another to trade policy issues. At the domestic level, environmental concerns would therefore be competing with many other non-trade objectives as negotiating targets for a new round of trade negotiations and, at the international level, any proposal to make the environment part of the negotiating objectives would be countered by proposals to take up other non-trade issues. There is nothing that can be said about the relationship between the environment and trade that does not apply also to the relationship of many of the competing policy objectives with the global trade order. The selection of the environment will therefore not emerge from the application of a principle that environmentalists could invoke to shield themselves against competing demands but from political struggles within and between trading nations.

The Uruguay Round negotiations on intellectual property rights illustrate that non-trade issues cannot be linked to trade issues for negotiating purposes without sacrificing trade to non-trade objectives. The countries in which the production of technological knowledge is concentrated and those to which this knowledge is disseminated or transferred took conflicting positions in these negotiations. The developed countries sought worldwide recognition of extensive intellectual property rights; the developing countries carefully weighed the economic costs and benefits that such a recognition entails. This difficulty was overcome by linking the negotiations on intellectual property rights with negotiations on market access and other matters in the Uruguay Round and incorporating the results of the Round in a legal framework that permits the withdrawal of obligations outside the field of intellectual property rights to respond to failures to observe the obligations in that field. Given the reciprocity principle guiding negotiators, the obligations in the field of intellectual property can reasonably be assumed to have been in part substitutes for market access and other trade obligations that would have been accepted by the developing countries had the linkage with intellectual property rights not been made.[27]

One of the main purposes of linking trade and environmental negotiations in the framework of the WTO would be to obtain the possibility of using trade sanctions as a stick to enforce obligations in the environmental sphere, to legalize – just as in the sphere of intellectual property – cross-retaliation. The principle of cross-retaliation has however inherent limitations. The main purpose of international bargaining in the WTO is to create regimes, systems of rules, and procedures making governmental actions more predictable. Each of these regimes cannot furnish predictability if it is constantly exposed to the need to adjust to a breakdown in other regimes. How can, for instance, an international regime governing intellectual property rights or trade in financial services function if the cooperation established under these regimes can at any time be disturbed by failures to observe obligations in the field of trade in textiles or agricultural products? Would it be satisfactory to link the operation of an agreement to curb sales of ivory to that of the WTO Agreement on Textiles and Clothing?

It is often forgotten that cross-retaliation under the WTO is a two-way street: WTO law permits trade sanctions to enforce intellectual property rights, but also the denial of intellectual property protection to enforce

[27] In the Uruguay Round the developing countries made substantially fewer market access concessions than the developed countries. Most of this discrepancy is of course attributable to the principle of non-reciprocity that has traditionally governed trade negotiations between developed and developing countries. However, in part it is no doubt attributable to the fact that the developed countries sacrificed to a certain degree their trade interests to their interest in a worldwide recognition of intellectual property rights.

trade rights. If market access and the protection of endangered species were to be successfully linked in WTO negotiations, trade concessions could be withdrawn in response to the non-protection of an endangered species *and* vice versa. If environmentalists seek in the WTO the "trade weapon" to further environmental goals, they must therefore accept that other nations obtain the "environmental weapon" to defend their trade interests. However, it is totally inappropriate to make commitments on such essential matters as the protection of endangered species, where the withdrawal from obligations may have irreversible effects, dependent on the ups and downs of commercial policies. Environmental organizations, now embracing the idea of a link between trade and environmental matters under the law of the WTO, might lose their enthusiasm once they realize that this linkage entails the risk of throwing vital environmental policy objectives into the crab basket of trade policymaking.

The inherent limitations of the cross-retaliation principle were recognized by the negotiators of the WTO agreements. Initially the United States, mainly with its interest in worldwide intellectual property rights protection in mind, proposed that there be an unbridled right of cross-retaliation under the WTO dispute settlement procedures. However, subsequently it revised its position to the effect that retaliation across sectors should be resorted to only if retaliation within the sector was not practical or effective. This change reflected the fear of the United States' banking sector that cross-retaliation resulting from failures to observe obligations in the field of trade in goods might upset the delicate balances of interest between nations in the field of financial services. The text of the dispute settlement procedures therefore now contains eight subparagraphs defining meticulously the circumstances under which a WTO Member may retaliate across sectors and the elements of the Uruguay Round package that constitute individual sectors.[28] This is the first indication that the broad linkages made in the Uruguay Round negotiations may not be sustained in the administration of its results.

## Opening the decisionmaking process in the WTO to environmental interests

WTO Members are required to conduct their policies transparently. They have the obligation to consider comments by other WTO Members before

[28] Article 22:3 of the DSU.

the adoption of technical regulations and sanitary and phytosanitary measures, to explain why an internationally agreed or equivalent national standard or measure was not chosen, to publish regulations in advance of their implementation so as to allow producers in other WTO Members to adapt their products or production methods to the regulations, and to respond to requests for information at inquiry points.[29] These procedural requirements ensure transparency in the adoption of policy measures, and therefore help maximize the information available to policymakers and administrators and minimize the information gap between domestic producers or service suppliers and those in other WTO Members.

The WTO however does not conduct its business transparently. Its meetings are closed to the public.[30] It is authorized to cooperate with non-governmental organizations[31] but has not yet decided to do so. Its dispute settlement procedures are confidential.[32] Even a WTO Member interested in a dispute settlement proceeding between two other WTO Members merely has the right to express its views but may not be present when the parties to the dispute exchange their arguments.[33] Most of the documents issued by the WTO are issued as restricted documents and are often derestricted only after a period of time sufficiently long to ensure that the decisions described in them are a *fait accompli.*

Some elements of the WTO's lack of transparency are justified. The intent to renegotiate a tariff concession cannot be made public without provoking speculative transactions anticipating the change. Conciliation procedures cannot be conducted in the limelight of the press and need not be subject to procedural rigors given their non-binding nature. And any organization needs a certain degree of privacy that permits consultations to explore ideas, seek reactions, or determine the common ground. So-called "non-papers," that is informal papers without any indication of authorship and distribution, and informal consultations without any records are therefore a

29 See Annex B of the SPS Agreement, Article 2 of the TBT Agreement, Article X of the GATT, and Article III of the GATS.

30 See for instance Rule 37 of the Rules of Procedure for Meetings of the General Council, which reads: "The meetings of the General Council shall ordinarily be held in private. It may be decided that a particular meeting should be held in public."

31 Article V:2 of the WTO Agreement.

32 Article 14 of the DSU.

33 Article 10 of the DSU. Third WTO Members that become co-complainants have full access to the proceedings (see Article 9 of the DSU); but there is no right to become a codefendant.

legitimate feature of the early, exploratory stage of decisionmaking in any international organization.

In the trade negotiations under the original GATT, complete transparency would not necessarily have entailed a better defense of the public interest. The original GATT imposed legal constraints merely on policies that discriminate between products as to their origin or destination. The process of decisionmaking in the GATT was therefore of primary interest only to import-competing and exporting industries, hardly ever to public interest organizations. The GATT's principal function was to provide a forum and legal framework for the negotiation of packages of market access concessions and rights, packages that could be submitted to legislators in their entirety so as to enable them to take into account broad economic policy interests rather than rent-seeking sectorial interests. That function would have been hampered by complete openness in the process of exchanging individual concessions.

The law of the WTO, however, goes beyond the mere prohibition of discrimination. It establishes numerous requirements for domestic regulations, that is regulations equally applicable to domestic and foreign goods, services, and service suppliers. The GATT's distinction between foreign trade policies, in respect of which governments are bound, and domestic economic policies, which they may conduct autonomously, is not made under the WTO agreements. Thus, the WTO Agreement on Technical Barriers to Trade (TBT Agreement) obliges Members to ensure that "technical regulations are not prepared, adopted or applied with a view to or with the effect of creating unnecessary obstacles to international trade. For this purpose, technical regulations shall therefore not be more trade-restrictive than necessary to fulfill a legitimate objective."[34] Similarly the Agreement on the Application of Sanitary and Phytosanitary Measures (SPS Agreement) obliges WTO Members not to impose measures that are "more trade-restrictive than required to achieve their appropriate level of sanitary or phytosanitary protection," a requirement which is met if there is no other "measure, reasonably available taking into account technical and economic feasibility, that achieves the appropriate level of sanitary or phytosanitary protection and is significantly less restrictive to trade."[35]

The objective of both the TBT and the SPS Agreements is not to prevent

[34] Article 2.2.

[35] Article 5:6.

the legitimate exercise of domestic regulatory authority, but to forestall protectionism in the guise of technical regulations and SPS measures. However, the broadly worded requirements of these Agreements need to be interpreted and applied both by the organs and the membership of the WTO, and in that process not merely the trade interests of exporting and import-competing industries of different nations have to be weighed against one another, as in the case of the interpretation of most GATT provisions, but the export interests of some WTO Members against the public policy interests of importing countries. It is legitimate, therefore, that environmental organizations wish that process to take place, not in a closed trade organization through which political forces representing producer interests have traditionally been channeled, but in the framework of transparent procedures that makes the WTO and its Members responsive to interests other than producer interests.

Under the original GATT, the dispute settlement procedures were based on the principle of consensus: any contracting party had the option of blocking the adoption of a panel report.[36] Given the contracting parties' control over the result, complete transparency in the process was not essential. Moreover, the dispute settlement process had strong elements of a conciliation procedure: its primary aim was the promotion of an agreed settlement. A certain degree of confidentiality is necessary to further that objective. However, under the WTO, the panel procedure is automatic; its result binding on the parties to the dispute; and the conciliation and panel procedures have been clearly segregated. The legitimacy of the panels' recommendations arose in the past mainly from their endorsement by the community of trading nations; now it can only be conferred upon them through the legitimacy of the procedures that lead to them. Openness is an essential part of that legitimacy.

The WTO, having ventured into the field of domestic regulations and administering procedures for the binding adjudication of disputes, must therefore become more transparent to ensure the legitimacy and public acceptability of its decisions. However, this will not be an easy step and will probably be taken only gradually and with many hesitations. There is no such thing as selective transparency: opening up to political forces representing legitimate public policy objectives therefore means also opening up

[36] Paragraph G.3 of the decision of 12 April 1989 on *Improvements to the GATT Dispute Settlement Rules and Procedures* (BISD 36th Supp., 61).

to rent-seeking, sectorial interests. When the United States proposed (unsupported by any other delegation) that the adoption of the Tuna panel be discussed by the GATT Council in the presence of environmental organizations, one delegation dryly remarked that setting this precedent would mean that the next panel report on import restrictions on dairy products might have to be discussed in the presence of farmers, possibly with their cows. There is no assurance that greater openness in the WTO's decision-making and adjudication process would enhance the relative influence of public interests. Domestic openness requirements have not resolved the basic problem of overrepresentation of special, rent-seeking interests in the governmental decisionmaking process, and it is unlikely that they would do so in the WTO. The great challenge of the WTO will therefore be to achieve greater openness without hampering its ability to further the public interest in rational trade policymaking.

## Summary and conclusions

The proposals to integrate environmental concerns in the substantive rules of the global trade order are not based on any principle that is capable of general application. Thus, the proposal to exempt domestic environmental policy measures from WTO obligations lacks any generalizable basis. Conflicts between domestic environmental law and WTO law only arise when a domestic environmental policy measure is applied discriminatorily in an effort to shift the economic burden of the measure to non-voters abroad. Conflicts consequently arise not for technical reasons but because of domestic political constraints. However, the principle that internal political constraints should override international market access commitments is not capable of incorporation into an abstract rule of conduct and a global trade order based on that principle is inconceivable.

The principle that nations should be permitted to offset through trade controls the economic consequences of differences in domestic environmental policies between them is equally incapable of universal application. The very purpose of the global trade is to permit nations to exploit their differences in resource endowments and preferences in accordance with the principle of comparative advantage, and diverging environmental policies often reflect such differences. With a general rule permitting all nations to offset the economic consequences of all differences between them, the world trade order could no longer perform its basic function.

WTO Members' domestic political constraints and the differences in the competitive position of their industries is taken into account in the WTO's procedures for the negotiation and renegotiation of market access commitments. Such commitments are made by product (GATT), sector (GATS), and procurement entity (Agreement on Government Procurement). Reciprocity is achieved not through equal but through equivalent commitments, and the schedules commitments of the different WTO Members therefore vary significantly. Moreover, the WTO Members are entitled to renegotiate their commitments. Both during the process of negotiating the commitments and after their acceptance WTO Members thus have the possibility of adjusting their obligations to their constraints and objectives. However, this modulation results from a negotiation and maintains the balance of rights and obligations among Members.

The use of market access as a source of carrots and sticks to induce nations to accept commitments to raise their environmental standards is incompatible with the principle of unconditional most-favored-nation treatment. An amendment of the provisions of the WTO agreements incorporating this principle requires acceptance by all WTO Members. To make the carrots and sticks legally available, a replacement of the WTO Agreement with a new agreement would therefore most likely be necessary. However, a replacement of the WTO Agreement is procedurally difficult and time-consuming and can therefore realistically be envisaged only in the context of a new negotiating round with a scope comparable to that of the Uruguay Round. The linkages proposed by environmentalists could therefore not be realized until an agreement has been reached on numerous other issues. The timing and success of negotiations on essential environmental matters would therefore be made dependent on political developments in unrelated areas.

The introduction to this chapter identified about two dozen worthwhile non-trade policy goals that governments have proposed for discussion in conjunction with market access issues. If market access under the WTO were made dependent on the attainment of all these policy goals, the source of carrots and sticks environmentalists propose to use would vanish. There is nothing that can be said about the relationship between the environment and trade that does not also apply to the relationship between many of the competing policy objectives and the global trade order. The selection of the environment as negotiating objective will therefore not emerge from the application of a principle that environmentalists could invoke to shield themselves against competing demands but from political struggles within and between trading nations.

Reciprocity and retaliation are mirror concepts and any linkage between environmental and trade issues in the framework of the WTO is therefore a two-way street: to propose that market access commitments be used to induce other nations to accept environmental commitments is to propose that the observation of environmental commitments be made dependent on the observation of market access commitments. Using the "trade weapon" in the pursuit of environmental objectives creates the "environmental weapon" in the pursuit of trade objectives. It seems however totally inappropriate to make commitments on such important matters as the protection of endangered species or the ozone layer dependent on the vagaries of trade policymaking. The idea of linking trade rights to environmental obligations under the global trade order is likely to lose its appeal once it is realized that it entails the risk of throwing essential environmental commitments into the crab basket of trade policymaking.

The environmentalists' quest for greater openness in the decisionmaking procedures of the WTO is based on principles capable of generalization. The law of the WTO now comprises obligations on domestic policy measures, such as technical standards and sanitary or phytosanitary measures, that must be interpreted and applied not only by weighing the trade interests traditionally channeled through the GATT, but by weighing trade interests against legitimate public policy interests. Only openness towards public policy interests can confer legitimacy on the WTO's decisions in these new policy areas. Under the original GATT, the dispute settlement procedures were based on the principle of consensus. However, under the WTO, the panel procedure is automatic. The legitimacy of the panels' recommendations arose in the past mainly from their endorsement by the community of trading nations; now it can only be conferred upon them through the legitimacy of the procedures that lead to them.

The WTO, having ventured into the field of domestic regulations and administering an automatic dispute settlement procedure, has no choice but to become more open. Its institutional survival depends on the acceptability of its decisions, which in turn depends on the legitimacy of the process leading to them. Openness is an essential part of that legitimacy. The challenge the WTO is facing is to achieve greater openness without hampering its ability to help governments further the public interest in rational trade policymaking.

# 5

# INTERNATIONAL TRADE LAW AND INTERNATIONAL ENVIRONMENTAL LAW: ENVIRONMENTAL TAXES AND BORDER TAX ADJUSTMENT IN WTO LAW AND EC LAW

ERNST-ULRICH PETERSMANN

PROFESSOR ROESSLER'S paper purports to "explore the systemic, legal, and institutional consequences of linking trade and non-trade issues in the framework of the WTO, taking the proposed linkages between environment and trade as an example." The first section of this comment on Prof. Roessler's paper addresses briefly the four conclusions reached by Roessler. The second section draws attention to additional "interface problems," notably advantages and problems of environmental taxes. The third section elaborates on the second conclusion of Roessler, i.e. that the WTO's border adjustment rules should not be changed, by analyzing in more detail the interrelationships between environmental taxes and border tax adjustment in the worldwide context of GATT and WTO law. The final section compares the worldwide GATT/WTO rules on border tax adjustment and tax discrimination with the corresponding rules and experiences in the regional context of EC law, and draws some tentative conclusions.

## Professor Roessler's four main conclusions

### CONSISTENCY OF WTO LAW WITH EFFICIENT ENVIRONMENTAL POLICIES

Roessler's first conclusion is that there is in principle no conflict between WTO law and the efficient pursuit of a domestic environmental policy

The comments on Prof. Roessler's paper refer to the draft paper presented at the Villa La Pietra symposium in July 1996.

objective so that there does not seem to be a need for exempting domestic environmental policies from WTO obligations. This view is widely shared today in environmental economics and among governments. As most environmental pollution arises at the level of production, distribution, consumption, or disposal of goods and services, efficient environmental policies should intervene directly at the source of the pollution, i.e. at the production, distribution, consumption, or waste disposal level rather than at the trade level where trade policy interventions risk causing welfare-reducing "by-product distortions." This "rectification at source principle" is also consistent with the ranking of trade and environmental policy instruments in GATT/WTO law, which leaves each WTO member country free to use efficient, non-discriminatory, internal policy instruments (see GATT Article III, GATS Article VI) and favors price-based trade policy instruments over non-tariff trade barriers (see Table 5.1).[1]

It is noteworthy in this respect that, after years of systematic examination of the various interface problems between trade and environmental policies in the WTO Committee on Trade and Environment and in the preceding GATT Committees, there are only a few proposals for amendments of WTO law for environmental policy reasons, and all these proposals remain controversial. The GATT and WTO dispute settlement practice regarding trade-related environmental and health protection measures (TREMS) is no less revealing: each of the more than ten GATT and WTO dispute settlement findings against unilateral TREMS over the past fifteen years concluded that unilateral discriminatory trade restrictions applied by the defendant country had not been necessary for achieving the specified environmental objective.[2] For instance:

1 The *1982 GATT panel report on the US prohibition of imports of tuna and tuna products from Canada* found that the import embargo was inconsistent with Article XI:1. As the US had neither catch limits for its own fishing fleets on most of the species of tuna nor restrictions on domestic

[1] For a more detailed explanation of the ranking of trade and environmental policy instruments in GATT/WTO law see E. U. Petersmann, *International and European Trade and Environmental Law after the Uruguay Round* (London and Boston: Kluwer Law International, 1995), 11–22.

[2] For a detailed analysis of these GATT and WTO dispute settlement reports see E. U. Petersmann, *The GATT/WTO Dispute Settlement System. International Law, International Organizations and Dispute Settlement* (London and Boston: Kluwer Law International, 1997), chapter 3.

Table 5.1 *The public choice of trade policy instruments*

| Instruments of import protection | Economic ranking (efficiency) | Political ranking (parliamentary control) | Legal ranking (GATT) |
|---|---|---|---|
| Non-discriminatory internal taxes and regulations accompanied by border adjustment measures | Optimal instrument for correcting *domestic* distortions | Non-discriminatory measures subject to legislation | Allowed (note to Art. III GATT) and not subject to countermeasures |
| Production subsidy | First-best trade policy instrument (production distortion) | Direct budgetary transfers subject to legislation | Allowed but possibly "actionable" and "countervailable" (Arts. VI, XVI:1, XXIII GATT and 1994 Subsidy Code) |
| Import tariff | Second-best trade policy instrument (production and consumption distortion) | Transparent taxes, government revenue, and protection rents subject to legislation | Allowed subject to tariff bindings (Arts. II, XXVIII) and safeguard clauses (e.g. Arts. VI, XIX) |
| Import restrictions<br>– global quota<br>– country quotas | Third-best trade policy instrument (additional distortions of price competition; private protection rents in lieu of tariff revenue; legal insecurity) | Less transparent, administrative distribution of market shares and protection rents to importers and foreign exporters | Prohibited subject to GATT's safeguard clauses (e.g. Arts. XI, XII, XVIII–XXI) and non-discrimination requirements (e.g. Arts. XIII, XX) |
| Voluntary export restraints (VER) | Fourth-best trade policy instrument (additional transfers of quota rents abroad, additional legal insecurity) | Non-transparent transfers of protection rents at home and abroad without parliamentary and judicial control | Prohibited (Art. XIII GATT) with only temporary exceptions (1994 Safeguards and Textiles Agreements) |

consumption of tuna and tuna products in the US, the US embargo on Canadian tuna had also not been "made effective in conjunction with restrictions on domestic production or consumption" of tuna as required by Article XX(g).

2 The *1987 GATT panel report on US taxes on petroleum and other environmental taxes* found that the taxes on petroleum discriminated against imported products in violation of Article III:2. The US did not even argue that this tax discrimination had been necessary for achieving the environmental objectives.

3 The *1988 GATT panel report on Canada's restrictions on exports of unprocessed herring and salmon* found the export prohibitions to be inconsistent with Article XI:1 and not justified under Articles XI:2(b) or XX(g) because, *inter alia*, the Canadian export restrictions were not "primarily aimed at the conservation of salmon and herring stocks and at rendering effective the restrictions on the harvesting of these fish."

4 The *1990 GATT panel report on Thailand's restrictions on importation of cigarettes* related to the protection of health; it found the import restrictions to be inconsistent with Article XI:1 and not justified under Article XX(b) because Thailand could avail itself of alternative, GATT-consistent non-discriminatory tobacco-control strategies applicable to both imported and domestic cigarettes, which – according to several World Health Organization recommendations – were more effective in protecting citizens against the risks of smoking: "Thailand's practice of permitting the sale of domestic cigarettes while not permitting the importation of foreign cigarettes was an inconsistency with the General Agreement not 'necessary' within the meaning of Article XX(b)."

5 The *1991 GATT panel report on US restrictions on imports of tuna* (Tuna I) concluded that the import embargo was inconsistent with Article XI:1 and not justified by Article XX(b) and (g) because, *inter alia*, a unilateral import embargo was not "necessary" for the protection of dolphins in the High Seas as long as the US "had not exhausted all options reasonably available to it to pursue its dolphin protection objectives through measures consistent with the General Agreement, in particular through the negotiation of international cooperative arrangements which would seem to be desirable in view of the fact that dolphins roam the waters of many States and the high seas."

6 The *1994 GATT panel report on US import restrictions on tuna* (Tuna II) found that neither the "primary nation embargo" nor the "intermediary

nation embargo" could be justified under Article XX because, *inter alia*, "both the primary and intermediary nation embargoes on tuna were taken by the United States so as to force other countries to change their policies with respect to persons and things within their own jurisdiction, since the embargoes required such changes in order to have any effect on the protection of the life or health of dolphins"; "the GATT contracting parties had not agreed to give each other in Article XX the right to impose trade embargoes to force other countries to change their domestic environmental policies."

7 The *1994 GATT panel report on US taxes on automobiles* found that the luxury tax on automobiles and the environmental "gas guzzler tax" on automobiles were non-discriminatory and not inconsistent with GATT Article III:2. By contrast, the "corporate average fuel economy" requirement was found to accord foreign cars and car parts less favorable conditions of competition than to like domestic products in a manner inconsistent with Article III:4 and not justified under Article XX (d) or (g).

8 The *1995 complaints by Chile, Peru, and Canada against French trade restrictions for scallops*, which were bilaterally settled in spring 1996 on the basis of a WTO interim panel report confirming the inconsistency of the restrictions with Articles 2.2 and 12.3 of the Agreement on Technical Barriers to Trade (TBT), concerned discriminatory restrictions on the use of trade names ("coquille Saint Jacques") rather than the environmental protection of the scallops concerned.

9 The *1996 WTO panel report on US standards for reformulated and conventional gasoline* found that certain regulations in the Clean Air Act, which aims at reducing air pollution caused by motor vehicle emissions in the US by means of setting standards for gasoline quality, treated imported gasoline less favorably than like domestic gasoline in a manner inconsistent with GATT Article III:4. These legal inconsistencies, by which imported gasoline was prevented from benefiting from as favorable sales conditions as were afforded to domestic gasoline by an "individual baseline" tied to the producer of gasoline, were not "necessary" or otherwise justifiable in terms of GATT Article XX on the basis of the evidence submitted to the panel by the USA. The panel findings on Article XX(g) were appealed in February 1996. The *1996 WTO Appellate Body Report on US standards for reformulated and conventional gasoline* found that the "baseline establishment rules" in the US Clean

Air Act fell within the ambit of GATT Article XX(g) but failed to meet the non-discrimination requirements of the chapeau of GATT Article XX, and accordingly were not justified under Article XX of GATT 1994. The Appellate Body report confirmed that "under the General Agreement, WTO Members are free to set their own environmental objectives, but they are bound to implement these objectives through measures consistent with its provisions."

10 The *1996 WTO panel reports on EC measures affecting meat and meat products (hormones)* found, *inter alia*, that the EC, "by adopting arbitrary or unjustifiable distinctions in the levels of sanitary protection it considers to be appropriate in different situations which result in discrimination or a disguised restriction on international trade, has acted inconsistently with the requirements contained in Article 5.5 of the Agreement on Sanitary and Phytosanitary Measures" (SPS). The *1998 Appellate Body report* reversed this panel finding, but upheld the additional panel finding that the EC ban on imports of meat and meat products from cattle treated with certain "growth hormones" was inconsistent with Articles 3.3 and 5.1 of the SPS Agreement.

11 The *1998 WTO panel report on the US import prohibition of certain shrimp and shrimp products* found the US import prohibition inconsistent with GATT Article XI and "not within the scope of measures permitted under Article XX" of GATT since the US made the import ban conditional on the adoption of US environmental standards by the exporting countries. The *1998 Appellate Body report* concluded that the US measure qualified for provisional justification under Article XX(g) but failed to meet the non-discrimination requirements of the chapeau of Article XX.

## WTO MEMBERS SHOULD NOT BE ALLOWED TO OFFSET THROUGH TRADE CONTROLS THE ECONOMIC IMPACT OF DIFFERENCES IN ENVIRONMENTAL STANDARDS

The second conclusion is that the WTO's border adjustment rules, and the WTO principle of unconditional most-favored-nation treatment, should not be changed so as to permit WTO Members to offset differences in environmental regulations and to make the access to domestic markets conditional on changes in foreign environmental policies. This conclusion, again, coincides with the current worldwide consensus among governments and among economists, as expressed for example in the principles adopted by the 1992 UN Conference on Environment and Development (such as "Principle 12"). The 1998 WTO panel report on the Shrimp–Turtle dispute applied the following principle in support of its finding that unilateral import restrictions designed to force exporting countries to adopt environmental production standards of the importing country are "not within the scope of measures permitted under Article XX":

> if an interpretation of the chapeau of Article XX were to be followed which would allow a Member to adopt measures conditioning access to its market for a given product upon the adoption by the exporting Member of certain policies, including conservation policies, GATT 1994 and the WTO Agreement could no longer serve as a multilateral framework for trade among Members as security and predictability of trade relations under those agreements would be threatened . . . if one WTO Member were allowed to adopt such measures, then other Members would also have the right to adopt similar measures on the same subject but with differing, or even conflicting requirements. If that happened, it would be impossible for exporting Members to comply at the same time with multiple conflicting policy requirements . . . Market access for goods could become subject to an increasing number of conflicting policy requirements for the same product and this would rapidly lead to the end of the WTO multilateral trading system.[3]

Roessler's paper does not analyze the GATT/WTO border adjustment rules and the need for clarifying and adjusting them so as to accommodate better eco-taxes on environmentally harmful emissions, process and production methods, products and their inputs. These important problems are discussed in more detail later in this comment.

## DOES INTERNATIONAL BARGAINING ACROSS TRADE AND ENVIRONMENTAL ISSUES REQUIRE A NEW WTO AGREEMENT?

International environmental law has evolved in a piecemeal manner without adequate coordination among the approximately 800 bilateral and multilateral environmental agreements. However, proposals for negotiating a General Agreement on the Environment, or for establishing a World Environment Organization, continue to lack sufficient political support. Roessler's third conclusion is that linking future trade and environmental

[3] United States–Import Prohibition of Certain Shrimp and Shrimp Products, report of the panel, WTO Document, WT/DS58/R of 15 May 1998, para. 7.44.

negotiations in the WTO framework might necessitate "the replacement of the WTO Agreement with a new agreement." Yet, "issue linkages" will continue to be made in international trade negotiations. They are even likely to increase in view of the "meshing of different international regimes" in the WTO Agreement, which includes numerous explicit references to other worldwide and regional agreements such as the UN Charter, the IMF Agreement, international commodity agreements, multilateral environmental agreements (like the International Plant Protection Convention), international services agreements (like the International Telecommunications Union and international air transport agreements), and intellectual property rights conventions.[4]

The discussions in the WTO Committee on Trade and Environment suggest that, in negotiations on the agenda of future "WTO Rounds," developed country proposals to negotiate environmental rules in the WTO (e.g. on eco-labeling, eco-packaging, waste disposal) will be linked by less-developed countries to their demands for further liberalization of existing import restrictions on textiles and agricultural products. Developing countries also point to the environmental benefits deriving from additional trade liberalization (e.g. of agricultural protectionism, coal subsidies, and tariff escalation on tropical timber). In certain areas, developing countries invoke health and environmental reasons for additional trade restrictions (e.g. for domestically prohibited pesticides and hazardous pharmaceuticals). In the context of the WTO Agreement on Trade-Related Intellectual Property Rights (TRIPS), developing countries call for preferential terms for the transfer of patented environmental technology, for instance if multilateral environmental agreements prohibit environmentally harmful process and production methods and the alternative "clean" technologies are patented and too expensive for poor countries.

The concept of "sustainable development," which is explicitly recognized in the preamble to the WTO Agreement, acknowledges that trade liberalization and environmental protection are complementary conditions for an efficient use of scarce resources and need to be integrated also in the context of WTO law and practices. There are also important political arguments for such policy integration: protection of global public goods (such as the

[4] See E. U. Petersmann and J. Chakarian, "Meshing Multilateral Regimes: GATT/WTO Law, Multilateral Environmental Agreements and Dispute Settlement," in D. Leebron ed., *The Multilateral Trade Regime in the 21st Century: Structural Issues*, forthcoming.

ozone layer), and correction of cross-border pollution (such as emissions of ozone-depleting substances), require multilateral cooperation as well as safeguards against non-cooperating countries ("free-riding"). While financial sticks and carrots (e.g. in the context of the World Bank Group) vis-à-vis non-cooperating governments are preferable, there are good economic, political, and legal arguments for better integrating trade and environmental law and policies. If such legal integration cannot be achieved by explicitly integrating trade and environmental rules into one single legal framework, as in the EC Treaty, WTO law needs to be coordinated with international environmental agreements negotiated outside the WTO.

## NEED FOR OPENING WTO DECISIONMAKING PROCESSES TO ENVIRONMENTAL INTERESTS

Roessler's fourth conclusion – that there is a need for additional transparency and legitimacy of WTO decisionmaking procedures – can hardly be contested. It must never be forgotten that governments and their policies derive their legitimacy from promoting the equal rights and "public interest" of all their citizens.[5] Transparency of governmental decisionmaking processes is a fundamental prerequisite for democratic citizen participation, public discussion, and parliamentary control. The traditional non-transparency of foreign policies, including GATT and WTO decisionmaking processes, may sometimes help governments to cooperate as a sort of "liberal cartel" so as to fend off protectionist interest group pressures better. Yet, the lack of transparency is also frequently abused for granting "protection rents" to powerful textiles, agricultural, steel, and other lobbies at the expense of the general interest of domestic citizens in liberal trade.

It is therefore to be welcomed that the WTO's General Council agreed in July 1996 on guidelines for improving transparency, furthering contacts with non-governmental organizations (NGOs), and for derestricting WTO documents more quickly. In 1997, and again in 1998, the WTO Secretariat organized public symposia with approximately seventy NGOs on trade-related environmental problems and the future WTO work on TREMS. The

[5] See E. U. Petersmann, "The Moral Foundations of the EU's Foreign Policy Constitution: Defining 'European Identity' and 'Community Interest' for the Benefit of EU Citizens," 51 *Swiss Review of International Economic Relations* (*Aussenwirtschaft*), 151–76 (1996).

opposition by WTO member countries to direct participation of NGOs in WTO meetings and negotiations is sometimes explained by the asymmetries in the organization and political influence of interest groups, which favor concentrated, "rent-seeking" producer interests over dispersed general interests (e.g. of consumers and taxpayers in liberal trade);[6] yet, the example of the "Economic and Social Committee" in the EC demonstrates that a balanced representation and participation of private interest groups in an advisory body can strengthen the transparency and legitimacy of international organizations without endangering legitimate public interests. There are also many other ways of enhancing the transparency and legitimacy of international agreements for the benefit of domestic citizens, for instance by treating citizens as legal subjects of international trade agreements rather than as mere objects of paternalistic government regulation, and by enabling them to invoke and enforce international guarantees of freedom and non-discrimination (such as those in WTO law) before domestic courts. The more the jurisdiction of the WTO extends beyond trade policy border measures and covers also internal economic and other regulations, the more the WTO should undertake additional efforts at improving the transparency and legitimacy of WTO law and policies for the benefit of the citizens and their democratic participation.

## Additional interface problems: advantages and problems of environmental taxes

In his concluding remarks, Prof. Roessler claims that "proposals to integrate environmental concerns in the substantive rules of the global trade order are not based on any principle that is capable of general application." This claim is hardly consistent with the actual trend in WTO law, EC law, and NAFTA law to integrate trade and environmental rules and principles (such as the polluter pays principle, the precautionary principle, "sustainable development") within the same treaty framework.[7] The fragmented and insufficiently coordinated development of international environmen-

[6] On this "producer bias" of trade policymaking processes as a "constitutional problem" see E. U. Petersmann, *Constitutional Functions and Constitutional Problems of International Economic Law* (Fribourg, Switzerland and Boulder, Colo.: University Press, Westview Press, *c.* 1991), at 12ff.

[7] See, e.g., the compilation of environmental provisions in the WTO Agreement and in the EC Treaty in Annexes II and V to Petersmann, *International and European Trade.*

tal rules and their inadequate implementation in domestic legal systems vis-à-vis private polluters and governmental administrations are among the major weaknesses of international environmental law. The objective of "sustainable development" requires not only integrating environmental costs into national and international economic and legal systems; it also requires a more comprehensive integration law with rights and obligations not only for governments but also for polluters, pollutees, and other citizens interested in a clean environment and in democratic participation in environmental decisionmaking processes.

There are thus good arguments for incorporating *substantive* environmental law rules into WTO law (such as the basic environmental law principles recognized in Article 174 of the EC Treaty) as well as *procedural* requirements for taking into account international environmental law and policies in the WTO context (e.g. interpretation of the "necessity principle" in GATT Article XX and in the WTO Agreement on Technical Barriers to Trade in conformity with multilateral environmental agreements). In contrast to the economic theory of optimal intervention, which argues in favor of separating trade and environmental policy instruments, there are "public choice" arguments in favor of integrating trade and environmental rules and policies in national and international environmental law so as to help governments to overcome the "free-riding problems" in the supply of international public goods, including protection of the international environment.[8]

Is there also a need for dealing with purely national instruments of environmental policy, such as environmental taxes, in the context of international agreements and organizations? Should the WTO review its rules on environmental taxes and border tax adjustments? Environmental economists and policymakers emphasize the potential economic and environmental gains to be reaped in certain areas of environmental policy by switching from direct "command-and-control regulation" to price-based, indirect policy instruments, such as taxes on emission of pollutants and on "dirty" types of production, distribution, or consumption of goods and services so as to ensure that market prices reflect the full cost to society of production and consumption, including the environmental costs.[9] OECD

[8] See on these problems the various contributions in Robert V. Bartlett, Priya A. Kurian, and Madhu Malik eds., *International Organizations and Environmental Policy* (Westport, Conn.: Greenwood Press, 1995).

[9] See *Managing the Environment: The Role of Economic Instruments* (OECD, 1994); *Evaluating the Economic Instruments of Environmental Policies* (OECD, 1997).

countries have introduced an increasing number of specific environmental *emission taxes* (e.g. on air, water, and soil pollution), *product taxes* (e.g. on petrol, other motor fuels, gas and other energy products, vehicles, batteries, plastic carrier bags, disposable containers, tires, disposable razors, disposable cameras), *input taxes* (e.g. on agricultural inputs such as fertilizers and pesticides), other *production taxes* (e.g. on CFCs and halons), *tax benefits* (e.g. for environmental investments, unleaded petrol) and *environmental charges* for public services delivered (e.g. water and sewage charges, waste disposal charges, noise charges, transport charges).[10] The OECD has also drawn attention to the economic and environmental advantages of reinforcing the complementarity of fiscal and environmental policies through a comprehensive restructuring of tax systems so as to achieve environmental objectives more efficiently, yet without increasing the overall tax burden.[11] Only a few countries (such as Denmark, Finland, the Netherlands, Norway, and Sweden) have, however, so far engaged in comprehensive "ecological tax reforms" away from income taxes towards taxation of production and consumption with negative effects on the environment.[12]

## ADVANTAGES AND ALTERNATIVE FORMS OF ENVIRONMENTAL TAXES

Environmental taxes serve to change relative prices so as to "internalize" environmental costs and reduce pollution and wasteful consumption of resources by inducing producers and consumers to take account of the effects of their activities on the environment. Compared with "command-and-control measures", environmental taxes offer important advantages such as:

1 *Greater flexibility* to polluters who remain free to adapt to market signals in a cost-effective manner (e.g. reducing emissions by means of reduced output, installation of better pollution abatement technology, better production efficiency, or lesser use of polluting substances in the production process).
2 *Permanent incentives* to reduce pollution below permitted levels, and to innovate in "cleaner" production methods and pollution reduction technologies, so as to reduce eco-tax payments.

[10] For an overview of environmentally related taxes and charges in OECD countries see *Implementation Strategies for Environmental Taxes* (OECD, 1996), 15–17.

[11] See *Taxation and the Environment: Complementary Policies* (OECD, 1993).

[12] See *Ecotaxes and Green Fiscal Reform* (OECD, 1997).

3 *Lesser overall social costs* of pollution abatement by means of tax instruments and price adjustments, provided environmental taxes are fixed at an appropriate level.
4 Generation of *government revenue* that would not arise with alternative regulations.
5 *More transparency* of tax instruments, which may also be less vulnerable to "regulatory capture" than alternative regulatory policies.

Just as, according to the economic theory of optimal intervention, government interventions should correct market failures (such as pollution externalities) directly at their source, pollution taxes should be linked as closely as possible to the source and amount of pollution. Ideally, polluting emissions arising during the production or consumption process should therefore be taxed directly at the source. Such direct taxation of polluting emissions through *emission taxes* may, however, not be feasible for practical reasons (e.g. in case of numerous small and varied pollution sources that are difficult or too costly to control). Environmental taxes may then be levied on the final product the production or consumption of which gives rise to pollution. Such *product taxes* can offer a convenient proxy for emission taxes; they may be an optimal policy instrument if pollution is generated in the process of consumption rather than production of goods and services. As an alternative to taxes on final products, governments may also resort to *taxes on inputs*, whose use is associated with pollution. Determining the optimal level of pollution taxes (e.g. at the producer, supplier, or consumer level) requires information about the pollution associated with the production or use of a product, and about where the marginal cost of reducing pollution equals marginal social damage. Such information will often not be available. Second-best approaches, such as the taxation of commodities (e.g. fossil fuels) rather than of emissions themselves (e.g. carbon emissions causing global warming), may also be preferred in view of the high cost of measuring pollutants and of enforcing emission taxes.

## INTERNATIONAL IMPLICATIONS OF ENVIRONMENTAL TAXES: BORDER TAX ADJUSTMENTS AND OTHER COMPENSATORY MEASURES

Emission charges, input taxes, and environmental product taxes, may raise the private cost of the polluting firm. In the case of international rather than national or local pollution, it may be politically difficult to impose the environmental taxes on all polluters and emissions at home and abroad. National eco-taxes may then deteriorate the international competitiveness of domestic producers and affect the prices of their traded goods and services. For instance, domestic taxation of CFCs so as to reduce greenhouse gases would most likely increase the production costs and prices of domestic refrigerators and prompt domestic consumers to switch to cheaper imports from countries that do not tax CFCs. If CFCs are released into the air also when refrigerators are being disposed of, such imports would again undermine the environmental objective of reducing emissions of harmful CFCs at home and abroad. There is so far little empirical evidence, however, that differences in environmental standards have had a significant adverse effect on competitiveness.[13] The issues of competitiveness, trade, and the need for supplementing eco-taxes by regulatory or compensatory measures, were nonetheless often at the center of the debate on the introduction of environmental taxes. Governments have dealt with these concerns in various ways, such as:

1 *Tax concessions and exemptions for exposed industries.* The Danish government, for instance, offered until recently a 100 percent refund of energy taxes to all VAT-registered business firms in Denmark so that energy taxes were ultimately paid only by the household sector.[14]
2 *Environmental subsidies.* In order to avoid a deterioration of international competitiveness, and the disincentives for investment in pollution abatement if polluting industries are exempted from environmental taxes, the revenue from pollution taxes may be used for subsidies in new abatement technologies and cleaner production methods. Such tax/subsidy schemes may enable some reduction of the accepted level of pollution, as well as of the private pollution abatement costs, without impairing the international competitiveness of domestic producers. The EC Guidelines for Environmental Subsidies explicitly deal with such subsidy schemes.[15]

[13] See *Implementation Strategies for Environmental Taxes* (OECD, 1996), at 41, with further references.

[14] On the example of the tax exemptions and automatic refund mechanisms in the Danish carbon tax on mineral oils, coal, gas, and electricity, which is designed according to principles similar to those underlying the EC Commission's 1992 proposal for a common tax on carbon dioxide in the EC, see P. B. Soerensen, "Pollution Taxes and International Competitiveness: Some Selected Policy Issues," in *Environmental Policies and Industrial Competitiveness* (OECD, 1993), 63–68.

[15] The text of the Community Guidelines on State Aid for Environmental Protection is reproduced in Annex VI to Petersmann, *International and European Trade.*

3 *Border tax adjustments (BTAs).* A BTA consists of the imposition of a tax on imported products equivalent to a tax borne by like domestic products, and the exemption from (or remission of) taxes on products if they are exported. Compared with general exemptions from eco-taxes, which run the risk of reducing the environmental effectiveness of eco-taxes, BTAs can increase the effectiveness of environmental taxes aimed at reducing emissions arising out of consumption. The underlying *destination principle* of indirect taxation does not, however, offer effective protection of the domestic environment if pollution is generated in the process of production and a major part of domestic production is exported. Taxation of domestic *production* according to the *origin principle* may, however, be politically acceptable only in the framework of multilateral BTA rules so as to avoid raising the costs of domestic producers relative to the costs of foreign producers.
4 *Production and import restrictions.* Protection of global public goods (such as the ozone layer) and correction of cross-border pollution (such as emissions of ozone-depleting substances) require multilateral cooperation and safeguards against non-cooperating countries ("free-riding"). In the case of the Montreal Protocol on the protection of the ozone layer, for instance, cooperating countries agreed to ban trade between parties and non-parties in controlled substances (such as CFCs); to ban imports from non-parties of products containing controlled substances (such as refrigerators); and to examine whether imports from non-parties of products produced with, but not containing, controlled substances should be restricted. Even though the parties decided to make no use of the latter provision, the trade restrictions under the Montreal Protocol do more than prevent competitive distortions (e.g. substitution of imports for domestic production) so as to induce third countries to cooperate in the protection of the environment.

## BORDER TAX ADJUSTMENTS AND ENVIRONMENTAL POLICY

BTAs, i.e. the application to imports of domestic taxes on like products and the remission of domestic taxes on exports of like products, raise three main questions with respect to environmental policy:

1 *To what extent can BTAs further the environmental objectives and effectiveness of eco-taxes?* For instance, the extension of domestic consumption taxes to imports can help to make eco-taxes on polluting consumption

more effective. The remission of eco-taxes on exports can, however, also reduce the effectiveness of eco-taxes, particularly if pollution arises from production processes and methods (PPMs) and domestic producers sell their products in the world market.

2 *To what extent are BTAs permitted by, and consistent with, the multilateral trade rules in GATT/WTO law?* GATT/WTO rules allow BTAs on products, including their physically incorporated inputs. They do not limit a country from using eco-taxes to address environmental problems occurring within its own jurisdiction. It remains to be clarified, however, whether and to what extent GATT/WTO rules allow BTAs for domestic emission and production taxes based on PPMs. If such BTAs are not allowed, countries may shift environmental taxes onto products even if emission taxes and production taxes are environmentally more efficient.

3 *To what extent are BTAs compensating for domestic emission and production taxes practically feasible?* For instance, how can the PPMs of imported products and the share of production taxes they bear be ascertained? The 1987 GATT panel report on US Petroleum and Chemical Taxes accepted that BTAs could be based on the "predominant production method" for chemicals manufactured using feedstocks in the exporting country.[16] Yet, many environmental emissions (such as carbon dioxide) are not characterized by a "predominant production method." Tax adjustments based on PPMs also risk being abused for protectionist purposes.

## GATT/WTO rules on border tax adjustment

### GATT 1947 RULES ON BORDER TAX ADJUSTMENT

The 1970 report of the GATT Working Party on BTAs used the following definition of BTAs applied in the OECD:

> border tax adjustments were regarded as any fiscal measures which put into effect, in whole or in part, the destination principle (i.e. which enable exported products to be relieved of some or all of the tax charged in the exporting country in respect of similar domestic products sold to consumers on the home market and which enable imported products to be sold to consumers to be charged with some or all of the tax charged in the importing country in respect of similar domestic products).[17]

[16] See GATT, BISD, 34th Suppl., 136–66.

[17] See BISD, 18th Supp., 97.

The *destination principle* is to be distinguished from the *origin principle*, whereby products destined for export are to pay the tax charged in the country of exportation and imported products are exempted from such taxes in the importing country as they would have paid at their point of origin. The Working Party examined the rules on BTAs in GATT Articles I–III, as regards imports, and Articles VI and XVI, as regards exports. While these rules codified practices existing at the time of the drafting of GATT 1947, the Working Party concluded that "the present rules served the purpose of trade neutrality of tax adjustment appropriately and that no motive could be found to change them." Environmental taxes were apparently not considered by the Working Party.

According to GATT Article II:2(a),

> nothing in this Article shall prevent any contracting party from imposing at any time on the importation of any product a charge equivalent to an internal tax imposed consistently with the provisions of paragraph 2 of Article III in respect of the like domestic product or in respect of an article from which the imported product has been manufactured or produced in whole or in part.

The interpretative note to GATT Article III confirms that

> any internal tax or other internal charge . . . of the kind referred to in paragraph 1 which applies to an imported product and to the like domestic product and is collected or enforced in the case of the imported product at the time or point of importation, is nevertheless to be regarded as an internal tax or other internal charge . . . of the kind referred to in paragraph 1, and is accordingly subject to the provisions of Article III.

The main legal disciplines on BTAs on imports arise therefore from the national treatment requirement in GATT Article III:2:

> The products of the territory of any contracting party imported into the territory of any other contracting party shall not be subject, directly or indirectly, to internal taxes or other internal charges of any kind in excess of those applied, directly or indirectly, to like domestic products. Moreover, no contracting party shall otherwise apply internal taxes or other internal charges to imported or domestic products in a manner contrary to the principles set forth in paragraph 1.

The interpretation and application of the BTA rules in GATT Article III raise various legal issues that remain to be clarified. The GATT Working Party on BTA reached broad agreement that taxes directly levied on products are eligible for BTA under GATT 1947; and that taxes or social security charges on employers and employees are not eligible for BTA. The eligibility for BTA of other taxes, such as "taxes occultes" on energy and machinery used in the production and transportation of taxable goods, has remained controversial.[18] The terms "like product" (Article III:2, first sentence) and "directly competitive or substitutable product" (Article III:2, second sentence and interpretative note to Article III:2) have been construed on a case-by-case basis taking into account, *inter alia*, the product's end-uses in a given market; consumers' tastes and habits, which change from country to country; the product's properties, nature, and quality; tariff classifications for products; and whether the tax distinction in question was "applied . . . so as to afford protection to domestic production" (Article III:1). The policy purpose of a tax has been considered not to be relevant for determining whether the tax was eligible for BTA. Since Article III:2 does not prescribe the use of any specific method or system of taxation, it has also been recognized that

> there could be objective reasons proper to the tax in question which could justify or necessitate differences in the system of taxation for imported and for domestic products . . . it could also be compatible with Article III:2 to allow two different methods of calculation of price for tax purposes. Since Article III:2 prohibited only discriminatory or protective tax burdens on imported products, what mattered was . . . whether the application of the different taxation methods actually had a discriminatory or protective effect against imported products.[19]

Legal issues in need of further clarification include:

1 *"Internal taxes" eligible for BTA.* For instance, what is the legal meaning of the terms "taxes on products" and "directly or indirectly" in Article III:2? Does the notion of a tax applied "indirectly" to a product include a tax on any input (including PPMs) to a final product, so that BTAs for such "input taxes" would be allowed under Article III?[20] How can non-discriminatory "internal taxes" (Article III:2), which are eligible for BTA,

[18] For a survey of the relevant GATT practice see Border Tax Adjustment. Note by the Secretariat (GATT, 1994).

[19] See the 1987 panel report on Japan – Customs Duties, Taxes and Labeling Practices on Imported Wines and Alcoholic Beverages, BISD, 34th Supp., 83, paras. 5.8–5.9. See also the 1996 WTO panel report on Japan – Taxes on Alcoholic Beverages, WT/DS8/R of 11 July 1996, para. 6.24.

[20] See, e.g., P. Demaret and R. Stewardson, "Border Tax Adjustments under GATT and EC Law and General Implications for Environmental Taxes," 28(4) *J. World Trade*, 7, at 18 (1994).

be distinguished from discriminatory "other duties or charges" (Article II), which cannot be adjusted at the border?

2 *The "like products" definition.* For instance, to what extent is it consistent with GATT Article III:2 to differentiate among seemingly "like products" according to the environmental impact of the products concerned (e.g. their waste disposal) and of their PPMs? Is it correct, as stated in the 1992 panel report on US – Measures Affecting Alcoholic Beverages, "that the like product determination under Article III:2 also should have regard to the purpose of the Article," and that it follows from Article III:1 that "the purpose of Article III is not to prevent contracting parties from using their fiscal and regulatory powers for purposes other than to afford protection to domestic production"?[21] Or should one follow from the wording of Article III:2 and from its systematic relationship to GATT Article XX that, as claimed by the 1996 WTO panel report on Japan – Taxes on Alcoholic Beverages,[22] the words "so as to afford protection" contained in Article III:1 do not justify interpreting the term "like products" in a functional manner depending on whether the regulatory product distinctions had the aim or effect of affording protection to domestic production?

3 *The "directly competitive or substitutable product" definition.* For instance, can one follow from the text of the interpretative note to GATT Article III:2 (notably from the words "where competition exists") that, as claimed by the 1996 WTO panel report on Japan – Taxes on Alcoholic Beverages,[23] "the appropriate test to define whether two products are

[21] BISD, 39th Supp., 206–99, at 276. The application of the "aims and effects test" in this dispute was based on the fact that the complainant Canada had not contested the argument of the defendant that the US product differentiation between "low alcohol beer" and "high alcohol beer" had been introduced for health policy reasons and differentiated among products depending on their alcohol content, i.e. regardless of their origin, without protectionist aims or effects "as a means of favouring domestic producers over foreign producers" (cf. para. 5.74: "there was no evidence submitted to the Panel that the choice of the particular level [of alcohol content] has the purpose or effect of affording protection to domestic production"). In the view of this panel, "it is imperative that the like product determination in the context of Article III be made in such a way that it not unnecessarily infringes upon the regulatory authority and domestic policy options of contracting parties" (para. 5.72).

[22] WT/DS8/R of 11 July 1996, para. 6.17: "In sum, the Panel concluded that for reasons relating to the wording of Article III as well as its context, the aim-and-effect test proposed by Japan and the United States should be rejected."

[23] *Ibid.*, para. 6.22.

'like' or 'directly competitive or substitutable' is the marketplace"? Are "supply-side criteria" (such as product characteristics) as important as "demand-side criteria" (such as consumer preferences) for the determination of the competitive relationship between the products concerned?

4 *The definition of taxation "in excess of" that imposed on like domestic products (Article III:2, first sentence), as well as of "dissimilar taxation" of "directly competitive or substitutable products" so as to afford protection to domestic production* (Article III:2, second sentence). For instance, is it justified to apply, as done in the 1996 WTO panel report on Japan – Taxes on Alcoholic Beverages,[24] a "de minimis test" to the prohibition of "dissimilar taxation" without applying the same test to the prohibition of discriminatory taxation in the first sentence of Article III:2? How can we examine whether the dissimilar taxation is applied "so as to afford protection"?

5 *The optional character of GATT rules on BTA.* For instance, is it consistent with the principles of environmental policy (such as the "polluter pays principle") that the GATT rules on BTA leave it to each contracting party to decide whether it wants to adjust internal taxes at the border (destination principle), whether instead it prefers to exempt imports from domestic taxes according to the origin principle, or whether it wants to practice double taxation of traded goods?

6 *Symmetry between import and export rules.* For instance, why were the GATT provisions on BTAs for exports in GATT Article VI:4 ("taxes borne by the like product"), as well as in the 1979 GATT Subsidy Agreement (cf. Annex (g): "remission in respect of the production and distribution of exported goods of indirect taxes"), formulated differently from the GATT rules on BTAs for imports (cf. Articles II:2 and III:2)? Does the text of GATT Article II:2(a)[25] imply that the border adjustment of input taxes must be limited to taxes on inputs physically incorporated into the imported final product? Is it nonetheless correct to state that, as claimed by the GATT Working Party on BTA, "GATT provisions on tax adjustment applied the principle of destination identically to imports and exports"?[26]

[24] *Ibid.*, para. 6.33.

[25] "Nothing in this Article shall prevent any contracting party from imposing at any time on the importation of any product . . . a charge equivalent to an internal tax imposed consistently with the provisions of paragraph 2 of Article III in respect of the like domestic product or in respect of an article from which the imported product has been manufactured or produced in whole or in part."

[26] Cf. BISD, 18th Supp., 97, 100.

## WTO RULES ON BORDER TAX ADJUSTMENT

According to Annex 1A of the 1994 WTO Agreement, the "GATT 1994" consists of the provisions of the "GATT 1947" subject to the various additional WTO provisions on trade in goods. The "general interpretative note to Annex 1A" states that "in the event of conflict between a provision of the General Agreement on Tariffs and Trade 1994 and a provision of another agreement in Annex 1A to the Agreement Establishing the World Trade Organization . . ., the provision of the other agreement shall prevail to the extent of the conflict." Notwithstanding the identical text of the BTA rules in GATT 1947 and in GATT 1994, the substance of the WTO provisions on BTAs seems to have changed as a result of the additional agreements in Annex 1A of the WTO Agreement, notably the 1994 Subsidy Agreement and the Agreement on Technical Barriers to Trade. While, under the GATT 1947, it was widely held that environmental taxes on PPMs and on "non-incorporated inputs" were not adjustable, the 1994 WTO rules appear to have brought about more flexibility for distinctions between seemingly "like products" based on their impact on the environment, as well as for BTAs for taxes imposed on elements of the production process.[27]

### *The WTO Agreement on Subsidies and Countervailing Duties*

The 1979 GATT Subsidy Agreement included provisions on remission of "indirect taxes . . . on goods that are physically incorporated in the exported product" (Annex (i)). The 1994 WTO Agreement on Subsidies and Countervailing Duties replaced the term "goods that are physically incorporated" in Annex (h) and (i) of the 1979 Subsidy Agreement with the phrases "goods or services used in the production of" and "inputs that are consumed in the production of" in paragraphs (h) and (i) respectively of its Illustrative List of Export Subsidies. The "Guidelines on Consumption of Inputs in the Production Process" in Annex II of the WTO Agreement on Subsidies elaborate on the meaning of paragraphs (h) and (i). A footnote in

[27] See Taxes for Environmental Purposes: The Scope for Border Tax Adjustment under WTO Rules (WWF, 1995); E. U. Petersmann, "Environmental Taxes and Border Tax Adjustment," in Jong-Soo Lim ed., *Trade and Environment. International Issues and Policy Options* (1996), 149–64; Taxes and Charges for Environmental Purposes – Border Tax Adjustment, Note by the WTO Secretariat, WTO document WT/CTE/W/47 of 2 May 1997.

these Guidelines clarifies: "Inputs consumed in the production process are inputs physically incorporated, energy, fuels and oil used in the production process and catalysts which are consumed in the course of their use to obtain the exported product."[28] As the 1994 Subsidy Agreement allows for exemption, remission, or deferral of prior stage cumulative indirect taxes not in excess of the amount of such taxes actually levied on inputs that are consumed in the production of the exported product, the text of this footnote seems to allow also for exemption, remission, or deferral of taxes levied on the energy, fuel, and oil inputs "consumed in the production of" an exported product, even if such energy inputs and catalysts are not physically incorporated in the final product.[29]

Thus, an environmental tax on the energy used in the production process could be eligible for BTA on both the product and the process even if the energy is not physically present in the exported product.[30] Moreover, notwithstanding the limitation of these rules to export subsidies and BTAs for exports, the need for symmetry of BTA rules for imports and exports may lead to the view that, for functional and systematic reasons, the broader interpretation of BTA rules for tax rebates on exports must also be applicable to equalizing taxes on imports. The actual scope of these new provisions in the Subsidy Agreement, and their impact on the traditional physical incorporation test, remains to be clarified in WTO practice and have not yet been tested in WTO dispute settlement proceedings.

### *The WTO Committee on Trade and Environment*

Item 3(a) of the work program of the WTO Committee on Trade and Environment includes the "relationship between the provisions of the

[28] Cf. Negotiating History of Footnote 61 of the Agreement on Subsidies and Countervailing Measures. Note by the Secretariat, WTO document WT/CTE/W/16 of 1 December 1995.

[29] In an informal letter, the US has taken the position that this footnote does not expand the right of countries to apply BTAs for a broad range of taxes on energy. This unilateral interpretation was, however, not recorded in the WTO Subsidy Agreement or in its preparatory documents and negotiations. See WT/CTE/W/47, paras. 75 and 76.

[30] In the 1987 GATT panel report on US Taxes on Petroleum and Certain Imported Substances, BISD, 34th Supp., 136–66, the panel decided that taxes on feedstock chemicals were eligible for BTA on the import of the like final product because the feedstocks had been "used as materials in the manufacture or production" of the final product. The panel report did not specify whether these chemical inputs were considered to be "physically incorporated" and still present in recognizable form in the imported final product.

multilateral trading system and charges and taxes for environmental purposes."[31] By 1997, no proposals had been submitted on this issue but some countries had stated that, given the importance of BTAs for international trade and environmental policies and the political opposition from domestic industries to proposals for carbon dioxide taxes (e.g. in Germany, the EC, and Switzerland), international coordination would reduce the risk of competitive distortions in some sectors. Reference was also made to the rules for standardization of technical regulations in the Technical Barriers to Trade Agreement as a possible model for environmental taxation standards and environmental border tax adjustments.

### *The WTO Agreement on Technical Barriers to Trade*

The 1994 WTO Agreement on Technical Barriers to Trade (TBT) defines "technical regulation" as: "Document which lays down product characteristics or their related processes and production methods, including the applicable administrative provisions, with which compliance is mandatory. It may also include or deal exclusively with terminology, symbols, packaging, marking or labelling requirements as they apply to a product, process or production method." According to the "general interpretative note to Annex 1A" of the WTO Agreement, the provisions of this TBT Agreement shall prevail to the extent of any conflict with GATT 1994. Does it follow from this that technical regulations consistent with the TBT Agreement must also be deemed to be GATT-consistent even if they differentiate between seemingly "like products" based on their respective PPMs? Does this also hold for environmental tax differentiations based on such "technical regulations"?

### *WTO law and international environmental law*

WTO law and WTO practice include an increasing number of references to international principles of environmental law and policy.[32] Article 3 of the

[31] On the work of this WTO Committee on Trade and Environment see: Report 1996 of the Committee on Trade and Environment (WTO, 1996); E. U. Petersmann, "Trade and the Protection of the Environment after the Uruguay Round: An Agenda for Future WTO Negotiations," in R. Wolfrum ed., *Enforcing Environmental Standards: Economic Mechanisms as Viable Means?* (Berlin and New York: Springer, c1996), 165–97.

[32] For a collection of these environment-related WTO provisions see Petersmann, *International and European Trade*, Annexes II and III.

WTO's Dispute Settlement Understanding explicitly requires interpretation and clarification of the provisions of WTO law "in accordance with customary rules of interpretation of public international law." If principles of environmental law and policy (such as the "polluter pays" and "rectification at source" principles) have been recognized by WTO member countries and have been used by them as a justification for taxing environmental pollution at the source (e.g. at the level of PPMs rather than on the resulting product), should WTO law be construed in conformity with such agreed principles of environmental law and policy? Should Multilateral Environmental Agreements, such as the World Climate Convention and any future decisions in the framework of this agreement on the introduction of carbon dioxide and energy taxes, be taken into account in the interpretation of the WTO rules on BTA? Should product differentiations based on internationally agreed PPMs (such as the prohibition of using CFCs) be presumed to be GATT-consistent? How can we deal with the problem, emphasized in the GATT Committee on Trade and Environment, that unilateral taxation of pollution and PPMs abroad by means of BTAs on imported products could lead to protectionist abuses and to "unacceptable interference in countries' sovereign rights to evaluate and internalize as appropriate their domestic environmental costs"?[33] Are the WTO rules on BTA consistent with environmental economics and policy? Do they require further adjustments?

## Environmental taxes and border tax adjustments in EC law: comparative aspects and conclusions

### ENVIRONMENTAL TAXES AND BORDER TAX ADJUSTMENT RULES IN THE EC

The EC Treaty objective of an "internal market without internal frontiers" (Article 14) requires the abolition not only of trade restrictions but also of tax adjustments at the borders. Article 93 of the EC Treaty therefore requires the Council to "adopt provisions for the harmonization of legislation concerning turnover taxes, excise duties and other forms of indirect taxation to the extent that such harmonization is necessary to ensure the establishment and the functioning of the internal market within the time-

[33] See Trade and the Environment, GATT document TE 010 of 11 October 1994, at 4 (statement by Brazil).

limit laid down in Article 14." As Article 93 does not apply to direct taxes and production or emission charges, EC Member States retain the right to maintain or introduce environmental taxes. EC harmonization of indirect taxes, as a necessary complement to the abolition of border controls and border tax adjustments, has led to uniform systems of value-added taxes, excise duties (notably on alcohol and alcoholic beverages, tobacco, and cigarettes as well as mineral oils), taxes on heavy goods vehicles, and tolls and charges for the use of motorways. The EC directives only introduce minimum levels of taxation and harmonized structures of taxation, and leave EC Member States with wide discretion to maintain their existing environmental taxes (e.g. on emissions such as sewage, waste, air pollution, or energy) or introduce new environmental taxes, provided they do not give rise to border-crossing formalities (such as BTA).[34]

The fifth "European Community programme of policy and action in relation to the environment and sustainable development" of 1993 recommends the increasing use of economic instruments (such as environmental charges, levies, state aids, environmental auditing, and liability) and fiscal incentives so as "to internalize all external environmental costs incurred during the whole life-cycle of products from source through production, distribution, use and final disposal, so that environmentally-friendly products will not be at a competitive disadvantage in the market place vis-à-vis products which cause pollution and waste."[35] The EC Council likewise agreed in 1993 "that fiscal instruments will play an important role in developing the Community's overall strategy to limit carbon dioxide emissions and to improve energy efficiency."[36] In the 1990s, some EC countries (notably Denmark and Sweden) and EFTA countries (such as Norway) initiated comprehensive environmental tax reforms and proposals for new energy taxes. The 1992 and 1995 proposals by the EC Commission for a common EC framework for carbon-energy taxes included provisions on BTA and exemptions for energy-intensive industries.[37] These EC proposals

[34] For an overview see A. Ziegler, *Trade and Environmental Law in the EC* (Oxford and New York: Clarendon Press, Oxford University Press, 1996), 190–96.

[35] *Towards Sustainability* (EC Commission, 1993), at 105.

[36] See Guy Corcelle and Stanley Johnson, *The Environmental Policy of the European Communities* (2nd edn., Boston: Kluwer Law International, 1995), at 176–77.

[37] The 1995 proposal is reprinted in Europe Environment, document supplement No. 455 of 23 May 1995. The proposal explicitly provides for tax adjustments so as to equalize anti-competitive effects of the tax. The 1992 proposal included a conditionality clause making the introduction of the tax dependent on similar taxes in other OECD states.

have, however, been opposed by EC Member States on the ground that, without similar commitments by other major trading countries (such as Japan and the USA), the proposed energy taxes could undermine the international competitiveness of EC industries. A recent EC analysis foresees, however, no significant negative competitiveness effects within the EC from the introduction of common energy taxes in EC Member States, *inter alia* due to the use of financial mechanisms to ease negative trade impacts.[38]

The regional EC experience in the field of trade, tax, and environmental laws and policies may be useful for the future clarification and development of the legal and political interrelationships between trade, tax, and environmental measures in the global WTO context. For instance:

1 *The distinction between direct and indirect taxes.* While the GATT/WTO rules on BTA govern the *external* relations of the EC, Articles 90–93 of the EC Treaty set out specific BTA rules for *intra*-EC trade among EC Member States. Under both GATT and EC rules, taxes on products (indirect taxes such as sales taxes) are eligible for BTA pursuant to the destination principle, and taxes on producers (direct taxes such as income taxes) are, in principle, not eligible for BTA pursuant to the origin principle. As in WTO law, this distinction between direct and indirect taxes has, however, not been strictly maintained in EC practice regarding the prohibition of tax discrimination (Article 90) and BTAs (Articles 91–93). In certain cases, BTAs have been made also for taxes on producers, PPMs, inputs, and transport services if such taxes were "sufficiently closely related to the product." But, as noted by some commentators, "this category is perhaps too undefined and subjective to be practicable in the GATT context, as it requires the presence of a strong decisional body."[39] As regards the distinction between environmental product taxes and environmental process taxes, the EC case law seems to be more flexible than GATT law in respect of eco-taxes on PPMs in view of the fact that an eco-tax on environmentally harmful PPMs could often also be imposed directly on the final product.
2 *Harmonization of indirect taxes and movement towards the origin principle for* intra-*EC trade.* EC law differs from GATT/WTO law, *inter alia*, in the EC Treaty provisions on harmonization of indirect taxes (Article 93)

[38] See *A Preliminary Assessment of Sectoral Implications of Regional $CO_2$ Energy Taxes within the EU* (EC, 1995).

[39] See Demaret and Stewardson, "Border Tax Adjustments under GATT and EC Law," at 42 ff.

and the ambitious EC Treaty objective of "an internal market characterized by the abolition, as between Member States, of obstacles to the free movement of goods, persons, services and capital" (Article 3, c). Following the abolition of all internal customs frontiers and physical border controls for *intra*-EC trade as of 1993, the EC continues to work towards the abolition of BTAs within the EC in the context of a new system whereby goods will be taxed in the country of origin at the tax rate of the country of origin. These Treaty objectives seem to have already influenced the EC Court's jurisprudence on BTAs.[40] The harmonization of indirect taxes and movement towards the origin principle for *intra*-EC trade may offer interesting experiences also for the WTO if, for instance in the implementation of the 1992 World Climate Convention, WTO Members should agree on an international harmonization of, for example, energy taxes and on adjustments to BTA rules for such taxes.

3 *Definition of indirect taxes eligible for BTA.* As in the GATT/WTO context, there is a vast EC case law on how to distinguish internal indirect taxes from customs duties, as well as on which taxes on inputs and PPMs are eligible for BTA and consistent with the prohibitions of tax discrimination and subsidies. A comparative analysis of the GATT/WTO and EC case law reveals numerous parallels (e.g. regarding the symmetrical application of BTA rules so as to avoid double taxation) as well as differences (e.g. due to the harmonization of value-added taxes within the EC).[41]

4 *Tax differentiations between like or competing products.* The prohibition of tax discrimination in Article 90 of the EC Treaty is almost literally copied from the corresponding prohibition in GATT Article III:2. The EC case law on determining "similar" or otherwise competing products, as well as on tax discrimination or other "internal taxation of such a nature as to afford indirect protection to other products" (Article 90), again reveals numerous parallels (e.g. regarding potential competition between imported and domestic products, the relevance of protectionist motives for the legal evaluation of product and tax differentiations) as well as differences in comparison with the corresponding GATT/WTO case law relating to GATT Article III:2 (e.g. the more permissive EC case law on tax rebates and tax differentiations among similar or competing products on the basis of PPMs and raw materials provided such differentiations do

[40] *Ibid.*, at 57.

[41] *Ibid.*, at 43 ff.

not discriminate against imports).[42] For instance, different taxation of beer depending on the size of the brewery, whether domestic or foreign, was held permissible by the EC Court,[43] but not permissible by the GATT panel report on US – Measures Affecting Alcoholic Beverages.[44] And actual trade flows were considered as a relevant criterion in the examination of material discrimination and protective effects by the EC Court,[45] but not for example in the unadopted 1994 GATT panel report on US – Taxes on Automobiles.[46] EC law thus seems to permit product and tax differentiations, provided they are based on objective criteria and do not protect domestic production through categories that are mainly applied to imported products, which may be held to be inconsistent with the prohibition of tax discrimination in GATT/WTO law.[47]

5 *The "necessity principles" in WTO and EC law.* So far, neither the "necessity principle" in the WTO rules on trade in goods (notably in the TBT and SPS Agreements) nor the "necessity" and "proportionality principles" of EC law (e.g. in the context of Articles 28 and 30 of the EC Treaty) seem to have influenced the GATT/WTO and EC case law on tax discrimination and BTAs.

## IS THERE A NEED FOR ADJUSTING BORDER TAX ADJUSTMENT RULES TO ENVIRONMENTAL NEEDS?

In both GATT/WTO and the EC, the rules on BTA were designed so as to avoid competitive and protectionist distortions. The increasing impor-

[42] For a comparative survey see P. J. Kuyper, "Booze and Fast Cars: Tax Discrimination under GATT and the EC," in *Legal Issues of European Integration* (Kluwer, 1996), 129–44.

[43] *Bobie Getränkevertrieb*, Case 127/75 [1976], ECR 1079, 1088.

[44] See above, note 21.

[45] Cf. Demaret and Stewardson, "Border Tax Adjustments under GATT and EC Law," at 54–56.

[46] Cf. WTO document WT/DS31/R of 14 March 1997, e.g. paragraph 5.10: "The effect of a measure in terms of trade flows was not relevant for the purposes of Article III, since a change in the volume or proportion of imports could be due to many factors other than government measures"; paragraph 5.14: "In the view of the Panel therefore the regulatory distinction of $30,000 did not create conditions of competition that divided the products inherently into two classes, one of EC or other foreign origin and the other of domestic origin."

[47] For detailed analyses of the EC Court's case law on tax discrimination see also M. Danusso and R. Denton, "Does the EC Court of Justice Look for a Protectionist Motive under Article 95?" in *Legal Issues of European Integration* (Kluwer, 1990), 67–120; M. Hedemann-Robinson, "Indirect Discrimination: Article 95(1) EC Back to Front and Inside Out?" 1 European Public Law 439 (1995), 439–68.

tance of environmental emission taxes, production taxes, and product taxes, might require further clarifications of, and adjustments to, the existing GATT/WTO and EC rules on BTA, whose focus on product taxes might discourage more efficient direct taxation of environmentally harmful emissions and PPMs.[48] Such clarifications and adjustments might be easier in the EC context than in the WTO context in view of the ever-increasing body of EC environmental law (e.g. in Articles 174–76 of the EC Treaty) and the EC rule-making powers in the field of environmental law and policy (see Article 175). The 1992 and amended 1995 proposals for an EC directive instituting an energy tax confirm that political concerns over international competitiveness and BTA rules may be important impediments on the way towards making environmental policies more effective and consistent with trade policies. As in the WTO and the OECD, it has been emphasized also in the EC that, because the costs of compliance with environmental regulatory requirements represent only 1–2 percent of overall production costs in the EC, and there is no evidence of countries deliberately resorting to low environmental standards to gain competitive advantages or attract investments, "differences in environmental policies should not result in the introduction of compensating duties or export rebates, or measures having an equivalent effect (i.e. so-called eco-duties) as a means of compensating for the cost of imposing more rigorous environmental requirements on domestic industries than those supported by foreign competitors."[49] In contrast to discriminatory trade policy instruments, non-discriminatory border tax adjustments are legitimate instruments of economic and environmental policies and require a close attention in the WTO context so as to ensure the mutual consistency of WTO law and efficient environmental policies.

[48] For a discussion of these problems see, e.g., C. Pitschas, "GATT/WTO Rules for Border Tax Adjustment and the Proposed European Directive Introducing a Tax on Carbon Dioxide Emissions and Energy," *Ga. J. Int. & Comp. Law*, 479–500 (1995); M. Düerkop, "Trade and Environment: International Trade Law Aspects of the Proposed EC Directive Introducing a Tax on Carbon Dioxide Emissions and Energy," in 31 *Common Market L. Rev.*, 807–44 (1994).

[49] *Communication on Trade and Environment from the Commission to the Council and the European Parliament* (EC Commission, 1996), at 6.

# 6

## "ENVIRONMENTAL PROTECTION AND THE GLOBAL TRADE ORDER": A DIFFERENT PERSPECTIVE

SCOTT BARRETT

### Introduction

THIS CHAPTER addresses the first three of the four issues analyzed by Professor Roessler: exempting domestic environmental policies from WTO obligations, permitting WTO Members to offset differences in environmental regulations, and reforming the WTO to allow the use of sanctions to coerce WTO Members into raising their environmental standards. On the fourth issue discussed by Professor Roessler – that the WTO should open its decisionmaking to scrutiny by environmental organizations – I have nothing to add to what he and others have already said.[1]

### Exempting domestic environmental policies from WTO obligations

Should domestic environmental policy be generally exempt from having to comply with the multilateral trading rules? The argument in favor of this proposal seems to be that the exemption would increase the demand for environmental policies by politicians, and that this would be good for the environment, even if it were not good for trade. In fact, the exemption would potentially be disastrous for trade, as it amounts to a giant loophole

[1] See D. C. Esty, *Greening the GATT* (Washington, D.C.: Institute for International Economics, 1994) for arguments in favor of opening the WTO decisionmaking process to environmental interests and J. Bhagwati and T. N. Srinivasan, "Trade and the Environment: Does Environmental Diversity Detract from the Case for Free Trade?," in J. Bhagwati and R. E. Hudec eds., *Fair Trade and Harmonization* (Cambridge, Mass.: MIT Press, 1996), vol. I, for arguments against.

in the trading regime. And there can be no presumption that the environment would be any better protected, either. The point is that, under this regime, environmental policy would serve the cause of protectionism. Environmental policy would be devised not only or perhaps even mainly to protect the environment but to protect domestic industry (at the expense, perhaps, of foreign industry). There can be no presumption that policies which protect markets would necessarily protect the environment.

Up to here, Professor Roessler and I are in agreement. Where we disagree is in regard to the example he cites of the Montreal Protocol phase-out mechanism for ozone-depleting substances like CFCs.

This seems an odd example of an inappropriate "domestic environmental policy." The restrictions on production and consumption (defined by the Montreal Protocol as production plus imports minus exports) were not taken unilaterally. The last time I counted there were 168 parties to this agreement. Moreover, and in contrast to the suggestion made by Professor Roessler, according to the chief US negotiator at the Montreal Protocol talks, Richard Benedick, the restrictions on production and "consumption" (as defined above) were *not* intended to win the support of domestic producers, except perhaps as regards the negotiating position of the European Community.[2] During the negotiations, the United States, Canada, Australia, Denmark, Finland, New Zealand, Norway, Sweden, and the Soviet Union argued for reductions in consumption only. The European Community (absent the support of Denmark) argued for reductions in production only. The combined restrictions on production and "consumption" were simply a negotiated compromise.[3]

Much more importantly, whether the reductions in production and consumption would generate rents for producers and importers – another claim in the essay – depends on national implementation of the Montreal Protocol obligations, and national implementation has varied widely. To take a particularly appropriate example, the United States implemented its obligations by allocating production and consumption entitlements to

[2] R. E. Benedick, *Ozone Diplomacy* (Cambridge, Mass.: Harvard, 1991).

[3] The decision to regulate production and consumption (as defined above) was not arbitrary. The great administrative advantage in these restrictions is that the number of producers and importers is small (in the US, only seven producers and sixteen importers were subject to the Montreal Protocol's original restrictions). It would have been much more difficult to regulate "thousands of consuming industries and countless points of consumption" (Benedick, *Ozone Diplomacy*, 79).

domestic producers and importers (and has allowed these to be traded). Of course, in doing so producers and importers could be expected to receive huge rents. But the United States recognized this, and taxed the windfall that would otherwise have been reaped by these firms. There was nothing in the Montreal Protocol which prevented national governments from denying producers and importers the rents associated with the increasing scarcity of ozone-depleting substances.

It is as well to note that the phase-out mechanism in the Montreal Protocol does *not* violate the national treatment principle, contrary to the impression Professor Roessler might give. What do violate this principle are the associated restrictions on trade as regards countries which are parties to the WTO but not the Montreal Protocol (Professor Roessler does not distinguish between parties and non-parties to the Montreal Protocol, but the distinction is vital). These restrictions were not needed to gain the support of the producers of ozone-depleting chemicals (though producers based in countries which were parties to the agreement would certainly have welcomed the restrictions); weaker restrictions (such as border tax adjustments: see below) would probably have sufficed for this purpose. I shall argue that the restrictions were needed for a different purpose: to deter free-riding. In contrast to what Professor Roessler asserts, I shall argue that the trade restrictions in the Montreal Protocol *were* needed to protect the ozone layer.

## Permitting WTO Members to offset differences in environmental regulations

Should countries be able to impose restrictions relating to how a product was made as opposed to what the product is? According to the WTO rules, on the whole the answer is "no," and as Professor Roessler notes, it is mainly for this reason that a GATT panel ruled in favor of Mexico in its famous complaint against the United States' ban on tuna imports. This was a controversial decision, but the tone of Professor Roessler's essay suggests that he believes the WTO rules do not need to be changed in the light of it. There are, of course, certain features of this particular case that do pose problems, not least the fact that the US action was unilateral.[4] But I shall argue that the

[4] Bhagwati and Srinivasan, ("Trade and the Environment") also draw attention to the fact that the cruel, incidental killing of dolphins affects utility relationships and not production relationships. As a point of principle, this should not matter: either way, welfare is affected. What does matter, and what Bhagwati and Srinivasan object to, is the imposition

principle that trade measures must not be based on how a product was made is not always appropriate.[5]

What matters in this context is not so much whether one country has lower standards than another. There is no reason why all countries should have the same standards.[6] The relevant issue is whether the standards are "fair." It is the claim that a country with lower standards has an "unfair" advantage in trade that has sparked demands for countervailing measures.

If a country suspects that one of its trading partners does have "unfairly" low environmental standards, it can respond in several ways: (1) it can lower its own standards to redress the imbalance (the response implicit in the notion of a "race to the bottom" to which Professor Roessler refers); (2) it can seek to intimidate its trading partner into raising its standards; (3) it can impose countervailing duties on imports which offset the "unfair cost advantage" associated with the weaker standards; or (4) it can subsidize domestic industries to compensate for the costs of meeting strong domestic standards. The first two responses are welfare-reducing. The third and fourth need not be. But countervailing duties based on how a product was made are WTO-incompatible.

of one society's values on another. Had the Tuna–Dolphin dispute been resolved by multilateral negotiation, however, it is likely that the resulting agreement would have involved not just a ban on the use of purse seines but a side payment to compensate Mexico for economic damages.

[5] Although Professor Roessler's concern and that of the literature has been with restrictions relating to processes, a case for reform can possibly be made even as regards the rules relating to products. As an example, the Danish law banning the sale of beer and soft drinks in cans, ostensibly for environmental reasons, would seem to be WTO-compatible, for neither Danish nor imported products can be sold in cans. But trade was harmed nonetheless (it was much less costly for local firms to comply with the restrictions than foreign firms), and it is not clear that the can ban was needed for environmental reasons. While it would seem sensible to adopt the presumption that product restrictions should be allowed provided they are not superficially discriminatory (as the WTO now allows), a case could be made that parties to the WTO should be able to challenge the need for product restrictions where trade is significantly damaged (perhaps with the burden of proof resting on the party or parties making the complaint).

Under European Union law, the Danish regulation can be challenged, and it was in fact challenged by the European Commission. The conflict between the desire to protect the environment and the desire not to distort trade was resolved in this case by the European Court. The Court ruled that the can ban was not "disproportionate." However, the Court did not articulate precisely how a "proportionate" or "disproportionate" environmental policy could be identified. In this respect the decision was, to my mind, unsatisfactory.

[6] See Bhagwati and Srinivasan, "Trade and the Environment."

Suppose that the environmental problem is local; there are no cross-border externalities. Then the only concern is with the effect of the differential standards on "competitiveness." For countervailing measures to be justified it must at the very least be shown that "competitiveness" really is harmed by the differences in standards This is an empirical question. A recent and thorough review of the empirical literature concludes that, "Overall, there is relatively little evidence to support the hypothesis that environmental regulations have had a large adverse effect on competitiveness, however that elusive term is defined."[7]

But even if a statistically significant and quantitatively important relationship between environmental standards and "competitiveness" did exist, there may still be no justification for countervailing measures. These could only be justified if low environmental standards were "unfair" – if the standards were set at a low level for the purpose of gaining a "competitive advantage." The question is: do countries have any incentive to weaken their environmental standards for reasons of "competitiveness"? I have shown that they do, but only under very special circumstances: competition must be imperfect; competition must be of a certain nature (firms must compete in quantities rather than in prices); there must not be too many domestic firms; and other instruments (such as production subsidies: see below) must not be available to governments.[8] Not only are these conditions very special, but I have also shown that concerns about competitiveness may even justify setting tougher, not weaker, environmental standards (with competition between countries leading to a "race to the top").

Three other considerations further weaken the case for distorting environmental standards for strategic reasons. The first is that such behavior may invite retaliation by other states, and the knowledge that other countries would retaliate may be sufficient to deter strategic behavior in the first instance. The second is that, once it became known that a government would distort environmental standards for competitiveness reasons, domestic firms would allocate resources to lobbying for protection, thus dissipating any rents that might be created by the intervention. The final reason is that there are non-strategic policies that can improve "competi-

[7] A. B. Jaffe, S. R. Peterson, P. R. Portney, and R. N. Stavins, "Environmental Regulation and Competitiveness of US Manufacturing: What does the Evidence tell us?" 33 *J. Econ. Lit.* 132–63 (1995).

[8] S. Barrett, "Strategic Environmental Policy and International Trade," 54 *J. Pub. Econ.* 325–38 (1994).

tiveness." In particular, the use of economic instruments can often lower costs without any of the harmful side-effects associated with strategic policy.[9]

To sum up: as regards local environmental problems, the evidence suggests that "competitiveness" is not harmed significantly by higher environmental standards and that attempts to improve well-being by lowering standards are likely to be self-damaging. Since countries cannot in most cases gain by imposing "unfairly" weak environmental standards, and since any effects on "competitiveness" would likely be negligible in any event, there is little justification for imposing countervailing measures of any kind, let alone countervailing duties. This conclusion is reinforced to the extent that, as Professor Roessler notes, suitable mitigation options already exist within the WTO, including the imposition of production subsidies.

So far, I have only considered the case where externalities are local. But where the pollution externality is cross-border, the case for trade restrictions is to my mind irrefutable.

Suppose that a group of countries (the "Abaters") impose a carbon tax in order to reduce their collective carbon dioxide ($CO_2$) emissions. The effect of this would be to make the manufacture of carbon-intensive goods relatively more expensive in these countries. Comparative advantage in manufacturing carbon-intensive goods would therefore shift from the Abaters to the Polluters.[10] It is likely that $CO_2$ emissions by the Polluters would rise, thus at least partially offsetting the abatement by the Abaters. This is known as the "leakage" problem.

How important is the leakage problem? A number of studies have estimated the magnitude of leakage in simulations, but a consensus is lacking. Estimates vary from the negative (emissions by Polluters *fall* in response to abatement by Abaters) to 80 percent (for every 10 tons of $CO_2$ abated by the Abaters, emissions by the Polluters increase by 8 tons, so that global emissions fall by only 2 tons). The estimates vary for many reasons but mainly because the studies examine different scenarios (the identities of the Polluters and Abaters vary, as does the extent and timing of unilateral abatement) and make different assumptions (most importantly perhaps in regard to substitution elasticities).

[9] R. B. Stewart, "Environmental Regulation and International Competitiveness," 102 *Yale L. J.* 2039–106 (1993).

[10] This shift would be exacerbated by the effect the tax would have on world energy prices.

In principle, leakage can be neutralized by a border tax adjustment. But if the Abaters were able to influence world prices of traded goods, they would want to go further than this; they would want to impose a tariff which reduced global emissions even more than in the leakage-neutral case.[11] Are non-neutral adjustments "fair"? That depends on whether the Polluters are free-riders – whether they benefit from the abatement of the Abaters. If the Polluters are free-riders, then it would seem that the adjustments are "fair."

If border tax adjustments were prohibited, then a carbon tax would become a second-best policy instrument, and it would be optimal to vary the tax by sector. All countries which have imposed carbon taxes do in fact vary the tax, with the residential sector bearing the brunt of the tax and energy-intensive, export-led industries typically paying the least. But sectoral differentiation may not be effective in reducing leakage. Oliveira-Martins, Burniaux and Martin show that the European Commission's proposal to exempt energy-intensive industry from paying a carbon tax would merely redistribute the leakage; the total amount of leakage would remain unchanged.[12]

The implication of these results is this: if leakage is a quantitatively significant problem, and if second-best policies are ineffective at correcting for leakage, then the case for allowing border tax adjustments is very strong.

Having established this principle, I should note as well that border tax adjustments are not easily implemented. The Montreal Protocol includes a provision for restricting trade in products made using ozone-depleting substances, such as electronics components which are made using CFCs as a solvent. However, this provision has not been implemented, and the secretariat to this agreement was advised in 1993 that to do so would not be feasible.[13] To implement the provision would require either sophisticated equipment capable of detecting trace residues of CFCs or certification of the manufacturing facilities of industries in countries which are not parties to the agreement. Constructing a border tax adjustment for a carbon tax

[11] See J. R. Markusen, "International Externalities and Optimal Tax Structures," 5 *J. Int'l. Econ.* 15–29 (1975); M. Hod, "Should a Carbon Tax be Differentiated Across Sectors?" 59 *J. Pub. Econ.* 17–32 (1996).

[12] J. Oliveira-Martins, J.-M. Burniaux, and J. P. Martin, "Trade and the Effectiveness of Unilateral $CO_2$-Abatement Policies: Evidence from GREEN," OECD Economic Studies, No. 19 (1992), 123–40.

[13] R. van Slooten, "The Case of the Montreal Protocol," in *Trade and Environment: Processes and Production Methods* (Paris: OECD, 1994).

would be even harder. Virtually all production results in the emission of $CO_2$, and not all production is characterized by a "predominant production method."[14]

But the fact that it is difficult to calculate the appropriate border tax adjustment does not mean that its use should be prohibited. Prohibition is an excessively blunt policy instrument. At the same time, allowing parties the right to impose border tax adjustments at will would also be inappropriate. Guidelines for allowing border tax adjustments would therefore need to be agreed.

## International bargaining across trade and environmental issues

Should the WTO be reformed to allow the use of trade sanctions to coerce WTO Members into raising their environmental standards? Professor Roessler discusses a number of linkages of this kind, but he ignores the most important challenge to the argument against linkage. As noted earlier, the Montreal Protocol bans trade between parties and non-parties in certain ozone-depleting substances (ODSs), products containing these ODSs, and products made using these ODSs. The bans violate the multilateral trading rules, but without them I do not think that the Montreal Protocol would have been as effective in protecting the ozone layer.

The GATT Secretariat has noted that the harmful competitive effects of unilateral abatement could have been addressed in a non-discriminatory way – by, for example, a consumption tax on ODSs.[15] A consumption tax would not disadvantage exports, but nor would it favor imports. The tax would thus be leakage-neutral. The GATT Secretariat claims that the trade sanctions were intended to address a different purpose: that of protecting the producers of ODSs. This is of course precisely the same claim made by Professor Roessler that I discussed above.

I also noted that countries seeking to provide a global public good such as ozone layer protection would want to do more than simply neutralize

[14] The GATT allowed the United States to impose a tax on imports of chemicals made from certain feedstocks which were taxed in the US, on the assumption that the feedstocks embodied in the chemicals were consistent with the "predominant production method" used by the industry (the US would allow exceptions where the importer could establish that less of the input in question had in fact been used). It is possible that the WTO would allow a similar procedure to be used in other cases.

[15] GATT Secretariat, *International Trade 90–91* (Geneva, 1992).

leakage; they would want to distort prices such that the environment was better protected. The tax on consumption alone would not do for this purpose. It would need to be supplemented by border tax adjustments. Furthermore, the countries imposing these adjustments would be justified in doing so provided non-parties to the environmental agreement were free-riding on the abatement undertaken by parties.

Trade sanctions, however, are a pretty blunt instrument for this purpose. Why were *they* used instead of a border tax adjustment? The purpose of the sanctions was not just to lower global emissions of ODSs as compared to the case where cooperating countries neutralize leakage. The purpose was to deter free-riding. According to Benedick, the trade sanctions "were critical. since they constituted the only enforcement mechanism in the protocol."[16] To see why the trade sanctions served the purpose of deterring free-riding requires a basic understanding of the theory of how nations interact in devising their environmental protection policies.[17]

The first rule of the game of international relations is that states are sovereign. This means that international agreements must be self-enforcing; they cannot be enforced by a third party. I have shown how collective abatement can be sustained by a self-enforcing agreement.[18] But an implication of this work is that self-enforcing agreements typically improve very little on the "anarchic" outcome if strategies are limited to abatement choices. The reason is simple. To deter free-riding, parties to the agreement must punish non-parties. With strategies limited to abatement, parties can only punish non-parties by lowering their own abatement. But in lowering their own abatement, parties punish themselves and not only non-parties. Credible punishments will therefore typically be small. It is because of this that agreements can only improve marginally on the non-cooperative outcome.

Linking global environmental protection to trade can alter this calculus.[19] To the extent that the trade sanctions hurt non-parties more than parties, they increase the magnitude of credible punishments. It turns out that trade sanctions will sometimes (but not always) be credible, but only if enough countries are parties to the agreement.

[16] Benedick, *Ozone Diplomacy*, 91.

[17] I am now preparing a book on this subject, tentatively titled *Environment and Statecraft.*

[18] S. Barrett, "Self-enforcing International Environmental Agreements," 46 *Oxford Econ. Papers* 878–94 (1994).

[19] S. Barrett, "The Strategy of Trade Sanctions in International Environmental Agreements," 19 *Resource and Energy Economics*, 345–361 (1997).

I can illustrate these points using just three simple diagrams, provided I assume that all countries are symmetric.[20] In Figure 6.1, there are 101 countries. From the point of view of any one country, there are therefore 100 other countries. Since the countries are symmetric, the situation facing each country is the same, and so we need only consider the decision facing one country. In general, any one country's best choice will depend on the choices made by the other countries. These choices are given by the horizontal axis. I focus on the decision to be a signatory or a non-signatory, and the horizontal axis indicates the number of other countries that are signatories. All other decisions – such as those regarding abatement levels – are subsumed within the payoff curves and need not concern us greatly.

Should one's own country be a signatory or a non-signatory? The answer depends on whether, taking the actions of other countries as given, the country's payoff to being a signatory is greater or less than its payoff to being a non-signatory. Figure 6.1 illustrates three possibilities in linear payoffs.

Figure 6.1A depicts the "prisoners' dilemma" game. The payoff to each country of being a signatory is less than the payoff to being a non-signatory, whatever all the other countries do. There is thus a unique equilibrium (indicated by the solid dot). It is that all countries are non-signatories. Each gets a payoff of 1. But the equilibrium is inefficient: if all countries cooperated and became signatories, each would get a payoff of 9 (this is the full cooperative outcome; it is indicated in the figure by the open dot).

Figure 6.1B depicts a game in which the signatories vary their abatement depending on the number of signatories. If the number of signatories is less than sixty, it would be in one's own country's interest to accede. If the number of signatories were greater than sixty, it would be in one's own country's interest to be a non-signatory. There is once again a unique equilibrium, but in this case it involves roughly sixty countries cooperating and the remaining forty or so "free-riding." What sustains cooperation in this case is the credible threat by signatories to lower their abatement in the event of a defection. As noted earlier, such a punishment may be very small because it harms signatories as well as free-riders. This means either that very few countries will be parties or that a lot of countries will be parties but abatement by each will be only slightly greater than in the non-cooperative outcome.

[20] The graphical representation of *N*-party symmetric games was developed by T. C. Schelling, *Micromotives and Macrobehavior* (Cambridge, Mass.: Harvard, 1978).

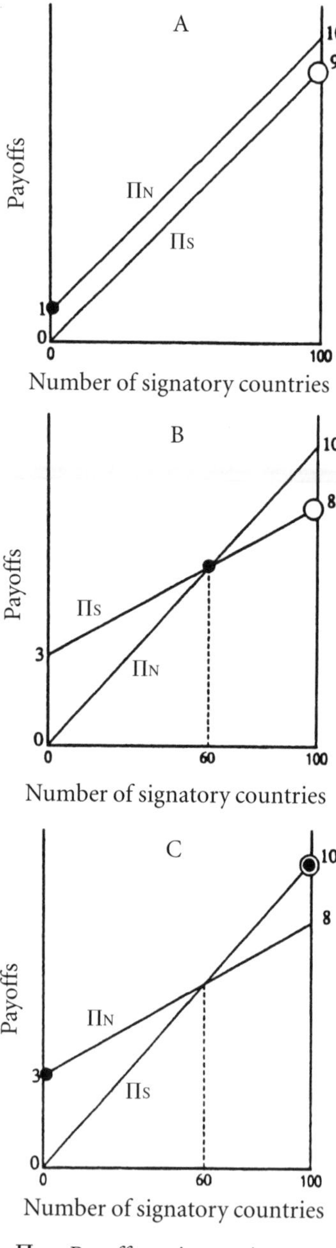


$\Pi_S$ = Payoffs to signatories
$\Pi_N$ = Payoffs to non-signatories

*Figure 6.1* Payments to signatories and non-signatories as a function of the number of signatories

Figure 6.1C depicts a game in which signatories not only vary their abatement depending on the number of signatories but where they also ban trade with non-signatories. If the number of signatories were small, the loss in the gains from trade to signatories would be huge and would exceed the net benefits of collective abatement. It would thus be in one's own country's interest to be a non-signatory. But if the number of signatories were sufficiently large, trade sanctions would harm non-signatories much more than signatories, and the increase in the gains from trade to signatories would exceed the loss in net benefits associated with free-riding. It would be in one's own country's interest to be a signatory.

There are thus two equilibria, one in which no country is a signatory and one in which all countries are signatories. The latter equilibrium is preferred by all countries to the former. To ensure that the preferred equilibrium is realized requires coordination. This is easily achieved. All that is needed is a clause in the agreement which says that the agreement will only be binding (in the legal, not the game-theoretic, sense) if the number of signatories surpassed a certain threshold – say sixty-five signatories. Then a country would have nothing to lose by acceding if the number of signatories were less than sixty-five and much to gain by acceding if the number of signatories were sixty-five or greater. The Montreal Protocol contains just such a clause: the agreement would not become binding on signatories until ratified by at least eleven countries accounting for at least two-thirds of global consumption. Benedick explains that this clause was written into the agreement to ensure full participation.[21]

What is particularly interesting about this result is that it suggests that the credible threat to invoke sanctions may be sufficient to deter free-riding; trade need not actually be restricted. In fact, participation in the Montreal Protocol is for all intents and purposes full, and trade has not been restricted.

Are the threatened trade sanctions responsible for this happy state of affairs? We will never know because we cannot observe the counterfactual, though anecdotal evidence suggests to me that the trade sanctions did play an important role. A representative of one important country told me that his country acceded to the Protocol because of the trade sanctions. An executive of a large ODS manufacturer told me that his company would have been reluctant to invest in the development of ODS-substitutes were it not

[21] Benedick, *Ozone Diplomacy.*

for the trade sanctions. The implication is that, if the Montreal Protocol had conformed to the WTO rules, and trade sanctions had not been threatened, the ozone layer would not have been as effectively protected.

I should note that the "stick" of trade sanctions was not the only incentive for accession. Developing countries were also offered the "carrot" of compensation for the "incremental costs" of complying with the Montreal Protocol. This carrot not only contributed directly to the effectiveness of the agreement but it also rendered the stick of trade sanctions legitimate. Developing countries could with some justification claim that they were not free-riders and so should not be punished for failing to accede to the agreement. It is only because of the carrot that the trade sanctions in the Montreal Protocol can be labeled "fair."

## Conclusion

The WTO *is* in need of reform, but it is not in need of the wholesale reform that some of its critics have demanded. The changes that are justified relate to policies to correct transboundary externalities. The WTO should allow for border tax adjustments, trade restrictions based on how a good was made, and the use of trade sanctions in multilateral environmental agreements. But such allowances need to be bounded. It would do no good to replace a regime which favored trade at the expense of the environment with one that favored the environment at the expense of trade. What the international system must do is strike a balance in its management of both trade and the environment. The suggested reforms should only be allowed where it can be demonstrated that their use would be both welfare-improving and fair.

# Part III

## CHOICE OF ENVIRONMENTAL POLICY INSTRUMENTS

# 7

# ECONOMIC INCENTIVES FOR ENVIRONMENTAL PROTECTION: OPPORTUNITIES AND OBSTACLES

RICHARD B. STEWART

## Introduction

THE FAILINGS of state socialism in the former Soviet Union, Eastern Europe, and many developing countries have stimulated renewed appreciation of the economic and political virtues of competitive markets in harnessing the efforts of managers to the demands of consumers, promoting efficiency in resource allocation, stimulating innovation, and avoiding undue concentration of political economic power. Many nations have taken steps during the past twenty years to dismantle central planning, privatize state-owned enterprises, and reduce or transform government control of economic activity.

Yet, during the same two decades governments have adopted and continually expanded far-reaching centrally planned command-and-control regulatory programs in order to limit air and water pollution, deal with toxic wastes, and solve other environmental problems. Seemingly oblivious to the inherent and well-documented failures of central planning, these programs aim to produce environmental quality by issuing detailed orders to thousands of individual facilities, prescribing their conduct in labyrinthine detail. This chapter seeks to help resolve this paradox by analyzing the advantages of economic incentive systems (EIS) for environmental protection including environmental taxes and tradable pollution quotas, identifying the types of environmental problems for which they are best suited, diagnosing structural factors that impede wider use of such instruments, and proposing regulatory reform strategies to promote such use.

The traditional instrument of choice for all types of economic and social regulation has been command and control. During the past twenty years, however, governments have, in the context of economic regulatory programs, increasingly come to the conclusion that the failings of command and control are often more serious than the market failures that those programs were supposed to correct. Accordingly, governments have either substantially deregulated or shifted to more flexible structural strategies, such as reliance on competition policy rather than price and entry controls. Environmental and other forms of social regulation, however, have been viewed quite differently. Unregulated competitive markets can generate seriously excessive amounts of residuals, including pollution, hazardous waste, and other forms of environmental degradation.[1] Such market failures are often much more serious than those addressed by economic regulation, justifying strong regulatory measures. This circumstance, however, cannot explain why governments have relied almost exclusively on command-and-control instruments to address environmental degradation, to the virtual exclusion of economic incentives systems (EIS) such as fees on pollution and tradable pollution quotas.

Several factors explain the relative disregard of EIS. Because they rely on market-based incentives, EIS tend to be perceived as a form of deregulation. Because regulatory failure in dealing with environmental and health risks can result in irreversible and serious harms, it is important that regulatory measures be effective. Command-and-control regulation is viewed as assuring such efficacy. The flexibility afforded by EIS is seen as a weakness. Because of the strong command-and-control regulatory tradition, EIS are relatively untried. As confirmed and explained by public choice analysis,[2] many politically and economically powerful interests have a vested stake in the perpetuation of the command regulatory status quo. There is also strong public sentiment that pollution and environmental degradation are wrongful and should be prohibited. Regulatory commands answer to this

[1] Hereinafter the term "residuals" will be used generally to include air and water pollution, wastes, and other forms of environmental degradation, including the adverse effects of development and other activities on natural resources. The term "source" includes not only facilities that generate pollution and wastes but also development and other activities that generate residuals. This chapter, however, focuses primarily on environmental regulatory instruments to address pollution and wastes. The use of economic instruments to protect and preserve natural resources and the ecological services that they provide are addressed in Geoffrey Heal's contribution to this book.

[2] See Nathaniel O. Keohane, Richard L. Revesz, and Robert N. Stavins, "The Choice of Regulatory Instruments in Environmental Policy," 22 *Harv. Env. L. Rev.* 313 (1998), discussed below at pp. 202–3.

condemnatory instinct. EIS, on the other hand, are often criticized as implicitly endorsing or condoning immoral behavior by selling indulgences to pollute.

Recent developments have nonetheless created conditions more hospitable to the use of EIS for environmental protection. In most developed countries, the public are demanding higher and higher levels of environmental quality. In order to achieve this goal and maintain continued economic growth, lower and lower levels of residuals per unit of output must be achieved, pushing command-and-control regulation relentlessly up the marginal control cost curve. As regulation becomes relentlessly more ambitious, the inherent administrative as well as economic dysfunctions of command-and-control instruments – including excessive complexity, delay, rigidity, and cost – become more serious and more obvious. Increasingly intense economic competition on a global scale has created increased political sensitivity to environmental regulatory burdens. Further, the public are increasingly skeptical about the capacities and performance of centralized government. There is growing awareness of the need to reconcile economic and environmental objectives by promoting more resource-efficient methods of production and consumption. There is also increasing appreciation of the regional and global character of environmental problems, including climate change, and their close connection with international trade and investment flows. For many types of environmental problems, EIS are substantially better suited than command-and-control methods to address the challenges posed by these developments. As a result of these factors, there has recently been increasing use of EIS in the United States and in Europe.

The basic argument traditionally made for EIS has been cost-effectiveness: EIS can achieve a given level of overall limitation on residuals at substantially lower cost than command-and-control regulation. This consideration alone, however, has generally not been sufficient to overcome the impediments to wider adoption of EIS. In making the case for EIS, the other important comparative advantages of economic incentives must be stressed. EIS can promote sustainable development by providing both the flexibility and the incentive for business innovation in less polluting, more resource-efficient technologies and methods. EIS economize on government. They limit its role to establishing and enforcing pollution prices or tradable quotas, and rely on the price system to decentralize to managers and consumers the legion of detailed production and consumption decisions which regulatory bureaucracies must make under command and control. EIS generate investment flows or revenues that can be reinvested to reduce pollution by upgrading outdated production processes.

Although the comparative advantages of EIS go far beyond static efficiency gains, they are not a panacea. For example, the flexibility which they afford is a disadvantage in dealing with localized pollution impacts that threaten serious damage if health or ecological thresholds are exceeded. Moreover, significant political barriers to greater use of EIS persist. Regulatory reform strategies must be developed to overcome these obstacles if EIS are to enjoy broad use.

This chapter addresses the opportunities for and obstacles to greater use of EIS in both the domestic and the international context, and offers suggestions as to how those obstacles can be overcome. The various available types of environmental regulatory instruments are summarized. The comparative performance advantages and disadvantages of EIS in relation to command-and-control regulation are analyzed in greater detail. Distributional and other ethical aspects of different regulatory instruments are then examined. The experience with environmental regulatory instruments and the political economy of regulatory reform are discussed. Next, the comparative advantages of EIS in dealing with regional and global environmental problems are examined. The final section takes the example of global climate change as an illustration of how EIS might be used to deal with global and regional environmental problems.

## Types of environmental regulatory instruments

The fundamental distinction between command-and-control methods and EIS is this: command systems limit, directly or indirectly, the quantity of residuals that each actor may generate; EIS establish, directly or indirectly, a price that must be paid for each unit of residuals generated but leave each actor free to decide on the level that it generates.[3]

Command systems typically – through regulations, permits, or licensing authorizations – impose quantitative limitations on the rate or amount of residuals that each source generates. These regulatory limitations may be based on the level of control which can be achieved by currently available technology, or that needed to achieve environmental quality goals or

[3] See Martin L. Weitzman, "Prices vs. Quantities," 41 *Rev. Econ. Studies* 477 (1974).

aggregate limits on pollution loadings. In practice, technology-based control requirements limiting the rate of residuals discharged in relation to process inputs or outputs predominate. Command regulations may also indirectly limit the quantity of residuals generated by mandating use of certain technologies, or controlling inputs, or otherwise prescribing conduct in such a way as to constrain the level of residuals generated.

EIS impose a price on residuals. *Fees or taxes* on pollution, wastes, and other residuals do so directly. A *tradable quota or credit system* does so indirectly. Under a tradable quota system, the government issues a fixed number of permits or allowances, limiting the aggregate amount of residuals that may be generated by all of the sources subject to the system. Permits are distributed by government to individual sources by auction or by legislative or administrative allocation. A source may not emit residuals in excess of the number of quota permits that it holds. Permits may be bought, sold, and traded by anyone. Because the demand for quota permits exceeds the supply, they carry a positive price. A tradable quota system effectively imposes a price on a source for each additional unit of pollution that it generates; it must either purchase an additional permit or incur the opportunity cost of foregoing sale of a surplus permit that it already holds. Under a tradable quota system, however, the price of pollution is set by market supply and demand rather than directly by the government, and the aggregate quantity of pollution is fixed. A variant of tradable quotas is a system of emission reduction credits (ERC); a source that reduces pollution below the levels fixed by command regulations can obtain a credit which it can sell to other sources which they can use to help meet their respective command obligations.[4]

Fees and tradable quota systems are not deregulation. They either require sources to pay discharge fees or forbid sources from generating residuals in excess of the permits that they hold. Violations of these requirements, like violations of command-and-control directives, are subject to administrative, civil, and criminal sanctions. But EIS differ fundamentally from command systems by allowing sources the flexibility to choose the level of residuals generated and the methods of limiting residuals that they prefer. By imposing a price on residuals, EIS also provide continuing incentives for

[4] Under a tradable quota system, the government sets a limit on aggregate residuals. Under an ERC system, the government initially sets required residuals limitations for each source through command regulation.

sources to reduce their existing residuals levels.[5] Tax and transferable permit systems are potentially powerful forms of EIS with broad applicability. But there are a number of other forms of EIS.

Under *environmental contracting*, the government and a source contractually agree on an aggregative, multi-media "umbrella" of residuals limitations for the facility in lieu of the uniform, technology-based requirements imposed by command-and-control regulation on specific residual streams into particular media.[6] The source-specific contract must ensure an overall limitation on residuals such that the health and environmental risks that they pose is equal to or lower than that provided by compliance with otherwise applicable command regulations. This risk "cap" creates economic incentives because higher levels of discharges by the facility of a given residual into a given medium carry an opportunity cost in the form of the resources that must be devoted to reducing other residuals in order to stay within the cap. In effect, the contract creates an implicit internal residuals trading market.[7]

[5] Regulation can also be viewed as imposing a price on pollution, in the form of fines or other sanctions for non-compliance with command requirements. Even if one accepts this characterization, however, an important difference between command regulation and EIS remains: sanctions for violation of command-and-control requirements impose a discontinuous price (fines are levied only if discharges exceed the permitted amount) whereas incentive systems impose a continuous price (e.g. a fee must be paid on each unit of pollution). This difference has significant implications for the structure of incentives generated by the two types of systems. Under a command system, sources face incentives not to exceed the regulatory limitation, but no incentive to reduce residuals further.

[6] Other forms of environmental contracts or covenants, including those between government and an entire industry, are discussed in Professor Rehbinder's contribution to this book. See also Jan van Dunné, ed., *New Instruments for a Realistic Environmental Policy?* (Institute of Environmental Damages, Erasmus University, Rotterdam, 1993).

[7] The plant-specific flexibility afforded by such programs, combined with large differences in the marginal costs of limiting different residuals from different waste streams into different media, can generate very substantial cost savings over command regulation. In one example, EPA concluded that allowing a source flexibility could achieve reductions in residuals equivalent to that required by existing regulations at only 25 percent of the cost of complying with the command requirements. See Dennis D. Hirsch, "Bill and Al's XL-Ent Adventure: An Analysis of the EPA's Legal Authority to Implement the Clinton Administration's Project XL," 1998 *U. Ill. L. Rev.* 129, 140–46 (describing history of Project XL); see also Benjamin Starbuck Wechsler, "Note, Rethinking Reinvention: A Case Study of Project XL," 5 *Env. L.* 255 (1998) (describing Project XL). But see Charles C. Caldart and Nicholas A. Ashford, "Negotiation as a Means of Developing and Implementing Environmental and Occupational Health And Safety Policy," 23 *Harv. Env. L. Rev.* 141, 186 (arguing that the site-specific nature of Project XL demands enormous resources from EPA and that EPA's enthusiasm for the XL project "has been tempered").

*Information-based strategies* represent another form of EIS. Under these strategies, government takes measures – such as imposing disclosure requirements on firms or instituting eco-label programs – to provide consumers and investors with information regarding the environmental performance of products and firms. To the extent that consumers or investors value superior environmental performance in their purchasing or investing decisions, the market will penalize firms with inferior performance through diminished sales and higher capital costs. There are, however, significant obstacles to providing information on environmental performance, especially to consumers, that is both accurate and concise.[8] Further, apart from organic food products, the extent to which consumers will in fact pay more for "green" products and processes is unclear. In addition, very few investors appear to base investment decisions on environmental performance.[9]

*Liability for environmental damage* imposed by tort law or statutory schemes of liability, such as the United States "Superfund" program of hazardous waste liability, can be viewed as a form of EIS because it imposes a price on conduct that causes harm or loss.[10] Liability systems generally operate *ex post* and require a showing that harm or loss was caused by a

Many scholars have questioned Project XL's legality under the existing statutory framework, and have suggested that project participation has been limited by companies' unwillingness to risk litigation. See, e.g., Hirsch, "Bill and Al's XL-Ent Adventure" (arguing that EPA can use its limited waiver authority to overcome legal barriers).

Regulatory provisions such as US fleet-wide fuel economy requirements, which require manufacturers to achieve a given average fuel economy for the cars which they sell but allow the performance of different models to be averaged in determining a manufacturer's compliance, represent another example of a regulatory program that creates an implicit internal residuals trading market.

8 See Peter S. Menell, "Structuring a Market-Oriented Federal Eco-Information Policy," 54 *Md. L. Rev.* 1435 (1995) (noting difficulties in educating consumers on manufacturing, use, and disposal impacts of myriad products, critiquing nationally implemented eco-labeling regimes in Canada and the EU, and advocating a market-oriented approach to eco-information policy through use of prices).

9 Some mutual fund firms have created "green" or "socially responsible" funds to attract environmentally conscious investors, but such funds attract only a small portion of mutual fund investments.

10 Strict liability in damages operates in a fashion analogous to discharge fees; the discharger is free to choose higher or lower levels of discharge, but must make correspondingly higher or lower payments in the form of damages liabilities. The payment, however, is based not on the level of discharges but the amount of harm caused, and is imposed only in those cases where harm occurs. Negligence liability exacts damages payments for harm caused only when an actor fails to observe a relevant standard of care, analogous to a regulatory standard.

given actor; these characteristics limit their effectiveness in dealing with some types of environmental harms.[11] On the other hand, the general and pervasive applicability of the incentives provided by the threat of damages liability are also an important advantage of liability systems as compared to regulatory measures that must be designed and targeted at particular risks *ex ante*.

*Pure subsidies* to polluters are another potential form of EIS, under which government would entertain bids from polluters for pollution reductions, and then purchase the desired level of reduction at the lowest total price. While this system would achieve cost-effective pollution control in a static context, it requires a baseline of what emissions would be in the absence of a subsidy program. It is extraordinarily difficult to establish and maintain such a baseline in a dynamic economy.[12] Moreover, there is likely to be strong political opposition to paying polluters not to pollute.

A variety of *mixed systems* of regulation, combining elements of both the command and EIS approaches, have been used or could be developed. For example, command regulation could require a minimum level of control by each source, while fees could be imposed or a tradable quota system established for remaining discharges. Deposit and refund measures to promote recycling or proper disposal of beverage containers or used batteries require consumers to pay a fee on purchase of disposable items, which is refunded when they comply with command requirements specifying the proper method of disposal or return. Similar mixed systems could be used to deal with other environmental problems such as hazardous waste generation and disposal.

For the sake of analytical clarity and expositional economy the remainder of this chapter will be limited to a discussion of command regulation and of fees and tradable quotas, which are currently the two most important forms of EIS.

[11] For example, damages liability is ill-suited to dealing with diffuse risks of harm to health or the environment generated by many sources, and is generally used as a supplement rather than an alternative to command regulation.

[12] See Thomas C. Schelling, "Prices as Regulatory Instruments" in Thomas C. Schelling, ed., *Incentives for Environmental Protection* (Cambridge, Mass.: MIT Press, 1983), 1, 33. In many cases, governments have allocated funds or given tax credits to polluters to defray a portion of the cost of complying with regulatory requirements. These programs are not EIS, because the required level of control is established for each source by command-and-control regulation.

## Comparative functional performance of command regulation and economic incentive systems

The comparative advantages and disadvantages of command regulation and EIS are a function of their respective techniques: source-by-source quantity restrictions, and prices on residuals.

The most important functional advantage of the command system is that it can be designed to ensure that the amount of residuals generated by a given source does not exceed a specified figure. Command regulation can also potentially be used to constrain the location of polluting facilities. The capacity of command systems to control local residual levels is potentially quite important in the case of environmental problems involving damage functions characterized by sharp thresholds, where serious harm will result if residuals concentrations exceed the threshold. In actual practice, however, command systems are often not designed or implemented in such a way as to achieve these objectives. Under EIS, the level of residuals discharged by a given source is not fixed, but rather is a function of the price imposed and the costs that the facility would incur in limiting residuals. Also, the location of facilities is not controlled. These aspects of the flexibility provided by EIS are a potential disadvantage in dealing with environmental problems that can create local pollution "hot spots," although EIS can be structured in various ways to address such problems. Moreover, many environmental risks are not characterized by such sharp thresholds; high residuals levels pose somewhat greater risks, lower levels pose somewhat lesser risks. There is no clear "safe" level. In such situations the use of EIS may be acceptable, even though some areas experience rather higher concentrations or loadings of residuals, if the cost savings and other advantages of EIS are sufficiently large, and especially if the cost savings are invested in more stringent regulation to reduce residuals further.

The command system's focus on source-by-source limitation of residuals quantities has important disadvantages, including high costs, impairment of innovation, structural distortions, administrative dysfunctions, and diminishing environmental returns from increased regulatory stringency. These disadvantages are relatively minor in the early stages of command regulatory programs but become progressively more acute as regulatory stringency is increased in the effort to reduce further residuals per unit of output. Because they allow individual sources flexibility while providing continuing incentives to reduce residuals further, EIS avoid many of these disadvantages. In the case of many environmental problems, EIS can achieve limitations on overall residuals at substantially lower cost than command systems, and also promote long-run goals of resource efficiency and sustainable development. The performance of command regulation and of EIS is also affected by various administrative factors discussed below.

## ENVIRONMENTAL PERFORMANCE

The choice between command-and-control regulation and EIS depends importantly on the type of environmental problem involved and the shape of the damage function. In cases where the environmental damage function exhibits sharp local thresholds, the ability of command regulation to ensure that such thresholds are not exceeded by limiting residuals from individual sources is a potentially important advantage that may outweigh its drawbacks. In situations involving a single source, command regulation could directly limit the quantity of residuals generated so as to avoid exceeding the damage threshold. In the more typical case where multiple sources contribute to the pollution of a given airshed or water body, matters are more complex. Ambient standards defining permissible sub-threshold levels of aggregate pollution concentrations are often adopted. In order to ensure that these ambient standards are not exceeded, controls on residuals from all the relevant sources must be devised and implemented. This is an often complex and information-intensive task. Furthermore, in practice most command source controls do not directly limit the total quantity of residuals generated by each source. For administrative reasons, source limitations are often expressed in terms of a rate: the amount of residuals generated per unit of a production input (such as fuel BTUs) or output (such as pounds of products). Furthermore, most command systems do not directly limit the number of sources or their location. Thus, in actual practice, the effectiveness of command systems in preventing aggregate pollution concentrations from exceeding damage thresholds and creating hot spots is far from optimal.

Typically, tradable quota systems establish an aggregate limitation on the total quantity of residuals discharges throughout a region but do not provide assurances about local residuals levels. Emission tax systems typically do not set assured limitations either locally or in the aggregate. Steps can, however, be taken to modify EIS in order to deal with the risk of local residuals "hot spots." For example, the level of fees or the amount of emissions allowed per permit can be adjusted by reference to total residuals loadings in each locality so as to ensure that ambient standards are not violated.[13] Establishing such limitations would, however, be administratively complex, especially when loadings originate outside of the locality. Alternatively, local pollution zones can be established, each with its own fee level or emissions/quota ratio. These measures, however, may introduce substantial administrative complexities and transactions costs and, in the case of tradable permit systems, may make it more difficult to establish well-functioning permit markets.[14] Alternatively, pollution fee or tradable quota systems can be established subject to the overriding regulatory constraint that ambient standards not be violated; this constraint could, however, limit the economic and other advantages that can be achieved by use of EIS.

Many important pollution problems, including local exposures to carcinogens and regional or global air pollution, are not characterized by sharp damage function thresholds; the damage function appears to be more linear in character. In these circumstances, the basic objective is to limit environmental damage by reducing aggregate residuals rather than to achieve a particular quantitative limitation in a given location.[15] In such cases, the ability of command regulation to achieve such a limitation is no longer important, and the cost, incentive, and other advantages of EIS tend to dominate.

[13] See Richard L. Revesz, "Federalism and Interstate Environmental Externalities," 144 *U. Pa. L. Rev.* 2341, 2412 (1996). Professor Revesz suggests marketing permits in "units of environmental degradation," where the emissions value of the unit would depend on the impact that emissions at each source would have on ambient air quality levels at affected locations, taking into account facility location, stack height, wind patterns, and topography. If the number of units available is determined by reference to the ambient standards at each affected location, then hot spots are prevented. See also Ger Klaassen, *Acid Rain and Environmental Degradation* (Cheltenham: Edward Elgar, 1996), 44–63.

[14] See Tom Tietenberg, "Tradeable Permits for Pollution Control when Emission Location Matters: What have We Learned?" 5 *Env. & Res. Econ.* 95 (1995). Alternatively, fees could be set high enough, or permit allocations low enough, to ensure that a given maximum level of pollution was not exceeded in any locality, but such a strategy would lead to unnecessarily high levels of control and cost in many localities that do not pose potential "hot spot" problems.

Another form of EIS, facility-specific environmental contracting, discussed at p. 176 above, has great promise for dealing effectively and efficiently with local pollution problems.

[15] This strategy may promote aggregate welfare but may also result in higher levels of residuals and harm in some locations than in others; such geographical differences may be challenged under certain conceptions of environmental justice. See pp. 193–94 below.

A still more fine-tuned approach to risk-based regulation would take into account not only residuals levels and the nature of the damage function but also the number of persons or the value and sensitivity of the ecosystems exposed to residuals. Thus, in order to target regulatory resources most effectively on reducing fatalities or illnesses, pollution control measures should be made more stringent in areas with higher populations. This objective can readily be achieved through a fee system by basing the level of the fee on the number of persons exposed and the average per person exposure.[16] Although there will be different fee levels in different localities, the system will equalize the marginal cost of risk reduction across locations. The stringency of command requirements or the emissions/permit ratio can be similarly adjusted. As discussed below, however, this approach may be opposed on the ground that each individual has a right to the same basic level of protection against risk regardless of where she lives and the number of other individuals who reside in the same locality.

## ECONOMIC PERFORMANCE

### *Flexibility and compliance cost savings*

For many types of environmental problems, EIS can achieve residuals limitations objectives at substantially lower cost than command systems by affording individual pollution sources flexibility in both the level of and the means of achieving limitations on the residuals that they generate.

Command regulations that consist of specification standards – for example, those that mandate limitations on certain inputs (such as the sulfur content of fuel) or adoption of specified control technologies – often prevent sources from choosing the least costly method of achieving a given level of residuals limitations. Even where command regulations consist of a performance standard that imposes a numerical limit on the rate or amount of a specific residual in specific waste streams to given media, such standards are typically based on particular control technologies, often end-of-pipe treatment methods. This circumstance strongly encourages use of the specific

[16] See Albert V. Nichols, "The Regulation of Airborne Benzene," in Schelling *Incentives for Environmental Protection* 145 (discussing use of emission fees for toxic pollutants based on local population and exposures).

control technologies upon which the standards are based and impedes use of alternative approaches, including process modifications and other pollution prevention techniques. The further circumstance that limitation requirements are imposed separately on discharges of different residuals from different waste streams to different media denies sources the flexibility to reallocate limitations across different waste streams, foreclosing or discouraging development and use of basic process charges and other innovative facility-wide measures of pollution prevention and resource efficiency.[17] In addition, dictating each source's level of residuals prevents overall limitations on the residuals generated by all sources from being achieved in the most cost-effective way. Command requirements are generally not tailored to variations among plants and industries in the costs of limiting residuals. In order to reduce information and decisionmaking costs, regulators typically adopt uniform requirements by industry categories, imposing the same limitations on those sources with high marginal control costs as on those with low marginal control costs. For the same reasons, standards for different industries are not coordinated. As a result, the marginal costs of complying with regulatory requirements for control of the same residual vary widely from industry to industry as well as from source to source within each industry.[18] The total costs to society of achieving a given overall level of

[17] See Hirsch, "Bill and Al's XL-Ent Adventure"; Stewart, "Environmental Regulation and International Competitiveness," 102 *Yale L. J.* 2039, 2090–93 (1993) and sources there discussed. In theory, under an integrated pollution prevention and control approach, regulators might adjust central command requirements to fit the circumstances of particular plants. But there are serious practical limitations on this approach because of the widely differing circumstances of the hundreds of thousands of regulated facilities subject to environmental regulation. See Damian Chalmers, "Inhabitants in the Field of European Community Environmental Law," 5 *Colum. J. Env. L.* 39, 71 (1998) (noting that early data from the United Kingdom's integrated pollution prevention and control efforts suggests that the program has "not altered industrial behavior patterns" as "industries with poor ecological performance records continue to behave poorly"). We can also attempt to introduce plant-by-plant flexibility on a decentralized basis. See Lisa Heinzerling, "Reductionist Regulatory Reform," 8 *Fordham Env. L. J.* 459, 472–75 (1997) (discussing the Clinton Administration's Project XL as an example of an attempt to extend greater regulatory flexibility by allowing cross-pollutant and cross-medium tradeoffs to satisfy compliance requirements); Kevin Martin, "Legislative Development, Integrated Pollution Prevention and Control," 3 *Colum. J. Env. L.* 331 (1997) (describing the EU's directive as regulating pollutants at the installation (i.e., factory or plant) level).

[18] See Robert W. Crandall, "The Political Economy of Clean Air: Practical Constraints on White House Review," in V. Kerry Smith ed., *Environmental Policy Under Reagan's Executive Order: The Role of Cost-Benefit Analysis* (Chapel Hill, N.C.: University of North Carolina Press, 1984), 205–25.

control of a given pollutant would be significantly reduced by shifting limitations requirements from sources with high marginal control costs to those with low costs, to the point where marginal control costs for all sources of the same residual were the same. Under a command system, however, it is neither administratively feasible nor equitable to accomplish such equalization. Imposing heavier regulatory burdens on sources with low control costs would be attacked by such sources as inequitable and would discourage firms from developing and adopting lower cost control measures.

EIS, by contrast, impose a price on residuals generated – a pure performance standard. Each facility enjoys total flexibility to select whatever level of residuals and method of residuals limitation that it chooses in order to minimize the sum of its limitations costs and the price imposed by an EIS on the residuals that it generates. EIS confront all sources of the same residual with the same price. Each source will tend to limit residuals to the level where its marginal cost of limitation equals the price that it must pay on its remaining residuals. Sources with low marginal control costs will have relatively high levels of control and pay less in fees or for permits than sources with high marginal costs, who will control less. Since all sources of the same residual face the same price, the marginal control costs of all sources tend to converge. The resultant cost savings, relative to a command-and-control system, can be enormous, running to tens of billions of dollars annually in the United States alone.[19] These savings can be invested in higher levels of environmental protection or other societal objectives.

### *Innovation and dynamic efficiency*

Achieving higher levels of environmental quality while maintaining economic growth will require far-reaching innovation and investment in less polluting, more resource-efficient methods of production and consumption.[20] Although command regulation may be quite effective in requiring sources to install existing control technologies, it is generally less success-

[19] See B. Ackerman and R. Stewart, "Reforming Environmental Law," 37 *Stan. L. Rev.* 301 (1985); see also pp. 213–14 and notes 105–10 below (summarizing cost savings of $SO_2$ trading program).

[20] See Ian W. H. Parry, "Pollution Regulation and the Efficiency Gains from Technological Innovation," 14 *J. Regulatory Econ.* 229 (1998).

ful in inducing innovation, particularly in the context of the US regulatory culture. Under command-and-control regulation, firms do not have a strong incentive to develop and adopt means for achieving higher levels of residuals limitation than required by law unless they anticipate that regulatory authorities will succeed in tightening standards in the future. Efforts to tighten regulatory commands successively to "force" technology have in many cases not been notably successful. As previously noted, the uncoordinated myriad of different command requirements on residuals in different waste streams to different media often prevents managers from using innovative process changes and other pollution prevention strategies. In response to environmentalists' demands for strict controls on the one hand, and political opposition to shutdowns of existing facilities on the other, legislators and environmental regulators tend to impose disproportionately stringent burdens on new products and processes over existing ones.[21] Also, new facilities and products must run the gauntlet of lengthy administrative and legal proceedings in order to obtain regulatory approval. Existing sources, on the other hand, can use the delays and costs of the legal process to challenge and delay implementation of new regulatory requirements. Technology-based command requirements, which take into account the ability of an industry to absorb the costs of a technology in determining whether it is "available," also tend to impose disproportionately costly regulatory burdens on more productive and profitable industries because they can "afford" more stringent controls. These features of command regulation penalize innovation and investment and impede

[21] See Bruce A. Ackerman and Richard B. Stewart, "Comment: Reforming Environmental Law," 37 *Stan. L. Rev.* 1333, 1336 (1985) (arguing that best available technology regimes tend to accommodate older firms' difficulties in complying with regulations, and compensate for this indulgence by placing disproportionate regulatory burdens on new facilities). See also Peter Huber, "The Old–New Division in Risk Regulation," 69 *Va. L. Rev.* 1025, 1054 (1983) (observing a tendency among courts and legislators to attempt to mitigate costs of compliance for existing facilities, without properly considering the social costs of stringently regulatory new risks); Bruce A. Ackerman and William T. Hassler, *Clean Coal/Dirty Air* (New Haven: Yale University Press, 1981) (arguing that the stringent scrubbing requirements for new facilities imposed by federal regulators made air dirtier by creating an incentive to keep older, dirtier facilities on-line longer due to compliance costs for new facilities). Because it is generally cheaper to build pollution prevention and control into a new plant or product than to retrofit an existing one, cost-effectiveness dictates that command regulatory controls on new facilities and products should generally be more stringent than controls on existing ones. The relative stringency of command regulatory controls on new facilities and products, however, is often substantially greater than would be justified by this consideration.

turnover of the capital stock, perpetuating older, more polluting products and processes.[22]

EIS, by contrast, provide positive incentives for innovation and investment in less polluting, more resource-efficient technologies.[23] Sources that succeed in such innovation can reduce the price that they pay for residuals and thereby gain a competitive advantage, making environmental protection a profit center. In addition, EIS tend to eliminate disproportionate burdens on new products or processes or on more profitable and innovative industries by charging all sources of a given residual the same price.[24]

### *Allocative efficiency*

Command systems do not impose a price on the residual pollution generated by sources that comply with limitations requirements. Residual pollution is "free" to the polluter. As a result, not only do sources lack a regulatory incentive to reduce residuals further, but the social costs associated with the residuals generated are not reflected in the prices of the goods and services produced by that source.[25] By contrast, EIS impose a price on all residuals generated. Although this price will rarely be exactly equal to the social costs of such pollution, it will tend to result in higher prices for goods and ser-

[22] See Richard B. Stewart, "Regulation, Innovation, and Administrative Law: A Conceptual Framework," 69 *Calif. L. Rev.* 1259 (1981); Huber, "The Old–New Division in Risk Regulation."

[23] Professor Requate models the relative incentives to introduce a cleaner technology under a tax or tradable permit regime and concludes that "under taxes welfare may go down if a new technology is introduced whereas this can never happen under permits." See Till Requate, "Incentives to Innovate Under Emission Taxes and Tradable Permits," 14 *Eur. J. Pol. Econ.* 139, 139 (1998). But see Vincenzo Denicol , "Pollution-reducing Innovations Under Taxes or Permits," 51 *Oxford Econ. Papers* 184 (1999) (finding taxes provide more incentives to innovate than permits in many cases).

[24] In Russia, however, political aversion to shutdowns has led officials not to apply or enforce in full pollution fees against older, economically marginal plants. See National Academy of Public Administration, *The Environment Goes to Market* (Washington, D.C., 1994). The tradable quota systems adopted in the United States favor established sources by giving them quotas without charge; this practice may impair the ability of such systems to promote cost-effectiveness and innovation. See pp. 215–16 below.

[25] To the extent, however, that regulatory requirements push control levels beyond those where marginal control costs equal marginal social benefits, command regulation imposes an implicit tax on residual pollution. See Richard Schmalensee, "Incentive Regulation for Electric Utilities," 4 *Yale J. Regulation* 1, 21 (1986).

vices produced by "dirtier" sources and industry sectors, moving consumer demand away from highly polluting firms and sectors towards less polluting firms and sectors.

### ADMINISTRATION AND GOVERNANCE

Command regulation requires the government to decide complex scientific, engineering, and economic issues in order to specify control requirements for different residuals in different waste streams to different media for many thousands of sources. Such determinations impose massive information-gathering and other decisional burdens on administrators. In the United States, they also provide fertile ground for complex litigation in the form of adversary rulemaking proceedings and protracted judicial review. This system creates a "democracy deficit" because important policy decisions are made through an arcane and costly bureaucratic–-regulatory–legal process accessible only to "insiders." Some of these drawbacks of command systems are less acute in those European and other developed countries that place greater reliance on negotiation between government and industry over regulatory requirements, although this corporatist approach suffers from its own form of democracy deficit. Further, as discussed by Stephen Breyer and Veerle Heyvaert and by Eckard Rehbinder in their contributions to this book, there has been an increasing centralization of command environmental regulation in Europe in the European Commission, which is beginning to create some of the same problems found in the US.[26]

Under EIS, detailed engineering and economic decisions about the appropriate level and method of pollution control for particular sources are decentralized, via the price system, to the source managers, who are generally far better equipped to make such decisions than are government officials, although this may not be the case for very small firms. Unlike government officials, managers of firms have strong incentives to achieve residuals limitations at least cost. EIS limit the role of government to basic "wholesale" decisions on the level of fees or the aggregate amount of pollu-

[26] See Richard B. Stewart, "Antidotes for the 'American Disease,'" 20 *Ecol. L. Q.* 87, 89–93 (1993) (arguing that the centralized environmental regulatory regime of the European Community is beginning to exhibit many of the problems characteristic of the US regulatory regime, such as the emergence of regulatory legalism and influential interest group lobbies).

tion quotas. In doing so, EIS can promote political accountability.[27] By invoking the price system, EIS also generate current, accurate, and public information as to the cost of environmental protection measures – an important consideration in any democratic decisionmaking process.[28]

Also, EIS can often be established and implemented more rapidly than command systems, which require thousands of detailed rules of conduct to be established. This feature of command systems makes them vulnerable to obsolescence in the face of changes in economic and environmental conditions. The greater flexibility associated with EIS makes them better able to accommodate such changes.

On the other hand, EIS deprive government of the power to dictate the residuals generated by individual sources. While this feature is in many respects a strength of EIS, regulators and environmental advocates often claim that there can be no assurance that regulation will be effective unless government has the power to exercise such source-specific control. Also, delegating pollution control decisions to market processes reduces the scope for public participation in and judicial review of particular control decisions at the "retail" level of the individual source, as pointed out by Professor Rehbinder in his contribution to this book.

Both command and EIS regulatory systems require that the government has accurate information about the residuals generated by sources in order to enforce compliance with regulatory requirements. The flexibility which EIS afford may require greater investment in monitoring of residuals, particularly if sources take advantage of this flexibility to change residuals limitations levels and/or methods frequently. Compliance with command regulations that rely on input-based or technology-based standards may be easier to monitor than requirements, including EIS requirements, based directly on the level of residuals generated. Direct, continuous monitoring

[27] See Ackerman and Stewart, "Reforming Environmental Law," at 1354 (arguing that EIS promotes more transparent decisionmaking by reducing environmental questions to "wholesale" determinations of what would constitute reasonable levels of pollution, which the authors contend is an issue both more relevant and more accessible to a democratic polity). But see Lisa Heinzerling, "Selling Pollution, Forcing Democracy," 14 *Stan. Env. L. J.* 300 (1995) (arguing that experience with the $SO_2$ trading provisions in the 1990 Clean Air Act Amendments reveals failure of market-based solutions to weaken special-interest dominance and promote democratic values in environmental policymaking).

[28] See Ackerman and Stewart, "Reforming Environmental Law," at 1342–43 (observing that EIS largely free central bureaucracy of information processing tasks, since most relevant information is internalized in prices).

of air pollution emissions can be costly, running to tens of thousands of dollars annually for large sources, although indirect methods of monitoring, including emissions factors and materials balances, may be feasible in some cases. Nonetheless, the significance of these burdens should not be overstated. The added costs of additional or more intensive monitoring under EIS are likely to be a fraction of the overall cost savings achieved by EIS.[29]

Unlike pollution fee systems, tradable quota systems require development of a well-functioning market to establish an accurate price for residuals and ensure that sources can readily buy or sell quota permits. The system must be designed to minimize transaction costs which would otherwise impede trading.[30] In order for a well-functioning market to develop, there must be a large number of sources; accordingly, a tradable quota system must generally cover a relatively wide geographic area. In order to keep track of the new property rights that it has created and ensure that sources' residuals levels do not exceed the number of quota permits they hold, the government must establish a system for recording trades and keeping accounts of permit holdings; the costs of doing so, however, are modest.[31] Government may also have to play an active market-maker role by promoting the development of exchanges, facilitating the establishment of futures markets by allowing "banking" for future use of issued but unused quotas, and maintaining a reserve of unissued quotas available for sale or auction in order to assure sources that a supply of permits will always be available. Steps may also be necessary to address potential problems of market power with respect to quotas.[32]

## GENERATION OF REVENUES FOR INVESTMENT

In the economist's view, sources that cannot afford the costs of complying with properly constituted regulatory requirements should shut down

[29] Generally, monitoring costs are borne in part by government whereas the costs savings associated with EIS accrue to the private sector. Under the US tradable quota system for $SO_2$ emissions, however, sources participating in the system are required to install monitoring equipment that continuously measures emissions.

[30] See Robert N. Stavins, "Transaction Costs and Tradable Permits," 29 *J. Env. Econ. & Mgmt.* 133 (1995).

[31] Some trading regimes are using electronic bulletin boards and other communications and clearinghouse mechanisms to reduce transactions costs substantially. See Timothy N. Cason and Lata Gangadharan, "An Experimental Study of Electronic Bulletin Board Trading for Emission Permits," 14 *J. Regulatory Econ.* 55–73 (1998).

[32] See Robert W. Hahn, "Market Power and Transferable Property Rights," 99 *Quarterly J. Econ.* 755 (1984).

because the environmental costs imposed on society by the residuals that they generate exceed the social benefits of continuing to operate the source, as measured by its profits. The political system, however, often fails to follow this logic. It is highly sensitive to the dislocation and other costs of closing plants or preventing individuals from continuing to engage in activities, such as driving automobiles, to which they have become accustomed. As previously noted, command regulation accordingly tends to impose less stringent regulatory requirements on older sources with relatively high control costs. From both an economic and an environmental perspective it would often be desirable to modernize or replace these sources with newer, less polluting, more resource-efficient substitutes. Because these existing sources are subject to less stringent requirements, however, they have no incentive to undertake such transformations, and might be unable to attract the private capital necessary to do so. Use by the government of general revenues to subsidize such efforts is subject to political constraints.

EIS can help to solve such problems by generating investment flows or revenue streams to finance environmental modernization. A tradable quota system automatically generates the necessary investment flows, as high-cost-control sources transfer funds and technology to low-cost-control sources in order to underwrite environmental modernization in exchange for surplus permits. For example, one of the objectives of the Los Angeles RECLAIM quota trading program for ozone precursor pollutants was to induce large sources such as refineries and chemical plants, which are already tightly controlled and face very high marginal control costs, to deploy their capital and know-how to finance and facilitate environmental modernization on the part of smaller sources that have lower marginal control costs but lack the know-how and capital to exploit this advantage.[33]

Under a fee system, revenues are collected by the government. These revenues can be used to reduce taxes on labor and capital to produce a tax structure with fewer distortions and reduce political opposition to environmental fees. Fee revenues, however, could also be recycled to promote environmental modernization at older, more heavily polluting sources. Fee revenues have been used for this purpose in some European countries and in developing countries such as China. Environmental taxes may be a politically more palatable way of providing such financing than use of appropriations from general revenues or reliance on tax preferences. A system of

[33] See Ackerman and Stewart, "Reforming Environmental Law," at 1360 (1985).

government grants to sources may, depending on the circumstances, be less successful than private sector investments and technology transfers under a tradable quota system in securing adoption of innovative, cost-effective means for limiting residuals.[34]

## REGULATORY EVOLUTION

The comparative performance of EIS and command systems also depends importantly on the evolutionary stage of a regulatory program. At an early stage, when there are few or no controls on residuals, use of technology-based command requirements can achieve impressive reductions at relatively low economic and administrative costs. As the regulatory program matures and efforts are made to achieve successively higher levels of residuals limitation, the command system yields diminishing returns relative to EIS.[35] The need to control sources more intensively and expand the scope of the command regulation system to include smaller sources creates increasing administrative and compliance costs. The rigidities and inefficiencies of the command system grow more acute. It becomes less and less effective in producing additional increments of environmental quality, and costs escalate. It is at this stage that the advantages of EIS become especially important. Freeing regulation from the command system's fixation on best available technology (BAT) measures will also promote better priority-setting, which also becomes more important as costs escalate. Under BAT, regulatory requirements tend to be driven largely by considerations of cost and technology, often ignoring differences in the seriousness of the environmental problem in question.[36] Under EIS, the level of fees or the amount of permits can readily be adjusted to take this important variable into account.

[34] The availability under tradable quota or fee systems of investment flows for environmental modernization can deflect political pressures that might otherwise operate to exempt older plants from permit or fee requirements altogether or to impose lower fees or allow them higher emissions per permit.

[35] Because the marginal costs of control generally rise, often sharply, as regulatory measures attempt to drive pollution levels towards zero, the cost of achieving additional increments of pollution reduction will increase no matter what regulatory instrument is used. The analysis here is comparative; command systems yield sharply diminishing returns relative to those obtained by EIS.

[36] See Ackerman and Stewart, "Reforming Environmental Law," at 1350.

## Principles of justice and other ethical issues

The primary claim made on behalf of EIS has been instrumental: that their use will significantly reduce the cost to society of achieving a given environmental objective. This claim has been challenged by those who are skeptical that EIS will provide effective environmental protection or that they will achieve the cost savings claimed. EIS, however, have also been criticized on non-instrumental grounds, including considerations of environmental and distributional justice and other ethical grounds, some of which appear to find substantial support in public sentiment.[37] These criticisms, however, do not disqualify EIS from use for environmental problems for which they are functionally well suited.

### PRINCIPLES OF JUSTICE

As previously noted, where there are sharp damage thresholds, "hot spots" created by high levels of residuals in a given locale may cause significant health and ecological damage. Under a welfare-maximizing approach to environmental regulation, such hot spots are a target of regulatory concern because the welfare losses that they cause may be high, although the costs of reducing such losses must also be factored into the regulatory decision. But, pollution hot spots also pose potential issues of justice. On one version of environmental justice, each individual has a right to a given minimum level of environmental protection, for example a right that her lifetime mortality risk from exposure to any given residual not exceed one in a million.[38] A second version of environmental justice focuses not on the absolute level of risk borne by any given individual but on the distribution of risks among individuals in different locations.[39] Thus, it may be argued that each indi-

[37] See generally T. H. Tietenberg, "Ethical Influences on the Evolution of the US Tradable Permit Approach to Pollution Control," 24 *Ecol. Econ.* 241–57 (1998).

[38] Such a standard would ignore increased risks from exposure to multiple residuals. See, e.g., Brian D. Israel, "Student Risk Assessment Article, An Environmental Justice Critique of Risk Assessment," 3 *NYU Env. L. J.* 469, 496 (1995) (arguing that the tendency to disregard multiple risks puts poor communities and communities of color at disproportionate risk).

[39] Legislation has been introduced in Congress calling for studies to identify those areas and population subgroups subject to the highest levels of toxic chemicals and to provide remediation for the people and property affected. See, e.g., H.R. No. 4584, "The Environmental Justice Act of 1998" (105th Cong., 2d Sess.).

vidual has a right to the same basic level of environmental protection regardless of where she lives. The provision in the US Clean Air Act for nationally uniform ambient air quality standards appears to reflect such a view.

For reasons previously noted, EIS, at least in the forms in which they have been applied in most cases, are not well suited to ensuring that residuals are below a given level and/or approximately the same in all localities.[40] In theory, command regulation could achieve either of these objectives. In practice, however, it fails to do so, in part for administrative reasons previously discussed,[41] and in part because of lack of political commitment to these objectives. Under the US system of nationally uniform ambient air quality standards, for example, there are many regions which have failed for decades to meet the standards. There are also wide and persistent variations in air quality among regions. The record in water pollution and toxic waste control is similar. This experience suggests that the two versions of environmental justice sketched above are not entirely compelling, and that the normative considerations underlying environmental protection policy are more complex than they allow. The claim that justice requires minimum levels of protection against specific environmental risks confronts the difficulty that any effort to define a "safe" exposure level or otherwise specify the content of right to environmental quality is arbitrary, particularly in the context of non-threshold risks. Although one can imagine gross levels of environmental insult that are morally repugnant, that is not a situation generally confronted, and accordingly should not dominate the choice of regulatory instruments in more typical situations. Further, as Professor Revesz notes in his contribution to this book, any sound right to health protection would have to be defined in terms of health risks in

[40] See generally Robert R. Kuehn, "The Environmental Justice Implications of Quantitative Risk Assessment," 1996 *U. Ill. L. Rev.* 103, 118–21 (discussing implications of current focus on individual pollutants for communities exposed to many differing pollutants and demographics of typically affected communities); Richard J. Lazarus, "Fairness in Environmental Law," 27 *Env. L.* 705 (1997) (arguing that "grandfathering" existing facilities, failing to assess cumulative exposure risks, and enforcing regulations more effectively in communities with political clout contribute to an inequitable environmental law system); Bradford C. Mank, "Environmental Justice and Title VI: Making Recipient Agencies Justify their Siting Decisions," 73 *Tul. L. Rev.* 787 (1999) (discussing environmental discrimination suits under Title VI of Civil Rights Act); Sandra Richardson, "Environmental Justice: A Tool for Community Empowerment," 27-Dec. *Colo. L.* 55 (1998) (surveying history of environmental justice and describing current trends).

[41] See p. 180 above.

general, or environmental health risks in general, rather than in terms of specific risk levels for each separate residual. Geographic disparities in risks are to some degree inevitable because of geographic, ecological, and developmental variables, and in at least some cases are arguably justified by countervailing variations in benefits, for example, the benefits of living in a warm and sunny climate such as that of Los Angeles notwithstanding high air pollution levels. Further, the existence and scope of the "hot spot" problem depends on the residual in question. In the case of some residuals, such as ozone-depleting chemicals and greenhouse gases, the hot spot problem does not exist at all. These considerations, taken together with the circumstance that the cost savings generated by EIS can in theory and have in practice, as discussed below, been used to provide overall higher levels of environmental protection, dictate that wide use of EIS should not be foreclosed by the justice-based considerations outlined above.

A third version of environmental justice has been advanced by advocacy groups in the United States, who contend that regulatory siting decisions have caused a disproportionate number of environmentally hazardous facilities to be located in poor and minority neighborhoods that lack political power or otherwise suffer from various forms of discrimination.[42] Adoption of EIS should ameliorate any such tendency because government would no longer control facility siting as a part of residuals regulation. Adoption of EIS would not, however, affect locational decisions that are driven as a function of lower land prices in localities where poor people and minorities tend to live.

Another justice-based consideration focuses on the distribution of environmental regulatory burdens among sources. Critics have objected to EIS on the ground that they enable wealthier sources to buy their way out of their obligations, much as the wealthy were able to buy their way out of conscription in the US Civil War. The premise underlying this criticism is that each source should do its best to reduce the discharge of residuals, and that the goal of "equal effort" is appropriately secured by command systems that tailor control requirements to the capabilities of each source. Assuming the justice of "equal effort," how is "effort" to be defined? In a market economy the prices of a firm's goods and services and its competitive position are determined primarily by its marginal production costs. Accordingly, the

[42] See generally Richard J. Lazarus, "Pursuing 'Environmental Justice': The Distributional Effects of Environmental Protection," 87 *Northwestern Univ. L. Rev.* 787 (1993).

increase in marginal costs attributable to regulatory measures is the most appropriate measure of burden, and hence of effort. Accordingly, environmental regulation measures should aim to equalize the marginal costs of residuals limitations among sources.[43] Command regulation results in wide variations in marginal control costs among different sources and industries. EIS, by contrast, promote "equal effort," appropriately defined, by imposing the same cost per unit of pollution on all sources, which will tend to equalize marginal control costs. There is no general reason to suppose that, under EIS, firms with large assets will, simply because they can "afford" to do so, choose to increase their total production costs and reduce their profits by paying additional sums to pollute at a level higher than the level at which marginal control costs equal the price of pollution.[44]

Still another justice-based consideration is the distribution of the costs and benefits of environmental programs among income classes. Environmental regulatory compliance costs generally have a regressive impact on overall income distribution. The incidence of benefits varies depending on the program in question, but many environmental programs confer disproportionate net benefits on wealthier people and are regressive in incidence.[45] Adoption of EIS in lieu of command-and-control regulation will lower the total costs of achieving a given overall level of residuals limitation, and in that respect have a relatively progressive effect. Fee systems, however, collect revenues from sources based on their residual pollution. Tradable quota systems in which quotas are auctioned off also require firms

[43] As explained previously, p. 182 above, a more sophisticated, risk-based regulatory system would equalize not the marginal costs of controlling pollution but the marginal costs of limiting the harms caused by pollution.

[44] Firms with large assets face strong competitive and capital market pressures to maximize profits. There may, however, be some types of sources, such as those owned and operated by public utilities or government authorities, which are not fully subject to such pressures and which may choose to pay to pollute above the cost-minimizing level in order to avoid disruptions of organizational routine. Since such sources will bear a greater economic burden than they would if they emulated the profit-maximizing behavior of other firms, there is no injustice presented by such behavior. Note that any such "slippage" must, however, be taken into account in the determination of appropriate fee levels.

[45] See, e.g., Lazarus, "Pursuing 'Environmental Justice'," 799 (1993) (arguing that environmental regulation frequently has a regressive distributional impact because it imposes significant controls on industry, which are borne in part by workers and consumers generally, in order to protect natural resources that often require leisure and wealth to be enjoyed, and also tends to concentrate harmful externalities in poor and minority communities, etc.). See also *Climate Change, Economic Instruments and Income Distribution* (OECD, 1995).

to make payments to the government in addition to the costs that they incur in limiting residuals. Although EIS reduce aggregate outlays for achieving residuals limitations, costs to regulated firms – control outlays plus government fees or permit costs – may well exceed control outlays under an equivalent command system. If so, and if these additional costs are passed on to consumers, the net impact may be regressive. The government, however, can use revenues from fees or auctions to offset this impact by, for example, reducing taxes on labor. Nonetheless, while fee payments or permit auction costs are transfer payments from the perspective of society as a whole, they are viewed as a costly burden by industry and will be strongly opposed.

One can design EIS to cushion the shocks involved in switching from a command system to EIS. Under a fee system, for example, revenues could be recycled to assist adversely affected plants and industries to modernize, or to retrain displaced workers. There may, however, be political impediments to such a strategy, at least in the US context. Recycling of fee revenues has, however, been practiced in a number of European nations and developing countries. Under a tradable quota system, transitional losses can be addressed by simply handing out quotas to existing sources, based on their existing permitted emissions or some other formula, rather than auctioning them off. All of the tradable quota programs in the United States have followed this "grandfathering" model, which may be objectionable on equity grounds by preferring existing firms over new entrants and making a "giveaway" of environmental resources that belong to the public.[46]

As discussed further below, the analysis of justice among sources of residuals is different in the international context where nations are often regarded as the "source" entity and the issue is one of relative effort and burden among different countries with sharply differing levels of wealth.

Intergenerational equity is another facet of distributional justice. As discussed by Geoffrey Heal in his contribution to this book, current rates of exploitation of renewable resources, including pollution of common resources such as the atmosphere and oceans, will in many cases have to be curtailed in order to ensure the sustainability of these resources and the ecological services that they provide for future generations. In principle, the decision on the extent to which exploitation should be curtailed could be made prior to and independent of the choice of implementing regulatory

[46] The potential economic inefficiencies associated with grandfathering are discussed at notes 116–17 below.

instrument. In practice, however, the use of EIS is likely to promote intergenerational equity by ensuring that resources are used more efficiently and lowering the costs of achieving sustainability objectives. By countering the "dead hand" of command systems and promoting innovation and investment in resource-efficient production methods and turnover of the capital stock, EIS can harness the market's creative destruction in the service of long-run environmental goals, as explained further in Professor Heal's contribution.

## OTHER ETHICAL OBJECTIONS TO ECONOMIC INCENTIVE SYSTEMS

EIS have been criticized on a number of ethical grounds in addition to the justice-based considerations discussed above. These criticisms, like the justice-based considerations, are not persuasive as applied to and should not preclude use of EIS to deal with environmental problems for which they are appropriate.

First, EIS, and in particular tradable quota systems, are critiqued on the ground that they improperly commodify the environment by treating it as an economic good on a par with products, disregarding and corroding the non-economic values that underlie public concern for the environment and government programs to protect it.[47] This criticism often rests on the mistaken premise that use of EIS necessarily implies that the environment should be treated as a commodity to human "consumers," and that the level of environmental protection should accordingly be determined by individuals' aggregate willingness to pay for environmental amenities versus other commodities. Economists have lent credence to this misapprehension by treating excessive environmental degradation solely as a market failure phenomenon and advocating use of EIS to supply the missing prices. But, use of EIS to promote environmental goals by no means implies that these goals should be determined by treating the environment on a par with marketed commodities. The goals of environmental protection programs should in principle and have in practice been based on non-commodity values.[48] In

[47] See Steven Kelman, *What Price Incentives?: Economists and the Environment* (Boston: Auburn House Publishing, 1981), 54–83.

[48] See Richard B. Stewart, "Regulation in a Liberal State: The Role of Non-Commodity Values," 92 *Yale L. J.* 1537, 1579 (1983) (pointing to the US Clean Air Act as an example of a program that properly considered non-commodity aspirations for a clean environment beyond the level that would be dictated by an interest analysis alone).

many instances, EIS are the most effective and appropriate means for realizing these non-commodity ends.

Critics of EIS nonetheless object that this means/ends distinction breaks down because the very act of pricing or trading things that have intrinsic, non-commodity values undermines those values. Thus, EIS have been analogized to the sale of sex or of babies.[49] This criticism is also off target. EIS do not involve sale of environmental quality. They deal with limited rights to use common resources for disposing of residuals generated by socially productive activities. The difference between EIS and command regulation is the mechanism for allocating these usufructory rights. The value that we place on distant vistas and clean water is the same whether the residuals limitations needed to preserve these environmental values are achieved through command regulation or through EIS.

A second ethical objection to EIS is that they assertedly endorse self-interest as the appropriate basis for actions with regard to the environment, and, as a result, "crowd out an individual's willingness to perform a task for its own sake."[50] Command regulation, by contrast, assertedly embodies judgments about right and wrong conduct, stigmatizes pollution and polluting activities, and bolsters "intrinsic motivation."[51] This criticism is also unpersuasive. EIS, no less than command regulation, have a firm moral as well as legal underpinning. Sources are obliged to pay discharge fees or obtain quota permits in order to make their appropriate contribution to the collective effort to limit aggregate residuals. Moreover, command-and-control regulation does not stigmatize or send any negative signal with respect to the residuals that are permitted by command standards. By contrast, EIS impose an economic cost on all residuals, reminding sources that any level of residuals may impose social costs. This message is most evident in the case of environmental taxes.

A third, related criticism is that EIS confer a "license to pollute [that] is

49 See generally, e.g., Margaret Jane Radin, "Market Inalienability," 100 *Harv. L. Rev.* 1849, 1857 (1987) (although Radin distinguishes market inalienability from the nontransferability of non-traditional property rights associated with various regulatory regimes, she points to the monetization of clean air and water to illustrate the scope of debate over market inalienability). Radin suggests that there are moral similarities between selling babies and selling environmental permits. See Margaret Jane Radin, "Address, What, if Anything, is Wrong with Baby Selling?" 26 *Pac. L.J.* 135, 142 (1995).

50 B. Free, "Motivation as a Limit to Pricing," 14 *J. Econ. Psych.* 635 (1993).

51 B. Free, "Tertium Datur: Pricing, Regulating and Intrinsic Motivation," 45 *Kykos* 161 (1992).

akin to selling indulgences" to sin.[52] Tradable permit systems have been equated with the sale of licenses to kill, maim, or engage in racial discrimination. It is asserted that EIS "seem to say, 'It is okay to pollute, provided you pay'; when the proper message is instead, 'It is wrong to pollute, even if you can afford to pay.'"[53] This objection has been raised in especially strong form by developing countries which have objected to global schemes for tradable permits in greenhouse gases (GHGs), whereby developed countries could satisfy their obligation to reduce GHGs by investing in reductions in developing countries.[54]

The discharge within proper limits of residuals from socially productive activities, however, can by no means be equated with sin or murder or racial discrimination. The laws of physics make such residuals an inevitable consequence of human activity. Zero residuals discharge is an unattainable and undesirable objective. Because all environmental regulatory systems allow some residuals to be generated, they all convey a "license to pollute." Under command regulation, such permissions are generally given away free, and no charge is imposed on the discharge of residuals that are permitted. Under EIS, by contrast, sources must pay or otherwise bear a cost for all of the residuals that they generate. Far from being a drawback, the requirement of payment for use of common resources is an important advantage of EIS on ethical as well as instrumental grounds.[55] Nor does use of EIS entail perpetuation of existing residuals levels. As discussed below, the US has successfully used tradable quota programs to eliminate lead in gasoline and reduce sulfur dioxide emissions by 50 percent.[56]

Critics of EIS invoke examples of repugnant conduct by an individual actor, such as destruction of a rare and beautiful ecosystem by a development project, or pollution by a factory at levels causing acute health injuries. They then contend that avoidance of such harm should be mandated, rather than leaving the matter to a contingent economic calculus by the actor. While correct, this observation affords no grounds against EIS for situations where their use is appropriate, including cases where the damage function does not pose sharp thresholds, many sources may be involved,

52 R. Goodin, "Selling Environmental Indulgences," 47 *Kykos* 573 (1994).
53 *Ibid.*, at 582.
54 See pp. 241–43 below.
55 Tradable permits programs that give away permits for free rather than auctioning them or otherwise requiring payment lack this ethical advantage.
56 See pp. 209–10, 212–14 below.

and the goal is to limit the aggregate residuals. In such cases, use of EIS is both functionally appropriate and ethically sound.

## Experience with economic incentive systems and regulatory reform

This section discusses the political economic obstacles to adoption of EIS to deal with environmental problems, reviews and evaluates the experience with EIS programs that have been adopted in Europe and the US, and outlines strategies of regulatory reform to promote wider use of EIS.

### OBSTACLES TO THE ADOPTION OF ECONOMIC INCENTIVES FOR ENVIRONMENTAL PROTECTION

Notwithstanding the advantages of EIS in addressing many environmental problems, environmental regulatory programs in most jurisdictions, including the US and the EU and under international environmental agreements, have relied almost entirely on command-and-control instruments. This pattern reflects tradition. Command measures have been the dominant regulatory instrument used to address other problems of industrialization, including unsafe and ineffective drugs, market power in sectors of the economy such as transportation and financial services, and unsafe vehicles and workplaces. Command regulation has a simple and appealing logic: people should be made to stop doing something bad. Command regulation promises effective control of behavior. Command environmental regulation has been successful in reducing substantially discharges of some air and water pollutants and preventing potentially large increases in others. It has also made significant progress in controlling hazardous wastes. Although crude and costly, the command system for environmental regulation has "worked."

The command regulatory tradition is reinforced by political and economic factors which impede widespread shift to EIS. For example, US environmental regulators have a strong vested stake in the command status quo. Adoption of EIS would reduce their power significantly. Decisions about how much each source should control would be delegated to sources via the price system. Although there is growing appreciation of the advantages of EIS, many regulators in the US and the EU as well as other jurisdictions still tend to believe that command systems are the best means of ensuring environmental protection, distrusting the uncertainty and "loss of control" associated with use of economic incentives. In Europe, where corporatist traditions are stronger, government officials have been receptive to using agreements with industry as a supplement or alternative to direct command regulation, as described by Eckard Rehbinder. On the other hand, as noted in the contributions to this book by Stephen Breyer and Veerle Heyvaert and by Roger van den Bergh, European Commission regulators have a strong interest in perpetuating and expanding centralized command controls.

Industry also has a substantial stake in the command regulatory status quo. Despite the burdens and other failings of command systems, the regulated community has devoted substantial efforts and resources towards managing them. A switch to EIS would create considerable uncertainty. Such a switch could also increase total regulatory compliance outlays, eliminate or reduce the regulatory advantages which older sources enjoy over new ones, and threaten older, economically marginal plants and industries. Moreover, politically powerful firms often are able to influence the structure and substance of command regulations in order to gain compliance cost advantages over competitors and thereby earn significant economic rents.[57] Fee and tradable quota systems can level the regulatory playing field by imposing the same price on pollution regardless of its source. But in doing so EIS would impose losses on those plants and industries which are subject to relatively less stringent regulatory burdens under the existing command regime; they and their workers will accordingly oppose a change in regulatory instruments. US quota trading programs have addressed this obstacle by giving quotas to existing firms gratis.

Environmental groups, especially in the United States, also tend to have a strong commitment to command regulation. Like regulators, they fear that EIS will produce uncertainty and "loss of control," along with enforcement difficulties. Under the citizen suit provisions found in all of the major US

[57] See Robert A. Leone and John E. Jackson, "The Political Economy of Federal Regulatory Activity, The Case of Water Pollution Control," in Gary Fromm ed., *Studies in Public Regulation* (New York: Basic Books, 1981), 231, 247. See also Robert A. Leone, *Who Profits: Winners, Losers, and Government Regulation* (New York: Basic Books, 1986), 3 (observing that different costs of compliance among firms might promote rent-seeking behavior on the part of firms who perceive opportunities to attain a competitive advantage through particular regulatory regulations). But see Leone and Jackson, "Political Economy," at 247 (observing that firms in practice frequently oppose even regulations that might give them a competitive advantage due to uncertainty over how regulatory agencies will implement regulations).

federal environmental regulatory statutes, environmental groups enjoy and frequently exercise the right to sue federal regulators to require them to issue regulations mandated by statute and to sue sources for non-compliance with command regulatory requirements. Under EIS, the role of citizen suits and other forms of litigation by environmental groups would be much reduced. Environmental advocates also fear that a system of discharge fees would make the cost of pollution control politically more visible, leading to a weakening of environmental protection programs.[58] In the European political context, environmental groups and environmentally oriented politicians appear to be less attached to command regulation and have shown increasing interest in environmental taxes.[59]

Recent work by Nathaniel Keohane, Richard Revesz, and Robert Stavins represents an attempt to create a more formal analytic framework to help explain the persistence of command-and-control regimes in spite of their acknowledged shortcomings and thus help explain the apparent paradox noted at the outset of this chapter.[60] They explain such regimes as the products of political markets in which legislators act as suppliers of environmental regulation, various interest groups provide the demand, and the "currency" of the market is support for a legislator's re-election.[61] Using this

[58] Robert N. Stavins, "What Can We Learn from the Grand Policy Experiment? Positive and Normative Lessons from $SO_2$ Allowance Trading," 12 *J. Econ. Persp.* 3, 75 (1998) (discussing preference by environmental groups for tradable permits over taxes because of the permits' tendency to "hide" the full costs of environmental regulation).

Adoption of discharge fees in the United States would also create political turf battles within both Congress and the administration. Would such fees be within the competence of the environmental committees of Congress and of EPA, or would they be subject to the jurisdiction of the taxing committees and administered by the Treasury? Similar problems do not exist in the case of tradable systems, which have been enacted by the environmental committees and administered by EPA.

[59] See Committee on Environment, Public Health and Consumer Protection of the European Parliament, Report: Environmental Taxes: Implementation and Environmental Effectiveness (1996) (recommending greater use of environmental taxes); Jonathan Golub, "Introduction," in Jonathan Golub ed., *New Instruments for Environmental Policy in the EU* (Routledge, 1998), 7, noting a "gradual conversion of environmental non-governmental organizations (NGOs) and Green Parties from an initial position of scepticism regarding new instruments towards one of guarded enthusiasm."

[60] See Keohane, Revesz, and Stavins, "Choice of Regulatory Instruments." The political and economic feasibility of economic instruments is also discussed in Todd J. Zywicki, "Environmental Externalities and Political Externalities: The Political Economy of Environmental Regulation and Reform," *Tul. L. Rev.* 845 (1999).

[61] See Keohane, Revesz, and Stavins, "Choice of Regulatory Instruments,"at 328–37.

model, they identify a number of factors favoring the perpetuation of command systems. Existing industry tends to favor command systems because they can be designed to impede entry of new competitors and allow existing firms to reap economic rents. EIS, especially environmental taxes, may impose higher costs on industry than equivalent command measures. The authors also find that many environmental groups have normative, strategic, and technical reasons for preferring command systems. Legislators are familiar with command systems: such systems tend to hide the costs of regulation compared to EIS; they are well suited for use in symbolic politics; they can assure politicians more control over administrative, economic, and social outcomes and their distributional consequences. The authors note, however, a number of emerging trends favoring use of EIS, including greater recognition by politicians and the public of the costs of command systems and the advantages of market-based incentive systems.

## THE DEVELOPMENT OF AND EXPERIENCE WITH ECONOMIC INCENTIVES FOR ENVIRONMENTAL PROTECTION

Notwithstanding the obstacles summarized above, there have been in recent years substantial moves to adopt EIS to deal with a range of environmental problems. In the United States, EIS have primarily taken the form of tradable quota systems. In Europe and elsewhere, the emphasis has been on taxes and fees on residuals. Thus, there is a striking disparity in the relative use of taxes and tradable quotas in Europe and the United States, notwithstanding the many functional similarities of the two types of EIS. This difference appears to reflect different political and social traditions. Europeans have tended to be more respectful of the power of the State and reluctant to see its responsibility for securing social and ethical objectives delegated to the market. Americans tend to take the opposite view.

### *Environmental taxes and fees*

Environmental taxes and fees are increasingly being used to address a variety of environmental problems in Western Europe, Russia, and a number of developing countries. Charges may be imposed directly on residuals, based on the amount of pollution discharged or waste generated. Alternatively, charges may be imposed on inputs to a polluting activity (such as a tax on motor vehicle fuels), or on polluting substances in an input (such as a tax on the carbon or sulfur content of fuels), or on a final product (such as a tax on motor vehicles or disposable products); in the latter case, the relation between the charge and residuals generated is more indirect.

Until recently, environmental taxes and fees were used primarily for revenue-raising purposes; they were generally set at levels too low to produce appreciable reductions in residuals levels.[62] For example, between 1980 and 1994, the use in OECD countries of environmental taxes, as measured in tax revenues as a percentage of GDP, rose only negligibly.[63] In countries such as Poland and China, the lack of strong government administrative capabilities for monitoring and enforcement has also been a factor. In recent years, however, a number of European countries have adopted significantly higher environmental taxes with the aim of reducing pollution and other residuals.

There is little evidence that environmental tax or fee schemes will entirely replace command regulation in the near term.[64] Such programs have been an "add on," imposing prices on residuals allowed by command programs. Further, nations have retained many of the subsidies which favor environmentally harmful activities, such as use of "dirty" coal, airline fuels, and pesticides.[65] Nevertheless, it is worth noting some of the efforts that have been undertaken to impose direct or indirect charges on tax residuals for incentive purposes.

Much of the focus of environmental taxes in Europe has been on air pollution, which has similarly been the focus of tradable quota systems in the US. European countries have imposed high taxes on gasoline, which has had the indirect effect of limiting automobile air pollution. They have also adopted higher taxes on leaded fuels; such taxes have been a major reason for the rise in unleaded gasoline use from below 1 percent in 1986 to over 65 percent by 1995.[66] Several European nations, including Sweden, Norway, and Denmark, have imposed taxes on the carbon content of fuels with the

[62] See National Academy of Public Administration, *The Environment Goes to Market*, 72–112 (analyzing pollution charge programs in Russia); *Environmental Taxes in OECD Countries* (OECD, 1995); *Managing the Environment: The Role of Economic Instruments* (OECD, 1994).

[63] See 25 *INTERTAX* 28 (1997).

[64] See *Environmental Taxes in OECD Countries.*

[65] See Jonathan Golub, "New Instruments for Environmental Policy in the EU, Introduction and Overview," in Golub, *New Instruments for Environmental Policy*, 1, 10.

[66] Jos Delbeke and Hans Bergman, "Environmental Taxes and Charges in the EU," in Golub, *New Instruments for Environmental Policy*, 245.

objective of limiting carbon dioxide ($CO_2$) emissions.[67] Efforts to implement an EC-wide carbon tax regime have foundered, however, on the unwillingness of some Member States to cede tax power to the European Community and incompatibilities among Member States' environmental priorities and industrial infrastructures, as well as opposition from industry sectors concerned about the impact of new taxes on their competitiveness.[68]

One successful example of the use of environmental taxes for incentive purposes is Sweden's tax on the sulfur content of fuel oil, which led to a 30 percent reduction in sulfur content between 1990 and 1992; administrative charges were reported as only 1 percent of revenue. Sweden has also instituted a significant tax on nitrogen oxide emissions, which resulted in a 40 percent reduction in emissions within two years.[69] The Netherlands has implemented levies on noise, air, and water pollution as well as taxes on motor vehicles,[70] and recently issued a white paper calling for further "greening taxes."[71] Denmark subjects CFCs and halons to environmental taxes, and has instituted a partial shift from taxes on wages to taxes on extraction of ground and surface waters, wastewater discharges, generation of solid waste, and shopping bags.

There is debate, however, as to whether taxes, taken alone, will effect change, or whether the revenues need to be earmarked for environmental protection investments in order to ensure environmental improvement.

67 See *$CO_2$ Emissions from Road Vehicles* (OECD, 1997), 60–83; *Economic/Fiscal Instruments: Taxation (i.e., Carbon/Energy)* (OECD, 1996); *A Comparison of Carbon Taxes in Selected OECD Countries* (OECD, 1993). One analyst found that the Swedish tax had resulted in limitations of $CO_2$ emissions in some sectors. F. Bohlin, "The Swedish Carbon Dioxide Tax: Effects on Fuel Use and Carbon Dioxide Emissions," 15 *Biomass and Energy* 213 (1998).

68 See Delbeke and Bergman, "Environmental Taxes and Charges in the EU," 242, 244–45; Angela Liberatore, "Arguments, Assumptions and the Choice of Policy Instruments," in Bruno Dente ed., *Environmental Policy in Search of New Instruments* (Dordrecht: Kluwer, 1995), 61–64.

69 See *Evaluating Economic Instruments for Environmental Policy* (OECD, 1997); *Managing the Environment: The Role of Economic Instruments* (OECD, 1994), 74; K. Lovgren, "Instruments for Air Pollution Control in Sweden," in G. Klaassen and F. Forsund eds., *Economic Instruments for Air Pollution Control* (Dordrecht and Boston: Kluwer Academic Publishers, 1994); T. Sterner and L. Hoglund, "Refunded Emission Payments: A Hybrid Instrument with some Attractive Properties" (Resources for the Future Working Paper, 1998).

70 *See Environmental Taxes in OECD Countries*, 10–11; sources cited in note 69 above.

71 See 27 *Financial Times World Tax Report* 21 (Feb. 1998).

The Dutch $CO_2$ tax revenues were not earmarked, and resulted in only negligible emissions reductions; on the other hand, the Dutch water and fuel levies, while not earmarked, were effective. The Swedish nitrogen oxides tax, whose revenues are recycled to sources based on their energy production (with the net result that sources with higher emissions effectively make payments to sources with lower emissions) has had a strong impact in reducing emissions.[72]

France's recent air pollution taxes earmark revenues for development of pollution prevention and reduction techniques and attendant monitoring techniques.[73] France has also taken steps to end anti-environmental tax subsidies, eliminating, for instance, a twenty-year land tax exemption to farmers who drained wetlands.[74]

Denmark implemented a treatment fee for polluted waste waters in 1987, and noted a 12 percent decrease in waste waters by 1989. When, however, the government attempted to expand the program by taxing more types of waste, the amount of waste taxed did not rise nearly as much as expected.[75] Instead, illegal dumping of waste increased, as did use of waste in road building; in other words, expanding the tax program merely increased noncompliance. Furthermore, it remains unclear whether the decrease in waste production that initially occurred was a result of the new tax regime or was due to unrelated technical innovations or regulatory changes.[76]

The experience of Poland also illustrates some of the difficulties in assessing the effectiveness of environmental taxes and charges. Although an extensive pollution fee system has been in place since the 1970s, evaluators lack basic data about administration, enforcement, and actual emissions under the program. Moreover, it is "difficult to identify the effect of the fee system separately," as it cannot be distinguished from the effects of changes

[72] See *Environmental Taxes in OECD Countries*, 38, 13.

[73] See *Environmental Taxes in OECD Countries*, 27.

[74] See Cyrille de Klemm and Clare Shine, *Biological Diversity Conservation and the Law: Legal Mechanisms for Conserving Species and Ecosystems* (Cambridge: IUCN, the World Conservation Union, 1993), 241. This trend extends beyond Europe; Brazil recently repealed a tax break for cattle farmers to convert rainforests to pastures. But other countries recently have increased tax subsidies in order to stimulate development investments in resource extraction and use. Following on the success of provisions providing incentives for mining, Argentina recently passed tax amendments heavily favoring logging projects. See 8 *Int. Tax Rev.* 41 (1997).

[75] See *Managing the Environment: The Role of Economic Instruments*, 64.

[76] *Ibid.*

in enforcement levels, shifts in economic policy, and growth in industry, although these same confounding factors also make it difficult to evaluate the performance of command systems.[77]

Environmental taxes suffer from the inherent problem that, as they succeed, tax revenue declines. If such revenues are used as substitutes for other revenues of other taxes, the reliability of the fiscal system may be undermined. If revenues are used to fund investments in residuals reduction, revenue declines may affect the success of the overall program. Further, there are, as noted previously, difficulties in properly recycling revenues to sources. If they go back to sources in the form of unconditioned subsidies, the effectiveness of taxes in reducing residuals may be blunted. If they are given to those enterprises with greatest need for assistance, they often end up wasted on old plants with dim prospects for environmental or economic success, and inhibit the ability of the market to cull inefficient performers. Several additional factors have limited the scope and effectiveness of environmental taxes in Europe. Governments are concerned that across-the-board tax increases on fuels and other such "basics" are regressive, and therefore care must be taken to avoid burdening low-income groups. Furthermore, political resistance from industry sectors that would be especially hard hit by environmental taxes has led governments to take steps to reduce their impact, and hence their incentive effect. An OECD study of carbon taxes indicates that while some of the taxes introduced were high, their ultimate effect was mitigated by adjustments of other energy taxes, extensive exemptions from the carbon tax, and grants of eligibility for various tax refunds.[78] In addition, governments try to avoid overly complicated tax structures. The net result is that the environmental taxes and fees imposed generally are below the levels needed to meet environmental goals.[79]

Nevertheless, the growing use of environmental taxes for incentive purposes in Europe is significant, even if it is too early to say that they have or will have an overall important role in providing incentives to limit residuals.

There has been no significant use of environmental taxes or fees in the United States, with the exception of taxes on CFCs and other ozone-depleting substances (ODS). These taxes were adopted not for incentive

[77] *Ibid.* at 136.

[78] See *A Comparison of Carbon Taxes in Selected OECD Countries.*

[79] See Diego Piacentino, "Carbon Taxation and Global Warming," in J. B. Opschoor ed., *Economic Incentives and Environmental Policies: Principles and Practice* (1994), 125.

purposes but to recoup the economic rents enjoyed by ODS producers as a result of the regulatory phase-out (through use of a tradable quota system) of ozone-depleting substances; nonetheless, the taxes have had incentive effects.[80] Fees for treatment of industrial water pollution discharges to municipal waste treatment plants have also had some incentive effects.

### *Tradable quotas and credits*

In contrast to Europe, the United States has made predominant use of quota and credit trading EIS rather than taxes or fees. The systems used in the United States have focused on air pollution control and have tended to follow a strategy of allocating quotas or credits by "grandfathering" existing sources.

The Environmental Protection Agency (EPA) has authorized, by regulation, various emissions trading and credit programs to introduce a degree of flexibility in the intricate command regulatory system for air pollution regulation imposed by the federal Clean Air Act.[81] When an entirely new plant is located in a region that does not comply with federal air quality standards, the Clean Air Act requires that its emissions be offset by reductions from existing sources. Under EPA's offset trading program, a new source can contract with existing sources for such reductions. Under the "bubble" program, an existing plant can reallocate existing command-and-control requirements for the same air pollutant among different emission sources within the plant. Also, two different plants located in the same region can similarly reallocate control requirements. Under EPA's "netting" program, an existing plant that increases its emissions by, for example, adding a new unit can avoid the regulatory requirements otherwise applicable to new or modified pollution sources by obtaining offsetting emissions reductions elsewhere in the same plant, creating an implicit internal market in emissions reduction credits (ERCs).

Under the netting and bubble programs, many internal trades of ERCs

[80] See note 114 below and accompanying text p. 215.

[81] *See* Richard Liroff, *Reforming Air Pollution Regulations: The Toil and Trouble of EPA's Bubble* (Washington D.C.: Conservation Foundation, 1986); Thomas H. Tietenberg, *Emissions Trading: An Exercise in Reforming Pollution Policy* (Washington D.C. and Baltimore: Resources for the Future; distributed by Johns Hopkins University Press, 1985).

have occurred within plants, resulting in significant cost savings estimated to run to billions of dollars.[82] External trades between plants have been much more limited. The development of a more robust external trading market has been impaired because such trades are often subject to stringent regulatory oversight and control on a case-by-case basis. Regulators, strongly backed by environmental groups, have generally insisted that trades must not worsen air quality in any location, even if the increase in local concentrations would not violate health-based ambient air quality standards, and also must not increase aggregate emissions. Such regulatory overhang significantly increases transaction costs, inhibiting trading and diminishing the benefits that it could provide.[83] This experience illustrates the reluctance of regulators and environmental groups to relinquish the particularized control over individual sources which command regulation affords.

The US EPA's program to phase out lead additives in gasoline during the 1980s used an emissions reduction credit system under which refiners who phased out lead faster or to a greater extent than required by the regulatory schedule could sell credits to other refiners who found it more costly or difficult to meet the schedule.[84] This program was highly successful and accomplished compliance cost savings running to several hundreds of millions of dollars.[85] Many of the savings came from "banking" provisions, added to the program in 1985, under which refineries could deposit credits for later use or sale.[86] Significantly, the cost savings and flexibility afforded

[82] See Vivien Foster and Robert W. Hahn, "Efficient Markets and Smog Control," 38 *J. L. & Econ.* 19, 21 (1995) (estimating cost-savings of $0.5 to $12 billion, in mid-1980s dollars, mainly from intrafirm trading).

[83] See Scott Atkinson and Thomas Tietenberg, "Market Failure in Incentive-Based Regulation: The Case of Emission Trading," 21 *J. Env. Econ. & Mgmt.* 17 (1991).

[84] See Barry D. Nussbaum, "Phasing Down Lead in the United States: Mandates, Incentives, Trading and Banking," in *Climate Change: Designing a Tradable Permit System* (OECD, 1992), 25.

[85] See Robert W. Hahn and Gordon Hester, "Marketable Permits: Lessons for Theory and Practice," 16 *Ecol. L.Q.* 361, 380–91 (1989); Robert W. Hahn and Robert N. Stavins, "Incentive-Based Environmental Regulation: A New Era For an Old Idea?" 18 *Ecol. L.Q.* 1, 17 (1991).

[86] EPA estimates that trading provisions saved industry about $65 million and banking another $200 million (on compliance costs of about $2.6 billion). See Tom Tietenberg, "Tradable Permits and the Control of Air Pollution in the United States, Written for the 10th Anniversary Jubilee Edition of the Zeitschrift Furangewandte Unweltforschung" (working paper downloadable at *http://www.colby.edu/personal/thtieten*) (visited 7 June 1999), 4–5.

by trading and banking secured industry agreement to a faster and deeper phase out schedule than would have been possible under a command system. This use of EIS enabled the EPA to "buy" a control level 50 percent more stringent than that which would be achieved under a traditional command approach, with "no increase in economic cost or political resistance."[87]

California has adopted a quota trading program (RECLAIM) to reduce emissions of sulfur dioxide, nitrogen oxides, and hydrocarbons in the Los Angeles basin in order to reduce high levels of ozone-type smog that are greatly in excess of federal air quality standards.[88] The program was endorsed by regulators, industry, and many environmental groups out of a belief that it would be too costly and administratively infeasible to achieve significant additional pollution reductions through further intensification of traditional command regulation. RECLAIM has achieved a mixed record of success.[89] Internal trading within firms is fairly vigorous; external trading among firms represents a much smaller share of all trades.[90] Critics suggest that expensive monitoring requirements and intensive regulations have hampered external trades.[91] Trading is also impeded by regulatory provisions designed to avoid "hot spot" problems; coastal facilities are restricted from using inland permits, driving up the costs of coastal permits.[92] Also, between 10 and 20 percent of any credits traded are automatically "retired," reducing emissions but also reducing the incentive to trade. RECLAIM provisions that allow stationary sources to obtain credits against their obligations by purchasing and retiring old, high-polluting automobiles have been challenged in court by environmental justice groups, who claim that nearby

[87] See Jonathan B. Wiener, "Global Environmental Regulation: Instrument Choice in Legal Context," 108 *Yale L.J.* 677, 715 n. 151 (1999) (citations omitted).

[88] South Coast Air Quality Management District ("SCAQMD"), Draft RECLAIM Executive Summary, 8 March 1993.

[89] See generally T. Klier et al., "A Mixed Bag: Assessment of Market Performance and Firm Trading Behavior in the NOX RECLAIM Programme," 40 *J. Env. Plan. & Mgmt.* 751 (1997).

[90] In calendar year 1997, RECLAIM oversaw 136 intercompany NOX trades (9.176 tons) and 17 intercompany SOX trades (5, 077 tons), compared with intracompany ("bubble") trades of 38, 652 tons of NOX and 15, 614 tons of SOX. See SCAQMD, Annual Reclaim Audit (March 1998), at 2–3.

[91] See, e.g., RECLAIM Critique Required Reading for Advocates of Emissions-Trading, Air Water Pollution Report, Efficient Markets and Smog Control (24 August 1995).

[92] Timothy N. Cason and Lata Gangadharan, "An Experimental Study of Electronic Bulletin Board Trading for Emission Permits," 14 *J. Regulatory Econ.* 55–73 (1998).

communities are disproportionately and unfairly affected by the continued emissions from the stationary sources.[93]

Experience with RECLAIM also demonstrates that thin trading markets in quotas and small volume trades suffer from high transaction costs.[94] For example, the costs of finding suitable trading partners are much higher in thin markets.[95] Fixed costs, such as administrative filing and compliance certification requirements, which do not vary by transaction size, disproportionately affect small volume trades. Learning costs are high; one study found that facilities must perform fifteen trades to build sufficient knowledge to lower transaction costs significantly.[96] One commentater, however, found that after several years of experience under the program brokers and electronic bulletin boards had succeeded in greatly reducing transactions costs.

Initially, RECLAIM's sulfur dioxide ($SO_2$) and nitrogen oxides (NOX) trading program was limited to a few hundred large facilities. However, its hydrocarbon trading program for emissions of volatile organic compounds (VOCs) included a much larger number of sources. One study found that the RECLAIM program for hydrocarbons purportedly failed because it tried to focus on very small emission units, and covered a wide variety of very small sources. As evidenced by the $SO_2$ trading program and the early EPA emission offset trading programs, emissions trading will only work for those industries with sufficient expertise to accurately monitor and quantify their emissions.[97] Another study found that problems with VOC monitoring hindered RECLAIM efforts to set up an independent market for VOCs.[98]

93 "Market Incentives; States to Expand Trading Programs," 159 *Chem. Wk.* (10 September 1997); see generally Perry S. Goldschein, "Going Mobile: Emissions Trading gets a Boost from Mobile Source Emission Reduction Credits," 13 *UCLA J. Env. L & Pol'y* 225 (1994/1995).

94 Vivien Foster and Robert W. Hahn, "Designing More Efficient Markets: Lessons from Los Angeles Smog Control," 38 *J.L. & Econ.* 19, 35 (1995).

95 Thomas H. Klier et al., "What can the Midwest Learn from California about Emissions Trading?," *Chicago Fed. Letter* (August 1997).

96 Lata Gangadharan, "Transactions Costs in Tradable Emissions Markets: An Empirical Study of the Regional Clean Air Incentives Market in Los Angeles" (University of Southern California Working Paper, 1997).

97 Jeffrey C. Fort and Cynthia A. Faur, "Can Emissions Trading Work beyond a National Program? Some Practical Observations on the Available Tools," 18 *U. Pa. J. Int. Econ. L.* 463 (1997).

98 See Barry D. Solomon and Hugh S. Gorman, "State-level Air Emissions Trading: The Michigan and Illinois Models," 48 *J. Air & Waste Mgmt. Assoc.* 1156, 1161 (1998).

There is growing interest in states other than California in developing state and regional programs for trading nitrogen oxide and hydrocarbon emissions. Illinois promulgated the final rule for its Emissions Reduction Trading Program for volatile organic materials (VOM) in November 1997. Under this "cap and allocate" program, major sources of VOM will receive allocations 12 percent lower than their baseline emissions and will be required to possess allocations equal to their actual emissions at the end of each season.[99]

The Illinois program offers two major advantages over RECLAIM. Illinois facilities had already developed the necessary capacity and expertise to monitor VOCs through long regulation of this aspect of air pollution. Also, the market is not limited to the larger sources that received the initial quota allocations; smaller sources, often hardest-pressed to meet controls, are free to purchase allocations.[100] Michigan and New Jersey have also recently instituted trading programs similar to those of Illinois.[101] The Ozone Transport Commission (OTC), a consortium of Northeastern states, has developed model rules to facilitate interstate emissions credit trading. Credits can be traded or banked, and facilities not initially covered by the program may opt in. The main restriction on trading is that facilities, irrespective of their credit holdings, are barred from exceeding federal and state ambient standards. While this constraint avoids "hot-spot" problems, it will also limit trades.[102]

The most far-reaching and successful US trading program is the sulfur dioxide allowance trading system adopted by the 1990 Amendments to the Clean Air Act. This program will reduce $SO_2$ emissions nationwide by 50 percent within ten years.[103] Existing fossil fuel electric generating plants are

[99] See Fort and Faur, "Can Emissions Trading Work?" (describing and critiquing Michigan and Illinois trading programs); Solomon and Gorman, "State-level Air Emissions Trading."

[100] See Soloman and Gorman, "State-level Air Emissions Trading," at 1162 (describing EPA disapproval of initial Michigan plan for failure to establish explicit baselines for emissions and control to prevent environmental regression in certain areas of state); Fort and Faur, "Can Emissions Trading Work?" at 469.

[101] See "First Open Market Emissions Trading Program Brings Brokers to New Jersey," *Energy Report*, 17 March 1997; "Airbank Completes First Michigan Emissions Credit Trades," *Energy Daily*, 5 May 1998.

[102] See Tietenberg, "Tradable Permits and the Control of Air Pollution."

[103] See Clean Air Act, Title IV; Nancy Kate, "The US Acid Rain Control Allowance Trading System," in OECD, *Climate Change: Designing a Tradable Permit System*.

given $SO_2$ allowances based on their energy input, rather than their historical emissions; under the allocation formula, sources with the same energy input receive the same number of allowances, regardless of their historical $SO_2$ emissions.[104] New sources are not given allowances but must purchase them. Allowances are issued annually. Each allowance entitles the holder to emit one ton of $SO_2$ in the year of issuance or a subsequent year. The number of allowances issued to sources is reduced over time in order to achieve the program's overall reduction target. Sources that reduce emissions more quickly or by greater amounts than required by the phase-down schedule can sell their excess allowances to others, or bank them for future use or sale.[105] In order to stimulate the development of an allowances trading market and assure a supply of allowances for new sources, EPA periodically auctions a limited stock of reserved allowances. By reducing compliance costs and giving existing sources valuable property rights, the use of tradable quotas helped to break a decade-long political deadlock on legislation to reduce sulfur emissions in order to curb acid deposition,[106] providing another example of how use of EIS can pay environmental dividends. A commodity market in sulfur allowances has been successfully established. In 1996, over 4 million tons of allowances were transferred between unrelated parties.[107] But most cost savings have come from internal trades within utilities and the flexibility which the program has afforded utilities to reduce emissions in the most cost-effective way, including through fuel switching, use of low sulfur or washed coal, energy conservation measures, and development of "scrubbers", alternatives that would not have been feasible under "one size fits all" BAT controls.[108] Overall, control costs under the program are billions of dollars less than they would be under the

[104] See Clean Air Act, Section 404(a)(2), 42 U.S.C. § 7651(a)(2).

[105] For detailed discussion of the $SO_2$ program, see Richard Schmalensee et al., "An Interim Evaluation of Sulfur Dioxide Emissions Trading," 12 *J. Econ. Persp.* 53 (1998) (summarizing empirical analysis of compliance costs and allowance market performance); Paul L. Joskow et al., "The Market for Sulfur Dioxide Emissions," 88 *Am. Econ. Rev.* 669 (1998) (finding that $SO_2$ trading market had become efficient by 1994).

[106] Schmalensee et al., "Interim Evaluation," at 56, suggest that allowances were given to utilities because the only alternative would have been an electricity tax that forced customers of "clean" utilities to help pay the clean-up costs of "dirty utilities."

[107] See Stavins, "What Can We Learn from the Grand Policy Experiment?" 69, 71 (1998) (surveying data on $SO_2$ trading program).

[108] Dallas Burtow, "Trading Emissions to Clean the Air: Exchanges Few but Savings Many," *Resources* (Winter, 1996), 3; Dallas Burtow, "The $SO_2$ Emissions Trading Program: Cost Savings Without Allowance Trades," 14 *Contemp. Econ. Pol'y* 79 (1996).

command-and-control alternative of requiring universal stack gas scrubbing.[109] It is expected that additional savings – up to 20 percent of baseline estimates, or another billion dollars – will be achieved as the trading program matures. The program has also been a success from an environmental perspective: for example, 1996 emissions, at 5.43 million tons, were well below the applicable regulatory cap of 8.12 million tons.[110]

While sulfur dioxide emissions are also subject to command-and-control limitations established by prior law, these limitations have not significantly constrained trading or the use of the flexibility provided by the allowance program.[111] Some states have attempted to limit allowance trading in particular regions in order to prevent the threat of "hot spots" or to insist on the use of local high-sulfur coal in order to protect local economies.[112] Although these efforts largely have been unsuccessful, the uncertainty that they engender may chill the trading market.

EPA has implemented a system of tradable emission permits in CFCs and other ozone-depleting substances under the Clean Air Act in order to phase out use of these chemicals pursuant to the requirements of the Montreal Protocol and the London Agreement, implemented domestically through the Clean Air Act.[113] Producers and consumers were allocated initial allowances based on 1986 levels; these allowances are reduced throughout the program's duration. Allowances are tradable between consumers and pro-

[109] See Stavins, "What Can We Learn from the Grand Policy Experiment?" 69, 70 (estimating savings of up to \$1 billion per year as compared to command-and-control baseline); Burtow, The "$SO_2$ Emissions Trading Program" (noting that estimated $SO_2$ trading program costs of \$1 billion in 1997, \$1.3 billion in 2000, and \$2.2 billion in 2010 represent savings of 40 percent from command-and-control baseline, with promise of substantially more savings as allowance trading increases).

[110] A. Denny Ellerman et al., *1996 Update on Compliance and Emissions Trading under the U.S. Acid Rain Program* (Center for Energy and Environmental Policy Research, Massachusetts Institute of Technology, 1997), at 2. 1996 emissions were, however, 6 percent higher than in 1995 as low allowance costs encouraged users to purchase cheaper, higher-sulfur coal and use allowances to lower their increased emissions.

[111] Ger Klaassen and Andries Nentjes, "Sulfur Trading under the 1990 CAAA in the US," 153 *JITE* 384, 407 (1997).

[112] See James J. Winebrake et al., "The Clean Air Act's Sulfur Dioxide Emissions Market: Estimating the Costs of Regulatory and Legislative Intervention," 17 *Resource & Energy Econ.* 239, 253 (1995); *Alliance for Clean Coal* v. *Miller*, 44 F.3d 591 (7th Cir. 1995) (striking down Illinois statute mandating use of local coal in some Illinois facilities).

[113] See Robert W. Hahn and Albert M. McGartland, "The Political Economy of Instrument Choice: An Examination of the US Role in Implementing the Montreal Protocol," 83 *Northwestern Univ. L. Rev.* 592 (1989).

ducers, and even across international borders. Although trades are confidential, estimates suggest that about 10 percent of the total permits were being traded by 1993. Congress, noting that the program had created "windfall profits" among the major producers allocated allowances, imposed an excise tax, providing further incentives to reduce CFC and halon use.[114]

There is also developing interest in the use of tradable quotas to deal with water pollution. There have been experimental uses of this technique in a number of countries, including China and the United States.[115]

If there are efficient markets for quotas and for the commodities produced by sources, then allocating quotas by "grandfathering" existing sources should not impede entry by new sources that must buy quotas from existing sources.[116] But to the extent that these conditions do not obtain, entry barriers and additional inefficiencies may be created by use of grandfathering rather than auctions. Because established firms receive rents from the sales of permits under such a system, it has also been argued that grandfathering may diminish the incentives for such firms to pursue innovations that might lead to a reduction in such rents.[117] Also, use of auctions rather than grandfathering creates revenues that government can use to offset existing distortionary taxes; recent work suggests that such

[114] See Tietenberg, "Tradable Permits and the Control of Air Pollution," at 6 (noting that program is unique in its "simultaneous application of permit and tax systems") (citation omitted).

[115] See United States Environmental Protection Agency, "Executive Summary, Draft Framework for Watershed-Based Trading," available at *http://www.epa.gov/owow/watershed/summary.html.*

[116] Under such conditions, existing sources will have neither the incentive nor the ability to discriminate against newcomers. Entrants will only enter the market if they are more efficient than an incumbent; this is the case under both auction and "grandfathering" schemes. See, e.g., Carolyn Fischer, Suzi Kerr, and Michael Toman, "Using Emissions Trading to Regulate US Greenhouse Gas Emissions: An Overview of Policy Design and Implementation Issues" (Resources for the Future, Discussion Paper, July 1998), 1, 6.

[117] See Peter Cramton and Suzi Kerr, "Tradable Carbon Permit Auctions: How and Why to Auction Not Grandfather" (Resources for the Future Discussion Paper, May 1998). Those who criticize grandfathering based on its dynamic effects on innovation argue that because established firms receive the rents from the sale of tradable permits under a grandfathering scheme, such firms will have less incentive to pursue innovations that might lead to less demand for tradable permits. Setting aside the fact that other firms would have incentives to innovate, there is also considerable ambiguity surrounding the effects innovation would have on the price of tradable permits.

"revenue recycling" may in fact be necessary for full efficiency gains to be realized.[118]

Another problem is uncertainty surrounding the nature of the property rights conferred by trading programs. Even in the $SO_2$ trading program, which has delineated property rights much more clearly than other trading programs,[119] the statute is explicit that allowances are not "property," but only a limited authorization, amendable by Congress. It is an open question whether government actions to revoke or limit existing allowances or credits could implicate the Takings Clause of the US Constitution and require payment of compensation.[120] At a more pragmatic level, the uncertainties and delays created by programs that require regulatory approval of individual trades and the risk of basic changes in emissions trading programs may chill investment. Furthermore, the property value of the credits depends also on ensuring widespread compliance with the program, which in turn requires extensive monitoring.[121] While monitoring adds to program costs, better compliance provides environmental benefits. Further, the interest of allowance or credit holders in preventing cheating, which would reduce the value of their holdings, creates an important new constituency in favor of effective implementation and enforcement.

Overall, the most successful US trading programs have been the lead credit program and the $SO_2$ allowance trading program. Their success is due to a number of factors. Each established a uniform, homogenous commodity – lead credits and sulfur allowances – which facilitated the development of trading markets as well as intra-firm transfers. Both programs used a pure emissions-based measure of performance – lead content in gasoline, or sulfur emissions – allowing firms complete flexibility in selecting the

[118] See Ian W. H. Parry, Robertson C. Williams, and Lawrence H. Goulder, *When Can Carbon Abatement Policies Increase Welfare? The Fundamental Role of Distorted Factor Markets* (Cambridge, Mass.: National Bureau of Economic Research, 1997). (Working Paper Series [National Bureau of Economic Research] Working Paper no. 5967.)

[119] Klaassen and Nentjes, "Sulfur Trading Under the 1990 CAAA," 384, 407.

[120] See Justin Savage, "Note, Confiscation of Emission Reduction Credits: The Case for Compensation Under the Takings Clause," 16 *Va. Env. L.J.* 227 (1997) (arguing in favor of viewing credits as property under Takings Clause); but see Susan A. Austin, "Comment, Tradable Emissions Programs: Implications Under the Takings Clause," 26 *Env. L.* 323 (1996) (arguing that most revocations or restrictions on credits would not implicate Takings Clause).

[121] See Jane V. Hall and Amy L. Walton, "A Case Study in Pollution Markets: Dismal Science vs. Dismal Reality," 14 *Contemp. Econ. Pol'y* 67 (1996).

means and levels of limiting lead content or sulfur emissions. In both programs trades and other transfers were accomplished by voluntary actions by private entities without the need for governmental review or approval before the trade or transfer became effective. Further, the risk of non-compliance was placed on sellers, not on purchasers or holders of credits or allowances. Under the lead phase-down program, if a refiner sold lead credits but failed to reduce the lead content in its gasoline in an amount sufficient to match the credit sold, the government took enforcement action against the seller; the buyer holding the credit could still claim the full value of the credit. Similarly, under the sulfur program, sellers of allowances who fail to reduce their emissions sufficiently to cover the amount of allowances sold face enforcement action and sanctions; the buyer who holds the allowances can continue to claim their full value. Placing the risk of non-performance on buyers or holders of credits or allowances is likely to chill trading. Finally, both programs mandated deep cuts in existing emissions, which helped to drive the trading programs.

The lower level of success of other programs, such as the EPA offset and bubble credit trading programs, is due in substantial part to crucial features in the design of these programs that differ from those in the lead and sulfur trading programs. The programs did not establish a uniform homogenous commodity or pure emissions-based performance measure. In order to qualify for recognition, a trade or other transfer had to be between two facilities in the same geographic vicinity, and the reductions at the one facility had to be at least equivalent environmentally, in terms of impacts on ambient concentrations, to that of the increased emissions at the other, as judged by regulatory authorities. Baselines for determining emissions reductions credits were often determined on a case-by-case basis, creating controversy between sources and regulators. Trades and transfers were subject to prior regulatory review and approval before becoming effective, creating regulatory overhang. Further, the risk of non-performance was imposed on the buyer or holder of credits. If the originating facility failed to reduce its emissions sufficiently to cover the credit, the receiving facility could face enforcement action on the ground that the credit that it was claiming was no longer valid. These several characteristics prevented development of a well-functioning commodity market for trading a uniform, homogenous commodity. Instead, trades and transfers had the character of a barter, with regulatory authorities reviewing and approving each barter in advance. Transaction costs as well as delay and uncertainty were correspondingly high.

These problems have been either absent or substantially less serious in the netting program, which helps to explain its relatively greater success. Netting is a form of intrafacility trading. Netting can be carried out unilaterally by a single actor without the need for prior regulatory review and approval. The "commodity" is homogenous – reductions and increases of the same air pollutant at the same facility. Under netting, however, the scope of the "market" is limited to a single facility, reducing the scope for cost-effective reallocation of abatement burdens and foreclosing the development of a trading market.

European experimentation with emissions trading schemes is quite limited. The UK's $SO_2$ reduction program provided for trading among utilities but inter-firm trading did not occur because the reductions were obtained relatively easily without it. Germany provided a credit trading scheme for certain air pollutants but it was not widely used because of regulatory limitations on trading.[122] Following the failure to secure agreement on an EU carbon/energy tax, the European Commission is studying the possibility of a Community-wide GHG trading system to meet the Community's Kyoto Protocol emissions reduction obligations. There has been limited use of trading mechanisms in connection with air pollution regulation in Sweden, Canada, and Australia.

## PROMOTING WIDER ADOPTION OF ECONOMIC INCENTIVE SYSTEMS

Because their use has been relatively limited, EIS still suffer under the burden of novelty. Despite the important theoretical advantages of such systems, in the absence of broader operational experience questions can be raised about their practicality. It is only in recent years that serious steps have been taken, primarily in Europe, to use environmental taxes for incen-

[122] See Wolfram Cremer and Andreas Fishan, "New Environmental Policy Instruments, Policy Instruments in Germany," in Golub, *New Instruments for Environmental Policy*, 68–69. See also Eckard Rehbinder's contribution to this volume, pp. 245–62 below.

For a description of developing Europe's initial attempts to implement emissions trading, see Ger Klaassen, "Prospects for Emission Trading in CEE," in Peter Kaderjak and John Powell eds., *Economics for Environmental Policy in Transition Economies* (Cheltenham, UK, and Lyme, N.H.: Edward Elgar, 1997), 95.

tive purposes. The future development of environmental tax systems must build on experience with these efforts. There is a larger record of experience with trading systems in the US. The record is on the whole positive, but mixed. Many of the programs have made valuable contributions. The most successful have been the $SO_2$ and gasoline lead additive trading programs. Other programs have been impeded by the perpetuation of command regulatory requirements. These requirements and other factors have inhibited external trading. Nonetheless, overall the programs have produced significant cost savings as well as environmental benefits.

The inherent drawbacks of centralized command systems have become increasingly manifest in developed countries as more stringent controls have been imposed, stimulating increased interest in EIS. These drawbacks have been especially serious in the United States because of its size and diversity, the adversary character of relations between regulatory government and business, and the pervasive overlay of formal legal procedures and litigation. The increasing centralization of command environmental regulation in the EU may also create significant dysfunctions, as discussed by Stephen Breyer and Veerle Heyvaert in their chapter, and there is growing interest in the use of EIS, especially taxes.[123] Although environmental regulation in most developing countries is at a far earlier stage, such countries may be increasingly interested in EIS because EIS can make more cost-effective use of the limited resources that such countries can devote to environmental protection. On the other hand, the need for accurate monitoring to implement EIS and for organizing quota trading markets may strain the limited administrative capabilities of some developing countries. Over the longer run, continued strong public demand both for higher levels of environmental quality and for continued economic growth are likely to exacerbate the limitations of the command system and create conditions conducive to wider adoption of EIS.

On the other hand, by the time established command regulatory programs have matured to the point where their inherent limitations create serious dysfunctions, powerful economic and political interests may have acquired such a vested stake in the regulatory status quo that a switch to EIS may be politically difficult. Further, the transition costs of abandoning one regulatory system for another may be high.

In these circumstances, there are a number of possible regulatory reform

[123] See also Stewart, "Antidotes for the 'American Disease.'"

strategies for promoting use of EIS. The most drastic is to scrap an existing command system in favor of an EIS replacement. The Los Angeles RECLAIM program is the only known instance of such a step, adopted out of conviction that the command system had reached its limits. This is not a strategy that could likely be adopted for environmental taxes, because uncertainties regarding the level of residuals that would be generated by a given tax rate would be great. A second reform strategy is to reform existing command regulatory programs partially by allowing sources to trade ERCs when they reduce residuals below levels mandated by command regulations; this is the strategy followed in the various EPA Clean Air Act emissions trading programs. This strategy introduces flexibility without scrapping the command system, but in practice often has the disadvantage of perpetuating regulatory overhang which significantly increases transaction costs and uncertainty and thereby reduces the benefits from trading. A third strategy, followed in Europe, is to adopt pollution taxes in addition to existing command regulatory programs. The tax level can gradually be increased over time to achieve further residuals reductions; command requirements can be maintained or phased out. If the proceeds of environmental taxes are used, on a revenue neutral basis, to reduce existing taxes on labor and capital that impair productivity, this strategy may have beneficial economic as well as environmental effects. This is a strategy that a number of European countries may pursue. A fourth strategy is to leapfrog the process of regulatory evolution and adopt EIS to deal with new environmental problems that have not yet been regulated. An example in the US is the use of tradable quotas to phase down the production and use of ozone-depleting chemicals. As developed in the following section, limitation of GHG emissions presents an important opportunity to use EIS at the outset to address a new environmental problem, that of climate change.

## The use of economic incentive systems in addressing global and regional environmental problems

A number of important environmental problems, including stratospheric ozone depletion, atmospheric warming, and loss of biodiversity, are global in character, affecting all nations. Other significant environmental problems are regional in character, including acid deposition, ozone smog transport, pollution of transboundary water courses, and land-based marine pollution. These regional problems often exist within a multi-jurisdictional political structure, including that of federal states, the European Union, or a regional group of nations. By their very nature, environmental problems of this sort require joint or coordinated measures among different jurisdictions. Otherwise, free-riders who do not join in such measures will continue to pollute, causing harm to the common or shared resources. The need for joint or coordinated measures is reinforced by economic factors. Typically, the jurisdictions involved in regional or global environmental problems are economically closely linked through free trade regimes. To the extent that control measures impose significant costs on industry, investment in search of competitive advantage may "leak" from jurisdictions that adopt control measures to those which do not, increasing the level of industrial activity in such jurisdictions and, consequently, the amount of regional or global pollution, further undermining the efforts of those jurisdictions that do agree to common or coordinated measures. The leakage problem is analytically distinct from the race-to-the-bottom issue, analyzed by Richard Revesz and Roger van den Bergh in their contributions to this book, which deals with economic rivalry among jurisdictions in cases where the effects of residuals are limited to the jurisdiction in which they are generated.

Any regional or international agreement on joint or coordinated environmental measures will involve conflicts over the distribution of the benefits and burdens of such measures. The difficulty of agreement is exacerbated by economic rivalries and concerns about the competitiveness impacts of environmental regulations, the temptation to free-ride, and geographic differences in the adverse impacts locally of shared environmental problems. It will generally be more difficult to resolve such conflicts in a federal or quasi-federal political system than in a single jurisdiction. It will be even more difficult in the international setting. Differences and rivalries among nations are likely to be greater than those among sub-units of a federal or quasi-federal system. Further, under the international law rule of voluntary assent, a nation generally is not bound by an international agreement unless it chooses to join it.[124] The selection of the policy instrument to deal with an international or regional environmental problem can, however, significantly affect the chances of reaching agreement among the relevant jurisdictions. The comparative advantages of EIS over command-and-control regulation are especially important in the context of regional

[124] See Wiener, "Global Environmental Regulation," 677, 771. An exception to this generalization may occur when an agreement embodies customary international law.

and global environmental problems; these advantages can promote agreement on joint or coordinated measures.

Many regional and global environmental problems, especially those characterized by extensive pollution mixing, do not present a serious risk of significant local "hot spots." In the case of some problems, such as stratospheric ozone depletion and climate change, the hot spot problem is non-existent. In these situations, the most important potential advantage of command regulation is either not relevant or not very important. Moreover, the greater the number and diversity of jurisdictions within which a regulatory system must operate, the greater the administrative and economic drawbacks of command regulation. At the same time, the advantages of EIS are likely to be greater when applied in a multi-jurisdictional context. For example, the cost savings advantages of EIS are likely to be substantially greater in a multi-jurisdictional context because marginal control costs generally vary more widely among different jurisdictions than within a single jurisdiction. Just as different jurisdictions benefit economically by participating in regional and global commodity markets, they benefit environmentally through use of EIS, which allows them to exploit the logic of comparative advantage and scale economies by channeling resources to locations where they can be used most cost-effectively in reducing pollution and waste. This factor is especially significant in addressing global climate change because GHG abatement costs vary quite widely among countries. The locational flexibility in reductions allowed by EIS produces large cost savings. These cost savings could amount to approximately $1 trillion over three decades.[125] Regional or global use of EIS also widens competition for innovation in environmentally superior technologies and promotes rapid diffusion of successful innovations. Further, EIS promote structural shifts in the output of goods and services to the emerging "green" sectors of the wider economy. In all of these ways, EIS can significantly reduce the costs of achieving a given international environmental objective and thereby increase the likelihood of agreement.

Whatever regulatory instrument is chosen to achieve environmental protection, there will be a need for regular collection of accurate information about residuals discharges.[126] Especially in the international setting, there

[125] *Ibid.*, at 716–17.

[126] See Tom Tietenberg, "Information Strategies for Pollution Control," keynote address at the Annual Conference of the European Association of Environmental and Resource Economists, Tilburg, Netherlands, 27 June 1996.

are substantial technical, institutional, and political obstacles to achieving this objective, particularly in developing countries. Such information is, however, necessary to ensure proper implementation and enforcement of any regulatory program, as well as to resolve scientific questions about the extent of residuals and their environmental effects. Collection of such information will also promote accountability and help mobilize public and political opinion against non-complying jurisdictions. The importance of publicly available information is especially significant in the international context because supranational enforcement is generally weak at best. Use of EIS can encourage collection of such information because governments and quota permit holders have a strong financial stake in accurate monitoring and reporting.

Command regulation systems for international environmental problems could take two basic forms. First, the system could impose uniform requirements, such as BAT limitations, on sources in all jurisdictions. These requirements could be specified in the international agreement establishing the system, but the agreement would have to contain a great degree of detail that would be difficult to negotiate. Alternatively, individual source limitations could be specified by an international administrative authority established pursuant to the agreement, but nations might be very reluctant to delegate such power to an international bureaucracy. Even if an institutional means could be found to specify international requirements for individual sources, such a system would present the dysfunctions of centralized "one size fits all" command regulation in an especially acute form because of the greater differences in circumstances among nations than within a single jurisdiction. Yet, departures from uniformity to accommodate differing national circumstances would be very difficult to negotiate or arrange.

By providing flexibility, EIS avoid many of the dysfunctions of international specification of limitations requirements for individual sources. Under EIS, there must be agreement by all jurisdictions on fee levels or permit caps and natural allocations, but once these are established, implementation is decentralized via the price system, with local reporting and monitoring overseen by appropriate regional or international authorities. Under a quota trading program, each national jurisdiction could decide on its own internal quota allocation. An international system of environmental taxes would provide less domestic flexibility in that all sources within each nation must pay the taxes established by international agreement.

A second version of an international command system would establish residuals limitations requirements for nations rather than for individual sources, allowing each nation the flexibility to determine how it will meet its international obligations through domestic regulatory measures for its sources. These measures may take the form of EIS as well as command requirements. This approach, which was the one adopted in the Kyoto Protocol, provides for more flexibility than the first version of international command regulation. But, domestic flexibility may lead to implementation and compliance problems, especially if government officials face pressures from domestic industry, based on international competitiveness concerns, to relax or not effectively enforce regulatory requirements. EIS, which rely on more impersonal and transparent mechanisms, may create relatively stronger incentives and constituencies for effective monitoring and compliance. Further, the second version of international command regulation provides flexibility within but not among nations; in effect, it treats each nation as a source. It thereby foregoes the ability afforded by EIS to take advantage of differences in marginal control costs among nations to achieve overall residuals limitations at lower cost. In theory, an international command system of the second type could seek to vary national obligations in accordance with national differences in marginal control costs, but it is likely to be very difficult to obtain the necessary information to determine the appropriate variations or to obtain agreement on them.[127]

Another important advantage of EIS in a multi-jurisdictional setting is their capacity to transfer fiscal and technological resources to jurisdictions, including economically less developed jurisdictions, who would otherwise oppose or refuse to agree to common measures because they believe that the burdens on them of complying with such measures would be greater than the benefits. Without these inducements, less developed jurisdictions may

[127] Europeans have had some success with such differentiated national emission ceilings in the Second Sulfur Protocol of 1994. See Klaassen, *Acid Rain and Environmental Degradation*, 197–99. The requirement that an international agreement generally must be beneficial to all signing nations, however, imposes a constraint that severely limits the efficiency gains that might be attained through command systems in an international context, since signing parties generally only sign agreements that lead to Pareto-dominant outcomes for their nation.

From a global economic and environmental perspective, it is of course a good thing to exploit low cost opportunities first. Technical and other assistance for developing country governments may, however, be necessary in order to help them negotiate and obtain a fair share of the economic rents associated with such opportunities.

elect to pursue economic growth through methods that may be cheaper in the short run but environmentally destructive and wasteful of resources over the longer run.

In many developing countries, the industrial infrastructure often consists of older, higher polluting technologies. If the adverse effects of the residuals generated are local, it may be entirely appropriate to apply less stringent requirements to such sources than to comparable sources in developed countries because the social benefits of reducing residuals may be less in a developing country.[128] When, however, pollution from sources in developing countries creates harmful transboundary environmental spillovers, such as stratospheric ozone depletion, marine pollution, or global climate change, the benefits of residuals reduction are greater, and more stringent regulatory measures may be appropriate. Yet, the countries where the pollution originates may be unwilling to adopt such measures because they will not capture all of the benefits. In addition, even though the marginal currency cost of achieving pollution reductions in a developing country may be substantially less than the marginal currency cost of achieving the same reduction in a developed country, the social opportunity cost to the developing country of diverting scarce capital away from other investments in its citizens' standard of living may be quite high, as pointed out by Professor Chichilnisky in her contribution to this volume.

There are four reasons why international regimes to address global or regional environmental problems must provide an effective means for transferring capital and technology to developing countries in order to upgrade their industrial infrastructure and limit their generation of residuals. First, it is important to secure developing countries' assent to the regime in order to avoid free-riding and leakage; transfers that provide economic as well as environmental benefits to developing countries can be an effective means of winning such assent. Second, without such transfers, developing countries may lack the resources and know-how to limit their residuals. Third, reductions that benefit all participants can often be accomplished more cheaply in developing than developed countries. Fourth, considerations of equity may demand that the richer countries, who have created significant global or regional environmental problems in the course of their

[128] See Richard B. Stewart, "Environmental Regulation and International Competitiveness," 102 *Yale L.J.* 2039, 2052–56 (1993) (addressing normative question of whether developing countries should be obliged to preserve natural resources for benefit of developed countries).

own development, bear a major share of the economic burden of addressing such problems.

If an international command system were adopted to address global or regional environmental problems, the need for transfers to developing countries could in principle be addressed through separate systems of multilateral or bilateral official assistance grants. There are, however, significant political and institutional limitations on the capacity of official assistance programs to meet this need. EIS have the advantage that resource transfers can be designed as an integral part of the regulatory system, rather than being accomplished through a separate and politically more vulnerable program. An international system of tradable quotas or credits can meet the need for transfers by stimulating market-based flows of capital and technology from firms in developed countries to projects to limit residuals in developing countries. A system of environmental taxes can generate revenues earmarked for environmental modernization in such countries.

Tradable quotas are likely to be superior to taxes in meeting the need for resource transfers to developing countries. Under a system of environmental taxes, the developed countries would have to hand over some of the revenues from the taxes that they collect to the jurisdictions receiving transfers. There may be greater political opposition to this method of redistribution than to a quota system, which could allocate a correspondingly greater number of quotas to transferee jurisdictions and accomplish the transfers through private sector investments in the transferee jurisdictions. The private firms benefiting from these investments would be an important political constituency favoring this approach. The latter approach is also likely to be significantly more cost-effective than a system of government-to-government transfers or the use of intermediary multilateral institutions. Further, transfers of tax revenues will increase the level of economic activity in transferee jurisdictions and thereby increase the overall generation of residuals. Tradable quotas avoid this problem by capping aggregate residuals discharges.

Some aspects of EIS may, however, make international agreement more difficult. Explicit differences in pollution fee levels or quota allocations may be needed to accommodate the circumstances and interests of different jurisdictions, including those of developed and developing countries. The need to recognize such differences explicitly may make agreement more difficult than under a command approach, which can seek to finesse conflict through agreement on a general principle – such as use of best available technology not entailing excessive cost – that can be flexibly interpreted and implemented by different jurisdictions. Such an approach can lead to varying interpretations by different jurisdictions of the principle adopted and controversies over compliance. Moreover, all agreements on residuals limitations, whether under a command-and-control approach or under an EIS, and whether expressed by reference to historical or current emissions baselines, or BAT requirements, or otherwise, involve an implicit allocation of entitlements to generate residuals. Recent international environmental agreements such as the Montreal Protocol and the Kyoto Protocol show that it is possible to reach international agreement on different obligations for different countries, combined with authorization for quota trading to provide flexibility and cost-effectiveness.

## Economic incentive systems to address global environmental problems: the example of climate change

The 1992 Framework Convention on Climate Change (FCCC)[129] and the Kyoto Protocol[130] are the latest of a new generation of international environmental conventions addressing global environmental protection; others include the Vienna Convention and Montreal Protocol for control of chemicals that deplete stratospheric ozone and the Biodiversity Convention. These agreements recognize the need for global solutions to global problems. Departing from the usual practice in international agreements to impose the same obligations on all Parties, these agreements accepted demands by developing countries that they incur less stringent obligations than developed countries and also receive financial assistance as a condition of their acceptance of such obligations. The developed countries have acceded to these arrangements in order to enlist the developing countries in the solution of global environmental problems in which they have a stronger interest.

129 United Nations, Framework Convention on Climate Change, 9 May 1992, 31 *I.L.M.* 849 (hereinafter FCCC).

130 United Nations, Conference of the Parties to the Framework Convention on Climate Change, Kyoto Protocol to the United Nations Framework Convention on Climate Change, UN Doc. FCCC/CP/1997/L.7/Add.1, 37 *I.L.M.* 22 (1997) (hereinafter Kyoto Protocol).

The FCCC and Kyoto Protocol are especially notable because they provide for the use of EIS, in the form of internationally tradable greenhouse gas (GHG) emissions quotas and credits, to implement an international environmental agreement.[131] This section of the chapter discusses the problem of climate change due to increased anthropogenic GHG emissions and the advantages of EIS in limiting such emissions; summarizes the FCCC and Kyoto Protocol and their EIS provisions; and discusses future options for implementing these provisions in order to limit GHG emissions.

## THE GLOBAL CLIMATE CHANGE PROBLEM

The threat of global climate change due to increasing anthropogenic emissions of GHGs poses an enormous challenge to the international community and to international law.[132] The most important GHG is carbon dioxide, but methane, nitrous oxide, CFCs and CFC-substitutes, and other gases are also important. GHGs are generated by a tremendously diverse range of industrial, commercial, agricultural, forestry, development, transportation, and other production and consumption activities, including activities that also destroy GHG sinks such as forests. Many of the GHG, including $CO_2$, have long residence times in the atmosphere; continuing increases in these gases threaten generations far into the future. Moreover, as discussed in John Houghton's contribution to this volume, empirical data as well as theoretical models have established that anthropogenic emissions of GHGs cause atmospheric warming, although the precise extent, rate, and distribution of warming remain uncertain, as does the magnitude of the adverse ecological and economic effects that

[131] The Montreal Protocol, for control of production and consumption of ozone-depleting substances, also includes certain limited trading provisions.

[132] See generally John Houghton, *Global Warming: The Complete Briefing* (2nd edn., Cambridge, 1997); J. T. Houghton, L. G. Meira Filho, N. Harris, A. Kattenberg, and K. Maskell eds., *Climate Change 1995: The Science of Climate Change* (Cambridge, 1996); R. T. Watson, M. C. Zinowera, and R. H. Moss eds., *Climate Change 1995: Impacts, Adaptation and Mitigation of Climate Change* (Cambridge, 1996); J. Bruce, Hoesung Lee, and E. Haites eds., *Climate Change 1995: Economic and Social Dimensions of Climate Change* (Cambridge, 1996); R. R. Churchill and David Freestone eds., *International Law and Global Climate Change* (London and Boston: Graham and Trotman, M. Nijhoff, 1991); William Nordhaus ed., *Economics and Policy Issues in Climate Change* (Washington, D.C.: Resources for the Future, 1998); *Greenhouse Gas Emissions Projections and Estimates of the Effects of Measures: Moving Towards Good Practice* (OECD, 1998).

warming might cause. Continued increases in GHG emissions at current projected "business as usual" rates have a potential for causing serious harm.[133] Given the long lead times necessary in order to build effective international and domestic measures and arrangements to limit GHG emissions, it is prudent to begin now to develop these measures and institutions as part of a "learning by doing" strategy. The FCCC and Kyoto Protocol represent such a beginning.

There are also significant uncertainties about the costs of measures to reduce GHG emissions, enhance sinks, or mitigate the consequences of climate change. Because GHG are emitted by many activities in different sectors, there is often no single "quick fix" available to reduce or limit such emissions. Although there are substantial opportunities in many countries for enhancing energy efficiency at low or even negative cost, significant limitations on GHG growth could entail very large costs running to many trillions of dollars globally over the next century.[134] The challenge of global warming is accordingly far more severe than that of stratospheric ozone depletion, where only a limited number of industrial uses were affected, CFC-substitutes were quickly developed, and switchover costs have been estimated at several billion dollars.[135]

Furthermore, serious obstacles to international agreement on effective measures to reduce GHG exist. Although many countries would, on balance, be harmed by global warming over the long run if the GHG emissions growth is not limited, the predicted level of harm varies greatly, and

133 Projected damages in the United States from a doubling of $CO_2$ levels are estimated at \$335.7 billion in the long term. See Clare Langley-Hawthorne, "An International Market for Transferable Gas Emission Permits to Promote Climate Change," 9 *Fordham Env. L.J.* 261, 294 (1998).

134 See generally William R. Cline, *The Economics of Global Warming* (Washington, D.C.: Institute for International Economics, 1992). A recent US Department of Energy study estimates that the effects of implementation of the Kyoto Treaty on the US economy range from a 0.1 percent drop in GDP to a 4.2 percent drop in GDP during the 2008–12 target period. See "Kyoto Protocol Major Economic Effects from 2008 to 2012," *Daily Environmental Report* (13 October 1998) at A6–7. A much more optimistic assessment is provided in Robert Repetto and Duncan Austin, *The Costs of Climate Protection: A Guide for the Perplexed* (World Resources Institute, 1997).

135 See Harold K. Jacobson and Edith Brown Weiss, "Assessing the Record and Designing Strategies to Engage Countries for Compliance with International Environmental Norms," in Edith Brown Weiss and Harold K. Jacobson, eds., *Engaging Countries: Strengthening Compliance with International Environmental Accords* (Cambridge, Mass.: MIT Press, 1998), 521.

many regions might actually benefit in the near future.[136] The distribution of the costs of GHG limitations would depend on the precise nature of any international agreement, but could vary widely among different countries. For example, stabilization of GHG emissions at current levels would impose significant costs on developed countries, but impose far greater penalties on developing countries' efforts to raise their standards of living.[137] Currently, emissions per capita in the developing countries are far less than in the developed countries. As the developing countries forcefully point out, most of the anthropogenic additions to GHG currently present in the atmosphere were contributed by the developed countries. If, however, per capita developing country emissions were to increase to current developed country levels, rapid warming and significant environmental dislocation would likely occur. Developing countries nonetheless maintain that they should have equivalent opportunities to industrialize and develop; if the developed countries wish to ensure that such growth occurs without increases in GHG, they should foot the bill for the necessary limitation measures.

GHG policy not only poses significant conflicts of interest between the developed and the developing countries, but also among the developed countries and among the developing countries. GHG emissions per capita or per unit of GDP vary widely among the developed countries. Not surprisingly, nations that are rich in fossil fuel resources, such as Canada, the United States, and Australia, have the highest emissions of $CO_2$ per capita or per unit of GDP. Other developed nations with fewer fossil fuel resources have been forced to develop more efficient patterns of energy use; they tend to view the high-emitting nations as environmental profligates that should assume a heavy control burden. Conflicts among the developing countries

[136] There are indications that the OECD countries on average may actually benefit from the limited degree of warming projected over the next several decades, while the developing countries would be harmed. In the longer run, most countries would be harmed by continued warming, especially if the rate of increase is rapid. See William D. Nordhaus and Joseph G. Boyer, "Requiem for Kyoto: An Economic Analysis of the Kyoto Protocol" (29 June 1998) (paper prepared for the Energy Modeling Forum meeting in Snowmass, Colo., 10–11 August 1998).

[137] This "bottleneck" effect is most evident in developing countries with rapid rates of economic growth, such as China, India, and Korea. Given the rates of growth in these countries, any environmental gains from less-polluting technologies would quickly be overcome by rapid economic growth rates. See Tom Kram, "The Costs of Greenhouse-Gas Abatement," in Nordhaus, *Economics and Policy Issues in Climate Change.*

are also rife. Some are rich in coal (China, India) or oil reserves (OPEC Members). Others, including small island states, states with low-lying coasts, and those threatened by desertification, are especially vulnerable to the adverse environmental effects of climate change. Because controls on GHG emissions could impose significant cost burdens on industry, competitiveness rivalries add a further confounding factor to the possibility of achieving and effectively implementing international agreement on GHG limitation measures.

## THE ADVANTAGES OF ECONOMIC INCENTIVE SYSTEMS IN ADDRESSING GLOBAL CLIMATE CHANGE

EIS are exceptionally well suited to dealing with the challenge of limiting net GHG emissions and securing international agreement on joint measures to accomplish this goal. GHGs are globally mixed throughout the entire atmosphere, eliminating any problem of local pollution hot spots, although the extent of warming and the effect of warming are not geographically uniform. The policy objective is to limit broadly the growth of GHG with a view to stabilization in order to slow or halt warming. There are many different types of facilities and activities that generate GHG, and very large differences in the marginal costs of controlling net GHG emissions among different activity sectors and among different nations. Because the costs of limiting net GHG emissions are potentially enormous, it is therefore extraordinarily important that limitations be achieved in a cost-effective fashion, which will in turn promote the chances of securing international agreement on limitations measures by reducing the costs of participation. EIS are best able to achieve this objective by capitalizing on differences in marginal control costs by providing both the flexibility and the incentives for targeting investments in GHG reductions on the lowest cost opportunities.[138] Limiting GHG while pursuing continuing economic

[138] See Nordhaus and Boyer, "Requiem for Kyoto," at 13 (estimating that while the abatement costs of the Kyoto GHG reductions would be approximately $276 billion under a scenario that allowed global tradable emissions, abatement costs in the absence of trading would be $1,971 billion). One study finds that countries acting alone would find it efficient to abate only 4 percent of the GHG emissions they would be willing to cut under an integrated global program. See William D. Nordhaus and Zili Yang, "A Regional Dynamic General-Equilibrium Model of Alternate Climate-Change Strategies," 86 *Am. Econ. Rev.* 741, 762 (1996); cited in Wiener, "Global Environmental Regulation," at 692 n. 60.

growth will require major sectoral changes in technologies, resource uses, and production and consumption patterns. For reasons previously discussed, these changes can best be accomplished through use of EIS rather than command regulation.

Further, use of EIS to address global climate change also could help meet the urgent need to generate large additional flows of capital and technology to developing countries in order to promote energy efficiency and other low-GHG-emitting paths to economic development and provide inducements for them to join an international agreement to limit GHG. As previously discussed, tradable quota and credit systems are likely to be most effective in meeting this need because they build supportive constituencies in developed countries. Some predict that the Kyoto Protocol could result in a $300 billion annual market for environmentally friendly technologies.[139]

Under a GHG tax system, charges would be imposed on net GHG based on their radiative forcing and atmospheric residence time. Credits would be given for sink enhancement. The tax level could be gradually increased over time. A potentially significant advantage in using taxes is that the damage function from increased emissions appears to be approximately linear, at least for the next several decades. Moreover, GHG are a "stock" pollutant; damage is a function of the total amount of GHG in the atmosphere rather than the flow of anthropogenic emissions into the stock or removals from the stock by natural processes in any discrete time period. On the other hand, the costs of achieving GHG emissions reductions are quite uncertain, and could present relatively sharp thresholds under scenarios for achieving significant reductions over the next decade or two. Use of taxes can avoid the problem of excessive compliance costs because such costs are capped by the level of the tax. Because they impose fixed limits on total emissions, command and tradable quota systems create the danger of excessive costs.[140] On the other hand, the total amount of GHG emissions reductions

[139] See Margaret Kruz, "After Argentina," *Nat. J.* (5 December 1998), at 2848. While the OECD countries have made financial commitments to the developed countries in the FCCC, and have established a Global Environmental Facility to facilitate funding transfers, the actual amounts of bilateral and multilateral aid provided have been and will be far too limited in relation to the gigantic task of limiting GHG growth in the developing countries. Use of EIS, and in particular tradable permits, could be a more politically palatable means of generating the large capital and technology transfers that will be necessary to deal with the challenge of GHG growth in developing countries.

[140] See William A. Pizer, "Prices vs. Quantities Revisited: The Case of Climate Change" (Resources for the Future Discussion Paper No. 98–02, 1997) (arguing that a GHG tax

achieved by a fee system in a given period will be uncertain. But, given the nature of the problem, certainty in limiting quantities within a specific time period may not be that important.[141]

GHG taxes, however, suffer from a number of significant disadvantages when used in the international context. There is no prospect that nations would agree to have such fees collected and spent by a supranational authority. Accordingly, there would have to be agreement on a schedule of fees that would be collected and spent by the participating nations. Developing countries, however, might not agree to impose fees at all or agree to do so only at significantly lower levels than in the developed countries, leading to leakage to developing countries of investment and additional increases in their emissions. If different GHG tax levels were adopted for different countries, the marginal costs of control would no longer be the same across all countries, sacrificing some of the cost savings achievable by EIS. Moreover, industry is generally strongly opposed to GHG taxes because they represent an added and potentially very significant economic burden.[142] There may be political and other obstacles to overcoming industry opposition to GHG fees by recycling revenues to the industries in question.

A system of tradable net GHG emission quotas or credits would be based on a common GHG unit such as a ton of carbon or equivalent. Sink enhancements could be addressed by issuing additional quotas or credits equal to the GHG sequestered or by allowing sources and countries to deduct the amount sequestered from their emissions. An international GHG trading system has several advantages over GHG emissions taxes in

system would in many respects be more economically efficient than a tradable quota system, although the economic benefits of a tax system must be balanced against the uncertainties of actual emissions).

141 *Ibid.*

142 The Congressional Budget Office has estimated that a fossil fuel $CO_2$ emission fee of $100 per ton, which would have significant incentive effects, would generate revenues of $120 billion annually. Even if GHG emission fees were initiated on a revenue-neutral basis, with compensating reductions in corporate income or payroll taxes, energy-using industries would be disproportionately burdened.

The European Commission proposed an energy/carbon tax in order to restrain GHG emissions. European industry, however, was extremely concerned that such a tax would impair its international competitiveness. In response to this concern, the proposal was made conditional on the imposition by the United States and Japan of GHG measures that would impose equivalent economic burdens on their industries. Even with this condition, the Commission's proposal has not been adopted. See note 68 above.

the international context. Transfers of capital and technology to developing countries can be accomplished by allocating relatively more quotas to them and relying on private sector investments to implement these transfers. Quota allocations to developing countries can also be used to meet equity concerns and obtain their assent to an agreement. Once the initial allocation is made, however, trading will channel investments to the lowest cost GHG-limitation opportunities and tend to equalize marginal limitations costs across all jurisdictions, promoting cost-effectiveness. The "leakage" problem is solved by the system's cap on overall emissions. Industry opposition can be moderated by giving quotas to existing sources. A system of tradable quotas or credits, as noted above, runs the risk of incurring costs that significantly exceed the benefits of achieving specific limitations requirements in a given period. This problem, however, could be addressed by renegotiating aggregate quotas periodically or by adopting a "safety valve" approach that would allow nations or sources to emit more emissions than the quotas they hold if they pay a set fee on the excess emissions.[143] Trading systems are also somewhat more complicated than tax systems; the commodity to be traded must be defined, trading markets developed, and trades and holdings recorded. For these reasons, the transactions costs of a trading system are likely to be greater than those of a tax system.

There are various forms which an international GHG trading system might take.[144] Under an emissions reduction credit approach, investor countries or firms would earn credits for emission reductions achieved as a result of investments in specific projects to reduce GHG emissions or expand sinks. Examples of such projects include construction of an energy-efficient electric generating plant or distribution network, conversion of a

[143] Raymond Kopp, Richard Morgenstern, and William Pizer, "Something for Everyone: A Climate Policy that Both Environmentalists and Industry can Live With" (Resources for the Future Working Paper, 1997); Richard G. Newell and William A. Pizer, "Stock Externality Regulation Under Uncertainty" (Resources for the Future Working Paper, 1998).

[144] See generally OECD, *Climate Change: Designing a Tradable Permit System*; United Nations Conference on Trade and Development, *Combatting Global Warming: Possible Rules, Regulations, and Administrative Arrangements for a Global Market in $CO_2$ Emission Entitlements* (UNCTAD, 1994); Robert W. Hahn and Robert N. Stavins, "Trading in Greenhouse Permits: A Critical Examination of Design and Implementation Issues," in Henry Lee ed., Shaping National Responses to Climate Change (Washington, D.C.: Island Press, 1995). Richard B. Stewart, Philippe Sands, and Jonathan B. Wiener, *Legal Issues Presented by a Pilot International Greenhouse Gas Emissions Trading System* (UNCTAD, 1996).

bus fleet from diesel fuel to natural gas, or a reforestation project. Credits would count against present or future domestic or international GHG limitation obligations and could be freely traded.[145] In order to determine the amount of ERC generated by a project, one must establish a baseline of what GHG emissions would have been in the absence of the project. Where there are pre-existing command regulations that limit emissions from the project in question, the regulatory limit can be used to establish the baseline. But in the absence of such requirements, there are significant conceptual and practical difficulties in determining what the level of emissions would have been in the absence of the specific project investment in question. What sort of power plant and distribution system would otherwise have been built? Would the bus system have switched to natural gas anyway because of local air pollution regulations? Will the afforestation project be offset by increased logging on existing forests? Will the trees grown in the afforestation project be cut down in twenty years? An international authority would have to develop criteria and procedures for resolving these questions and certifying credits.

The basic alternative to a GHG ERC system is a full-fledged allowance trading system. For example, nations could agree, through an international treaty, to an overall cap on aggregate GHG emissions, expressed in terms of $CO_2$ equivalents, and an agreed allocation of net emissions quotas to each Party. An international agency established pursuant to international agreement would issue GHG emission allowances to each participating nation consistent with its quota. The allowances, for example, might consist of the right to emit one ton of $CO_2$ or its equivalent in a given or subsequent year. Each Party could then distribute its allocation of allowances to its domestic sources. International trading could be limited to governments, but the advantages of trading would be much greater if private entities were also allowed to participate and allowances could be bought, sold, and held by anyone. The baseline problem would disappear. Allowances would be included in the compensation received by investors in projects to reduce or sequester GHG. Nations party to the agreement would be required to monitor their domestic emissions annually and ensure that total emissions did not exceed the allowances held by their sources. An international

[145] A more limited version of an ERC program would require new sources of GHGs to obtain offsets for their emissions from existing sources or from GHG sequestration projects.

authority established pursuant to the agreement would review national reports, conduct independent monitoring and verification, and certify each Party's compliance. If a Party's net emissions exceeded the permits held by its sources, the allowance-issuing agency could reduce its quota of allowances for the following year to offset the deficit.[146]

A third approach is an emissions budget system.[147] Nations would agree to specified limitations on GHG to be achieved by Parties by some designated future year or period of years. Each Party would be authorized to establish an emissions budget path, setting emission limitations for each year or other period leading up to the year in which the agreed limitations must be achieved. If a Party's emissions were limited to a greater extent and/or earlier than called for by its budget path, savings would be created. Savings could then be traded. The budget path would create the baseline for measuring savings. Savings created by investments originating in other countries could be recognized in determining the investor countries' compliance with their own budget paths and with their limitations obligations under the agreement.

Whatever form of EIS were adopted to address GHG emissions, a key design issue is whether they should be limited to energy-sector $CO_2$, emissions of which can be readily measured, or extended to include non-energy-sector $CO_2$ emissions, other GHG emissions, and sinks. A comprehensive approach is in principle highly desirable so as to bring all GHG within the program in order to maximize cost-effectiveness and avoid cross-sector or cross-gas "leakage" problems.[148] Different fees or emissions/quota ratios could be adopted for different GHGs with different global warming impacts based on their radiative forcing and atmospheric residence time. An index could be developed to determine the amounts of other gases that would be the equivalent in global warming impact of a ton of $CO_2$. Such an index has been developed under the Montreal Protocol for different ozone-depleting chemicals. A similar approach could be used for GHG sinks. It is, however, significantly more difficult to develop and implement means of accurately

146 See Stewart, Sands, and Wiener, *Legal Issues*, at 44–45.

147 *Ibid.* at 9–11.

148 See Richard B. Stewart and Jonathan B. Wiener, "The Comprehensive Approach to Global Climate Policy: Issues of Design and Practicality," 9 *Ariz. J. Int. & Comp. L.* 83 (1992) (citing cost savings of 70–90 percent in the US and India when controls are broadened beyond energy-sector $CO_2$ to encompass energy-sector $CH_4$ and forest-sector $CO_2$, as estimated in a study by the US Department of Energy and the World Bank).

monitoring GHG emissions other than energy-sector $CO_2$ emissions. It is also difficult to measure the amount of carbon sequestered by different types of forests.[149] A potential solution is to set emission fees or emissions/permit ratios for non-energy-sector $CO_2$ emissions, other GHGs and sinks, on a conservative basis to take into account monitoring and measurement uncertainties. Fees or ratios could be adjusted as monitoring techniques improve, although such changes could be politically difficult because they could alter the relative burden of agreed GHG limitations for different countries.[150]

## USE OF ECONOMIC INCENTIVE SYSTEMS UNDER THE FRAMEWORK CONVENTION ON CLIMATE CHANGE AND KYOTO PROTOCOL

The United Nations Framework Convention on Climate Change, signed at Rio in 1992, did not establish quantitative targets and timetables for limiting GHG emissions. It did, however, establish an international system for cooperation in addressing GHG emissions, including provisions for information-gathering, reporting, and the development of national plans for control of net GHG emissions. The developed countries and countries with economies in transition listed in Annex I to the FCCC are required to develop and submit inventories of their net GHG emissions and develop national programs to limit net GHG emissions with a vaguely stated aim of returning GHG emissions to 1990 levels. The developing countries are subject to much less specific obligations to gather and report information and develop national programs to mitigate climate change. Moreover, their discharge of these obligations is conditional upon receipt of financial assistance from developed countries. The OECD group of nations agreed to meet the developing countries' costs of complying with their obligations to prepare plans and make reports, and also to provide funds to meet the incremental costs of developing country projects to limit net GHG emissions.[151]

149 See Rob Swart, "Greenhouse Gas Emissions Trading: Defining the Commodity," in OECD, *Climate Change: Designing a Tradable Permit System*, 137.

150 See Jonathan B. Wiener, "Solving the Precautionary Paradox: Policy Approaches to Improve Measurement of Greenhouse Gas Sources and Sinks," in J. Van Ham et al. eds., *Non-$CO_2$ Greenhouse Gases* (Dordrecht and London: Kluwer Academic, 1994).

151 For a detailed review of the FCCC and its negotiation, see Daniel Bodansky, "The United Nations Framework Convention on Climate Change: A Commentary," 18 *Yale J. Int. L.* 521 (1993).

The Kyoto Protocol, negotiated by 160 countries in December 1997, provides a far more substantive framework for reducing GHG emissions.[152] The Parties agreed to quantitative emissions reductions targets and timetables for the FCCC Annex I countries, who agreed to limit their aggregate GHG emissions to an average of approximately 7 percent below 1990 levels during the period 2008–12, termed the first commitment period. The agreed-to limitations, known as quantified emissions reduction and limitation commitments (QERLCs), vary among individual countries.[153] The developing countries are not subject to any emissions limitations obligations. The Protocol authorizes four different types of EIS which developed countries can use to meet their QERLCs. Article 17 of the Protocol authorizes emissions trading among Annex I countries that have agreed to emissions limitations obligations. Under Article 4 such countries may implement their limitation obligations jointly. Under Article 6 they may trade project-based emission reduction units. Article 12 defines a Clean Development Mechanism (CDM) under which Annex I countries that invest in emissions limitations and sink enhancement projects in developing countries obtain certified emission reduction credits (ERCs) that count against their QERLC obligations. Article 12 also provides that private entities can participate in the CDM.

The development of effective international market-based mechanisms for limiting net GHG emissions can and should profit from the US domestic experience. That experience indicates that while there may be appreciable up-front costs in establishing an emissions trading market, as opposed to relying on case-by-case credit trades, these costs are well justified by the superior efficiency of trading markets. GHG emissions reduction programs should accordingly aim to build such markets. To that end it would be desirable for the various Annex I trading systems and the CDM to be based on a single, fungible tradable emissions unit (TEU), consisting of a ton of $CO_2$ or the equivalent (in terms of warming potential) in other

152 For a discussion of the Kyoto Protocol provisions, see Clare Breidenich et al., "The Kyoto Protocol to the United Nations Framework Convention on Climate Change," 92 *Am. J. Int. L.* 315 (1998). The Protocol has not yet been ratified by a sufficient number of countries to have entered into force.

153 Kyoto Protocol, Art. 3 and Annex B. The United States agreed to a binding target of 7 percent below 1990 levels by 2008–12, the EU 8 percent, and Japan 6 percent. A few countries are allowed small increases or permitted to maintain their emissions at the 1990 baseline. Article 3(2) also provides that Annex I countries should, by 2005, have made "demonstrable progress" in achieving their QERLCs.

GHG or sinks (in terms of GHGs sequestered). The scope for trading and for market participation should be as broad as possible. Under the CDM, administrative certification prior to issuance of ERCs will be required. There must also be an international system of accounting for TEU holdings and trades. There should, however, be no requirement for *ex ante* regulatory review and approval before a trade of ERCs or other TEUs can be made effective, which, as the US experience shows, could significantly impair the benefits of a trading system.[154] The US experience also demonstrates the necessity of establishing strong systems of monitoring and enforcement, including sanctions, to ensure the integrity of the market and the achievement of environmental protection objectives. Such systems are, however, necessary to ensure Parties' compliance with their QERLC obligations even in the absence of trading.

Other requisites of an international trading regime include the need to develop liability rules to govern situations where TEUs are issued or traded but the emissions reductions on which they are based are not achieved or maintained; procedures for resolution of disputes among Parties, private entities participating in the international trading regime, and FCCC/Protocol authorities responsible for administering the regime; and arrangements to ensure compatibility of the trading regimes with GATT/WTO and regional free trade regimes.

The circumstance that developing country Parties, unlike Annex I Parties, are not subject to emissions limitations obligations has important implications for the development of trading pursuant to the CDM. In the absence of an overall emissions cap, there must be a system for awarding credits (ERCs) for emissions reductions achieved by specific projects.[155] Thus, Article 12(5) of the Protocol provides that in order for ERCs to be certified, projects must provide emissions reductions that are "additional" to any that would occur in the absence of the project and that provide "[r]eal, measurable and long-term benefits related to the mitigation of climate

[154] The need for any such review and approval in the case of GHG is especially weak because GHG mix globally; unlike other air pollutants with local effects, there is no problem of "hot spots" associated with radiative forcing. Some GHG, such as tropospheric ozone, may have local effects that require limitations based on local ambient concentrations. This problem, should, however, be addressed through generic domestic regulation of the pollutant in question rather than review of individual trades by an international authority under an international GHG emissions limitation and trading program.

[155] The need for project-based accounting of emissions reductions credits also arises under Article 6, providing for trading of project-based credits among Annex I countries.

change." In addition, under Article 12(7), the Parties to the FCCC/Protocol must provide for independent monitoring and verification of project activities, through "modalities and procedures with the objective of ensuring transparency, efficiency, and accountability," to ensure that certified ERCs are valid.

In order to certify a project's ERCs, the relevant authority must first determine the extent of the emissions or sequestration services that a project has generated or will generate.[156] In addition, a certifying authority must establish a baseline that defines the level of net emissions that would have occurred if the project had not been undertaken. The difference between the baseline and the net emissions generated by the project is the amount of the credit. Establishing the baseline for a project is, as discussed previously, a complex and often controversial undertaking.[157] It would be highly desirable to develop generic rules of thumb to resolve these baseline issues by developing international benchmarks rather than attempting to determine baselines on a project-by-project basis, which would drive up administrative costs and uncertainty. For example, an international benchmark could specify a given level of energy efficiency that would normally be achieved in a given type of new project, such as an electricity distribution system, in developing countries at a given level of development. This benchmark would then establish the baseline to determine the extent to which a CDM project in a given nation would achieve reductions.

There are many other political, legal, and institutional issues that must be resolved in order to implement the various Protocol provisions for international GHG trading. There is a need for a tremendous amount of international institution and capacity building that must go far beyond what has thus far been attempted in respect of international efforts to address environmental problems. Contentious, cross-cutting political issues regarding

[156] In many instances, projects will be designed to operate over many years, requiring a degree of predictive uncertainty and a risk of future project failure. One approach to this problem is to make the best prediction possible and certify, *ex ante*, a stream of credits over a future period of years. If the project fails, then liability for the shortfall would be imposed on the project sponsor, the buyers of credits, or both. An alternative is to certify credits *ex post*, on the basis of actual emissions reductions achieved. While this approach may offer investors somewhat less certainty, the uncertainties should be manageable if transparent and predictable criteria and procedures for certifying ERCs are established. Those concerned to ensure that the CDM mechanism will achieve the Protocol's environmental goals have insisted on *ex post* ERC certification.

[157] See pp. 234–35 above.

international GHG emissions trading must be resolved. Two of these issues are especially important.

First is the issue of the role of private entities in international trading. Should only governments be allowed to trade internationally? Or, may business and financial firms and other non-governmental entities be authorized to do so? Articles 4, 6, and 17, dealing with trading arrangements among Annex I countries, are silent on this issue. Article 12(9) states, with arguable ambiguity, that "participation" in the CDM "involves private and/or public entities." China has recently indicated that international trading should be limited to governments or that any role for the private sector should be circumscribed and tightly controlled. Such a restriction would severely limit the advantages of GHG trading, including, in the case of the CDM, the transfer through market mechanisms of capital and technology to developing countries for environment-friendly sustainable forms of development. For these reasons, the Annex I countries and a substantial number of developing countries strongly favor private sector participation in international trading. The issue, however, has yet to be definitely resolved in the negotiations for implementation of the Protocol, and government officials in many developing countries remain suspicious of international market arrangements, fearing that they will be dominated by rich developed countries and their multinational companies.

A second contentious and cross-cutting issue goes under the label of supplementarity. Articles 6 and 7, which provide, respectively, for project-based credit trading and emissions trading among Annex I countries, state that these arrangements should be "supplemental to domestic actions" for the purpose of determining compliance by Annex I countries with their QERLCs. Furthermore, a number of Parties have sought to introduce the concept of supplementarity into the Article 12 CDM in order to limit the extent to which Annex I countries can use ERCs to meet their QERLCs.

Developing countries and some EU countries have argued that the Annex I developed countries should be required to reduce their domestic GHG emissions rather than using trading, including CDM investments in developing countries, in order to fulfill their Protocol obligations. Limiting the use of trading mechanisms in this fashion would involve needless economic waste and is not otherwise justified. Because GHG are globally mixed, the environmental benefit of reducing GHG is the same regardless of where the reduction occurs. Justice does not require the developed countries to achieve reductions within their borders if they can be obtained elsewhere at lower cost (a cost underwritten by the developed countries) and equivalent global environmental benefit. Of course, developed countries will save money as a result of the flexibility afforded by trading. But this is an advantage, not a drawback of the scheme. Under a properly constituted trading system, the developing countries as well as the developed countries would share in the economic benefits of such savings. These global savings are extremely important in securing wide agreement by nations on effective GHG limitations measures.

Trading would raise legitimate concerns about distributional equity if it allowed the developed countries effectively to avoid their just share, vis-à-vis the developing countries, of the collective burden of dealing with global environmental problems. But equity can be secured by appropriately adjusting the allocation of obligations between the developed and developing countries rather than by prohibiting trades that will lower the total global costs of addressing climate change and harness market forces to channel badly needed capital and environmentally appropriate technology to the developing countries. One ground for developing country objections to widespread use of trading that involves developing countries is that such countries inevitably will be made subject to emission limitation obligations; without such limitations, emissions reductions achieved by CDM investments in specific projects in developing countries could be wiped out by unchecked increases in emissions elsewhere in those countries. Some developing countries have, however, recognized this implication but have announced their willingness to adopt domestic emissions limitations in order to benefit more fully from international trading.[158]

Opposition to trading is also rooted in resentment of "profligate" lifestyles in some developed countries, especially the US, and the view that trading would allow the rich to perpetrate such profligacy. This criticism should not stand in the way of the practical business of securing international agreement on cooperative, cost-effective measures for GHG limitations. The likely alternative is that countries like the US would simply refuse to participate in international arrangements to limit emissions. Another

[158] At the Buenos Aires Conference of the Parties, two developing countries, Argentina and Kazakhstan, announced that they would adopt binding emissions targets for the 2008–12 period. See "Fact Sheet: Buenos Aires Climate Change Conference" (Bureau of Oceans and International Environmental and Scientific Affairs, United States Department of State, December 1998). As the Kyoto Protocol contains no provisions for countries to so volunteer, future conferences will need to address this issue. *Ibid.*

concern over trading is "cream skimming" – the fear that developed countries might exploit the lowest cost opportunities in developing counties for reducing net GHG emissions, leaving developing countries with a heavy economic burden when they are subsequently forced to limit GHG in order to meet later international obligations. This criticism appears to lack strong factual justification. Obsolescent industrial infrastructure in the developing countries must be replaced in the near-to-medium future for economic reasons; this non-recurring opportunity should be used, via trading, to ensure that the replacement stock is resource-efficient and environment-friendly. Furthermore, from a global perspective, it is of course a good thing to exploit low cost opportunities first. Technical and other assistance for developing country governments may, however, be necessary in order to help them negotiate and obtain a fair share of the economic rents associated with such opportunities.

It appears that, under the relevant Protocol provisions, the three Kyoto systems for trading among Annex I countries will not come into operation until the 2008–12 first commitment period, coincident with the effective date of those countries' QERLCs. Article 12 of the Protocol, however, provides that ERCs issued pursuant to the CDM can be certified as early as 2000; these credits can be banked and applied by Annex I countries subsequently against their QERLC obligations during the first commitment period. Accordingly, an essential component of learning-by-doing with respect to international GHG emissions trading is to initiate the CDM and ERC trading, including a vigorous secondary ERC market, as soon as possible.

A second essential component of learning-by-doing is to foster the development of emissions trading among Annex I countries in advance of the 2008–12 first commitment period and the various Protocol Annex I trading programs. A number of Annex I countries are considering domestic adoption of GHG emissions trading programs. These programs could provide the basis for the evolution of international trading if these countries mutually recognized TEUs generated under each others' domestic systems. Arrangements for mutual recognition could pave the way for the emergence of a plurilateral international GHG trading system involving a number of Annex I nations and their private firms. In order to facilitate such an evolution, the domestic systems should be designed to be as compatible as possible, consistent with differing countries' views about the appropriate design of domestic systems. Agreement on certain minimum common arrangements, such as an international bookkeeping system to keep track of TEU trades, might also be required. If such a plurilateral international trading system were to develop over the near term, it could form a sound basis for the design of Annex I trading programs under the Protocol that could be ready for launch by the beginning of the first commitment period in 2008.

Notwithstanding the significant political, legal, and institutional difficulties that remain, the Kyoto Protocol has taken a major step forward by authorizing emissions trading among Annex I countries and, via the CDM, between Annex I countries and developing countries. These various trading programs should, to the extent feasible, be designed as functional components of a single global GHG emissions trading system that will mobilize resources and technology efficiently and effectively to address the climate change threat and promote sustainable development.

## Conclusion

EIS can make important contributions to reconciling environmental and economic objectives. These contributions are especially notable with respect to regional and global environmental problems. While the superior cost-effectiveness of EIS over command instruments is an important and often decisive consideration in favor of their adoption, it is essential to exploit the broader array of advantages which they possess and devise creative strategies of regulatory reform in order to promote their wider adoption to address environmental problems for which they are well suited. These include many pressing regional and global environmental problems.

# 8

## MARKET-BASED INCENTIVES FOR ENVIRONMENTAL PROTECTION

ECKARD REHBINDER

### General remarks

PROFESSOR STEWART presents a very detailed and refined theoretical analysis of the pros and cons of (mainly market-based) economic incentive systems for environmental protection (EIS) with which, by and large, I agree on theoretical grounds, and to which adding some nuances in this short comment would not make much sense. However, since the United States has pioneered certain EIS, especially transferable permit systems of various kinds (lead in gasoline program, emissions trading policy, transferable permit program under the Clean Air Act Amendments, RECLAIM program in Southern California, and Illinois VOM program), I would have expected a more systematic treatment of the practical problems and difficulties that have arisen with respect to these programs.

One problem analyzed theoretically by Professor Stewart in various contexts but perhaps not sufficiently emphasized is that of regionally disproportionate distribution of pollution. "Hot spots" may arise where a certain concentration of emissions presents either an unacceptable risk or – which is true of carcinogens where safe concentration levels cannot be determined – an undesirable risk to individuals. This is by no means an atypical but, rather, the typical situation in air pollution (except for greenhouse gases and ozone depletion) and water pollution (even regarding nutrients, since eutrophication largely depends on the varying physical and physico-chemical characteristics of water courses and lakes). Therefore the American experience in coping with this problem (the Clean Air Act) is extremely important if one envisages spreading the message of EIS. It is clear that the "hot spot" problem can be taken care of by building strict ambient quality-related safeguards into an emission-based transferable permit system. For example, emission reduction credits or transferable permits could then be used by a particular source only if and insofar as ambient quality standards were not exceeded or non-deterioration increments not consumed. Of course, there are other possibilities for considering locally different pollution levels in designing tradable permits, such as zoning concepts that determine in advance the number of credits that are necessary to comply with ambient requirements, but here the "development" expenses may be prohibitive. What is interesting to know, though, is the impact of this conceptual separation of long-distance pollution from local pollution on the functioning of the markets for pollution rights, the efficiency gains, including the administrative costs, the incentives for technological innovation, and the investment flows. Professor Stewart refers to two studies[1] which suggest that ambient quality-related safeguards impair the functioning of the permit market, and for this reason he seems to consider these safeguards as somewhat excessive. However, while the (proposed) introduction of EIS may induce us to reconsider protection concepts, such as the ambient quality standards concept, hitherto taken for granted, it should not make us deflect environmental protection only for the market's sake.

A particularly problematic case in this respect is that of carcinogens. Professor Stewart does not have any objections to EIS in this field because he thinks exclusively in terms of general risk reduction. However, there might be a need for a more refined approach. Where a legal system grants every individual a right to minimization of individual risk, EIS must be ruled out entirely. Where a level of tolerable, albeit undesirable, exposure of the individual is recognized and minimization is undertaken in the public interest only, EIS may be used provided a local excess of this level is effectively prevented. However, irrespective of basic risk policies, it would seem that there is no reasonable basis for allowing unfettered use of EIS where and when their use imposes on individuals a high degree of cancer risk. This would run counter to the very rationale of public health policy which in its "hard core" is designed – and for constitutional reasons must be designed – to protect individuals rather than the public at large against

[1] Tom Tietenberg, "Tradeable Permits for Pollution Control When Emission Location Matters: What Have We Learned?" 5 *Env. & Res. Econ.* 95 (1995); Scott Atkinson and Tom Tietenberg, "Market Failure in Incentive-Based Regulation: The Case of Emission Trading," 21 J. *Env. Econ. & Mgmt.* 17 (1991).

unacceptable risks. The very fact that it is not easy to draw a clear line between safe (tolerable) and unsafe (unacceptable) levels of pollution does not warrant the verdict of "arbitrariness," the more so since, by the same token, environmental policy objectives that aim for a determined quantitative reduction of total emissions could also be treated as "arbitrary."

In the second place, it appears – and this is partly confirmed by Professor Stewart – that under the EIS practiced in the United States internal transactions within firms or corporate groups have always represented the bulk of all transactions effectuated, while full-fledged market transactions have been of clearly secondary importance. This experience under the Emissions Trading Policy prompted renowned commentators to ask "Where did all the markets go?"[2] It would seem that this question can be extended as well to the Clean Air Act's Acid Rain Program and to RECLAIM where the original euphoria about creating a true market for pollution rights has ended in a sort of crapulence about the overhang of rights offered for sale and the ensuing decline of the market price.[3] Of course, the increased flexibility that tradable permits offer firms to select efficient pollution prevention strategies within the firm is valuable in itself, but arguably, this does not require a sophisticated and expensive EIS of the type chosen under the Clean Air Act or in Southern California. As long as one believes in the superiority of the "invisible hand" of competition in the market (rather than within the firm), the full advantages of tradable permit systems can only be reaped if a sufficient number of true market transactions actually occur. Hence, the question arises as to what are the reasons for this unexpected development. Purely speculatively, one might think of an "insufficient" liberalization of the permit market, impediments stemming from the regulation of the public utilities' pricing system, lack of incentives because the emission reduction requirements are so low that they can easily be complied with by use of existing technology or of low-sulfur coal, decreases of transport prices for such coal, irrationality of firms which prefer expensive certainty to efficient uncertainty through dependence on the permit market, or banking as an insurance against future

[2] Robert W. Hahn and Gordon L. Hester, "Where Did All the Markets Go?" 7 *Yale J. Regulation* 109 (1989).

[3] See Dallas Burtraw and Byron Swift, "A New Standard of Performance: An Analysis of the Clean Air Act's Acid Rain Program," 26 *Env. L. Rep.* 10411, at 10416–20 (1996); as to RECLAIM see Pascal Bader and Fritz Rahmeyer, "Das RECLAIM-Programm handelbarer Umweltlizenzen," 19 *Zeitschrift für Umweltpolitik und Umweltrecht* 43, at 60–63 (1996).

uncertainties. Recent studies[4] suggest that a variety of reasons account for the unexpectedly slow development of markets for pollution rights.

In any case, the partial failure – as I see it – of the types of EIS practiced in the United States is liable to discourage the introduction of similar devices elsewhere in the industrialized world. This may explain why in Europe, outside the arcane community of academic economists, nobody had ever thought of using tradable permits for addressing global warming at national or supranational level. Rather, both nationally (Denmark, Netherlands, Norway, and Sweden) and at European Community level, the focus has always been on taxation of $CO_2$ emissions and/or energy consumption, which does not make global cooperation and harmonization of efforts to reduce greenhouse gases easier. It remains to be seen whether in the aftermath of the Kyoto Conference tradable permits will become more acceptable.

Finally in this context, it should be noted that the introduction of EIS, especially of tradable permits, leads to a far-going alteration of the established system of legal protection of rights and may require a modification of institutions that safeguard these rights. One problem arises in connection with the distribution of rights to pollute. In order to overcome political obstacles and also to mitigate difficulties of transition, the initial distribution of rights will normally be gratuitous, while most tradable permit systems provide that newcomers must acquire rights on the (free or organized) market. In this respect, EIS perpetuate the traditional unequal treatment of existing and new sources. Theoretically, this inequality is remedied by the need to include the calculatory costs of rights in the loss and earnings calculation of existing sources, but a legal requirement to do so does not seem to exist. It would be interesting to know more about the practice as it has developed in the United States in this respect. In any case, the question arises whether the state, because it has "artificially" created barriers to access of newcomers by establishing an EIS, has a residual obligation of ensuring market access, for example by intervening in the market if it does not function properly and by holding (gratuitous?) rights in reserve.

[4] Bernd Hansjürgens, "Wie erfolgreich ist das neue Schwefeldioxid-Zertifikatesystem in den USA? – Erste Erfahrungen und Lehren für die Zukunft," 21 *Zeitschrift für Umweltpolitik und Umweltrecht* 1–32 (1998); Douglas R. Bohi and Dallas Burtraw, "$SO_2$ Allowance Trading: How Experience and Expectations Measure Up" ( Resources for the Future Discussion Paper No. 97/24); A. Denny Ellerman et al., *1996 Update on Compliance and Emissions Trading under the US Acid Rain Program* (Center for Energy and Environmental Policy Research, Massachusetts Institute of Technology, 1997).

Another aspect of the problem is that of judicial protection of affected citizens.[5] EIS deeply affect the traditional system of judicial review. This is especially true of legal systems that do not limit judicial review to the protection against unacceptable risk but extend it to risk reduction for precautionary reasons. Also for preserving a minimum of judicial review, ambient quality-related safeguards would seem absolutely necessary and any attempt to curtail them should be resisted. Beyond that, the legal order must tackle the problem that in most EIS macro-decisions, such as the determination of caps on total emissions, are the essential element of the whole system.[6] By contrast, micro-decisions which have traditionally been subject to judicial review are replaced by the market mechanism. In order to avoid an undermining of judicial protection of individuals, these macro-decisions – similar to environmental standards – should be subject to judicial review, both at the request of affected citizens (too little environmental protection) and firms (excessive protection). Not all legal systems are well equipped for this new task – at least not in Europe.

## Contractual instruments as an alternative to market-based EIS

Market-based EIS rely on the "invisible hand" of competition as shaped by "artificial" framework conditions set by the state (taxes, tradable permit requirements, etc.). Contrary to widespread understanding, EIS are instruments of an interventionist environmental policy (from "top to bottom") in which the state retains a major role. In particular, caps on total emissions, which are at the core of most systems of tradable permits, amount to a severe "political" restraint of access to natural resources, although the rigor of this restraint is mitigated at the instrumental level by the flexibility built into the system by enabling market transactions. Environmental taxes fare

[5] See Eckard Rehbinder, "Übertragbare Emissionsrechte aus juristischer Sicht," in Alfred Endres, Eckard Rehbinder and Reimund Schwarze, *Umweltzertifikate und Kompensationslösungen aus ökonomischer und juristischer Sicht* (Bonn: Economica, 1994), 92, at 128–36.

[6] However, a trading system can postpone setting caps and provide for recognition of "early action" reductions by awarding credits for such reduction that can be "banked" and used later against future regulatory obligations; for a description of this "open trading" method see Environmental Protection Agency, 60 Fed. Reg. 39,668; Robert U. Ayres, "Developing a Market in Emission Credits Incrementally: An 'Open Market' Paradigm for Market-Based Pollution Control," 25 *BNA Environment Reporter* No. 31 (December, 1994).

better in this respect because there is no strict linkage between an amount of permissible total pollution and the artificial price to be paid per pollution unit. On the other hand, under a tax system, industry may have to pay for pollution that is below the threshold of intolerability. In contrast to the US, European countries have long preferred environmental taxes to tradable permits. Except for limited use of emission trading techniques in the field of air pollution control in Germany,[7] tradable permits have never played a role in Europe. By contrast, in the more recent past there has been a certain trend towards introducing environmental taxes which are no longer conceived as sources of finance for environmental investments but, rather, now clearly are designed to provide incentives for reducing pollution and waste. A good example are the taxes imposed on $CO_2$ emissions/energy use in various (smaller) European countries.[8]

An alternative to market-based EIS that claims to avoid some of the disadvantages of EIS by relying on the "visible hand" of negotiation and consensus is self-regulation by industry. Its purest forms are voluntary agreements by industry. They may be concluded or issued either in lieu of (future) administrative regulation or EIS (regulatory agreements) or as substitutes for measures of implementation or enforcement (implementation agreements).[9]

Professor Stewart briefly mentions contractual arrangements at plant level as an alternative to market-based EIS without going further into details, probably because there is not much experience in the United States in this respect. By contrast, various European countries such as the Netherlands, Germany, Denmark, and France have gained some experience which is worth discussing. In doing so, I will focus on Germany with which I am most familiar,[10] and limit the discussion to regulatory agreements

[7] See Eckard Rehbinder, "Environmental Regulation Through Fiscal and Economic Incentives in a Federalist System," 20 *Ecol. L.Q.* 57, at 75–76 (1993).

[8] See *Der Rat von Sachverständigen für Umweltfragen, Umweltgutachten 1996*, Nos. 963–82 (Metzler-Poeschel Verlag, Stuttgart, 1996); see also Rehbinder, "Environmental Regulation," at 72–74.

[9] See, e.g. Jan van Dunné ed., *Environmental Contracts and Covenants* (Vermande, Lelystad, 1993); Eckard Rehbinder, "Self-Regulation by Industry," in Gerd Winter ed., *European Environmental Law* (Dartmouth, 1996), 239–67.

[10] The following text summarizes findings of an EC-wide empirical study in which I have been responsible for Germany, see COWI (Consulting Engineers and Planners AS), *Study on Voluntary Agreements Concluded Between Industry and Public Authorities in the Field of the Environment, Final Report* (Copenhagen, January 1997); see also European Environmental Agency, *Environmental Agreements – Environmental Effectiveness*

which are more important and at the same time more suitable as substitutes for abstract-generic regulation or EIS than implementation agreements.

In Germany, "self-commitments" rather than formal agreements are the normal form of concerted self-regulation by industry in the field of environmental policy. Public authorities are not formally involved in these commitments which take the form of unilateral declarations of national branch associations or the national industry federation and in some cases of individual firms. However, these declarations are normally the outcome of intensive discussions with the competent ministries; more recently, but also sometimes in the past, these discussions have taken the form of veritable and long-lasting negotiations. Moreover, the declarations are addressed to the relevant public bodies, they are recognized by them in an informal way, for instance a press release, a press conference of the ministry concerned, or correspondence, or even flanked by a "lean" regulation. Finally the relevant public bodies exercise a major degree of control over the achievement of the targets set by the declarations.

Industry has issued about eighty self-commitments (and some formal agreements) in the field of environmental policy since the early 1980s (excluding about twenty purely internal self-commitments that are not addressed to, and not recognized by, the relevant authorities). The 1995 self-commitment of German industry concerning the protection of global climate, as amended and extended in 1996, now comprises nineteen separate self-commitments of the relevant branch associations which are quite different in character; if one included these self-commitments, the figures would have to be increased accordingly. The number of self-commitments is relatively high, with major increases in recent years. Quite a number of self-commitments were issued between 1995 and 1998 (e.g. in 1995: global climate protection, fuel efficiency of cars, cycle pool for taking back electronic equipment, detergents, and a comprehensive covenant in Bavaria; in 1996: amendment and extension of the self-commitment on protecting the global climate and various chemical substances; in 1997: end-of-life cars, global climate protection in the aluminum industry, production of paper, various detergents, and other chemical substances; 1998: various detergents and other chemical substances).

(Copenhagen, 1997), at 64–68; for an analysis of older self-commitments (issued in the 1980s) see Sylvia Lautenbach, Ulrich Steger and Peter Weihrauch, "Evaluierung freiwilliger Branchenvereinbarungen im Umweltschutz," in Bundesverband der Deutschen Industrie ed., *Freiwillige Kooperationslösungen im Umweltschutz* (Cologne, 1991).

There are two interrelated reasons for the increasing importance of self-commitments in Germany. First, there was a clear political commitment of the previous federal government in favor of self-commitments. After the federal elections of 1994, the political parties forming the ruling coalition agreed on a greater reliance on this informal instrument of environmental policy, and the federal executive was committed to a policy of deregulation, including self-regulation by industry. This stance corresponded to widespread demands by industry which opposed both administrative regulation and market-based EIS. The second reason for the emergence of self-commitments was that environmental policy, in the present state of widespread unemployment and a staggering economy, had a difficult position in conflicts with other policies; one can even say that the wind blew into the face of environmental policy. Self-commitments were considered as a sort of policy of the impossible, as a way out of the impasse in which environmental policy is presently situated. This, of course, theoretically means that the pendulum may also swing back to administrative regulation. However, given the general tendency towards recognizing the limits of regulation, it is not very probable that self-commitments will fall into disgrace in the foreseeable future, provided they can demonstrate an adequate degree of effectiveness, as compared to administrative regulation on the one hand and market-based EIS on the other. Although the new socialist–green coalition government that came into power after the election in September 1998 takes a somewhat more sober attitude towards self-commitments, the new coalition agreement expressly recognizes them as a useful instrument of environmental policy.

Among the more recent self-commitments, the declaration of German industry on protection of global climate of 1995, as amended and expanded in 1996, is of particular importance. It is seen as a test case for the effectiveness and acceptability of self-commitments as instruments of environmental policy in lieu of command-and-control regulation. It was first issued in view of the World Climate Conference in Berlin. The original declaration contained a commitment by German industry to reduce specific $CO_2$ emissions or specific energy consumption (i.e. emissions or energy per production unit) by 20 percent by the year 2005, the base year being 1987; the amended declaration stiffens this commitment by choosing the year 1990 as base year, which means that “windfall profits” in emission reductions from plant closures after the German reunification can no longer be credited. Moreover, in addition to the fifteen industrial sectors, four new sectors joined the declaration. The new declaration contains a rather detailed and complex monitoring system which is supervised by an independent economic research institute. It is provided that the data generated shall also be made public.

The declaration is an "umbrella" declaration which is concretized by nineteen individual self-commitments of various sectoral associations which describe the reduction potential and promise to make the best technical efforts to use this potential fully; they have also agreed in a second declaration to report on previous progress and indicate further measures envisaged. The whole system accounts for about 70 percent of industrial energy consumption and close to 100 percent of public electricity supply; moreover, due to the participation of the associations of the German gas and electricity supply industries and the municipal enterprises, it indirectly comprises most households and small commercial consumers. The individual self-commitments describe the potential for the reduction of $CO_2$ emissions and increase of energy efficiency and promise to make the best technical efforts to use this potential fully, sometimes in the form of detailed measures. Most self-commitments indicate quantitative targets which may be below, or beyond, the general target of 20 percent; often, there is differentiation between the old Federal Republic and Eastern Germany (where the reduction/saving potential is much higher). Moreover, in contrast to the 1995 declaration, individual self-commitments do not only promise the reduction of specific $CO_2$ emissions or the increase of specific energy efficiency; there are fifteen commitments that are also couched in absolute terms.

At the origin of the $CO_2$ self-commitment was the desire of the German government to have something to present to the Berlin Conference that demonstrated the firm will of Germany to comply with its unilateral commitment of reducing $CO_2$ emissions by 25 percent by 2005. Since both the introduction of a $CO_2$ and/or energy tax and the promulgation of the regulation for the reutilization of excess process heat mandated by the Federal Emission Control Act were very controversial, the self-commitment was seen as a way out of the impasse in which environmental policy was caught at that time. In the view of industry, the self-commitment presents important efficiency gains, its major advantage being the possibility of differentiating between the respective commitments of the various industrial sectors according to their (average) cost structure and reduction/saving potential. It is argued that administrative regulation as well as environmental taxes would lead to uniform – or at least less differentiated – requirements or effects. This problem is mirrored by various proposals made in the discussion on the EU $CO_2$ emissions/energy use tax to the extent that energy-intensive sectors be entirely exempted or at least granted some tax advantages.

The political, economic, and legal assessment of self-commitments has always been controversial and their increasing use in recent years is seen by many not as a sign of the growing need for a flexible environmental policy that is considerate of the needs of the affected industry, but, rather, as a sign of regulatory weakness of the state. The primary problem of a political and economic evaluation of self-commitments is the development of an adequate reference system for comparing the design (the objectives) and the performance of self-commitments on the one hand, and administrative and economic regulation, on the other. Possible criteria include:

what would have been achieved by hypothetical administrative regulation or EIS,
the technical emissions reduction potential,
the trend scenario ("business as usual" scenario),
the level of pollution before and after the self-commitment.

However, making this comparison is less easy than it appears at first glance.[11]

In comparing alternative instruments of environmental policy, it is methodologically incorrect to compare an ideal situation – what could theoretically have been achieved by using administrative regulation, eco-taxes, or tradable permits – with a real one – what one will achieve by accepting a self-commitment. This neglects the contingency of the political process. Nobody knows whether the executive or parliament would have been able politically to impose administrative regulation, eco-taxes, or tradable permits that ensure meeting its political targets. The $CO_2$ self-commitment is criticized because it aims at lower energy savings than envisaged by the federal executive and achieved on the average of the last few decades as a consequence of economic change.[12] However, one should not take it for granted that a mere prolongation of energy-saving trends

[11] European Environmental Agency, *Environmental Agreements*, at 12, 52–54, 83–87; Eckard Rehbinder, "Environmental Agreements – A New Instrument of Environmental Policy," 27 *Env. Pol. & L.* 258, at 263–64.

[12] Klaus Rennings et al., *Nachhaltigkeit, Ordnungspolitik und freiwillige Selbstverpflichtung* (Physica, Heidelberg, 1997); for an appraisal of an advanced draft of the $CO_2$ self-commitment see Michael Kohlhaas, Barbara Praetorius et al., *Selbstverpflichtungen der Industrie zur $CO_2$-Reduktion* (Berlin: Duncker & Humblot, 1994).

from the past to the future already represents a valid prognosis. It is true that the theoretical disadvantage of self-commitments is that the state must pay for them by a lessening of the desirable level of environmental protection. However, the possible drawback of watering down environmental policy targets may be offset by the advantage that a (prompt) solution of the problem is possible.

Furthermore, due to the acceptance by the most directly affected firms, there may be fewer compliance problems. This advantage of self-regulation is of a psychological nature. Where industry develops solutions through self-commitments it will later have to comply with self-created, rather than heteronomous, rules; this increases the degree of compliance. Of course, this requires participation of virtually all affected members of the relevant branch of industry which is not always ensured because small and medium-sized firms are sometimes not sufficiently represented in industrial associations. While some self-commitments issued so far have ultimately failed, there are many examples of quite successful self-commitments. Since the reasons for the failure of self-commitments have largely been "atypical," such as the lack of acceptance of an environmentally friendly product by consumers or the collapse of the calculatory basis of participants due to later developments, one cannot argue that self-commitments are doomed to failure because they are not enforceable. Rather, it would seem that self-commitments are indeed capable of contributing to the implementation of a precautionary environmental policy.

In any case, there are a number of prerequisites for the environmental success of self-commitments that substantially limit their applicability, although these factors are not absolute, but relative and not necessarily cumulative: industry and distributors must not expect considerable disadvantages (costs, competitive disadvantages, loss of turnover) as a consequence of the self-commitment; there must be a certain homogeneity on the part of the committed industry; there must be fairly uniform attitudes among the public as to the assessment of the environmental problem to be solved by the self-commitment so that industry is under pressure; and the agency must dispose of a considerable threatening potential, which means that in case of lack of consensus or compliance with the self-commitment the adoption of a more disadvantageous administrative regulation must be probable.[13]

[13] Cf. Pieter Winsemius, "Environmental Contracts and Covenants: New Instruments for a Realistic Environmental Policy?" in van Dunné, *Environmental Contracts and Covenants*, 5–15.

In order to compensate for "competitive" disadvantages of the state in this respect, the more recent self-commitments all provide for rather sophisticated monitoring systems; it is thought that the interim monitoring results will enable the state to intervene where there is no reasonable further progress towards achieving the relevant environmental targets.

Industry favors self-commitments on the ground that they achieve efficiency gains as compared to both administrative regulation and environmental taxes. Arguably the major advantage of self-commitments relates more to equitable distribution of regulatory burdens and avoidance of distortive effects on competition (e.g., dislocation of energy-intensive industry to low energy-efficiency countries, which would run counter to the environmental goal of achieving total net benefits for global climate). Since, except for some Dutch agreements, the association commitments are not formally translated into requirements for individual firms, it would seem that part of the alleged efficiency gains achieved by self-commitments differentiated sector by sector will be lost at firm level.[14] However, in developing a proposal for a self-commitment, the relevant industry association largely relies on the individual membership firms' self-assessment of their respective reduction potential. Provided these self-assessments reflect the firms' marginal costs and the firms, because they have a self-interest in the success of the self-commitment, reduce their emissions accordingly, one cannot rule it out that there are some merits to the efficiency argument.

Another advantage of self-commitments as compared to market-based EIS is the greater possibility for industry to foresee and calculate the economic consequences of required reduction of pollution. In particular, industry does not depend on the varying market price of tradable permits nor does it have to spend money on taxes at the very moment when it would be appropriate to use this money for investment in process changes, and industry is more flexible as regards the exact timing of environmental investments.

A related argument in favor of self-commitments is that they grant industry an option for self-regulation within the framework of targets set by the state. Self-regulation means that industry can shape the design of the relevant rules. This is particularly important in areas such as $CO_2$ reduction

[14] Peter Börkey and Matthieu Glachant, *Les engagements volontaires de l'industrie dans le domaine de l'environnement: nature et diversité* (CERNA (Centre d'économie industrielle), Paris, 1997), at 40; Rennings et al., *Nachhaltigkeit*, at 217.

and energy efficiency where quite different solutions are possible. Although industry can also influence the design of administrative regulation in the bargaining process as to relevant governmental proposals, the bargaining position of industry with respect to negotiated self-commitments is better and hence its influence on the design of the solution greater. However, market-based EIS are equivalent in this respect.

From a legal point of view, one may object to contractualization of environmental policy for various reasons, especially on the grounds that the state gives away its regulatory prerogatives, inequality is promoted, there is a danger of capture of agencies by industry, participation of the public is excluded, and competition is restricted.[15] The two latter aspects are the most important and shall be briefly dealt with. Public participation is generally seen as a major prerequisite for broadening the information basis of the executive, achieving a more rational decision, and securing public acceptance. Self-commitments are negotiated behind closed doors with virtually no public participation, except for isolated press coverage accompanying some more controversial negotiations. To the extent that the executive assumes a major role in the process by concluding formal agreements or initiating and recognizing self-commitments, it is arguable that this amounts to a circumvention of the participation requirements. A real remedy for the malaise is not in sight. Granting the public the right to participate in the negotiation might impede the success of negotiation, although fewer objections can be raised against a simple right to comment on an advanced draft of the self-commitment. In any case, "reformalizing the informal" is always problematic. Therefore, a viable solution might have to be sought in *ex post* controls, for example, extensive transparence and public participation in monitoring the achievements of the particular self-commitment. The strong emphasis laid recently on monitoring and transparence of the performance of self-commitments points in this direction.

As regards competition, self-commitments may be associated with restraints of competition where they fix prices, bar certain materials access

[15] See, e.g., Gerd Winter, "Bartering Rationality in Regulation," 19 *Law and Society Rev.* 219 (1985); Alfred Rest, "The Integration of Environmental Covenants and Contracts in the Public Law System," in van Dunné, *Environmental Contracts and Covenants*, 225–30; Ellen Basse, "The Contract Model – The Merits of a Voluntary Approach," 2 *Env. Liability* 74, at 81–82 (1994); Rehbinder, "Environmental Agreements," at 266–68; Udo Di Fabio, "Selbstverpflichtungen der Wirtschaft – Grenzgänger zwischen Freiheit und Zwang," 52 *Juristen-Zeitung*, 969, 970–73 (1998).

to the market, establish pools for collecting and recovering product-related waste, decide on the introduction of new products, or hamper innovation competition. In the practice of the German and European antitrust authorities, there has been a certain tendency to exempt self-commitments – except for cases of price-fixing and severe market foreclosure – from the scope of application of antitrust laws, on the grounds that the adverse impact on competition was not appreciable or the self-commitment was on balance beneficial and therefore could be tolerated or formally permitted.[16] Whatever the merits of this permissive balancing approach in individual cases, it is safe to say that the problem of adverse effects on competition can be tackled by antitrust enforcement. Of course, an orthodox antitrust philosophy that does not accept that there may be reasonable restraints of competition for the sake of environmental protection would be the death of self-commitments.

## Global problems and EIS

As Professor Stewart points out, EIS, especially tradable permit systems, can also be used as instruments for implementing international policies for tackling global warming. Already the Montreal Protocol provides that a Party which overcomplies with its production reduction (not consumption) quota can transfer the unused part of the quota to another Party and this Party can comply with its obligations by using the credit. Similar arrangements have been widely discussed in the Framework Convention on Climate Change.[17] The Kyoto Protocol (Art. 16 *bis*) now gives countries

[16] See, e.g., Alexander Riesenkampf, "Die private Abfallentsorgung und das Kartellrecht," 50 *Der Betriebs-Berater* 933 (1995); Ludwig Krämer, "Die Integrierung umweltpolitischer Erfordernisse in die europäische Wettbewerbspolitik," in Werner Rengeling ed., *Umweltschutz und andere Politiken der Europäischen Gemeinschaft* (Cologne: Heymanns Verlag, 1993), 47, at 56–58; Anja Verena Steinbeck, "Umweltvereinbarungen und europäisches Wettbewerbsrecht," 48 *Wirtschaft und Wettbewerb* 554 (1998).

[17] See, e.g., *Climate Change: Designing a Tradable Permit System* (OECD, Paris, 1992); Johannes Heister, Peter Michaelis et al., *Umweltpolitik mit handelbaren Emissionsrechten* (Tübingen: Mohr, 1990), 146–75; Henning Rentz, *Kompensationen im Klimaschutz* (Berlin: Duncker & Humblot, 1995); Christopher Stone, "Beyond Rio: 'Insuring' Against Global Warming," 86 *Am. J. Int. L.* 445 (1992); Scott Barrett, "Negotiating a Framework Convention on Climate Change: Economic Considerations," in *Convention on Climate Change. Economic Aspects of Negotiations* (OECD, Paris, 1992), 9, at 60–62; Axel Michaelowa, *Internationale Kompensationsmöglichkeiten zur $CO_2$-Reduktion* (Berlin: Duncker & Humblot, 1995); Alfred Endres, "Designing a Greenhouse Treaty: Some

whose emissions are above the limits stipulated in the agreement the option of purchasing emission quotas from countries who are below and who thereby have created credits. The principle of "carbon trading" must still be defined, its limits determined and specific procedures worked out for its application.

EIS in the field of protecting global climate require the explicit setting of national quotas or quota-like reduction obligations, ideally with respect to all greenhouse gases (expressed in $CO_2$ equivalents), but at least relating to $CO_2$.[18] As demonstrated by the long-lasting (ultimately successful) bargaining over the tradable permit system in the framework of the US Clean Air Act Amendments, the (unsuccessful) negotiations on an EC-wide $CO_2$ emissions/energy tax use, and most recently the Kyoto negotiations, the initial allocation of pollution rights is the real bottleneck in devising interregional and international EIS. Criteria such as emissions per capita, historic cumulative or present emissions, emissions per GNP, emissions per square kilometer, or need-oriented allocation schemes have been discussed as regards the Framework Convention on Climate Change. They all meet with major objections.[19]

A per capita allocation is out of proportion to the future needs of developing countries and would lead to massive transfer payments between industrialized countries and populous developing countries; moreover, it would equip states having low marginal emission reduction costs disproportionately with rights. Such an allocation criterium would at best be conceivable if not only $CO_2$ but all greenhouse gases and $CO_2$ sinks were included in the EIS. On the other hand, allocation according to historic cumulative or present emissions would favor industrialized countries in an inappropriate manner and practically maintain the present disproportion between industrialized and developing countries in world energy consumption and ensuing emissions. The GDP test has similarly distortive effects but would in addition lead to a differentiation within the group of industrialized states, favoring both states with high energy efficiency, which

Economic Problems," in Erling Eide and Roger van den Bergh eds., *Law and Economics of the Environment* (Oslo: Juridisk Forlag, 1996), 201–24.

18 Stone, "Beyond Rio," at 462–64, 470–74.

19 Michael Grubb and James K. Sebenius, "Participation, Allocation and Adaptability in International Tradeable Emission Permit Systems for Greenhouse Gas Control," in OECD, *Climate Change*, 185, at 201–02, 207–10; Scott Barrett, "Economic Instruments for Climate Change Policy," in *Responding to Climate Change* (OECD, Paris, 1991), 51, at 92.

is desirable, and states with a high share of nuclear energy, which might appear less desirable. Criteria relating to national territory disadvantage populous states having a small national territory. Recourse to energy need is devoid of any rational determination. Given this background, it is to be expected that only a combination of the criteria just denoted might meet with acceptance by the international community in the context of global climate policy.[20]

The experiences so far with the setting of differentiated emission reduction quotas for existing facilities in the framework of the EC Directive on Major Fuel-Burning Facilities,[21] the Second Protocol under the Economic Commission for Europe Convention for the Control of Sulfur Dioxide Emissions,[22] the allocation formula developed by the Greek presidency in the bargaining over the EC-wide $CO_2$ emissions/energy use tax,[23] and the internal allocation of the EC reduction proposal ("EC bubble") for the Kyoto negotiations between the EC Member States[24] presented examples of possible solutions. However, in the field of global climate policy, the global dimension added much more complexity to bargaining over, and allocation of, pollution rights.[25] Of particular importance in this respect also were the still existing uncertainties as to cause–effect relationships, the consequences of global warming and costs for reducing emissions, the unequal distribution of costs and benefits of preventive measures, and the interface of environmental and development policy implications. The final solution reached at Kyoto – differentiated reduction quotas for most industrialized countries, stabilization obligations for some of them, and increased allowances for a few others – reflects these difficulties.

The task now is to work out the procedures for the application of carbon trading. The implementation of the obligations assumed could be left to the states.[26] Rather than establishing a worldwide EIS system accessible to firms, there might be a coexistence of national administrative regulation, environmental taxes (which are favored by many European countries),

[20] See the authors cited in note 19 above.

[21] Directive 88/609/EC, OJ L 336/1 (1988).

[22] 24 *Envt. Pol'y & L.*132, 231 (1994).

[23] 24 *Envt. Pol'y & L.*190 (1994).

[24] *EC Bulletin* 10/1997, 57; Bundesministerium für Umwelt, Naturschutz und Reaktorsicherheit, 1997, *Umweltpolitik aktuell*, 3/23; as to the final internal allocation see *EC Bulletin* 6/1998, 72.

[25] Cf. Barrett, "Negotiating a Framework Convention," at 91–92, 93–94.

[26] This option is suggested by the wording of Art. 17 of the Kyoto Protocol.

transferable permits and voluntary agreements, and emission rights which are only to be traded between states. The alternative would be a worldwide trading system directly accessible to firms. In contrast to what Professor Stewart seems to suggest, I think that in view of the fundamentally different instrumental responses states subject to reduction obligations under the Kyoto Protocol have given to the challenge of global warming, the rather modest technique of carbon trading between states presently constitutes a good solution. It offers prospects for achieving a reasonable degree of efficiency, promoting dispersion of technological innovation and generating investment flows, while not compelling the states to give up already established patterns of implementing national global warming policies. Of course there could also be an option for states to choose between a trading system open only to states or also to private firms.[27]

The mechanisms for joint implementation between states have also been extended by the Kyoto Conference, allowing joint implementation between industrial and developing states ("Clean Development Mechanism"). Objections raised against this type of joint implementation by numerous NGOs as well as some developing countries[28] ultimately do not appear to be conclusive, if certain framework conditions are respected. First of all, it is a gross miscalculation of the cost-saving potential of joint implementation to expect that the bulk of required emission reductions could be covered by joint implementation projects. For example, a country review of China rendered the result that joint implementation might be economically much less attractive than hoped for.[29] Therefore, the fear that joint implementation will hamper technological innovation in industrial states because these states can comply with their reduction obligations through cheap joint implementation projects is largely unfounded. Furthermore, the anticipated opportunity costs in terms of lost economic use developing countries

[27] Inclusion of private firms is advocated in the proposal of the so-called Umbrella-Group submitted to the Bonn Conference of Subsidiary Bodies, June 1998: see "Non-Paper on Principles, Modalities, Rules and Guidelines for an International Emissions Trading Regime," UNFCCC/SB/1998/MISC.1/Add. 1.

[28] Herrmann Ott, "Tenth Session of the UNC/FCCC: Results and Options for the First Conference of Parties," *ELNI Newsletter* 2/1994, 3, at 4; see also Reinhard Loske and Stefan Obertür, "Joint Implementation under the Climate Change Convention," 6 *Int. Env. Affairs* 45 (1994).

[29] See Johannes Heister and Frank Stähler, "Globale Umweltpolitik und Joint Implementation: Eine ökonomische Analyse für die Volksrepublik China," 18 *Zeitschrift für Umweltpolitik und Umweltrecht* 205 (1995).

# 9

# EQUITY AND EFFICIENCY IN GLOBAL EMISSIONS MARKETS

GRACIELA CHICHILNISKY

THIS ESSAY examines the issues of equity and efficiency in the use of global environmental resources, with the atmosphere as a case in point. It shows a somewhat unexpected connection between the two issues in the context of international greenhouse gas emissions trading markets. Contrary to common wisdom, achieving a more even distribution of property rights to environmental assets is more than a matter of equity. Property rights also influence market efficiency. I show that a precondition for market efficiency is that more property rights in the global commons should be given to those regions that own fewer private goods. This connection leads to recommendations to implement the greenhouse gas emissions trading regimes authorized by the Kyoto Protocol to the United Nations Framework Convention on Climate Change (FCCC).[1] In order to ensure an efficient trading market, developing countries should be allocated proportionately more emissions rights than industrial countries. In

This paper was presented at a workshop organized by New York University Law School at the Villa La Pietra in Florence, Summer 1996. I thank the participants of the workshop, particularly Richard Stewart, Stephen Breyer, and Richard Revesz, for valuable comments and suggestions.

[1] The recommendations in this essay were presented at the May 1994 Workshop on Joint Implementation organized with the support of GEF and the FCCC at Columbia University, New York, and in various FCCC meetings. In these recommendations I benefited from the discussions of several members of the Intergovernmental Negotiating Committee (INC) of the FCCC, who provided important insights: Minister Raul Estrada Oyuela, Chair of the INC/FCCC, H. E. Ismail Razali, Ambassador, Permanent Mission of Malaysia to the United Nations (UN), Mr. Xialong Wang, Third Secretary, Chinese Permanent Mission to the UN, Mr. James Baba, Deputy Permanent Representative of Uganda to the UN, and Dr. John Ashe, Counsellor, Permanent Mission of Antigua and Barbuda to the UN.

addition, there is a need to create an International Bank for Environmental Settlements (IBES) as a self-financing institution that can obtain market value from environmental resources while preserving them. Emissions trading, the global reinsurance of environmental risks, and securitization of the earth's biodiversity resources are financial instruments that merge the interests of the private financial markets with international sustainable development policy. These instruments and institutions should help to redefine economic progress in a way that is compatible with a harmonious use of the world's resources and with equity among rich and poor nations.

## From industrial society to knowledge society

Since the Second World War, newly created institutions including the World Bank, the International Monetary Fund (IMF), and GATT, have led the world economy into an unprecedented period of industrialization, material expansion, and global commerce. These Bretton Woods institutions are creatures of the post-war reconstruction.[2] During this period economic progress has resulted in an ever-increasing use of energy and natural resources. A consensus is emerging that the main origin of the global environmental problems that the world faces today is the process of industrialization, which has been very resource-intensive. As the century turns, industrial societies' intensive use of the earth's resources has reached its logical limits. For the first time in history, economic activity has reached levels at which it can alter, in many cases irreversibly, the atmosphere of the planet and the complex web of species and ecosystems that constitutes and supports life on earth. Humans have the ability to destroy in a few decades much of the massive ecological infrastructure that supports the survival of the human species on the planet, the global habitat to which humans have adapted throughout the ages.

Industrial society's intensive use of the planet's resources is now under close scrutiny. At the same time, industrial society is in the process of transforming itself into a knowledge society, not a service economy as previously thought. To an increasing extent, humans can now achieve a new form of economic organization where the most important input of production is no

[2] See G. Chichilnisky, "The Greening of Bretton Woods," *The Financial Times*, 10 January 1996, and C. Bernandes, "Environmental Assets and Derivatives," 5 *Derivatives Week* No. 22 (3 June 1996).

longer machines, but human knowledge. Instead of burning fossil fuels to power machines, we could burn information to power knowledge. Information is a much cleaner fuel than coal or petroleum. This circumstance puts humans rather than machines at the center of economic progress.

The most dynamic sectors in the world economy today are not resource-intensive but knowledge-intensive: biotechnology and entertainment, software and hardware, communications and financial markets.[3] These sectors are friendly to the environment, use relatively few resources, and emit little carbon dioxide ($CO_2$). They are the high-growth sectors in the US and in the most industrialized countries, and are developing rapidly in other regions of the world. Some of the most dynamic developing countries are making a swift transition from traditional societies to knowledge-intensive societies. Mexico produces computer chips, India's Bangalore is fast becoming one of the world's largest exporters of software (current exports are about $2 billion), Barbados and Bermuda have recently unveiled a plan to become an information society within a generation. There is nothing new about such policies. These are precisely the policies followed by the Asian Tigers – Hong Kong, the Republic of Korea, Singapore, and the Taiwan Province of China – all countries which have achieved extraordinarily successful economic results over the last twenty years by relying not on resource exports but on knowledge-intensive products, such as consumer electronics. By contrast, Africa and Latin America have emphasized natural resource exports and have lost ground.

The lessons of history are clear. They dictate abandonment of reliance on resource exports as the foundation of economic development. Africa and Latin America must update their economic focus. Indeed, the whole world must shift away from resource-intensive economic processes and products. In doing so, fewer minerals (including fossil fuels) and other environmental resources will be extracted, and their price will rise. This is as it should be because today's low resource prices are a symptom of overproduction and inevitably lead to overconsumption and excessive environmental degradation.[4] In the future, resource producers will sell less but at higher prices.

[3] See G. Chichilnisky, "The Knowledge Revolution," *J. Int. Trade & Econ. Development* (1996) and *The New Economy* (London: IPPR, Spring 1997).

[4] See G. Chichilnisky, "Development and Global Finance: The Case for an International Bank for Environmental Settlements," keynote presentation at the Third Conference on Effective Financing, World Bank, 6 October 1995, Discussion Paper no. 10, UNESCO/UNDP–ODS (New York, 1996).

This is not to say that all will gain in the process. If the world's demand for petroleum drops, petroleum producers may lose unless they have diversified into other products and services that rely less on natural resource exploitation and have higher value. Many international oil companies (British Petroleum is a case in point) are investigating this strategy. The point is that nations cannot reliably develop on the basis of resource exports, and at the end of the day development based on knowledge-based strategies rather than natural resource-based stereotypes can make all better off. As the trend is inevitable, the sooner the transition is made, the better. Economic development means achieving more with less.

The question is how to promote the transition from an industrial, resource-intensive society to a much more environment-friendly knowledge society in the developing as well as the industrialized countries. New institutional arrangements, including international greenhouse gas emissions trading and the creation of an IBES, will be needed in order to facilitate this transition. The basic principles discussed in this essay apply very widely to the use of all environmental assets, including biodiversity, soil, and forests. However, the examples and data used here focus primarily on the use of the atmosphere of the planet through the emission of greenhouse gases, which are in large part derived from the burning of fossil fuels to generate energy.

## International cooperation and conflict in addressing climate change

Widespread concern with ozone depletion, biodiversity destruction, and global climate change led to the 1992 Earth Summit in Rio de Janeiro. Over 100 nations agreed to work together to reduce the threat of global warming by signing the FCCC, which establishes a framework of cooperation that looks forward to binding international obligations for reductions of greenhouse gas emissions. At the same time that it embraced environmental protection objectives, the Earth Summit also emphasized the importance of achieving sustainable development. United Nations Agenda 21 has, as an explicit objective, a pattern of consumption oriented towards the satisfaction of basic needs.[5]

[5] The concept of development oriented towards the satisfaction of basic needs was introduced theoretically and developed empirically by the author in 1994, in the context of studies of sustainable development in five continents: G. Chichilnisky, "North–South Trade and the Global Environment," 84 (4) *Am. Econ. Rev.* 427–34 (1994). The Brundtland

In December 1997 the Third Conference of the Parties (COP3) to the FCCC in Kyoto took matters a great deal further. It reached for the first time an agreement for hard quotas from industrial nations by which they will decrease their emissions by an average of 5.2 percent by the period 2008–12, using as a baseline the level of emissions prevailing in 1990 (the developing nations are currently not subject to any emissions limitations obligations). At the same time that it limits industrial nations' emissions, the Kyoto Protocol provides four market-oriented "flexibility" mechanisms to help achieve these limits: pooling of commitments among industrial country Parties to achieve compliance jointly (Article 4.1); transfer among industrial country Parties of joint implementation project-based emissions reduction units (Article 6); the Clean Development Mechanism (Article 12); and emissions trading among industrial country Parties (Article 17). Of these, only the Clean Development Mechanism (CDM) incorporates both the industrial and the developing nations. It enables industrial countries to obtain credits against their Protocol emissions limitation obligations by investments, including investments by private firms, in projects in developing countries to reduce net greenhouse gas emissions.

The flexibility mechanisms of the Kyoto Protocol are still in a somewhat embryonic form. The Conference of the Parties 4 (COP4) in Buenos Aires, in November 1998, attempted to achieve more definition. The agreement reached in Buenos Aires calls for a firm deadline to achieve this clarification within two years. In addition, the US signed the Kyoto Protocol in Buenos Aires and two developing nations, including the host of COP4, Argentina, declared their intention to participate voluntarily in the emissions trading provision. However these nations have little impact in terms of present or future emissions, and the unwillingness of developing nations to participate in emissions reduction commitments was reinforced in Buenos Aires by the largest emitters, such as India and China, and by the OPEC countries. Following Buenos Aires COP4, the need to achieve a solution that is attractive to both industrial and developing nations seems as compelling as ever.

Despite these steps towards cooperation, and the interest of all nations in dealing with the common problem of climate change, there are significant conflicts within the international community over the measures that

Report's definition of sustainable development is also anchored to basic needs: sustainable development satisfies the needs of the present without compromising the needs of the future. World Commission on Environment and Development, *Our Common Future* (1987), chapter 2, para. 1.

should be taken. Developing countries fear the imposition of restrictions on their growth in the form of emissions limitations that would curtail their use of their own energy and other national resources. Since most net greenhouse gas emissions currently originate and originated historically in the industrialized countries, whose patterns of development are at the root of the environmental dilemmas we face today,[6] the developing countries have consistently insisted that the industrial countries take the lead in reducing emissions. To a certain extent the Kyoto Protocol has met this requirement.

The members of OPEC are particularly concerned with the adverse effect of the Protocol limitations on their export markets if petroleum prices increase. A similar position is taken by other resource-intensive exporters, such as Australia. On the other hand, many industrialized countries fear excessive population growth, environmentally uncontrolled industrial growth, and sharply increasing energy consumption in developing countries and the environmental damage that they could bring. While recognizing their historical responsibility for excessive environmental resource use, they focus on a future in which global environmental problems could originate mostly in developing countries. Indeed, the future of industrialization is in the hands of the developing nations. Industrialization has led to the global environmental problems we have today. If the developing nations, with their much larger populations, were to retrace the steps of the industrial nations, the severity of the problems would increase several fold. Yet, the Bretton Woods institutions have traditionally advocated resource-intensive development policies in the developing nations. The traditional style of development, based on the intensive and extensive extraction of resources that are exported to and overconsumed in the industrial nations, has come to its logical end. It must be replaced by another form of development, the aspiration for which is reflected in "sustainable development" or "clean industrialization." This form of development can be promoted through the knowledge revolution as it evolves and is transmitted throughout the world economy. Nonetheless, the current and near-term negotiations for addressing climate change face a north–south divide. The road

[6] For carbon dioxide, the most important greenhouse gas, the breakdown is as follows: 60–70 percent of all emissions originate from industrial nations currently and about 70 percent historically, even though these countries contain about 25 percent of the world's population. Indeed, the 60 percent reduction in current emissions that many scientists believe may be required to have a substantial effect in lowering the risks of climate change can only come from decreasing the industrial nations' emissions: all developing nations together add up to only about 35 percent of emissions, and therefore nothing within their power could decrease emissions as required.

ahead is long and steep. International agreements are customarily adopted by consensus. How can this be achieved?

One essential step is to develop and eventually connect the various emissions trading mechanisms in the Kyoto Protocol in innovative ways in order to provide the transfers of technology and capital to developing countries that are crucial to break the historical link between carbon emissions and economic progress. The aim is to view the Kyoto Protocol's goals as part of the redefinition of the development strategies for developing nations, and trading mechanisms as a means to accomplish this objective.

A second essential step is to establish what I call an International Bank for Environmental Settlements, or IBES. The emergence of global and environmental problems and their close relation to international trade and investment means that new institutional arrangements are needed to complement the Bretton Woods institutions. An institution such as the IBES proposed here is needed in order to implement the Kyoto Protocol and to help set up a cooperative process for industrial and developing nations in the achievement of its goals. The role of the IBES complements markets but goes much further than anything that unaided markets can achieve. The Bank will use as collateral the environmental assets of the planet, perhaps the most valuable of all assets known to humankind. Among other matters, it will facilitate the execution and settlement of the trading of environmental assets and related financial instruments within the global emissions ceilings stipulated by the Protocol.

## The economics of the global environment: the link between efficiency and equity in international greenhouse gas emissions trading systems

The implementation of the various emissions trading regimes authorized by the Kyoto Protocol requires a measure of consensus about the policy instruments to be used and how they are deployed. These instruments share a novel and unusual characteristic. They trade rights to use the atmosphere of the planet, which are rights to use a public good: the quality of the earth's atmosphere is the same for all and cannot be chosen in different quantities for different people. Although different regions are affected differently, the concentration of greenhouse gases in the atmosphere is the same worldwide.

Another new aspect of this environmental problem is that emissions, although functionally related to a public good in the quality of the atmosphere, are not centrally produced by government, as are public goods like law and order. In contrast with the classic case examined by Lindahl, Bowen, and Samuelson,[7] in which public goods are provided by governments, the public good that interests us here is privately produced. Indeed every person on the planet emits greenhouse gases through driving a car, heating their home, or consuming energy produced by burning fossil fuels. Reduction in these emissions will require changes in private behavior. Such changes can be induced by a variety of regulatory instruments, including emission caps and trading systems, adopted and enforced by governments, but the public good of atmospheric quality must ultimately be produced by private conduct. Emissions markets are therefore markets to trade *privately produced public goods.* Such markets are quite different from classical markets.

To understand the issues presented by these novel circumstances and develop appropriate policy, conceptual advances in economics and institutions are needed to address challenging questions such as:

What property rights regimes and market structures will lead to allocational efficiency?

How can an acceptable degree of equity in the global use of carbon be ensured?

How would market-based approaches for dealing with climate change have an impact on developing countries? Should developing countries have more property rights in the global "common," and if so, why and how?

Which institutional arrangements may be needed to support and regulate the trading, clearing, and settlement of emission rights and related assets, and to ensure the efficiency and integrity of the market?

To abate carbon emissions means, in the short term, burning less fossil fuel and producing less energy. This means less economic output in terms of conventional goods and services. Both industrialized and developing countries face significant abatement costs in the short run because current patterns of development are resource-intensive and it is costly to change them. Although the outcome of current practices is uncertain because we know relatively little about the impact of human activity on the environment of the planet, the risks we face are nevertheless sufficient to make it compelling that precautionary steps be taken now.

[7] See, e.g., A. Atkinson and J. Stiglitz, *Lectures in Public Economics* (Maidenhead: McGraw Hill, 1980).

As developed in Richard Stewart's chapter and in Chichilnisky and Heal,[8] an important argument for the use of emissions trading systems to limit net greenhouse gas (GHG) emissions is that it sets an overall ceiling to world emissions and within this ceiling it tends to equate marginal costs of abatement across countries so that it can improve the cost-effectiveness of emission reductions.[9] Regardless of how entitlements to emit GHG are initially allocated, trading will ensure that resources are allocated to the lowest cost GHG-reducing opportunities, wherever in the world they are located. For example, if abatement of carbon emissions costs less in developing countries, then trading would tend to ensure that a substantial amount of abatement would be carried out in those countries.[10] This approach would of course have limitations: the developing nations emit at most 40 percent of the world's emissions while scientific evaluations require a 60 percent reduction to make a dent in the climate change problem. Therefore in practice the environmentally appropriate reduction targets cannot be reached without a substantial reduction of emissions on the part of the industrial nations, which generate most emissions, as well.

The question of who should abate emissions first and by how much leads to the issue of who should bear the burden of decreasing their use of energy and potentially decreasing economic growth. Analysis points to the conclusion that under current conditions the industrial nations may have to abate first. This conclusion tallies with the views of 166 nations that agreed in the Kyoto Protocol to require emission reductions solely from Annex B countries, which are mostly industrialized countries. However the generally held view in industrial nations is, not surprisingly, that it would be more efficient for developing nations to abate first. To support this view it is argued that the costs of abatement are lower in developing countries, and thus more abatement can be achieved at a lower cost if the reduction in emissions takes place in those countries. The economic approach invoked to support this

[8] G. Chichilnisky and G. Heal, "Tradable Carbon Emissions: Principles and Practice," Report to Working Party No. 1 of the OECD (OECD Economics Working Paper, Paris, 1995).

[9] See J. Coppel, "Implementing a Global Abatement Policy: Some Selected Issues," OECD/IEA conference on "The Economics of Climate Change," published in T. Jones ed., *The Economics of Climate Change* (Paris: OECD, 1993), and, in response, Chichilnisky's article in the same book as well as Chichilnisky and Heal, "Tradable Carbon Emissions."

[10] It is however an open question whether emission reductions are less expensive in developing nations, and if so under what accounting system, see Coppel, "Implementing a Global Abatement Policy," and Chichilnisky and Heal, "Tradable Carbon Emissions."

view arises from the standard theoretical position that efficient allocations require that marginal costs be equated throughout, and that accordingly, more abatement activity should take place in the lower cost regions.

The approach is sound when only the supply side is taken into consideration, but it neglects the fact that efficiency as usually defined involves both demand and supply.[11] When demand for environmental quality is taken into consideration, the standard approach is incomplete because it ignores the special character of public goods (such as reduced threats of climate change) that are privately produced. The implications of differences in wealth among nations alter the alignment of entitlements required to produce in an efficient manner the reduction in emissions needed to protect the climate system. Following Coase, the usual assumption is that it does not matter for purposes of efficiency how the initial set of entitlements to a joint resource is allocated; so long as those entitlements can be traded at low cost, an efficient allocation of entitlements and resource use will be achieved. As a result, the issue of property rights in emissions has until now been left to the political arena, with the understanding that it involves exclusively a transfer of wealth between countries, and has nothing to do with efficiency. The two issues, efficiency and distribution, have been seen as separate.

Recent advances in the economics of climate change,[12] however, have disclosed a new role for distributional issues: an appropriately equitable distribution of emissions rights is needed for markets to function efficiently.[13]

[11] The notion of efficiency used here is the standard notion of Pareto efficiency, under which a feasible allocation is *efficient* when there is no other feasible allocation that makes everyone better off.

[12] See G. Chichilnisky, "Economic Development and Efficiency Criteria in the Satisfaction of Basic Needs," 1(6) *Applied Mathematical Modelling* 290–97 (1997); G. Chichilnisky, G. Heal, and D. Starrett, "International Emissions Markets: Equity and Efficiency." Center for Economic Policy Research, publication no. 81 (Stanford University, Fall 1993).

[13] As stated above, a distribution is efficient (or Pareto efficient) if it cannot be improved so as to make one better off, or to make some better off and none worse off. Somewhat surprisingly, it can be shown (Chichilnisky, Heal and Starrett, "International Emissions Markets"; G. Chichilnisky and G. Heal, "Who Should Abate Carbon Emissions? An International Perspective," *Economic Letters* 443–49 (Spring 1994)), that a shift to an allowance distribution that is relatively more favorable to developing countries could make developed countries better off as well. This happens in two ways: by leading to a superior environmental quality that increases the welfare of industrial and developing nations, as well as by increasing the exports from industrial to developing nations thereby increasing industrial countries' economic growth. These results hold in a model of a market in which the utility of the traders depends on the consumption of private goods as well as on atmospheric quality.

The unexpected link between efficiency and equity emerges from an idiosyncratic economic property of markets for public goods such as the total biodiversity of the planet and the quality of the planet's climate. Like other public goods, such as the security provided by police forces, these global environmental goods are public goods in that their consumption is not rival. The benefit obtained by one person from atmospheric quality does not diminish the benefit obtained by others. This situation is unlike that in the case of private goods, where if one person obtains a car, the stock of cars available for others is reduced. But global public goods such as atmospheric quality are also different from many standard public goods because they are necessarily provided to everyone in the same quantity.[14] In this respect, they also differ from private goods, which afford an individual the opportunity to consume more or less of a given commodity quite independently of the others.

Markets allocate goods efficiently when the marginal rate of substitution among all goods for each individual is the same. Economic efficiency is achieved in markets for private goods because individuals adjust the amount that they consume of each to the point where the marginal utility derived from all goods consumed is the same. But matters become more complicated when atmospheric quality, which can only be enhanced by reducing the amount of private goods that would otherwise be produced, is included in the picture. In this situation, efficiency requires that the marginal rate of substitution between private goods and the public good of climate quality be the same for each individual.[15] This is difficult to achieve. There are large differences in average wealth among poor and rich nations. From the viewpoint of human welfare, what counts for purposes of efficiency is not the dollar value of the cost of abating greenhouse gas emissions in order to produce climate quality, but rather the opportunity cost of that dollar value in terms of the utility that it can provide. The marginal utility of income decreases with income. The more income we have, the less our utility increases with the additional dollar. Accordingly, the utility that a poor person would derive from spending a dollar to consume more private goods rather than better atmospheric quality is significantly greater

[14] Because the impacts of climate change may vary regionally, atmospheric quality is not absolutely uniform, but it is reasonable to assume uniformity for purposes of this analysis.

[15] Marginal rates of substitution must all be equal across markets, and must equal the marginal rates of transformation in those markets.

than the utility that a rich person would obtain from the same increase in private goods. Thus, even assuming that poor and rich persons have the same preference for atmospheric quality, poorer people would, other things being equal, prefer to consume relatively more private goods than to reduce such consumption in order to enjoy enhanced atmospheric quality, while wealthier people would prefer to consume relatively fewer private goods and have better atmospheric quality. Yet atmospheric quality is the same for all individuals, rich or poor, who consume it. In this circumstance, efficiency will not be achieved by equalizing the marginal monetary costs of limiting greenhouse gas emissions and of producing private goods, for example, through a market in emission rights, unless all countries and their populations have the same marginal utility of income, which they do not.[16]

For example, suppose that the marginal opportunity cost of abating a ton of carbon is $1 worth (in market terms) of private goods of output in India and $2 of private output in the United States. Standard efficiency analysis dictates that the abatement should occur in India, where the monetary cost is less. Yet, the real loss of utility from abatement in India can be much higher than in the United States because devoting $1 of resources to improving climate quality rather than producing private goods can have a major impact on the welfare of the average citizen of India, while devoting $2 less in the United States to the same goal has only a small impact on the average citizen. From the viewpoint of economic welfare, it may be preferable to abate in the United States. Thus, a focus on the dollar cost of abatement alone, while ignoring the distributional dimensions of the issue, will not ensure an efficient outcome. Requiring even proportional abatement from all countries in proportion to their emissions would thus be a regressive measure, because it would impose a relatively heavier burden on the poor. In addition to thwarting efficiency in producing climate quality, regressive measures of this sort can cause problems because environmental degradation and poverty are closely connected. Anything that worsens poverty is likely to lead to further environmental degradation.[17]

[16] See Atkinson and Stiglitz, *Lectures in Public Economics.* The rule is typically that the sum of marginal rates of substitution equals the marginal rate of transformation when the government produces the public good. See Chichilnisky, Heal, and Starrett, "International Emissions Markets," for the case where free international trade in permits is allowed. The answer is the same.

[17] For example, a policy that lowers the price of wood and therefore the income of harvesters can lead to more, rather than less, extraction of wood. Since the purpose of taxing the price of wood is to discourage extraction of wood, by decreasing the income of the

One possible solution to the problem of achieving efficiency in the production of the public good of climate quality is directly to transfer wealth from wealthier to poorer countries, through bilateral or multilateral assistance programs, in order to equalize their wealth and hence their marginal utility from private consumption. Such transfers, however, are not realistic on the scale that would be required.[18]

Another, potentially more realistic, solution is to distribute the burden of greenhouse gas abatement so as to equalize the marginal rate of substitution between atmospheric quality and private goods among rich and poor countries. This can be achieved by allocating relatively more emission allowances to poorer countries, which can use those allowances to obtain more private goods either by producing them domestically and using these allowances to cover the emissions increases caused by increased productive activity or by selling them to wealthier countries in exchange for private goods.[19] Under general conditions, the proportion of income dedicated to greenhouse gas emissions abatement should increase with the level of income; this goal can be achieved by an appropriate allocation of emissions allowances.

The Program on Information and Resources of Columbia University has carried out computer simulations based on a model that incorporates the factors summarized here and on a different model, the OECD Green model, modified to incorporate the possibility of trading emissions permits between the countries. These modeling exercises have confirmed the results discussed above; the most efficient model runs, in terms of minimizing the loss of economic welfare that abatement of GHG emissions induces, are those in which the distribution of permits favors the developing countries.[20]

harvesters the tax could achieve the opposite effect from that which is intended. See, e.g., *World Development Report* (World Bank, 1992); G. Chichilnisky, "North-South Trade and the Global Environment," 84(4) *Am. Econ. Rev.* 427–34 (1994); G. Chichilnisky, "Trade Regimes and GATT: Resource Intensive vs. Knowledge Intensive Growth," *J. Int. Comp. Econ.* 147–81 (1994).

18 Paid transfers, such as those which occur within international markets, need not equate the marginal utility of consumption across trading regions.

19 See Chichilnisky and Heal, "Who Should Abate Carbon Emissions?"

20 Those readers interested in the details of these models and the modeling results should review the references to the economic literature. See Chichilnisky, "Economic Development and Efficiency Criteria"; Chichilnisky and Heal, "Who Should Abate Carbon Emissions?"; Chichilnisky, Heal, and Starrett, "International Emissions Markets"; G. Chichilnisky and G. Heal, "Economic Returns fromn the Biosphere," 391 *Nature* (February 1998).

## An International Bank for Environmental Settlements

An IBES could be created in order to promote sustainable development, environmental protection, and global equity among nations. The existing Bretton Woods institutions are not currently discharging these functions and are not well equipped to do so.

An IBES could perform a number of important roles in structuring and facilitating efficient and equitable international greenhouse gas emissions trading markets. Since more sophisticated market structures are required to trade emissions, an institution like an IBES with the role of regulating the markets and ensuring their integrity is needed. In promoting the development of CDM trading between developed and developing countries, an IBES could operate under the aegis of the Executive Board established under Article 12 of the Kyoto Protocol to implement the CDM.

The Bank could serve as a forum for recording environmental accounts that could be used to monitor the successes and failures of implementation. It could fulfill the role of a clearing and settlement institution. It could also determine which type of instruments will be traded – for example, derivative securities (options, futures) – and how. The Bank could offer credit enhancements for the carbon emissions permits sold by adding creditworthiness to contracts sold, and perhaps by ensuring that the counterpart to each contract is the Bank rather than another country or corporation, as is the case in the commodities clearing house. The Bank could regulate the relationship between primary and secondary markets, a matter of great importance in ensuring market liquidity. It could run open market operations and, in general, have an impact on borrowing and lending rates.

The trading of emissions rights should not conflict with humanitarian aid or other international aid flows. An IBES should provide more access to capital for development. It should have the role of ensuring fair markets and equal access to information and to trading. It should also ensure market integrity and depth. Deals should be structured so that they can be reversed without undue penalty to the traders of countries, especially developing countries, which may revise their priorities in the future. In order to ensure fair prices for developing countries, it may be desirable for the Bank to establish a market rate of interest on emissions permits in a market open only to industrialized countries and then to pay this rate on deposits from developing countries.

The trading of GHG emissions rights should not compromise the future ability of developing countries to change their development strategies. In order to achieve this objective, emissions rights could be *loaned*, instead of or in addition to being *sold*, with the lending and borrowing managed by the Bank. The key aspect of a loan rather than a sale of emissions rights is that developing countries need not be concerned about unforeseen long-term consequences of an irreversible transfer of their emissions rights to other countries, nor need they be concerned that they will make irreversible deals today at prices that will subsequently look unreasonable. Lending rather than selling these rights avoids many uncertainties faced by developing countries entering into an emissions abatement agreement. Lending rates can also be regulated by the IBES.

Developing countries are likely to want to lend emissions rights for limited periods until their needs for such rights are clarified, whereas industrialized countries are likely to want to borrow for longer periods. The IBES and other institutions managing this market would match these positions by "borrowing short and lending long" in the traditional manner of financial intermediaries. In exchange for the risk involved, they would charge a borrow–lend spread. Commercial capital and international financial institutions, private or public, would undoubtedly be attracted to such an operation. The IBES should facilitate securitizing carbon emission reductions from new technologies and products, so as to attract investments from global capital markets and generate self-funding mechanisms to finance such technologies and products, thus fostering clean industrialization and advancing the knowledge revolution in developing nations.[21]

Joint implementation and other project-based credit trading schemes are bilateral agreements and a natural extension of the economic practice of barter trading. However, bilateral trading is typically inferior to multilateral trading through open, transparent, and widely accessible markets, where all parties have access to all possible deals that could in principle be made. Bilateral trading eventually leads to multilateral trading. Yet a widely expressed concern is that during the development of multilateral markets, the price may turn against the developing countries. Initially, developing countries will typically be sellers of permits when prices are lower. If they buy permits later in order to industrialize, they may be paying much more

[21] See G. Chichilnisky, "Technology Transfer and Emissions Trading: A Win–Win Approach to the Kyoto Protocol," United Nations Foundation Grant to Columbia University's Program on Information and Resources (September 1998).

for the same permits that they initially sold. Selling a country's rights to emit is the same as selling its rights to industrialize. There is a chance that the first buyer could reap unfair "rents" or "bargains" over later buyers. A response to this concern is to implement a strategy for "leapfrogging" into multilateral trading sooner rather than later and attempting to establish fair trading practices, such as uniformly distributed price information and other practices that are widely adopted in the most successful markets, in order to ensure equal access to information and trading opportunities, efficiency, market integrity, and depth. An IBES could play a key role in implementing this strategy.

The IBES can also promote efficiency and equity by playing a similar market-making role with respect to environmental assets other than the global atmosphere. For example, it has been established that at present most forests are destroyed in order to produce minerals or to grow agricultural products for sale on the international market.[22] The right financial mechanisms are needed to realize their value without destroying them. The IBES could help developing countries, which own most of the forests and biodiversity on the planet, to obtain economic value from these assets without destroying them. This may include securitization of commercial applications of biodiversity, such as the Merck-INBIO deal in Costa Rica. An analogy is provided by traditional mortgages, in which assets (such as buildings) serve as collateral for obtaining financial value from the asset (the building) without destroying the asset itself. This may require institutional arrangements for organizing, executing and monitoring the trading of emissions permits, loans on them, and associated derivative instruments. An IBES could also promote securitizing the world's watersheds, in order to attract private funding for the conservation of clean water resources.[23] It could similarly promote securitization of the planet's biodiversity, and global reinsurance of environmental risks.[24]

## Conclusion

This essay has examined the issues of equity and efficiency in the use of global environmental resources. A somewhat unexpected connection arises

[22] See Chichilnisky, "North–South Trade and the Global Environment."

[23] See Chichilnisky and Heal, "Economic Returns from the Biosphere."

[24] See G. Chichilnisky and G. Heal, "The Future of Global Reinsurance," *J. Portfolio Mgmt.* (August 1998).

between the two issues in the context of international greenhouse gas emissions trading markets: achieving a more even distribution of property rights to environmental resources can influence market efficiency. Because atmospheric quality is a privately produced public good, achieving market efficiency may require that more property rights in the global commons should be given to those regions that own fewer private goods. Accordingly, in implementing the greenhouse gas emissions trading regimes authorized by the Kyoto Protocol, proportionately more emissions rights should be allocated to developing nations than to industrial countries. In order to carry out such policies, I have suggested the creation of an IBES, a self-financing institution that can obtain market value from environmental resources without destroying them. Emissions trading, the global reinsurance of environmental risks, and securitization of the earth's biodiversity resources are financial instruments that merge the interests of the private financial markets with international sustainable development. These instruments and institutions could help redefine economic progress in a way that is compatible with harmonious use of the world's resources and equity among rich and poor nations.

# Part IV

## THE ENVIRONMENTAL STANDARD-SETTING PROCESS

# 10

# INSTITUTIONS FOR REGULATING RISK

STEPHEN BREYER AND VEERLE HEYVAERT

THIS CHAPTER examines three types of models for centralized risk regulation at different stages of their development: the first mature (the US model), the second maturing (the EU model), and the last in the early stages of centralization (the GATT/WTO and NAFTA models). The study focuses on questions of institutional design. It draws upon the discussion of environmental, health, and safety risk regulation in the United States presented in *Breaking the Vicious Circle*, a book by Stephen Breyer, co-author of this chapter.[1] The chapter reiterates the book's central, apparently paradoxical thesis, as developed in the US institutional context: that one can more rationally deal with problems of risk regulation – including serious problems of overregulation – by granting more, not less, discretionary power to an administrative bureaucracy. It then asks those willing to accept this thesis (even if they do so only hypothetically) to consider its applicability and ramifications in other, non-US institutional settings. To this end, the chapter first examines its potential consequences for the European Union. Is it desirable to give EU administrators more authority and discretion in the risk regulatory process? Is it politically feasible to do so? What might the result be? We hope that this essay, though it rests in substantial part upon American experience, will stimulate thought on these questions in Europe. Continuing, the chapter addresses these issues in the context of multilateral

Veerle Heyvaert would like to thank the Centre for Socio-Legal Studies, and Keble College, Oxford, for their support during the preparation of this chapter.

[1] See S. Breyer, *Breaking the Vicious Circle: Toward Effective Risk Regulation* (Harvard University Press, 1993). This Chapter is based in significant part on that book and a paper prepared for the Mentor Conference in London, September 1995, and was also presented at the New York University Conference at La Pietra in July 1996.

agreements – in particular international trade agreements such as GATT/WTO and NAFTA – and international dispute resolution mechanisms and their impact on the development and implementation of risk regulation policies. Again, the object of the discussion is not to provide definitive answers but to broaden the ongoing debate on risk regulation to incorporate an increasingly relevant global dimension.

The chapter is divided into three sections. The first begins with an overview of the basic elements of the US environmental, health, and safety risk regulatory system, followed by a summary of the essential arguments of *Breaking the Vicious Circle.* This summary covers current deficiencies in US risk regulation, the causes of these deficiencies, and the reasons why the author believes that increased bureaucratic flexibility would help solve some of risk regulation's problems. The second section discusses the reasons for increasing centralization of risk regulation in the European Union, as well as the obstacles and challenges EU risk regulators will have to face. It asks whether and how the lessons from the US experience might be of use to improve risk regulation in Europe. The last section addresses the risk regulatory scope of multilateral trade agreements, and explores the interplay as well as the tension between administrative discretion for risk regulation and compliance with international free trade standards.

## The problem of regulating small risks: lessons from the US experience

### AN INTRODUCTION TO THE US REGULATORY PROCESS

Before discussing the symptoms and causes of regulatory failure, we will sketch the regulatory "backbone" against which they should be reviewed. In a nutshell, health, safety, and environmental risk regulation in the United States is characterized by: a prevalence of federal over state regulation; copious but often fragmented legislation mandating regulatory action towards risk reduction; regulation and implementation through an array of separate federal agencies, and adherence to formal administrative procedures; and high levels of regulatory oversight exercised by the three branches of government.

1 *Federal regulation.* While the first modern regulatory agency in the United States – the Interstate Commerce Commission – dates back to 1887, the regulation of health, environmental, and safety issues only really gained

impetus during the 1960s.[2] The 1960s and '70s were marked by a veritable explosion of both regulatory institutions and issues falling under their competence. Among the latter, health, safety, and environmental questions were particularly prominent. The most important regulatory initiatives were – and still are – mandated by federal legislation, and carried out by federal rather than state regulatory authorities.[3] Seminal federal statutes that mandate regulation include the Occupational Safety and Health Act (OSHA),[4] the National Traffic and Motor Vehicle Safety Act (NTMVSA),[5] the Clean Air Act (CAA),[6] the Federal Water Pollution Control Act or "Clean Water Act,"[7] the Safe Drinking Water Act (SDWA),[8] the Resource Conservation and Recovery Act (RCRA),[9] the Toxic Substances Control Act (TSCA),[10] the Federal Insecticide, Fungicide, and Rodenticide Act (FIFRA),[11] and the Atomic Energy Act.[12] As a rule, the enactment of federal rules and standards does not preclude the adoption of more stringent requirements at the state level, although in practice federal law dominates. Moreover, federal statutes frequently delegate implementation and enforcement tasks to the states, which reduces the amount of time and resources states can spend on local regulatory initiatives.[13] The scope for state-level regulation is not only practically, but also legally narrowed in the area of product regulation. Statutes containing or calling for the adoption of product standards in some cases pre-empt state regulation, on the grounds that different product standards adopted by different states might constitute trade barriers. For example, FIFRA pre-empts diverging state regulation with regard to pesticide labeling. In the

2 See, e.g., S. Breyer, *Regulation and its Reform* (Harvard University Press, 1982), 1.

3 See R. Stewart, "Environmental Quality as a National Good in a Federal State," *The University of Chicago Legal Forum* (1997), 199 (analyzing why, in contradiction with conventional public choice expectations, environmental regulation occurs predominantly at the federal, and not at the state level). See R. Brickman, S. Jasanoff and T. Ilgen, *Controlling Chemicals. The Politics of Regulation in Europe and the United States* (Ithaca and London: Cornell University Press, 1985), 64–65.

4 29 U.S.C. §§ 651(b) ff. (1970).

5 15 U.S.C. §§ 1381 ff. (1976).

6 42 U.S.C. §§ 7401 ff. (1994).

7 33 U.S.C. §§ 1251 ff. (1994).

8 42 U.S.C. §§ 300f ff. (1994 & Supp. 1996).

9 42 U.S.C. §§ 6901 ff. (1994).

10 15 U.S.C. §§ 2601 ff. (1994).

11 7 U.S.C. §§ 136 ff. (1994).

12 42 U.S.C. §§ ff. 2011 ff. (1994).

13 Stewart, "Environmental Quality as a National Good," 200.

absence of pre-empting federal legislation, different product standards for the protection of health, safety, or the environment could result in the establishment of undue trade barriers between states. American courts are competent to adjudicate such conflicts, and if necessary set aside state legislation under the "dormant commerce clause" jurisprudence established by the US Supreme Court, which has held that the Constitution's grant of authority to Congress to regulate commerce among the several states empowers courts, in the absence of congressional legislation, to strike down state regulatory and other measures that prohibit or restrict the import of goods from other states in a discriminatory or otherwise unjustified manner. Hence, federal courts can act as additional centralizing forces in US risk regulation by invalidating state measures that interfere with national free trade, potentially setting the stage for congressional adoption of uniform national regulation.

2 *Fragmentation.* As the enumeration of federal statutes above suggests, there is no unified legal framework for risk regulation.[14] Legislation is enacted piecemeal, often focusing on one medium (water, air, soil) or one issue (worker protection, waste management, cleanup, etc.) at a time.[15] The fragmentation of legal statutes pertaining to health, environmental, and safety issues is echoed at the regulatory level: risks are regulated by a variety of agencies and administrations.[16] In the United States, regulation of these risks takes place within a legal framework created by at least twenty-six different statutes administered by at least eight different federal agencies, including the Food and Drug Administration (FDA), the Environmental Protection Agency (EPA), the Occupational Safety and Health Agency (OSHA), and the Nuclear Regulatory Commission. While all regulatory agencies must comply with the dictates of the Administrative Procedure Act (APA) (see below),[17] the different legal statutes may set different regulatory standards, require different regulatory approaches, and prescribe different regulatory outcomes for the

[14] See S. Rose-Ackerman, "Environmental Policymaking and the Limits of Public Law in Germany and the United States," 6 *Revue Européen de Droit Publique* 36–37 (1994).

[15] See J. Dernbach, "The Unfocused Regulation of Toxic and Hazardous Pollutants," 21 *Harv. Env. L. Rev.* 7 (1997), referring to the "crazy quilt covering of pollutants" under various statutory programs.

[16] The US Congress has a penchant for adopting statutes that create or modify regulatory mandates and simultaneously provide for the establishment of new regulatory agencies to carry out these mandates.

[17] Administrative Procedure Act, 5 U.S.C. §§ 551–706.

agencies to pursue. It takes little imagination to envisage the enormous potential for inconsistency, conflict, and inefficiency resulting from this fragmented structure and these differentiated requirements. This problem will be further explored in the following subsection.

3 *Formality.* As indicated above, the APA directs the actions of regulatory agencies, both when they are adopting regulations with the force of law, and when they are deciding individual cases. In accordance with the APA, agencies are required to give "notice" and provide an opportunity for states, local communities, and interest groups to "comment" prior to the adoption of a rule, which rule or decision must be accompanied by a reasoned opinion.[18] Over time, Congress, the judiciary, and the Presidency have made the procedural requirements for regulatory decisionmaking both more elaborate and more demanding.[19] The advantages of the increased level of formality resulting therefrom are that the regulatory process has become fairly transparent with clear access points for interested parties that will be affected by forthcoming regulation, that every step in the regulatory process is extremely thoroughly documented, and that enormous efforts are poured into the gathering of scientific evidence and additional information on the basis of which rules and decisions are justified.[20] On the down side, high levels of formality can turn the adoption of every single rule into a war of attrition, making the regulatory process excessively rigid, sluggish, even "ossified."[21]

[18] *Ibid.*, § 553.

[19] See S. Breyer, R. Stewart, C. Sunstein, and M. Spitzer, *Administrative Law and Regulatory Policy* (4th edn., New York: Aspen Law & Business, 1998), 594–642 The notice-and-comment requirements were introduced to broaden regulatory "outreach" by extending agencies' opportunities for information gathering and exchange with interested parties. Reflecting this philosophy, the decisionmaking process that incorporated notice-and-comment procedures was dubbed "informal rulemaking." The courts, however, responded to the increasing use by agencies of rulemaking rather than adjudication to make basic law and policy by requiring agencies to develop a comprehensive record for the rulemaking, including comments submitted by outside parties as well as agency documents, and to provide a full explanation for the rule issued, answering adverse comments and demonstrating substantial support in the rulemaking record for the rule chosen. Congress has imposed similar requirements in a number of specific agency statutes. As described below, Presidents have imposed requirements that agencies examine the costs and benefits of major rules.

[20] See Rose-Ackerman, "Environmental Policymaking and the Limits of Public Law," 72–75; Brickman, Jasanoff, and Ilgen, *Controlling Chemicals*, 40–45.

[21] *See* T. McGarity, "Some Thoughts on 'Deossifying' the Rulemaking Process," 41 *Duke L.J.* 1385 (1992).

4 *Oversight.* The numerous reviews, controls, and oversights to which regulatory agencies are subjected constitute perhaps the most distinguishing feature of the American risk regulatory process. Heads of major regulatory agencies are appointed by the President and can, with exceptions for some "independent" agencies like the Nuclear Regulatory Commission, be removed by him. But this power does not necessarily translate into effective White House control over the thousands of regulatory decisions made every year by federal agencies. Ever since President Nixon, both Republican and Democratic Presidents have been concerned about the potential impact on the overall economy and the competitiveness of US industry of myriad regulatory requirements imposed by different agencies under different statutes. They have instituted a system of regulatory analysis and review which requires agencies to prepare a cost-benefit analysis of both proposed and final rules that will have major economic impacts and submit the analysis for review by the Office of Information and Regulatory Affairs (OIRA), within the President's Office of Management and Budget (OMB).[22] Essentially, the Offices check compliance with presidential guidelines for agencies to evaluate the economic and social costs of proposed regulations.[23] Although the OMB does not have the power to amend or reject deficient proposals, its approval needs to be obtained before planned or final rules can be published in the Federal Register, and major unresolved conflicts between OMB and an agency may have to the resolved by the President.

A second institution keeping a watchful eye on regulatory agencies is the US Congress. In contrast to the parliamentary system that prevails in most European nations, the political party of the US President does not always hold a majority in Congress. In fact, since 1980, in only the first two years of the Clinton administration did the executive and congressional majority political parties overlap. Considering the ability of the White House to control agency decisions (see above), Congress has little

[22] See Breyer et al., *Administrative Law and Regulatory Policy*, 102–23. See also S. Shapiro, "Political Oversight and the Deterioration of Regulatory Policy," 46 *Admin. L. Review*, 8–9 (1994); J. O'Reilly and P. Brown, "In Search of Excellence: A Prescription for the Future of OMB Oversight of Rules," 39 *Admin. L. Rev.* 421–41 (1987).

[23] A succession of US Presidents, starting with Richard Nixon, have insisted that regulatory proposals should pass through a form of "regulatory impact analysis." See Brickman, Jasanoff, and Ilgen, *Controlling Chemicals*, 40–45.

reason to assume that its interests and viewpoints will always be fully reflected in the regulatory process. It therefore tries to control and constrain the regulatory process. It enacts detailed statutory directives to agencies and imposes implementation deadlines, which requirements in turn furnish grounds for judicial review.[24] It also oversees the agencies' compliance with regulatory mandates, primarily through the organization of congressional hearings and investigations performed by its many committees.[25]

Finally, we should take care to mention the prominent tradition of judicial review of administrative decisions. In contrast to Europe, where such review is relatively rare, the legality of US regulations, rules, and administrative decisions is frequently contested in court. The legal foundations for judicial review of informal rulemaking are listed in the APA, which directs courts to set aside decisions that are "arbitrary, capricious, an abuse of discretion, or otherwise not in accordance with the law."[26] Additional grounds for review are supplied in legislative statutes that contain detailed and specific assignments to regulatory agencies. In addition, the APA (as judicially interpreted) and specific statutes impose significant procedural requirements that agencies must follow in regulatory decisionmaking. Federal courts – in particular the US Court of Appeals for the District of Columbia – have deepened judicial review by developing what became known as the "hard look doctrine," advocating that courts should exercise close scrutiny on the policies, data, and assumptions that drive regulatory decisions, and that agencies should keep detailed records and extensive data to illustrate and justify the decisionmaking process. Although, since the early 1990s, courts have slightly shifted towards a more deferential attitude, the threat that insufficiently reasoned agency decisions will be annulled remains very real.[27]

[24] See R. Stewart, "Regulation, Innovation and Administrative Law: A Conceptual Framework," 69 *Calif. L. Rev.* 1277 (1981).

[25] Additionally, Congress can exercise influence on regulatory decisionmaking through the appropriations process, reauthorization and statutory amendment proceedings, and formal as well as informal inquiries. See Brickman, Jasanoff, and Ilgen, *Controlling Chemicals*, 45–55.

[26] APA 5 U.S.C. § 706. Cf. D. Lee Davis, "The 'Shotgun Wedding' of Science and the Law: Risk Assessment and Judicial Review," 10(1) *Colum. J. Env. L.* 71 (1985).

[27] See, e.g., R. Glicksman and C. Schroeder, "EPA and the Courts: Twenty Years of Law and Politics," 54 *L. & Contemp. Problems* 249–309 (1991).

## THE VICIOUS CIRCLE: DIAGNOSING THE PROBLEMS OF RISK REGULATION

One might roughly summarize the first part of *Breaking the Vicious Circle*[28] as follows: Its subject matter is small risks to health, typically caused by, for example, food additives, pesticides, industrial chemicals, radiation, and similar activities and substances. The book focuses upon federal regulatory programs that primarily seek to avoid rather small risks of cancer, risks of the order of, say, ten in a million or less. That regulation, were it to work well, might save (to report very impressionistic and highly controversial sets of estimates) somewhere between 10,000 and 50,000 lives per year (out of a population of about 250 million, with 2.2 million deaths annually, of which cancer causes approximately 500,000).

An examination of the literature on US risk regulation suggests that it is plagued with three serious problems. The first, "tunnel vision," involves spending considerable resources to reduce a risk to zero or close to zero, when the risk could be substantially, but not entirely, reduced at far lower cost. (A former US EPA Administrator described the problem well in noting that about 95 percent of the toxic material could have been removed from "Superfund" hazardous waste sites in a few months, but years were spent trying to remove the last little bit at enormous additional cost.) The second, called "random agenda selection," involves the regulatory system's failure to approach problems in a rational order, i.e., a failure to optimize the resources and efforts devoted to risk reduction. The result is a set of regulatory priorities that ignores health or environmental problems that experts consider to be serious while focusing upon others that they would consider less serious. The third, called "inconsistency," involves regulators using different methods of calculating risk; creating programs that vary dramatically in the expenditure made to save a single life; ignoring one program's negative impact upon another, sometimes increasing, rather than reducing, the net risk to human health; and, considered as a whole, ignoring many less expensive ways to save human life.

Although these three problems will plague any regulatory program to some extent, and although they do not warrant questioning efforts to reduce large, known risks to human health (such as smoking), they seem serious (relative to the programs' results) where small risks are at issue.

[28] *Ibid.* at 3–29 and sources cited therein.

There, they seem sufficiently widespread that they apparently entail a vast expenditure of funds (perhaps hundreds of billions of dollars over a period of years) to achieve far less safety than this sum, if otherwise directed, could purchase. Moreover, the cost of such misguided regulation is not merely financial; large-scale wasteful regulatory expenditures undermine public confidence in the regulatory system as a whole and may lead to popular calls to end a wide range of beneficial (not just wasteful) environmental and health regulation.

## CAUSES: DECONSTRUCTING THE VICIOUS CIRCLE

Because the second part of *Breaking the Vicious Circle*[29] is of greater relevance to this chapter, we summarize it in somewhat greater detail. It looks for causes of the three sets of problems that plague the effort to regulate small risks. And, it finds three such causes.

First, consider public perceptions. Numerous studies show that the public's view of the comparative seriousness of different risk problems differs dramatically from the views of experts. In Breyer's opinion, this difference, in large part, stems not from some enormous desire for super-safety, but rather from the public's uncertainty about whether risks are indeed small. Certain psychological features of human nature make it difficult for the ordinary citizen – without much time to study the intricacies of risk – to evaluate the comparative significance of a "small risk" problem. These include:

1 *Rules of thumb.* Human beings want to categorize through the use of simple heuristic devices that will produce binary choices: yes/no, friend/foe, eat/abstain, safe/dangerous. This "quick and dirty" approach to complex problems often helps decisionmaking by cutting a navigable path through the information jungle, but, in the area of small risks, it creates confusion by asking regulators to produce answers that are more categorical than the relevant science will allow.
2 *Prominence.* People react more strongly to events that stand out from their background. They will more likely notice the (low-risk) nuclear waste disposal truck driving past the school than the (much higher risk) gasoline delivery truck on its way to the local service station.

[29] *Ibid.* at 29–50 and sources cited therein.

3 *Ethics.* The strength of feelings of ethical concern diminishes with distance. One feels more strongly obliged in relation to one's family than, in diminishing order, to next door neighbors, friends, community, state, nation, the world, those whom we see, those whom we read about, and those whom we know only as statistical numbers. Thus, risks that are closer to home tend to be perceived as more important.
4 *Trusting experts.* When experts disagree, most people do not know whom to trust.
5 *Fixed decisions.* Once a person makes up his mind, he is reluctant to change it.
6 *Mathematics.* As Holmes pointed out, "most people think dramatically, not quantitatively."

Now apply these considerations to a typical environmental hazard, a toxic waste dump. In a large pool of samples, such as US towns and cities, a great many will have a higher (or a lower) cancer rate than the average cancer rate. Now, given the number of toxic waste dumps in the United States (26,000), combined with the fact that many regions in the US have a cancer rate above the average, it is hardly surprising that some locations with an elevated cancer rate and some locations in the vicinity of a toxic waste dump may coincide. Will the public understand this "mathematical" fact? And what sells newspapers? Interesting stories do, and thus one can be fairly certain that the press will point out the "prominent" fact of a seriously elevated cancer rate. Will it be easy to convince the family of a cancer victim living close to the waste dump that in terms of probabilities ("mathematics") it probably did not cause the cancer, particularly when the expert cannot say definitely "yes" or "no" ("rules of thumb")? And, how will the public react to the image of an understandably angry family member on television – a person the public has seen and who, therefore, is more than a mere statistic ("ethics") – particularly if experts disagree ("trust in experts"), as they might? If further study tends to exonerate the dump, will the viewing public change its mind ("fixed decision"), particularly when the dump, after all, *might* have caused the cancer?

These (and other related) propositions suggest that "risk communicators" face an uphill battle. Over time, as science and communications improve, the "communications" effort may become more rather than less difficult. Science will become able to identify more easily ever tinier risks (for instance, that of a single molecule of plastic migrating into a soft drink). The press will be able quickly to discover, and write about, unusual accidents and events. With the progress of science, there will be a plethora of new, if often small, risks to report. To change public reaction, one would have to institute widespread public education in risk analysis or generate greater public trust in some particular group of experts or the institutions that employ them. The first alternative seems unlikely. The second poses a significant political challenge. Nevertheless, in the absence of alternatives, and considering that the problems of "small risk regulation" are likely to increase over time, this option should be explored.

Second, consider the legislative reaction. Congress has responded to the public's perception by enacting legislation that seeks to control the regulatory agendas of regulatory agencies, at times dictating particular regulatory outcomes. Some statutes will simply list specific materials, such as dioxin, arsenic, cadmium, chromium, etc. (e.g., "dioxin-containing hazardous wastes numbered F020, F021, F022, and F023") and instruct the regulators to create standards for those substances within a specific period of time. Others will lay down a standard (e.g., to be "clean," a toxic waste site must meet Safe Drinking Water Act "goals" as long as they are "relevant and appropriate") that is visionary (the Safe Drinking Water Act "goal" is a total absence of any carcinogenic substance, ignoring the fact that, for example, spinach, coffee, etc. are carcinogens) but with an escape hatch ("relevant and appropriate") that becomes difficult or impossible to apply in the bureaucratic context. Sometimes the statute will simply say, for example, that "no" carcinogenic substance may be used (e.g., as a food additive), again ignoring the fact that vast numbers of substances are, to some small extent, carcinogenic in large doses.

The problem with this legislation is that it amounts to taking rifle shots in the dark. It tries to dictate the EPA's cleanup agenda in detail, through directions that later experience may show to be inappropriate because they overemphasize some risks to the exclusion of others. Yet, it is difficult to insist that Congress write less specific legislation. As previously noted, when different political parties control the legislative and executive branches of government, the former branch may not trust the latter properly to exercise broad discretionary powers. Individual members of Congress, moreover, may wish to indicate, through support of specific, detailed legislation, that they are particularly responsive to the public's specific concern and more committed than average to making certain the regulator deals with it effectively. Dependence on different geographically based electoral constituencies (for instance, rural or urban communities, poor or affluent regions, etc.) may further reinforce the inclinations of members of Congress to champion causes which are particularly salient to their voters, even if this results in regulatory inefficiencies and inconsistency. At the same time, the structure of Congress (with legislation originating in any one of many different subcommittees, with one statute enacted at a time, without any institutional need or structure to consider risk, safety, or cancer prevention coherently as one composite problem, and members highly responsive to public opinion) makes it difficult for Congress to resist the temptation to legislate in detail, on a piecemeal basis.

Third, consider the technical regulatory uncertainties. Regulation, as presently carried out, approximates a system that, idealized and in principle, is divided into two parts, the first called "risk assessment" and the second called "risk management." Risk assessment involves (1) identifying the potential hazard, (2) drawing a dose/response curve, (3) estimating the amount of human exposure, and (4) categorizing the result in terms of potential danger. Predicting small risks, however, involves not what scientists do best (developing theories about the relation of x to y, *other things being equal*) or what epidemiologists may be happiest doing (looking for large differences in samples of populations over short periods of time). Rather, it asks for predictions in a world where other things are not equal, where expertise involves many disciplines (e.g., toxicology, epidemiology, meteorology, hydrology, engineering, etc.), and where scientists must search for small differences in large populations over long periods of time. Risk analysts often have no choice but to make simplifying, but scientifically questionable, assumptions (sometimes called "default assumptions").

Certain of these assumptions tend to overstate risks. For example, investigators tend to use a model that uses a straight line to extrapolate from high doses of a substance (say, saccharin) given to a test animal (say, a rat) to the likely effects of a low dose on a human being. If, for example, a 5 percent saccharin diet causes tumors in 30 percent of all rats exposed (i.e., 300 per thousand), the model might indicate that one hundredth of the dose, a 5/100 of 1 percent saccharin diet, would cause tumors in 100 times fewer rats, i.e., 0.3 percent of all rats (3 per thousand). Critics argue that use of such a mathematical approach is like saying "if ten thousand men will drown in ten thousand feet of water, then one man will drown in one foot of water." Indeed, though some substances (perhaps cyanide) are proportionately as deadly in small doses as large ones, others (such as butter) are harmful only when consumed in large quantities, and still others (such as iodine) kill in high doses, are harmless in small doses, and in tiny doses are necessary for life. But, which of these substances does saccharin resemble? Scientists may simply not know. Yet, the differences matter enormously. For example, two different but scientifically plausible models for the risks associated with aflatoxin in peanuts or grain may show risk levels differing by a factor of 40,000.

One can find similar difficulties with other "default assumptions" in risk assessment, such as those that use "upper confidence levels," those that look to the results on whatever animal is most sensitive to the substance, and those that assume particularly high human exposure to a substance. Still other assumptions may understate the risks that attach to special combinations of circumstances, for example, where human beings have more pathways through which a substance comes into contact with the body than do, say, rats. Risks may furthermore be underestimated in cases where humans are subjected to unusually lengthy exposure, where they are exposed to multiple substances, or where they have special sensitivities. Similarly, the analysis may focus only upon cancer, leaving other potential harms, such as neurotoxicity, aside. How reasonable these various assumptions are, how serious the limitations of the analysis may be, will vary from area to area, from substance to substance, from case to case. When errors arise, they do not offset each other (except by accident).

A regulator must take this risk analysis, and, in light of its possibly oversimplified conclusion (e.g., that a substance, say a pesticide, is a "known" or "suspect" carcinogen), must decide how to manage the risk, asking such questions as: (1) what will it cost to ban the substance (for example, what are the compliance costs and costs of alternative pesticides)? (2) What benefits would we thereby lose (do pesticides produce healthier, cheaper crops)? (3) Would a ban create other significant risks (will farmers grow pest-resistant crops, say, "organic celery," with riskier natural carcinogens)? (4) What are the practicalities of enforcement (such as the cost of measuring pesticide residues)? The answers to these questions too involve assumptions, guesswork, subjectivity. The resulting uncertainties, knowledge gaps, default assumptions, and guesses produce a regulatory system that, where small risks are involved, generates results (sometimes overstating, sometimes understating) that may be close to random.

Scientists and regulators, understanding the difficulties inherent in the system, can exacerbate the public's difficulties with the system when they honestly communicate their own uncertainty. When, for example, the press reported that EPA had begun to regulate the pesticide EDB and state regulators began to regulate tiny doses, television news displayed a skull and crossbones along with pictures of chemical workers exposed to *pure* EDB. Scientists had to respond truthfully that EDB in large doses is carcinogenic and that some small risk may attach to small doses, but, as EPA's Administrator added: "The truth is we don't know. We're operating in an area of enormous scientific uncertainty." Here, the truthful word "uncertainty" itself implies "risk"; the denial thereby carries with it a kind of self-refutation that does not alleviate public concern. The Administrator continued: "We are operating with substances that the public is terribly afraid of. If they want absolute information, we can't give it to them."

The end result is that scientifically inevitable uncertainties, meeting with the administrative demands of a regulatory process, make it particularly difficult for Congress, and the public it represents, to disentangle the complex combination of science, fact, value, and administrative need underlying the agency's risk conclusion, and to determine whether or not the agency is effectively dealing with the problem.

We shall simply repeat the book's conclusion as to how these three causes, for a set of complex reasons, create a "vicious circle."[30]

The three elements of the vicious circle – public perception, congressional reaction, and the uncertainties of the regulatory process – reinforce each other. Obviously, public perception influences Congress. Congress (through press reports of its activities in particular) helps to shape public perception, and both influence the response of agency administrators to the problems they consider important.

It is less obvious, but equally true, that the regulatory system's inherent uncertainties make it more difficult for agencies to resist piecemeal congressional or public efforts to target particular risks and to insist upon particular results. These uncertainties, accompanied by scientific statements of doubt, along with administrative practices such as default assumptions that differ among agencies and among programs, give the appearance of subjective decisionmaking. For example, in the 1980s both OSHA and EPA embarked on lengthy and expensive projects to assess the hazards of benzene, relying on different methodologies and arriving at vastly differing outcomes. This appearance of subjectivity can encourage outside groups, such as environmentalists who monitor agency performance, to try to gen-

[30] *Ibid.* at 50–51 and sources cited therein.

erate congressional interest in particular agency decisions. Any such congressional interest, in turn, will help to generate public interest, which tends to move the particular problem at issue towards the top of the agency's agenda ("random agendas") and creates more political pressure for stricter regulatory solutions ("tunnel vision"). At the same time, particularly on less visible issues where industry groups provide effective countervailing political pressure, lenient rules (or no regulation) may be adopted for other risks, in spite of their being very similar in magnitude to the risks targeted for strict regulation ("inconsistency").

This circular process is reinforced by the fact that the more outside pressures seem to control agency results, the less confidence the public will have in the agency. The less confidence the public has in the agency, the greater the perceived need for outside action, the greater the pressure upon the agency to prove it has erred on the side of safety, and the greater the tendency to adopt the public's risk agenda of the moment. Yet, because of their irrational and counterproductive elements, the latter tendencies will not help build public confidence.

Scientific uncertainties, together with default assumptions that "err on the safe side," may also help to convince environmentalists, press, and public that more should be done about known risks – particularly known carcinogenic risks – even when those risks are tiny. Public pressure may thereupon encourage Congress to enact standards or to supervise agencies by setting agency agendas and encouraging strong action in respect of those programs or substances that catch the public eye. Congressional reaction provokes further public concern. All of the above make it more difficult for agencies to resist overkill and random agenda setting. The famous Delaney Clause, which imposed an absolute ban on carcinogens in food additives, no matter how small the risk, could be seen as the congressional expression of an understandable but partially misguided public preoccupation with cancer, resulting in overly stringent regulatory goals and inefficient, inconsistent regulatory outcomes.

Given the uncertainties and regulatory methods, are "tunnel vision" results surprising? Given congressional statutes, likely agency reactions, and public pressures, should we not expect random risk-reducing agendas? Should we not expect regulators to react to what Congress, or the public, puts on their plates? Since Congress created different safety regulatory programs at different times, under different circumstances, with differing statutory language, administered by different agencies, with different institutional environments employing different scientists from different disciplines, involving different publics with differing degrees of interest, why should we not expect to find inconsistent treatment of health and safety risks and inconsistent results?

This, then, is our predicament: a kind of regulatory gridlock, whose mutually reinforcing causes tend to generate agency regulation that suffers from the three serious "tunnel vision," "random agenda," and "inconsistency" problems.

## BREAKING THE VICIOUS CIRCLE: A PROPOSAL FOR INSTITUTIONAL CHANGE

Although *Breaking the Vicious Circle* strongly criticizes the present US risk regulatory system – a bureaucratic system – its suggestions for change would nonetheless retain an essentially administrative apparatus for regulating risk, though they would change the present administrative structure significantly.[31] On the one hand, the author does not think that simply "deregulating risk" – abandoning the effort to regulate small risks – is possible. The public demand for regulation is strong.[32] In large populations even small risks mean many deaths. And, at least some of those risks might be reduced significantly at low cost. Where small risks are involved, labeling is not a substitute for regulation. The eagle-eyed label reader who sees "Cancer risk 1 in 100,000" does not want this warning so much as he wants to know what to do: eat the food, or leave it?[33] While some less restrictive methods of regulation, such as taxes on dangerous substances, or simplified labeling proposals, may help, the need for classical command-and-control regulation will likely remain.

One cannot effectively reform the system without re-examining the bureaucratic structure of regulation itself. One cannot, for example, hope that increasing the power of courts to examine, and to set aside (as unreasonable), regulatory actions will significantly improve the results of regulation.[34]

[31] The following discussion borrows from *Breaking the Vicious Circle*, 55–81.

[32] *Ibid.*, 33–42.

[33] See T. McGarity, "Risk and Trust: The Role of Regulatory Agencies," 16 *Env. L. Rep.* 10198, 10199 (1986).

[34] See *Heckler* v. *Chaney*, 470 U.S. 821, 831–32 (1985) ("The agency is far better equipped than the courts to deal with the many variables involved in the proper ordering of its priorities.")

It is important to understand why courts are not well suited to review closely the results of administrative regulatory activities in highly technical areas. Consider the critical differences between the standard-creating process as it takes place within an agency, and the standard-reviewing process that takes place in a court. A regulatory agency, trying to develop a new standard in a technical field, faces several typical difficulties:

1. The agency must obtain accurate information about the problem. But where is it to find that information? From industry? Is it a biased source? From independent experts? Who are they? From university professors? Will they have sufficiently detailed and relevant information? Where did they obtain it? From industry? From environmental or consumer groups? Do they suffer an anti-industry bias? Should the agency develop the information in-house? Does it have the resources to do so? Consider, too, the enormous uncertainties in the "risk assessment" process described earlier.
2. The agency must face a host of technical questions related to the type of standard it wishes to promulgate. Should it ban a substance? Set an upper limit? Promulgate a standard that aims at a surrogate (e.g., biological oxygen demand as a measure of water pollution)? Set a "technology forcing" standard that industry presently cannot meet? Set a "performance" standard or a "design" standard?
3. The agency must take account of enforcement concerns. Who will actually enforce its standard? How? What are the costs of doing so?
4. The agency must consider competitive effects, for particular standards will favor some competitors over others, or perhaps favor all existing firms at the expense of new entrants.
5. The agency may have to negotiate a final standard. It finds before it different parties – industry, suppliers, consumer groups, members of Congress, its own staff – each with slightly different objectives. Different parties see different aspects of the problem as particularly important: industry groups may emphasize costs; suppliers, competitive fairness; consumer groups, life saving; staff, administrative ease and enforcement. Moreover, each party has a special bargaining chip: industry, information; consumers and environmentalists, political action; the staff, future cooperation; all, recourse to courts, Congress, or the press. The resulting standard may (and from an administrative perspective probably should) reflect compromises among the positions held by these, or other, relevant groups.

The courts, in trying to review the results and determine the rationality of such administrative action, work under very different institutional constraints. For one thing, courts work within institutional rules that deliberately disable them from seeking out information relevant to the inquiry at hand. For, while a judge, expert in the law, is permitted to scan all forms of legal authority and learning in reaching conclusions of law (and is given the resources to do so in the form of libraries and law clerks), in factual matters the judge is limited to review of a cold record created by those over whom he has no control. An appellate judge cannot ask an expert to answer technical questions or go outside the record to determine the present state of scientific or technical knowledge.[35] The record itself tells only part of the story, the part that the lawyers have chosen to present to the court. The judicial system, emphasizing "fairness," will normally insist only that the advocates have a "fair" opportunity to present their side of the case; it will not insist that the court obtain sufficient information to reach the "truth," at least when "legislative facts" (those general factual propositions that underlie a regulatory rule) are at issue. For another thing, a cold record, even if complete, will not necessarily permit the judge to study the case in depth. A judge can spend a week reading a 4,000 page record and yet still feel somewhat unfamiliar with highly technical facts. Moreover, docket pressures are such that federal appellate judges may not have that much time to study the case.[36] A typical federal appellate judge will write forty or more full opinions in an average year, an average of about one per week. How then are they to analyze fully a record with studies and comments sufficient to answer the difficult risk-regulatory questions mentioned above (p. 299)? Can they do more than ask, somewhat superficially, whether the agency's results are reasonable? And, how does the judge's view of "reasonableness," based on the logic of his legal perspective, correspond with the agency's view of a "reasonable rule," based in part upon instinct and negotiation? Finally, courts create precedent. Even if a court cautiously avoids saying that a rule is unreasonable while returning the matter to the agency for further consideration, the reasons the court gives

[35] See, e.g., *Camp* v. *Pitts*, 411 U.S. 138, 142 (1973); *Valley Citizens for a Safe Environment* v. *Aldridge*, 886 F.2d 458, 459–60 (1st Cir. 1989) (explaining reasons for courts' reliance on administrative record, and describing circumstances warranting consideration of additional evidence).

[36] See S. Breyer, "The Donahue Lecture Series: 'Administering Justice in the First Circuit,'" 24 *Suffolk U.L. Rev.* 29, 33 (1990).

for doing so will be used as precedent by advocates in other cases. Thus, a court's stating that the agency must consider "alternatives" (as in an important environmental case) may be understood as creating a legal rule that requires agencies to do so, even when doing so may waste considerable time and effort.[37] Ultimately, while courts may find and correct fairly obvious mistakes, they are not institutionally well suited to reviewing agency decisions closely or to evaluating for themselves the complicated factual circumstances that determine the reasonableness of a risk-regulating agency action.

The upshot is a need to reform the administrative regulatory system itself. We shall not describe here in any detail the suggestion for reform made in *Breaking the Vicious Circle* – a proposal that would modify the present regulatory system in two generally unpopular ways: (1) through greater centralization; and (2) by granting administrators greater *discretionary* authority.[38] By way of brief summary, it would create a small administrative group, charged with a "rationalizing" mission. The group would be composed of civil servants with experience in health and environmental agencies, Congress, and the central "administrative managerial agency," OMB. Its model, roughly speaking, is the French Conseil d'Etat, though it would focus more on regulatory policy than on administrative law and procedure.

However, we shall try to explain, in general institutional terms, the grounds for suspecting that this kind of administrative system might alleviate the risk-regulatory problems described elsewhere.

First, the problems themselves seem to call for an administrative organization with certain characteristics:

1 *A system-building mission.* The organization would have to build a "system" – a general way of dealing with small risks – adaptable for use in different risk-related programs administered by the same or different "line" regulatory agencies. The organization would have to create priorities within as well as among programs, and it would have to compare programs to determine how better to allocate resources to reduce risk.

[37] See *Breaking the Vicious Circle*, 58 (providing examples).

[38] *Ibid.*, 59–72; cf. J. Mashaw, *Bureaucratic Justice: Managing Social Security Disability Claims* (London: Yale University Press, 1985), 226–27 (discussing the idea of a "superbureau" that would employ elite public managers, oversee agency operations, and provide a model for bureaucratic governance).

2 *Interagency jurisdiction.* In order to build a sound risk-regulatory system, the organization would require interprogram and interagency jurisdiction, to bring about the actual transfer of resources from areas where they are saving fewer, to areas where they will save more lives (or enhance the quality or length of lives). Interagency jurisdiction would help assure that compromises within or among agencies reflect scientific rather than purely bureaucratic imperatives. Additionally, it would help the organization find examples of comparable risk-related problems in different areas for use in building its system. Such jurisdiction is also needed if the group is to suggest priorities among and within separate programs.[39]

3 *Political insulation.* The organization would have to be insulated to a degree from political pressures that are exerted by the public directly or through Congress and other political sources. Guaranteeing insulation would be particularly important in cases where public pressure calls for piecemeal action on individual substances.

4 *Prestige.* The organization should be prestigious, and thus have the ability to attract a highly capable staff, which ability would further strengthen its prestige. A capable staff is one that understands science, some economics, administration, and possibly law, and has the ability to communicate in a sophisticated way with experts in all these fields.

5 *Authority.* The organization should have sufficient authority to give it a practical ability to achieve results. Such authority may arise in part out of a legal power to impose its decisions. But, it may also stem from informal contacts with line agency staffs, from its perceived knowledge and expertise, from "rationalizing" successes that indicate effectiveness, and from the increased public confidence that such successes may build.

To summarize, the problems of risk regulation call for the creation of an administrative organization that is mission oriented, with the goal of bringing about a degree of uniformity and rationality to decisionmaking in highly technical areas, with broad authority, somewhat independent, and with significant prestige. Such a group would make general, government-

[39] Coherent control of the entire regulatory process would help ensure that the government would treat problems holistically and not, for example, clean up the ground by shifting pollution to the air. See G. Edwards, *Implementing Public Policy* (Washington, D.C.: Congressional Quarterly Press, 1980), 134–41 (describing "fragmentation" of programs among numerous agencies and the tendency towards excessively narrow focus within each agency and towards inefficiency in the system and in achievement of program goals).

wide rationalizing efforts of a kind that EPA is now trying internally to achieve.[40]

Second, a civil service – a bureaucracy – has several characteristic virtues that seem especially helpful when viewed in light of the risk regulation problems described. These characteristic virtues include:

1 *Rationalization.* Bureaucracies rationalize the problems and processes with which they work, allowing them to develop systems. For example, over several decades, bureaucracies charged with setting rates for electricity, communications, and transportation developed a complex but fairly uniform system of "cost-of-service ratemaking." That system does not consist simply of rules and regulations. Rather, its mission is accomplished by standards, practices, guidelines, prototypes, models, and informal procedures, all shaped to some extent by a general goal (that of replicating a competitive marketplace) but more directly guided by goals internal to the system (efficiency, fairness, fair return on investment). The system solves roughly similar problems in roughly similar ways irrespective of the particular regulatory program or regulated industry at issue.[41]

   The problems of health and safety risk regulation could well benefit from the development of a similar system. Such a system would recognize the differences between, say, unusually high risks to specially placed individuals and risks to the general population. It would neither reduce all lives saved to a common dollar-value, nor duck out of hard choices by claiming incommensurable differences among different health programs

[40] See S. Jasanoff, *The Fifth Branch: Science Advisers as Policymakers* (Cambridge, Mass.: Harvard University Press, 1990), 89–100 (discussing the role of the Science Advisory Board to the EPA in reviewing scientific evidence and recommending research strategies); see also Committee on the Institutional Means for Assessment of Risks to Public Health, National Research Council, *Risk Assessment in the Federal Government: Managing the Process* (Washington, D.C. and Springfield, Va.: National Academy Press, 1983), 150–60 (recommending interagency coordination of cancer risk assessment broader than that EPA currently undertakes, but less comprehensive than that proposed here).

[41] See Breyer, *Regulation and its Reform*, 36–39 (describing cost-of-service ratemaking and the choices regulators must make in determining rates); T. McCraw, *Prophets of Regulation* (Cambridge, Mass.: Harvard University Press, 1984), 239–70 (practice of cost-of-service ratemaking and its reform in electric power industry and airlines); see generally A. Kahn, *Economics of Regulation: Principles and Institutions* (Cambridge, Mass. and London: MIT Press, 1988) (providing an economic and institutional analysis of traditional ratemaking issues).

and circumstances. It would compare experiences under different programs to create a common approach, while embodying that approach in models, examples, and paradigms that permit local variation. Ratemaking problems are somewhat simpler, yet they suggest a parallel.

2 *Expertise.* Bureaucracies develop expertise in administration, but also in the underlying subject matter. They normally understand that subject matter at least well enough to communicate with substantive experts, to identify the experts, and to determine which insights of the underlying discipline can be transformed into workable administrative practices, and to what extent. A unified group charged with developing a system for addressing health risk regulation might bring together people familiar with science, risk analysis, economics, and administration – expertise that now is divided among different agencies, such as EPA and OMB.

3 *Insulation.* A civil service automatically offers a degree of insulation or protection from politics and public opinion. Of course, tenure rules tend to insulate its members, to some extent, from the force of public criticism. More importantly, administrators of a system can rationalize or justify particular results in particular cases in terms of the system's rules, practices, and procedures. Just as a doctor justifies a dose of bitter medicine by reference to medical theory and practice that indicate it will help the patient, so regulators explain and justify highly unpopular individual decisions, such as a decision that means a significant rate increase for the public. They do so through reference to the rules and practices of a system that, considered as a whole, helps the public by keeping rates within reason. Use of a coherent, well-worked-out system changes the focus of political questions. It becomes more difficult simply to ask: "Isn't this specific result terrible?" The relevant question becomes: "Is this a good *system*, and, if so, does the system generate this particular result?" Bureaucratic solutions that emerge from sound, coherent, and well-constructed comparisons among different substances offer administrators the promise of a modest increase in independence, through greater insulation from public criticism of individual decisions.

4 *Authority.* A bureaucratic solution offers the hope of creating authoritative decisions that may, in turn, help break the vicious circle. Respect for decisions as authoritative is not easy to create in this era of political distrust, an era that since 1970 has seen Americans' confidence in virtually every institution – government, business, the press (but surprisingly, not

the military) – plummet,[42] and an era in which different political parties typically control Congress and the executive branch. Still, it appears that public respect depends not only upon the perception of public participation, but also, in part, upon an organization's successful accomplishment of a mission that satisfies an important societal need.

A third argument in favor of a bureaucratic solution is that it seems fairly easy to create an agenda for a central administrative organization, which agenda would take advantage of these inherent bureaucratic virtues. A centralized administrative group, charged with helping to develop a uniform system, could do the following:

1 *Develop standards.* The organization could usefully try to make explicit, and more uniform, controversial assumptions that agencies now – implicitly and often inconsistently – use in reaching their decisions. Regulators should investigate carefully in order to avoid actions that kill more people than they save. Comparative program experience is likely to suggest more uniform relevant standards.[43] The organization would seek to develop consistent approaches to answering questions such as the following: is there some *de minimis* level of risk below which any program ought to consider a substance safe?[44] Is there some level of expenditure beyond which a program should not go in its efforts to save a single statistical life? And how are these two questions related? To work out a *de minimis* standard involves considering both the extent to which small doses of a substance pose risks to the population at large (for instance, "substance x threatens 100 additional deaths across the nation"), and the extent to which exposure poses certain special risks to particular individuals (for example, "only 200 people are exposed to substance x, but each of them

42 See Louis Harris, Inc., "Confidence in the Military is Up While Confidence in the White House Falls," *The Harris Poll* (March 22 1992); see also *Breaking the Vicious Circle*, 64, figure 4.

43 The FCCSET Ad Hoc Working Group on Risk Assessment, a high-level body set up in 1991, involving eleven federal agencies, has made efforts to pool experience and harmonize approaches. See EPA, *Intergovernmental Public Meeting on Risk Assessment in the Federal Government: Asking the Right Questions*, Final Report (10 June 1992).

44 See F. Cross, D. Byrd, and L. Lave, "Discernable Risk – A Proposed Standard for Significant Risk in Carcinogen Regulation," 43 *Admin. L. Rev.* 61 (1991) (discussing possible standards for identifying significant risks); Federal Focus, Inc., *Toward Common Measures: Recommendations for a Presidential Executive Order in Environmental Risk Assessment and Risk Management Policy* (Washington, D.C., 1991), 93; see generally C. Whipple ed., *De Minimis Risk* (New York: Plenum Press, 1987).

has a fifty–fifty chance of death"). Furthermore, the costs of reducing risks through regulation, broadly defined (in that tiny costs may warrant stricter standards aimed at tiny risks, and vice versa), should be taken into consideration. Currently, permitted risk levels vary widely – even ranging between one in 10,000 and one in a million within a single proposal – both between and within programs and agencies, against a vague legislative background whose statutes simply announce the criteria of "acceptable," "safe," or "significant" levels of risk, typically tempered by concerns of economic and technical feasibility expressed in vague, general terms.[45] The *de minimis* problem is complex but it does not defy efforts to create a more uniform, common-sense standard, if only a presumptive standard that would permit exceptions, or even a set of examples of frequently found tradeoffs and acceptable risk levels that would help agencies develop their own rules.[46]

2 *Tap expert opinion.* A central administrative organization could make conscious efforts to draw upon scientific and technical work found outside the government. Some outside experts, for example, have developed systematic and sophisticated methods of factoring different kinds of uncertainty into risk analyses; others have developed methods for assessing how particular communities value different health-risk reduction programs.[47] Working with existing science advisory boards, it could

[45] EPA has set forth four different measures of "acceptable risk." EPA National Emission Standards for Hazardous Air Pollutants, 53 Fed. Reg. 28,496, 28,523, 28,527, 28,529 (1988) (proposed rule and notice of public hearing); see also EPA, Airborne Radionuclides, 54 Fed. Reg. 9,612 (1989) (same). Not surprisingly, courts have found open-ended statutes to allow agencies substantial flexibility (and thus disparity) in determining permissible levels of substances posing health risks. See, e.g., *American Textile Manufacturers* v. *Donovan*, 452 U.S. 490, 508, 512 (1981) (Occupational Safety and Health Act provisions requiring standards to assure no "material impairment of health" to "the extent feasible" and measures "reasonably necessary or appropriate to provide safe or healthful employment" did not mandate cost-benefit analysis).

[46] See also Committee on the Institutional Means for Assessment of Risks to Public Health, *Risk Assessment in the Federal Government*, at 162–75 (arguing for the development of "uniform inference guidelines" in cancer risk assessment, and for a central board on risk assessment to lead the process); C. Powers, J. Moore, and A. Upton, *Improving the Coherence of Federal Regulation of Risks from Hazardous Substances* (background paper prepared for the Task Force on Science and Technology in Judicial and Regulatory Decision Making, Carnegie Commission on Science, Technology, and Government, 1991), 24–26 (discussing need for "inference guidelines").

[47] See, e.g., R. Mitchell and R. Carson, "Valuing Drinking Water Risk Reductions Using the Contingent Valuation Method: A Methodological Study of Risks from THM and Giardia" (unpublished manuscript, 1986) (contingent valuation study with focus groups and in-

select and disseminate such work, which could help inform the judgmental risk-regulatory process in much the same way that good econometric models inform, but do not determine, judgmental "rate of return" decisions.[48]

3 *Build sensible models.* A central administrative organization could help develop models that aim to achieve higher-quality analysis and better results in a range of regulatory applications. Models build uniform systems, while recognizing that different circumstances may call for different treatment. For example, exposures of specially sensitive populations (or exposures through multiple pathways, or dose extrapolation models with thresholds) will sometimes, as a matter of common sense, be highly relevant to a regulatory judgment, and sometimes not. To create uniform, multi-program rules in advance about such matters can provoke heated but unenlightening debate and threaten to be procrustean; yet for each agency to go its own way means serious inconsistency. Models, prototypes or examples, flagging key assumptions and providing options at key points, can produce a system with uniform aims which is also adaptable.

Models based upon interagency experience could help regulators decide how to find some kind of natural regulatory stopping place, short of zero risk or the destruction of an industry, which does not depend upon the regulator's subjective reaction to the facts of a particular case. The models might use comparisons that would themselves create, without specifically defining, standards that the human mind can grasp, that limit arbitrary action, and that achieve consistency. Models and examples might explain how usefully to "unpack" crude risk-assessment numbers and supply qualitative conclusions through comparisons that illuminate the nature of relevant uncertainties.[49] All this is to suggest a

depth interviews, using a risk-ladder as a visual aid). Mitchell and Carson found that a majority of respondents would vote against spending any extra money to reduce drinking water risks by 2.4 in 100,000. *Ibid.* at 66.

48 See Powers, Moore, and Upton, *Improving the Coherence of Federal Regulations*, 49–52 (affirming need for a central organization to build a risk inventory of risk-related information). But cf. Carnegie Commission Staff Report, "Relative Risk and Regulation of Toxic Substances," 13–14 (Preliminary Draft, 16 May 1991), in *Task Force Binder* (Carnegie Commission, 24 May 1991) (arguing for decentralized risk inventories in various agencies).

49 See, e.g., J. Graham, "Improving Chemical Risk Assessment," 14(4) *Regulation* 14, 15–16 (Fall 1991) (urging consideration of multiple factors in determining carcinogenic potency).

need for a system that provides neither a single set of rules nor a myriad of approaches, that simplifies but recognizes the need for a few major variations, and that guides through standard, paradigm, and example, but does not directly command.

4 *Set an agenda.* The central administrative organization might create a "risk agenda" that helps to prioritize different programs and different activities within programs, and that looks for tradeoffs among programs that will lead overall to improved health or safety. It might look for ways to reallocate, transfer, or combine health resources so that they perform more effectively.

In sum, it seems possible to harness certain inherent virtues of a civil service in order to improve risk regulation. The listed characteristics of a bureaucracy match the problem's needs. A bureaucracy's rationalizing tendencies match the need for consistency through system-building and prioritizing; a bureaucracy's use of expertise matches the need for technically related regulatory improvement; a bureaucracy's insulation matches the need for protection from the vicissitudes of public opinion based on a single substance or a single issue; and a successful bureaucracy can begin to build public confidence in its systems, thereby making its results more authoritative.

There are, of course, important objections to these suggestions. Also, there are many who reasonably believe that increased bureaucratic discretion will hurt more than it will help. We shall not consider these objections in detail here. Nor can we prove that the direction suggested in *Breaking the Vicious Circle* is the right one. Rather, for purposes of generating discussion, we simply want to make plausible the view that a civil service will continue to regulate small risks, and that it is important (and possible) to encourage and empower that civil service to operate a regulatory system that is coordinated, rational, and coherent.

## Risk regulation in the European Union

### THE CHANGING LANDSCAPE OF RISK REGULATION

The problems of risk regulation – tunnel vision, random agendas, and serious inconsistency – currently seem less serious in Europe than in the United States. Judging solely on the quantity of publications on the subject,

US scholars and policymakers appear far more preoccupied with risk regulation and its reform than their European counterparts. Of course, the relative scarcity of European studies on risk regulation is to some extent related to the fact that, until the beginning of the 1970s, there was hardly any "European" risk regulation to speak of; rather, each nation adopted and implemented its own health, safety, and environmental regulatory framework. Since that time, the situation has changed drastically. The causes and consequences of this change for European risk regulation are studied in detail below.

Still, even looking at European countries individually, the problems that beset American regulators are – or at least are perceived to be – less pressing. A profound analysis of the reasons for this difference would by far exceed the scope of this chapter. One can nonetheless suggest a number of factors that probably contribute to the more "benign" climate for risk regulation in Europe.

### *"Old style" European risk regulation*

In most European countries, general risk policies are developed by the executive branch of government, in other words, the ministries – usually divided into ministerial departments – and their cabinets. Administration, implementation, and enforcement are officially considered politically "neutral" tasks, and are in the hands of a body of non-elected civil servants who enjoy considerable prestige and authority. Government and administrators traditionally enjoy a higher degree of insulation from public and political pressure than US regulatory agencies, for the following reasons.[50] First, in many European nations, the political party controlling the government (or parties in countries with coalition governments) also holds a majority in parliament.[51] Consequently, there is less cause for close scrutiny by the legislative branch of regulations developed by the executive. This relative freedom from parliamentary oversight may in turn cause the government to relax its grip on the administration. Second, regulatory decisionmaking procedures are usually less open, less accessible to special

[50] See V. Heyvaert, "The Changing Role of Science in Environmental Regulatory Decisionmaking in the European Union,"9 *Law & Eur. Aff.* 426, 428–31 (1999).

[51] See, e.g., Rose-Ackerman, "Environmental Policymaking and the Limits of Public Law," 41–46.

interest groups, and therefore less confrontational in nature, than in America. Europe is characterized by a strong corporatist tradition, where interested parties are either drawn into the black box of government decisionmaking, thus becoming internal to the process, or denied access.[52] Third, judicial oversight of regulations and administrative acts is marginal, and instances of litigation are relatively rare.[53] Finally, it has been claimed that Europeans generally have more tolerance and respect for public administration, and are less suspicious of the motives behind and overall soundness of regulatory decisionmaking.[54] Naturally, such claims are highly speculative. Nonetheless, it is hard to deny that a young professional choosing a career in public administration in France is more likely to have fulfilled her parents' highest aspirations than her American colleague.

In sum, European regulators and administrators are on average less exposed to public scrutiny and pressure, two elements feeding the vicious circle diagnosed in the United States. The relative freedom from oversight, and the greater prestige of the public office, would allow European regulatory bodies and administrations to develop risk-regulatory strategies in a more systematic, pragmatic, and coherent manner, thus reducing incidences of tunnel vision, random agenda setting, and inconsistency.

It would, however, be prematurely optimistic to conclude that the vicious circle is a uniquely American problem that need not concern European policymakers. European risk regulation is undergoing a period of rapid and profound transformation, both at the national and at the European Union level. Significant changes in the way health, safety, and environmental policy is developed, and in the institutions involved in the regulatory process, gradually cause the relations between the legislative, executive, administrative, and judicial branches of government to shift. Tried and tested notions of administrative discretion, corporatism, and judicial deference are being reassessed and reinterpreted in the light of changed circumstances. It therefore becomes highly relevant to examine whether, in a changing Europe, ingredients are brewing that could lead to the development of a European vicious circle for risk regulation.

52 See Brickman, Jasanoff, and Ilgen, *Controlling Chemicals.*

53 Cf. Rose-Ackerman, "Environmental Policymaking and the Limits of Public Law," 45–46.

54 See, e.g., J. Salomon, "Science and Government: A European Perspective," in H. Brooks and C. Cooper eds., *Science for Public Policy* (Pergamon Press, 1987), 34.

## *A changing environment*

Briefly, when we review developments at the national level over the past two decades, two phenomena stand out: first, the growing emphasis on institutional decentralization of regulation and administration, which has characterized restructuring efforts in, for example, France;[55] second, European regulation that is marked by the recent emergence of agencies that are structurally similar to US agencies, and that profess a more managerial, entrepreneurial style of decisionmaking.[56] The Environment Agency for England and Wales, which was established in November 1995, and its Scottish counterpart, introduced at the same time, are the pre-eminent examples.[57]

Although the changes in risk regulation at the national level are certainly worthy of further exploration, they are not the focal point of this section of the chapter. Instead, we will concentrate on the developments at the European Union (EU) level, and their present and potential ramifications for the treatment of small risks in Europe. Accordingly, the second part of this section begins with a brief overview of certain basic features of the EU, concentrating on those necessary to understand the ensuing study of EU risk regulation. The third part contains a discussion of the reasons why it is likely that the EU's involvement in risk regulation will deepen over time. Because the integration dynamics at play are not only operative within the European Union, but are also relevant for other forms of international association or federation (such as NAFTA and WTO), the mechanisms pushing towards an intensifying Europeanization of risk regulation are examined in greater detail. The part concludes with a summary overview of the current state of play in EU risk regulation. In the fourth part, we examine whether EU risk regulation might potentially nurture the same weaknesses as the ones prevalent in the US system (tunnel vision, random agenda setting, inconsistency). The final part investigates whether, if EU risk regulation were indeed likely to develop some of the same flaws as observed in the US, American experience in dealing with these problems could help to devise an EU system that handles risk rationally.

55 See Institut International d'Administration Publique, *An Introduction to French Administration* (La Documentation Française, 1996).

56 See S. Zifcak, *New Managerialism. Administrative Reform in Whitehall and Canberra* (Buckingham and Philadelphia: Open University Press, 1994).

57 See, e.g., W. Howarth, "Self-Monitoring, Self-Policing, Self-Incrimination and Pollution Law," *Modern L.Rev.* 201–09 (1997).

## SOME BASIC ELEMENTS OF THE EUROPEAN UNION

In summary, the European Union joins fifteen European nations (with more expected to join in the future) in the establishment and maintenance of a customs union, a common market, and, most recently, a monetary union; the development of common policies in a range of major policy areas (such as transportation, agriculture, nuclear energy policy, antitrust, social and environmental policy); and cooperation in others (for instance, defense and foreign affairs).[58] The Member States' commitment towards these goals is expressed in a series of treaties and protocols, of which the Treaty establishing the European Community ("EC Treaty") is the most important.[59] It is the EC Treaty that contains the principles most relevant to European risk regulation,[60] as well as a description of the tasks, competencies, and operating procedures of EU institutions.

The core institutions of the European Union are the Council, the Commission, the European Parliament, and the Court of Justice, which is assisted by a Court of First Instance. The Council consists of ministerial

[58] See generally, P. Craig and G. De Burca, *EU Law. Text, Cases, and Materials* (2d edn., Oxford University Press, 1998); J. Shaw, *Law of the European Union* (2d edn., Basingstoke: MacMillan, 1998); P. J. G. Kapteyn, P. Verloren van Themaat, and R. Barents, *Inleiding tot het Recht van de Europese Gemeenschappen: na Maastricht* (5th eds., Deventer: Kluwer, 1995); S. Weatherill and P. Beaumont, *EC Law* (2d edn., Harmondsworth: Penguin, 1995); T. C. Hartley, *The Foundations of European Community Law: An Introduction to the Constitutional and Administrative Law of the European Community* (3d edn., Oxford: Clarendon Press, 1994). Current EU Member States are: Austria, Belgium, Denmark, Finland, France, Germany, Greece, Ireland, Italy, Luxembourg, the Netherlands, Portugal, Spain, Sweden, and the United Kingdom. Countries likely to join during the next EU enlargement round, which is planned for the beginning of the new millennium, are: the Czech Republic, Cyprus, Estonia, Hungary, Poland, and Slovenia. Cf. European Commission, *Agenda 2000 – Volume II: the Challenge of Enlargement* (COM/97/2000 final – Vol. II).

[59] The most recent version of the EC Treaty is contained in the Treaty of Amsterdam, which was finalized in late 1997, and entered into effect in mid-1999. The Amsterdam version of the EC Treaty changes the numbering of the Treaty articles. The following discussion uses the new numbering system, but refers to the old article numbers with the indication "old" in the footnotes.

[60] The EC Treaty lays down Community policies for the free movement of goods and elimination of trade barriers, which may be at cross-purposes with national risk regulatory measures (see below), common rules on the approximation of laws, regulations, and administrative provisions between the Member States, and the basic principles for the development of common agricultural, social, health, consumer protection, and environmental policies.

representatives from the Member States, and functions as the main legislative body for the European Union. Article 271 of the EC Treaty[61] charges the Council to ensure that Treaty objectives are attained, and to this effect confers on it the power to take decisions. On most issues, including market integration, health, and environmental matters, the Council decides by qualified majority voting. It should however be noted that, in a growing range of areas, the Council must share decisionmaking power with the European Parliament. The Parliament consists of 626 members, all directly elected by the citizens of the Member States. It was originally set up as a "weak" institution with an advisory and supervisory function. Yet, as the European Union has developed, the European Parliament has acquired greater importance, and its legislative prerogatives have gradually expanded. As will be discussed in greater detail below, the growing powers of the European Parliament and its changing position vis-à-vis other EU institutions may complicate risk regulation at the EU level.

Arguably the most interesting and certainly the most idiosyncratic of the institutions is the Commission. The Commission defies classification in one of the classic branches of government; it performs a range of different tasks, covering executive, as well as legislative, administrative, and even judicial functions. The Commission is the European Union's principal strategist: it drafts broad, long-term policy programs for the EU (which are later submitted to the Council for endorsement) and plays a major role in outlining the Union's legislative plan for any given year. Its competencies in these areas make the Commission a crucial player in the European regulation of small risks. Moreover, the Commission has the right of legislative initiative by making proposals to the Council and Parliament. Hence, it is able to ensure that the policy lines it developed earlier are indeed translated into proposals for secondary EU law.[62] The Commission also functions as the EU watchdog: it sees to it that Treaty provisions as well as secondary provisions are respected in the Member States, and functions as the main supervisor and overseer of EU policy implementation. Implementation itself, however, is almost always left to public authorities in the Member States. This scattering of tasks between national and supranational institutions constitutes one of the most challenging, and often trying, complications for European policy

[61] Old Article 202.

[62] Primary EU law covers the Treaty articles and general principles to which the EU adheres. Secondary law refers to the plethora of acts adopted by EU institutions to carry out their tasks under the Treaty.

integration. As to the institutional architecture, it is useful to know that the Commission is headed by a College of twenty Commissioners, which is in turn chaired by the Commission President. The permanent officials working in the Commission – the Commission bureaucracy – are organized into Directorate-Generals or "DGs", covering the different major EU policy areas. At present, there are twenty-four DGs, including one for Industry (DG III), Agriculture (DG VI), Environment, Nuclear Safety, and Civil Protection (DG XI), Science, Research, and Development (DG XII), and, a most recent addition, Consumer Policy and Consumer Health Protection (DG XXIV).

The fourth core institution is the European Court of Justice (ECJ), to which the Court of First Instance (CFI) is attached. The Court represents the judicial branch of the European Union, and its task is essentially one of assessing and deciding whether EU institutions, as well as the Member States and public and private entities within the Member States, are in compliance with EU law. Compared to other international judicial bodies (such as the International Court of Justice in The Hague), the ECJ commands a noticeably high level of authority; its judgments count as "hard law" rather than respectable but often ineffectual moral condemnations. Important in this regard is the Court's power, established in the Maastricht version of the EC Treaty, to impose fines on a Member State that has failed to comply with a previous Court judgment.[63] The Court has played a famously active role in the process of European market integration and the development of European environmental law and, as will be examined below, has the potential to become a major actor in the development of EU risk regulation.

We should briefly mention the different legal acts that EU institutions adopt to carry out the objectives of the EC Treaty. The two most important instruments are the regulations and directives adopted by the Council and the European Parliament. Regulations are binding on all the Member States and are directly applicable; they do not require transposition into national law. Directives, in turn, are binding as to the ends to be achieved, while leaving the Member States discretion as to the forms and method of implementation. They do need transposition into national law.[64] While the

[63] Article 228 of the EC Treaty (Old Article 171).

[64] Directives can be addressed to any one Member State. In practice, however, the overwhelming majority of directives are addressed to all Member States.

differences between regulations and directives are theoretically clear, the boundaries between the two have become quite blurred in legislative practice. Although directly applicable, regulations often need to draw upon national authorities to be put into effect, which creates a *de facto* national implementation stage and opens opportunities for national variation. Directives, on the other hand, can include such level of detail that Member State discretion as to implementation is reduced to a bare minimum. Detailed directives – sometimes dubbed "regulation-type directives" – are particularly prevalent in areas affecting risk regulation: technical harmonization, safety, health, consumer and environmental protection. In addition to regulations and directives, EU authorities act through decisions (binding in their entirety for those to whom they are addressed), recommendations, and opinions. The latter two have no binding force.

Finally, a word about the relation between EU and Member State law. As a general rule, EU legislation and decisions have supremacy over and preempt national legislation. However, there are quite a few exceptions to this rule, not in the least in the area of environmental risk regulation. These will be discussed at the end of the following section.

## THE EU'S GROWING INVOLVEMENT IN RISK REGULATION: PATTERNS FOR INTEGRATION

Although risk regulation was not part of the original European agenda, which focused almost exclusively on economic integration, the development of health, safety, and environmental policies has over the years matured into a major European project. Moreover, we may safely predict that, at the very least, EU involvement in risk regulation will remain as high in the future as it is today. An even more likely scenario is that, as Europe makes its way towards an "ever closer union," EU administrators will be drawn ever more deeply into the small-risk regulatory business.

A first reason for the continuing past and likely future "Europeanization" of risk regulation flows from the basic objective of the European Union (or, as it was called in the early days, the European Economic Community): the establishment of a single, common market within which boundaries goods (as well as services, people, and capital) could circulate freely.[65] To attain the

[65] See, e.g., S. Farr, *Harmonization of Technical Standards in the EC* (2d edn., John Wiley, 1996), 3–4.

goal of market integration for goods, two major paths present themselves.[66] The first, "positive integration," entails the adoption of harmonized product standards, which are usually enacted in the form of EU directives (for example, Directive 88/378 on toy safety; Directive 93/42 on medical devices; Directive 89/686 on personal protective equipment; etc.). A great number of EU institutions participate directly or indirectly in this enterprise. The Council of the European Union is responsible for the adoption of harmonization directives. An equally important role is reserved for the European Commission, which drafts legislative proposals and to which the task of detailing harmonized standards may be delegated. The European Parliament supervises the legislative process, tables amendments to proposed harmonization directives, and, since the entry into force of the Maastricht Treaty in 1993, has veto power over their adoption. Additionally, a variety of European, pluri-national and regional agencies, committees, advisory groups, and non-governmental organizations – such as the European standardization body (CEN) – contribute more or less informally to the process. Since harmonized product standards as a rule include requirements for health, safety, and, increasingly, the environmental friendliness of products, it is easy to see how positive integration draws European Union institutions into the regulation of small risks. Harmonization of, say, food laws in Europe inevitably involves issues of risk regulation, such as the adoption of a positive list for allowable food additives, colorants, and contaminants, the establishment of maximum levels for pesticide residues on fruit and vegetables, and even the development of an EU-wide pesticides authorization scheme.[67] Because of the harmonization process, these issues are now no longer within the exclusive competence of national authorities, but are at least partially settled by European institutions.

The harmonization process does not prevent national authorities from implementing risk policies for products (and services) that have not yet been "Europeanized" through EU legislation. Member States have adopted laws and regulations that forbid the importing of certain (non-harmonized) products from other Member States, with the stated objective of pro-

[66] See, e.g., E. J. Kirchner, *Decision Making in the European Community. The Council Presidency and European Integration* (Manchester and New York: Manchester University Press; distributed in the US by St. Martin's Press, 1992), 9.

[67] See, e.g., C. Lister and D. Vaughan, *Regulation of Food Products by the European Community* (Butterworths, 1992).

tecting public health or the environment in the first state. Article 28 of the EC Treaty, however, prohibits Member States from imposing measures "having equivalent effect" to "quantitative restrictions on imports."[68] Yet Article 30 of the EC Treaty[69] provides that Article 28 shall not "preclude prohibitions or restrictions" on imports that are "justified" on grounds that include "the protection of health and life of humans, animals or plants," provided that such measures do not constitute "a means of arbitrary discrimination or a disguised restriction" on trade. Articles 28 and 30 of the EC Treaty thus mark out the second path towards market integration: they enable the European Union to outlaw those national rules and regulations that hamper the functioning of the internal market and are not appropriately or adequately justified by environmental, health, and safety objectives.[70] This method of integration (commonly referred to as "negative integration") is exercised by the European Court of Justice, the ultimate authority in charge of assessing the validity of national protective measures against the parameters of Articles 28/30.[71] Where product harmonization requires the Council, Commission, and Parliament to deal with risk issues, negative integration compels the Court to review national, often quite technical environmental, health, and safety measures. Thus, the Court becomes another authority involved in risk regulation in Europe, exercising an authority similar to that exercised by US courts over state regulation under "dormant commerce clause" jurisprudence.

In a string of Article 28/30 judgments spanning more than two decades, the Court has developed a number of principles (or rules of thumb) to

[68] Article 28 of the EC Treaty (Old Article 30): "Quantitative restrictions on imports and all measures having equivalent effect shall, without prejudice to the following provisions, be prohibited between Member States." Article 30 of the EC Treaty (Old Article 36): "The provisions of Articles 28 to 29 shall not preclude prohibitions or restrictions on imports, exports or goods in transit justified on grounds of public morality, public policy or public security; the protection of health and life of humans, animals or plants, the protection of national treasures possessing artistic, historic or archaeological value; or the protection of industrial and commercial property. Such prohibitions and restrictions shall not, however, constitute a means of arbitrary discrimination or a disguised restriction of trade between Member States."

[69] Old Article 36.

[70] See, e.g., C. Joerges, "Scientific Expertise in Social Regulation and the European Court of Justice: Legal Frameworks for Denationalized Governance Structures," in C. Joerges, K. H. Ladeur, and E. Vos, *Integrating Scientific Expertise into Regulatory Decision-Making* (Nomos, 1997), 298.

[71] See generally, P. Oliver, *Free Movement of Goods in the EEC* (2d edn., London: European Law Centre, 1988).

assess whether a national product requirement that applies to products coming from other Member States is a legitimate measure intended to regulate risks threatening health, safety, or the environment, or whether it is an unacceptable barrier to trade. Thus, these court-developed principles set qualitative standards for risk regulatory decisionmaking within the Member States.[72] Undoubtedly one of the most famous is the proportionality principle, which advocates that public interest goals, such as health and safety objectives, should be attained by the least restrictive means available.[73] Equally well known is the principle of mutual recognition, laid down in the landmark *Cassis de Dijon* decision.[74] Mutual recognition embodies the idea that, while the particulars of mandatory product requirements (including health, safety, and environmental prescriptions) may differ between the Member States, one should assume that they are generally equivalent.[75] Therefore, if a product is lawfully produced and marketed in one Member State, it presumptively can be sold freely throughout the Community. Regulatory restrictions on lawfully produced imports are only allowed by way of exception, and are to be interpreted restrictively. But in the case of risk regulation, case law indicates that the Court displays considerable willingness to accept that measures justified on the basis of health, safety, and environmental reasons constitute exceptions to the mutual recognition principle of presumed equivalence (*mutual recognition*). Accordingly, the Court usually grants Member States broad margins of discretion in the adoption and implementation of national risk regulation, provided however that there exists a "genuine risk" and that the restrictive measures are necessary and effective for risk reduction.[76] Unfortunately, those are precisely the most difficult elements to establish in the area of

[72] *Ibid.*, 187–203; J. Jans, *European Environmental Law* (Kluwer, 1995), 214–35; C. London and M. Llamas, *EC Law on Protection of the Environment and the Free Movement of Goods* (London: Butterworths, 1995), chapter 3.

[73] *De Peijper*, Case 104/75 [1976] ECR 613; *Commission* v. *Denmark*, Case 302/86 [1988] ECR 4607 (*Danish Bottle Case*).

[74] *Rewe-Zentral AG* v. *Bundesmonopolverwaltung für Branntwein*, Case 120/78 [1979] ECR 649.

[75] See Farr, *Harmonization of Technical Standards in the EC*, 10–12.

[76] See, e.g., *Frans-Nederlandse Maatschappij voor Biologische Produkten*, Case 272/80 [1981] ECR 3277; *Nijman*, Case 125/88 [1989] ECR 3533; *Albert Heijn*, Case 94/83 [1984] ECR 3263; and *Gourmetterie v.d. Burg*, Case C–169/89 [1990] ECR I–2143 (*Red Grouse Case*). See generally M. Hession and R. Macrory, "Balancing Trade Freedom with the Requirements of Sustainable Development," in N. Emiliou and D. O'Keefe, *The European Union and World Trade Law. After the GATT Uruguay Round* (John Wiley, 1996), 198–202.

small risks. Not surprisingly, the Court is wary of pinning down more detailed, substantive criteria for risk regulation, and wherever possible restricts itself to offering essentially procedural prescriptions, for example, that risk regulation should take into account the findings of (international) scientific research, and that regulatory restrictions should be reviewed as new scientific information becomes available.[77]

Faced with the prospect that market integration may proceed either through positive harmonization measures adopted by the EU Council and Parliament or, in their absence, "negatively" through Court rulings tearing down national barriers to trade, EU Member States may well favor the former scenario. First, Member States may justifiably feel that they retain a firmer grip on the development of European risk and safety standards (which resonate in national risk regulation policies) through a political process of EU legislation in which they are explicitly represented,[78] than in one governed and arbitrated by an independent judicial authority.[79] Second, for the reasons set forth earlier in the US discussion,[80] EU administrators will often prove better able than EU judges to decide whether technical statutes and regulations are "disguised restrictions on trade."[81]

Consider the kinds of questions that can arise under Articles 28 and 30.[82] Is a rule that insists on the use of particularly sturdy metal for lift cables aimed to protect workers or to help the local steel makers (who, by chance, produce especially sturdy steel)? The 1986 *Woodworking Machines* case provides another illustration of this actual dilemma. Here, the conflict revolved around different national safety philosophies. To ensure the safety of their

[77] *Van Bennekom*, Case 227/82 [1983] ECR 3883; *Motte*, Case 247/84 [1985] ECR 3887; *Bellon*, Case C–42/90 [1990] ECR I–1747; *The Upjohn Company and Upjohn NV* v. *Farzoo Inc. and Kortmann*, Case C–112/89 [1991] ECR I–1703 (reliance on scientific evidence); and *Ministère publique* v. *Mirepoix*, Case 54/85 [1986] ECR 1511 (review on the basis of new information).

[78] The EU Council is, after all, an assembly of the governments of the Member States.

[79] See Kirchner, *Decision Making in the European Communtity*, 9.

[80] See pp. 299–301 above.

[81] Article 30 of the EC Treaty (old Article 36). A possible solution is for the Court to make the decision, but to rely heavily on briefing from the Commission in its role as *amicus curiae*. However, this solution is likely to be imperfect: for political or other reasons, the Commission may not always fulfill that role as the Court might wish, and even with all the relevant legislative facts, the Court may well be faced with making a decision implicating a wider range of political and economic factors than judges are accustomed to dealing with. See, e.g., *3 Glocken GmbH* v. *USL Centro-Sud*, Case 407/85 [1988] ECR 4233.

[82] Old Articles 30 and 36.

workers, French regulatory authorities insisted on stringent design and operational standards for woodworking machines. Germany, in contrast, opted for a combination of somewhat less stringent product safety standards and vocational training of machine operators. Given these differences, was France's decision to deny German woodworking machines access to the French market genuinely intended to protect the safety of local machine operators, or the interests of local woodworking machines manufacturers?[83] Similarly, is a regulation that prohibits the importing of trout infected by certain bacteria aimed at protecting the physical health of other local trout or the economic health of those who raise them?[84] Is a restriction forbidding the importing of peaches with a certain pesticide residue aimed at helping those who might eat the peach or the local peach growers? These questions are all the more thorny since, as the Court confirmed in 1991, there exists no European Union definition of illness or disease. The only possible definitions for those terms, the Court added, are those most commonly accepted on the basis of scientific knowledge.[85] While the criterion of scientific acceptability may be of help to sift out the more obvious trade restrictions adopted under the guise of health protection measures (consider the mythical Swiss restriction, stipulating that anyone may sell milk in Switzerland but only if it comes from cows that graze in fields more than 2,500 meters high), it provides insufficient guidance for more technical – hence less transparent – regulations.

American courts have had to deal with similar concerns in applying the "dormant commerce clause." In light of the institutional difficulties courts face in trying to answer these kinds of questions, it is not surprising that judges reach results that are sometimes inconsistent,[86] or that Congress has often had to change judicial results through legislation.[87] Indeed, Congress itself has found that, in certain technical areas, administrators are better

[83] *Commission* v. *France*, Case 188/84 [1986] ECR 419. In this case, the Court ruled in favor of France.

[84] See *Maine* v. *Taylor*, 477 U.S. 131 (1986); *United States* v. *Taylor*, 752 F.2d 757 (1st Cir. 1985).

[85] *Delattre*, Case C–369/88 [1991] ECR I–1478.

[86] See, e.g., L. Tribe, *American Constitutional Law* (2d edn., Mineola, N.Y.: Foundation Press, 1988), 418–19 (comparing *South Carolina State Highway Department* v. *Barnwall Brothers*, 303 U.S. 177 (1938), which upheld a South Carolina statute limiting the width and weight of trucks, with *Southern Pacific Co.* v. *Arizona*, 325 U.S. 761 (1945), which struck down a statute limiting train lengths).

[87] See G. Bermann, "Taking Subsidiarity Seriously," 94 *Colum. L. Rev.* 331, 424–27 (1994).

able than judges, or than Congress itself, to assess the need for such restrictions. Congress has therefore at times exercised its power to pre-empt state laws that interfere with interstate commerce by delegating to a federal agency the authority to decide whether or not a particular state's regulatory rules unreasonably interfere with commerce. Thus, a state that imposes strict rules on trucking dynamite across its territory (for example, by permitting dynamite trucks only between midnight and 4 a.m.), in doing so, both interferes with interstate commerce and helps protect the lives of its citizens. A congressional statute gives the Department of Transportation the legal authority to decide which of these effects is predominant, and authorizes the administrators to set aside a state law when they believe that it unreasonably interferes with commerce.[88]

The same factors that have led Congress to give agencies, rather than courts, the authority to make this kind of decision might lead EU Member States to charge a European institution, such as the Council or the European Commission, with the development of centralized risk regulation standards that would then be used to determine whether, or when, an environmental regulation unreasonably interferes with trade among Member States.[89] They might empower the European Commission to apply these standards to practical cases. Of course, the European Court of Justice can review regulatory and administrative acts adopted by other EU institutions.[90] But, aware of their comparatively greater ability to make rules and provide expertise in the policy issues involved in the particular regulatory context, the Court will likely defer considerably to the administrative results.[91]

[88] See *New Hampshire Motor Transport Ass'n* v. *Flynn*, 751 F.2d 43, 50 (1st Cir. 1984) (discussing 49 U.S.C. § 1811).

[89] The Commission would be the most likely candidate for this task, since it is the most "expertise oriented" of the European institutions, and officially represents the Community viewpoint. Alternatively, the Council might decide to broaden the competencies of one of the newly established European agencies, for instance the European Environmental Agency, to draw up these national regulation assessment standards.

[90] See Article 226 of the EC Treaty (authorizing the Commission to bring a Member State's non-compliance with legislation before the Court of Justice) (old Article 169); Article 230 of the EC Treaty (Court of Justice to review the legality of acts of the Council and Commission) (old Article 173); Article 234 of the EC Treaty (Court of Justice's jurisdiction to give preliminary rulings concerning the interpretation of the EC Treaty and the validity and interpretation of acts of EC institutions) (old Article 177).

[91] See Bermann, "Taking Subsidiarity Seriously," 391–95 (advocating procedural, rather than substantive, "subsidiarity" review by the Court of Justice to ensure that administrators have taken subsidiarity into account).

A second reason for EU involvement in risk regulation relates to the transboundary effects of pollution emanating from industrial and other processes and production methods as well as from certain end-products, such as motor vehicles.[92] Even if individual Member States can protect themselves fairly easily against imports of products from other States that may harm their environment or the health and safety of their citizens, they cannot easily protect themselves against production processes in other Member States that may do the same. If Member State A dumps toxic waste into the North Sea, it may threaten fishermen from Member State B, or threaten those who come into contact with it as it washes up on State B's shores. Or, those who live in State B may feel a kind of "moral harm" as they contemplate the dolphins caught up in nets of fishermen from State A. In the first scenario, the inhabitants of Member State B suffer from a physical externality generated by Member State A's waste disposal policy; in the second the externality is of a psychological nature.[93] While it is commonly accepted that exposure to physical externalities gives the exposed Member State, Member State B in our example, a legitimate interest in the offending Member State's risk regulation policies, it is far more contested whether psychological distress should also warrant international interference with Member State A's policies.[94] In either case, however, State B would like to stop the harm that State A is causing its citizens. For reasons explored below, one of the most effective ways of doing so is by securing environmental legislation, promulgated by the EU, which will apply uniformly to State A and to State B.[95]

92 See M. Faure, "Harmonisation of Environmental Law and Market Integration: Harmonising for the Wrong Reasons?" 7(6) *Eur. Env. L. Rev.* 169, 170–71 (1998); D. Esty, "Revitalizing Environmental Federalism," 95 *Mich. L. Rev.* 570, 593–97 (1996); Jans, *European Environmental Law*, 9–10; H. Siebert, "Environmental Policy and European Integration," in Siebert, *Environmental Scarcity: The International Dimension* (J. C. B. Morh, 1991), 57, 64–66; E. Rehbinder and R. Stewart, *Integration Through Law. Vol. II. Environmental Protection Policy* (Walter De Gruyter, 1985), 4.

93 See Esty, "Revitalizing Environmental Federalism," 593–97.

94 *Ibid.*; Faure, "Harmonisation of Environmental Law and Market Integration," 173; but cf. W. Wils, "Subsidiarity and the EC Environmental Policy: Taking People's Concerns Seriously," 6 *J. Env. L.* 85–90 (1994).

95 Interestingly, Giandomenico Majone describes this phenomenon as the result of international *regulatory failure* rather than market failure: "[M]arket failure with international impacts, such as transboundary pollution, could be managed in a decentralized fashion, without delegating regulatory powers to a supranational authority, *provided* that national regulators were willing and able to take into account the international effects of their choices, that they had sufficient knowledge of one another's intentions; that the costs of organizing and monitoring policy co-ordination were not too high, and especially pro-

The EU now has considerable authority to promulgate regulations of this sort.[96]

Third, even where transboundary aspects are negligible, individual Member States may still want uniform EU regulatory laws that will assure them that other Member States' production processes are regulated as strictly as their own. If Member State A, for example, insists that its chemical manufacturers dispose of certain wastes in a costly risk-diminishing way, Member State A will want Member State B to do the same, lest the chemical manufacturers in State B enjoy a competitive advantage and the industry relocate to Member State B. That is so even if the toxic wastes in State B do not pose risks to citizens of State A. To protect and preserve its chemical industry, Member State A will seek to "level the playing field" for competition by securing the adoption of internationally uniform process standards, thereby ensuring that other States will not reap the benefits of their environmentally irresponsible behavior.[97] The creation of a level playing field is a major European preoccupation; the preamble of virtually every health and environmental measure adopted at the EU level refers to it as a legislative rationale. The underlying concern is that, if the European playing field were not leveled through uniform health, safety, and environmental regulations, a "race to the bottom" would ensue. In a nutshell, the race-to-the-bottom hypothesis posits that, in the absence of harmonization, Member States would compete for industrial investment by offering lenient health and environmental standards.[98] Caught in a downwards spiral of competitive deregulation, no country would in the end still manage to enact or enforce adequately protective legislation.

The validity of the race-to-the-bottom hypothesis is one of the most hotly debated questions of contemporary regulatory theory. Opponents of the hypothesis, such as Richard Revesz, insist that race-to-the-bottom claims

vided they could trust each other to implement in good faith their joint agreements." See G. Majone, "A European Regulatory State?" in J. Richardson, *EU Power and Policy-Making* (Routledge, 1996), 269.

96 See Articles 34, 95, 174, 175 of the EC Treaty (old Articles 100, 100a, 130r, 130s).

97 See J. Golub, "Introduction and Overview," in Golub ed., *Global Competition and EU Environmental Policy* (Routledge, 1998), 5; Faure, "Harmonisation of Environmental Law and Market Integration," 170; Siebert, "Environmental Policy and European Integration," 60–61.

98 See Golub, "Introduction and Overview" 5; D. Esty and D. Geradin, "Environmental Protection and International Competitiveness," 32(3) *J. World Trade* 16–17 (1998); Faure, "Harmonisation of Environmental Law and Market Integration," 170; Esty, "Revitalizing Environmental Federalism," 607–09; A. Ogus, "Quality Control for European Regulation," 2 *Maastricht J. Eur. and Comp. L.* 326 (1995).

are not borne out by any economic model, and maintain that decentralized systems of environmental regulation would increase social welfare – including environmental health – more than centralized styles of policymaking.[99] Furthermore, commentators claim that, even if decentralized policymaking would inspire Member State B to compete for investment by reducing social and environmental burdens, this phenomenon should not worry Member State A, much less compel it to reduce its own health and environmental standards.[100] One might expect environmentalists in State A to be pleased if toxic-waste-producing chemical plants moved to State B; and one might also expect that State A's consumers would be pleased, for they would benefit from less costly chemicals in that State B's citizens are willing to run the risks chemical production creates without the more costly, price-raising, waste disposal rules needed to satisfy the citizens of State A.[101] Indeed, from a purely "free trade" perspective, if one assumes the different Member States' different regulatory rules reflect their different citizens' differing levels of concern about risk and/or differing levels of need for jobs, and if one further assumes low transaction costs which make it possible for industry in Member State A to relocate with relative ease to Member State B, there is a net "economic" benefit to all should the chemical industry move, thereby supplying the same chemicals to all at lower real cost.[102] In addition, some commentators have claimed that competition in regulatory standards will not necessarily lead to lower standards; in cases where the development of new, resource-efficient technologies confers a competitive advantage, states may engage in a "win–win" regulatory "race to the top."[103] Finally, there are

[99] See R. Revesz, "Rehabilitating Interstate Competition: Rethinking the 'Race to the Bottom' Rationale for Federal Environmental Regulation, " 67 *NYU L. Rev.* 1210 (1992); W. Oates and R. Schwab, "Economic Competition among Jurisdictions: Efficiency Enhancing or Distortion Inducing?" 35 *J. Pub. Econ.* 333 (1988). In Europe, see Siebert, "Environmental Policy and European Integration," 57.

[100] See Golub, *Global Competition and EU Environmental Policy*, 20; M. Porter and C. van der Linde, "Green and Competitive: Ending the Stalemate, " *Harv. Business Rev.* 120 (September–October, 1995).

[101] See Golub, *Global Competition and EU Environmental Policy*, 20; Porter and van der Linde, "Green and Competitive," 120.

[102] W. Nordhaus, "Locational Competition and the Environment: Should Countries Harmonize Their Environmental Policies?" (discussion paper No. 1079 of the Cowles Foundation for Research and Economics, Yale University, 1994).

[103] *See* Revesz, "Rethinking the 'Race to the Bottom' Rationale"; Oates and Schwab, "Economic Competition among Jurisdictions." In Europe, see Siebert, "Environmental Policy and European Integration."

those who argue that, even if the goal of leveling the playing field is legitimate, it will not be achieved through the imposition of uniform, technology-based standards. Where environmental standards are identical, the cost of complying with environmental regulation may still differ substantially, depending on, for example, the type of industry to which they are applied, or the flexibility with which they are implemented.[104]

In sum, there is no consensus on the necessity or appropriateness of centralizing risk regulation to "level the playing field" for competition in Europe. Most existing empirical evidence suggests that the impact of environmental regulation on competitiveness is low.[105] This supports the claim, voiced by opponents of centralized regulation, that fears for a race to the bottom are without ground. On the other hand, a minority of studies do spot a significant negative correlation between stringent regulation and a decline in competitiveness for some industries. Furthermore, and perhaps more importantly, virtually all available studies – those establishing a negative correlation as well as those denying one – display methodological or factual limitations, which means that they may well understate or overstate the link between regulation and competitiveness.[106] The debate is far from settled at this stage, and it is unlikely that this situation will change in the near future.[107]

Yet, it is undeniable that the European Union has in the past and will most probably continue to adopt health and environmental process and quality standards, even when the transboundary dimension of the matter to be regulated is tenuous. One of the possible explanations for this phenomenon is that, as long as the correlation between environmental regulation and competitiveness is not entirely and conclusively disproved, fears of a race to the bottom prevail over arguments in favor of decentralization. This outcome may in turn be explained when one considers who benefits and who gets hurt if a race to the bottom unfolds. In the chemical industry example above, the beneficiaries of a race to the bottom are consumers and environmentalists in Member State A. The chemical industry of Member State A, on the other hand, faces bleaker prospects: it may well be forced

104 See R. Stewart, "Environmental Regulation and International Competitiveness," 102 *Yale L. J.* 2069–70 (1993).

105 *Ibid.*, 2061–84; Esty, "Revitalizing Environmental Federalism," 607.

106 Esty, "Revitalizing Envrionmental Federalism," 627–38. Cf. Stewart, "Environmental Regulation and International Competitiveness," 2069–70.

107 See Faure, "Harmonisation of Environmental Law and Market Integration," 172.

either to relocate to Member State B, or to dismantle its operations. Considering that the chemical industry forms a highly specialized and well-organized interest group in Europe, whereas the interests of consumers are more diffuse, the chemical industry will most likely be more successful in pleading its cause and affecting the agenda of European political institutions.[108] And, industry efforts to promote uniform European regulation may well be favored by environmentalists who fear a race to the bottom. Moreover, European institutions may well be receptive to interest groups lobbying for European regulatory action because they have an institutional interest in promoting centralization.[109]

Concerns about national competitiveness, targeted pressure exercised by well-organized industry interest groups with environmental group support, and promotion by a European policy entrepreneur, may persuade Member States with high environmental standards to back up centralized policymaking. These factors, however, do not adequately explain how Member States with lower environmental standards – who do not have to fear the consequences of a race to the bottom, and whose industries certainly will not exert pressure in favor of restrictive EU standards – can be made to agree to stringent EU regulatory standards. One possibility is that the governments of the latter Member States are swayed by the Commission's "win–win" predictions, and see EU-level action as a good opportunity – or excuse – to "sell" tighter regulatory standards to their own citizens. Alternatively, their cooperation (or acceptance) may be obtained during negotiations in the Council. Since the introduction of qualified majority voting rules governing health and environmental matters, they can simply be outvoted in EU Council ses-

[108] See, e.g., Ogus, "Quality Control for European Regulation," 332–34, on EU Regulation and public choice analysis.

[109] It is in this regard interesting to observe how the European Commission – which, of the three main EU institutions (Council, Commission, and Parliament), has the weakest ties to national governance structures – has embraced the concept of "win–win" solutions (see above) and uses it to sell European environmental regulation, glossing over the fact that, essentially, the concept pleads the case of decentralization. (See J. Golub ed., *New Instruments for Environmental Policy in the EU* (Routledge, 1998).) After all, if tight environmental standards create a competitive advantage, there is no need for Member State A, which has strict regulations, to worry about losing business to states with more lenient standards. Hence, there is no reason for State A to insist on uniform, EU-wide application of its own high standards. On the contrary, the imposition of stringent environmental standards on a European scale might make Member State A lose its competitive edge!

sions. Or, reluctant Member States may receive side-payments. For example, less affluent Member States, on which compliance with EU environmental standards weighs comparatively heavier, might be induced to agree with them in exchange for a promise of additional funds from the EU for regional development. Similarly, Member States may engage in intergovernmental bargaining and package dealing, agreeing to high regulatory standards in one area in exchange for concessions in another. Finally, one should not overlook that the centralization of risk regulation may be driven by aspirations of a more ideological nature, overriding national economic interests in Member States A and B. Centralization may be the expression of a growing feeling of unity among the citizens of Europe, of a growing desire to protect the common European cultural and ecological heritage across national boundaries, and of a rising expectation among Europeans that, when they move from one country to another, they will benefit from the same high level of health and environmental protection.[110]

## THE STATE OF PLAY IN EU HEALTH, SAFETY AND ENVIRONMENTAL REGULATION

Considering the different rationales propelling EU Member States towards deepening forms of integration, it should come as no surprise that, half a century after its inception, the European Union has developed extensive health, safety, and environmental policy programs. The original Treaty on the European Economic Community made no explicit mention of "risk" policies, but very soon – and with increasing regularity from the 1970s onwards – EU institutions began to adopt secondary legislation that incorporated health or environmental protection goals. This was accomplished by linking health or environmental measures to other objectives that were listed in the Treaty (such as the establishment of a common agricultural policy,[111] social policy,[112] and the approximation of national laws for market integration purposes[113]), or by adopting them on the basis of the

110 See, e.g., Faure, "Harmonisation of Environmental Law and Market Integration," 173–74; Esty, "Revitalizing Environmental Federalism," 645; M. Cassan, *L'Europe communautaire de la santé* (Economica, 1989), 18–19.

111 Articles 32 to 38 of the EC Treaty (old Articles 38 to 47).

112 Articles 136–37 of the EC Treaty (old Articles 117–18).

113 Articles 94–95 of the EC Treaty (old Articles 100/100a).

Council's residual power, confirmed in Article 308 of the EC Treaty, to take appropriate measures to advance Community objectives.[114] Thus, by the time the 1987 and 1992 Treaty amendments (contained in the Single European Act and the Maastricht Treaty respectively) formally recognized health, safety, consumer, and environmental protection as Community goals,[115] a great deal of European risk regulation was already in place. In the area of environmental protection, over 200 pieces of Community legislation have been adopted.[116] They cover air, water, and noise pollution, dangerous substances, pesticides and biocides, environmental impact assessment, packaging and waste treatment, major accident hazards from industrial activities, access to environmental information, etc.[117] In the areas of health and safety, major efforts have been undertaken towards the harmonization of product safety rules, food safety, and health protection in the workplace.[118]

While the level of centralization of risk regulation is still lower than in the United States, it is substantial and still on the rise. This does not imply, however, that national lawmaking and regulatory authorities have become insignificant in the risk regulation process. National law applies in those areas that have not, or not yet, been harmonized. Moreover, Articles 153(5), 176, and 95(4) to (6) of the EC Treaty allow Member States to maintain or adopt consumer, health, and environmental protection measures that are more stringent than the Community measures, thereby creating exceptions

[114] Article 308 (old Article 235): "If action by the Community should prove necessary to attain, in the course of the operation of the common market, one of the objectives of the Community and this Treaty has not provided the necessary powers, the Council shall, acting unanimously on a proposal from the Commission and after consulting the European Parliament, take the appropriate measures."

[115] See Articles 138 (health and safety for workers; old Article 118a), 152 (public health; old Article 129), 153 (consumer protection; old Article 129a) and 174 to 176 (health and environmental protection, old Articles 130r to 130t) of the EC Treaty.

[116] Cf. House of Lords Select Committee on the European Communities, *Community Environmental Law: Making it Work* (Session 1997–98, 2d Report), 9.

[117] See, e.g., L. Krämer, *Focus on European Environmental Law* (2d edn., London: Sweet & Maxwell, 1997); G. Winter, *European Environmental Law. A Comparative Perspective* (Dartmouth, 1996).

[118] See, e.g., S. Weatherill, *EC Consumer Law and Policy* (London and New York: Longman, 1997); R. Baldwin and T. Daintith, *Harmonisation and Hazard. Regulating Health and Safety in the European Workplace* (London, Dordrecht, and Boston: Graham & Trotman, 1992); S. Slacke, "Foodstuffs Law and the Precautionary Principle: Normative Bases, Secondary Law and Institutional Tendencies," in Joerges, Ladeur, and Vos, *Integrating Scientific Expertise into Regulatory Decision-Making*, 169–86.

to the principle of pre-emption (see above).[119] Finally, as with the vast majority of EU legal acts, implementation and enforcement of EU risk regulation is secured predominantly by national public authorities. For example, the rules for notification of new chemical substances prior to their release on the Community market have been harmonized, but the bodies receiving and reviewing notifications are public authorities of the Member States.[120]

## THE TENSION BETWEEN CENTRALIZING AND DECENTRALIZING TENDENCIES IN THE EUROPEAN UNION

Up to now, our analysis has concentrated on the factors that tend to increase the authority of central EU regulators, in particular the Council and the Commission. They imply a "centralizing" tendency. The move towards centralization is offset, however, by important tendencies that work in the opposite direction: the trend towards greater "democracy" within the EU and the trend towards local control reflected in the demands for "subsidiarity" and, more recently, for "simplification" and "flexibility." The bottom

119 Articles 153(5) (old Article 129a(3)) and 176 (old Article 130t)) establish Member States' prerogatives to opt up from Community consumer, health, or environmental measures in a general, unconditional way. The situation is somewhat more complicated in the case of Article 95(4) to (6) (old Article 100a(4)). Since Article 95 enables harmonization of national measures (typically laying down product standards) for the purposes of market integration, national derogations from Community measures adopted under Article 95 might hinder the functioning of the common market. To minimize the potential detrimental effect of the opt-up clause in Article 95(4) to (6) on free trade within the European Community, its application has been limited: Member States wanting to opt up from harmonized environmental standards need to obtain Commission approval. The Commission, in turn, has been instructed by the Court of Justice to provide reasons for its decision, showing that the appropriate procedures have been followed and substantively justifying the grounds for derogation on the basis of scientific evidence. See *French Republic* v. *Commission*, Case C–41/93 [1994] ECR I–1829. Cf. H. Somsen, "Applying More Protective National Environmental Laws after Harmonization," 3(8) *Eur. Env. L. Rev.* 238–42 (Comment on Case C–41/93) (1994); and R. Sloan and P. Cardonnel, "Exemptions from Harmonization Measures under Article 100a(4): The Second Authorization of the German Ban on PCP," 4(2) *Eur. Env. L. Rev.* 45–50 (1995).

120 See Council Directive 79/831/EEC of 18 September 1979 amending for the sixth time Directive 67/548/EEC on the approximation of the laws, regulation, and administrative provisions relating to the classification, packaging, and labeling of dangerous substances, OJ L 259/10 (1979), last amended by Council and European Parliament Directive 96/548/EEC of 3 September 1996 amending for the eighth time Directive 67/548/EEC, OJ L 236/35 (1996).

line is that the European Union has not yet reached a stable point in the distribution of national and international decisionmaking authority respectively. The continuous flux, caused by simultaneous but conflicting centripetal and centrifugal forces, poses particular challenges to the development of a European framework for risk regulation. More precisely, we will argue that the need to reconcile both centralizing and decentralizing approaches within the EU legal system may give rise to problems very similar to the tunnel vision, random agenda setting, and inconsistency problems that encumber US risk regulation.

The first of these trends, that of increased democracy, is related to the problems of risk regulation in an interesting way. The notorious "democratic deficit" with which the EU now struggles appears ironic when one considers that the founding fathers of the European Economic Community deliberately emphasized technocracy over democracy.[121] Wary of over-democratization, which had become associated with many of the excesses of political decisionmaking during the Second World War, they felt more sympathy for the philosopher king than the voice of the people.[122] The original institutional structure of the Community reflected as much: the main political bodies were the Council, an intergovernmental body joining the executive rather than legislative branches of the Member States, and the Commission, a supranational body of highly trained civil servants who were insulated from the pressures of national politics. Interestingly, the Commission shares more than a few characteristics with the "super civil service" proposed in *Breaking the Vicious Circle.* If the logic of that proposal is sound, then those similarities bode well for the future of European risk regulation.

Premature optimism should, however, be tempered by the reminder that, as the powers of EU institutions expanded, the elitist and technocratic nature of EU decisionmaking came under severe attack.[123] Efforts have been undertaken to boost the democratic credentials of the European Union, most prominently by strengthening the powers of the European Parliament. The Parliament, we recall, is the one EU institution of which the members are directly elected,[124] and is therefore arguably the one with

[121] See, e.g., E. Haas, *The Uniting of Europe* (Stanford University Press, 1958), 16.

[122] See J. Golub, "Sovereignty and Subsidiarity in EU Environmental Policy," 44(4) *Political Studies*, 697 (1996); D. Obradovic, "Policy Legitimacy and the European Union," 34(2) *J. Common Market Studies* 192 (1996).

[123] See, e.g., J. McCormick, *The European Union* (Westview Press, 1996), 103–04.

[124] See, e.g., J. Lodge, *The 1994 Elections to the European Parliament* (Pinter, 1995), 13–20.

the strongest claims to democratic legitimacy.[125] Through a series of Treaty amendments adopted between 1972 and 1998, the role of the European Parliament in the EU legislative process evolved from that of a glorified consultant to an active decisionmaker in a growing range of policy areas.[126] The Parliament has embraced its new powers with enthusiasm, and vigilantly defends itself against usurpation by the Council or Commission. A growing body of European case law furthermore confirms that the European Court will not hesitate to annul EU legislation that has been adopted in breach of parliamentary prerogatives.[127] Finally, whereas there used to be very limited public awareness of the existence and functions of the European Parliament, its media share is growing slowly but steadily, which makes it a more visible – and therefore more influential – player in European politics.

The increase in parliamentary authority, however desirable as a general matter, might create difficulties in the small world of risk regulation. In particular, it could tend to bring about some of the same problems that plague American regulation. Like Americans, Europeans fear illness and disease. They read the press which, as in America, is interested in dramatic news about risks to health posed, for example, by chemical substances. European as well as US environmental groups worry about such matters. Scientific development is characterized by uncertainty on both sides of the Atlantic, leaving scope for controversy and discord within scientific communities.

125 See R. Dehousse, "European Institutional Architecture after Amsterdam: Parliamentary System or Regulatory Structure?" 35 *Common Market L. Rev.* 598 (1998).

126 The corresponding legislative procedures granting progressively greater powers to the Parliament are the consultation procedure (which granted the Parliament the right to give a non-binding opinion on certain Community proposals); the cooperation procedure (which added the right to a second reading for certain laws adopted by the Council); the co-decision procedure (which enabled the Parliament, under specified circumstances, to block the adoption of EU legislation in selected areas); and the assent procedure (which formally places the Parliament on equal footing with the Council). On the gradual expansion of the European Parliament's powers and the different procedures, see, e.g., D. Earnshaw and D. Judge, "From Co-operation to Co-decision. The European Parliament's Path to Legislative Power," in Richardson, *EU Power and Policy-Making*, 97–111; McCormick, *The European Union*, 157–59; G. Ress, "Democratic Decision-Making in the European Union and the Role of the European Parliament," in D. Curtin and T. Henkels eds., *Institutional Dynamics of European Integration. Essays in Honour of Henry G. Schermers*, vol. II (Martinus Nijhoff Publishers, 1994), 161–62.

127 See, e.g., *European Parliament* v. *Council of the European Union* Case C–303/94 [1996] ECR I–2943; *European Parliament* v. *Commission of the European Communities* Case C–156/93 [1995] ECR I–2019; *Albert Romkes* v. *Officier van Justitie for the District of Zwolle* Case 46/86 [1987] ECR 2671.

Moreover, even if scientists agree, Europeans would seem no more likely to become experts in the technical intricacies of risk than their American counterparts.

The recent "mad cow" or BSE (bovine spongiform encephalitis) scare which haunts Britain and the European continent shows that the possibility of a European-wide health panic is anything but academic. The BSE controversy displays many of the ingredients which, following the reasoning in *Breaking the Vicious Circle*, may obstruct rational risk decisionmaking. On the one hand, the precise relation between BSE, beef consumption, and the incidence of the Kreutzfeldt-Jakob disease remains partially shrouded in scientific uncertainty.[128] Furthermore, since preliminary evidence indicates that only a tiny proportion of beef consumers in Britain or abroad have contracted the disease, the BSE risk may be much smaller than the risk of, say, illness from exposure to pesticide residues. These factors would normally warrant caution in the regulation of beef products.[129] Yet, on the other hand, the unfamiliarity of the threat, the cruelly debilitating course of the disease, the apparent randomness with which it strikes, and massive media exposure have European consumers deeply worried and clamoring for tight regulations and export bans.[130] A European Parliament with enhanced powers, interested in environmental matters, can respond to constituency pressures with committee hearings, with oversight of EU administrators, and even, like the American Congress, with insistence on legislation that focuses on individual substances, or otherwise creates regulatory priorities based upon the public's immediate interest in a particular risk. The European Parliament certainly asserted itself during the BSE crisis, when it deployed its new powers (conferred on it in the Maastricht Treaty)[131] to keep a close and critical watch on the Commission's risk management activities. Two consecutive Parliamentary Committees of Inquiry

[128] See, e.g., C. Goybet, "Ces vaches qui affollent l'Europe," 398 *Revue du Marché commun et de l'Union européenne* 350–51 (1996).

[129] See, e.g., A. Dnes, "An Economic analysis of the BSE Scare," 43(3) *Scottish J. Pol. Econ.* 343–48 (1996).

[130] See, e.g., B. Viale, "En réponse à la crise de la 'Vache folle', plaidoyer en faveur d'une politique communautaire de l'alimentation," 125 *Revue de droit rural* 161–62 (1997); N. De Grove-Valdeyron, "Libre Circulation et Protection de la Santé Publique: La Crise de 'la Vache Folle,'" 403 *Revue du Marché commun et de l'Union Européenne* 759 (1996); *Consumers Shun Beef as "Mad Cow" Panic Spreads* (*http://www.nando.net/newsroom/nt/328consume.html*, published on 28 March 1996).

[131] See Article 193 of the EC Treaty (old Article 138c).

investigated how the Commission was handling the crisis, issued recommendations for reform and improvement, and monitored the implementation of its recommendations.[132] Parliamentary scrutiny was instrumental in the Commission's re-evaluation of its working procedures for dealing with health risks in foods, which resulted in a number of important institutional reforms, including the creation of a group of Commissioners, chaired by the Commission President, with overall responsibility for food health matters, and the thorough reform of DG XXIV, which deals with consumer health issues.

The BSE crisis illustrates that European regulators are not immune to problems of "public perception," of "legislative reaction," and of "uncertainties in the regulatory process" – problems roughly similar to those found in the United States. Europeans, too, will have to ask how to design a rational form of environmental risk regulation, i.e., a system of regulation that more effectively delivers what, in our view, the public in fact wants: more safety.

In developing such a system, the EU begins with certain advantages. Europe's historically strong tradition of central administrative authority, and comparatively lesser reliance upon adversary legal proceedings, may help. Furthermore, having a centralized bureaucracy concentrated in Brussels, the EU might be able to avoid the coordination problems and resulting inconsistencies that thwart risk regulation in the US. Yet, recent trends in EU institutional development indicate a move towards jurisdictional fragmentation and geographic decentralization: since 1990, a string of European regulatory or quasi-regulatory agencies, offices, and bureaus have sprung up in Copenhagen (the European Environment Agency), Bilbao (the European Agency for Safety and Health at Work), London (the European Agency for the Evaluation of Medicinal Products), Ispra (the European Chemicals Bureau), Alicante (Office for Harmonization in the Internal Market), and Brussels (Community Plant Variety Rights Office).

132 The main themes of the Parliament's recommendations were a call for greater transparency of Commission decisionmaking procedures, the need to place consumer protection on equal footing with market integration as Community goals, and the need for tough Commission action against fraudulent imports of beef products. See European Parliament, "Report on Alleged Contraventions or Maladministration in the Implementation of Community Law in Relation to BSE" (Docs. PE 220.544 A/FIN, Annexes I–IX, and B, Brussels, 7 February 1997). Cf., e.g., M. Westlake, "Mad Cows and Englishmen. The Institutional Consequences of the BSE Crisis," 35 *J. Common Market Studies* 11–36 (1997).

Most of these are directly or indirectly involved in the regulation of small risks.[133] While the establishment of European regulatory bodies, staffed with EU civil servants as well as Member State representatives,[134] may indeed promote coherence of regulatory policies across countries, the benefits of this approach might be overshadowed by the inconsistencies emerging between distinct but overlapping policy areas (such as market harmonization, environment, consumer health, health and safety at work), which are parceled out to different agencies scattered throughout Europe. It remains to be seen whether the agencies' frequently proclaimed networking and coordinating capacity will safeguard them from regulatory inconsistency.[135]

Linking up agencies located in different countries may simply be a problem of logistics. However, in the European context, the geographic decentralization of regulatory and advisory bodies is symptomatic of a far more fundamental challenge confronting the development of a central EU risk regulation program. This "anti-centralizing" challenge is simply the continued (perhaps growing) demand for local (Member State) control of regulation. From its inception, the European Union has had to reconcile the

[133] Council Regulation (EEC) No. 2062/94 of 18 July 1994 establishing a European Agency for Safety and Health at Work, OJ L 216/1 (1994); Council Regulation (EEC) No. 1210/90 of May 1990 on the establishment of the European Environment Agency and the European Environmental Information and Observation Network, OJ L 120/1 (1990); Council Regulation (EEC) No. 2309/93 of 22 July 1993 laying down Community procedures for the authorization and supervision of medicinal products for human and veterinary use and establishing a European Agency for the Evaluation of Medicinal Products, OJ L 214/1 (1993); and Commission communication (93/C 1/02) to the Council and the European Parliament, OJ C 1/3 (1993), regarding the European Chemicals Bureau. See, e.g., J. Gardner, "The European Agency for the Evaluation of Medicines and European Regulation of Pharmaceuticals," 2 *Eur. L.J.* 54–63 (1996).

[134] The European Agency for the Evaluation of Medicinal Products (EMEA), for example, comprises an Executive Directive and Secretariat, a Management Board, and two scientific committees responsible for drafting the Agency's opinion on questions relating to the evaluation of medicines for human or veterinary use. The Director and Secretariat staff are civil servants. The Management Board and Committees, however, are predominantly staffed with members appointed by the fifteen Member States. See EMEA homepage: *http://www.eudra.org/abouemea.htm.*

[135] See, e.g., R. Dehousse, "Regulation by Networks in the European Community: The Role of European Agencies," 4(2) *J. Eur. Public Pol'y* 254–57 (1997); G. Majone, "The New European Agencies: Regulation by Information," 4(2) *J. Eur. Public Pol'y* 271–74 (1997); M. Shapiro, "The Problems of Independent Agencies in the United States and the European Union," 4(2) *J. Eur. Public Pol'y* 282–90 (1997); and J. Peterson, "Decision-Making in the European Union: Towards a Framework for Analysis," 2(1) *J. Eur. Public Pol'y* 69–93 (1995).

drive towards international decisionmaking with respect for considerations of national sovereignty and regional autonomy. This need to balance and combine different levels of authority is reflected in increasing Commission use of "framework" and other directives that leave to Member States the implementation of generally stated regulatory goals.[136] It is reflected in the practical fact that the EU, with fewer than 20,000 employees, depends upon each Member State's own administrative civil service to implement the EU's rules.[137] It is reflected in the EU's willingness to permit Member States to enact local environmental rules that are more demanding than their EU counterparts. It is reflected in the dispersion of agencies and other bodies across the European landscape. And, it is reflected in the concepts of "subsidiarity and flexibility."[138]

The simple fact that the EU is not a federal state, and that most governmental powers remain in the hands of the Member States, can make efforts to centralize and rationalize risk regulation more difficult than in the United States in certain obvious ways. The EU lacks significant budgetary powers. The EU, therefore, will find it more difficult to compensate for less strict regulation in one area (for instance, less than "zero risk" toxic dump standards) by spending more (of the saved resources) to save more lives elsewhere (say, through mammogram subsidies). This undercuts the most powerful argument for rational risk regulation, namely that rationalizing and prioritizing will provide more, not less, total safety. The fact that Member States themselves apply, and enforce, EU regulations also makes the EU regulatory job

136 Amended proposal for a European Parliament and Council Directive establishing a framework for Community action in the field of water policy, COM (97) 49 final; Council Directive 96/61/EC of 24 September 1996 concerning integrated pollution prevention and control, OJ L 257/26 (1996) Article 249 of the EC Treaty (old Article 189); see, e.g., R. Wägenbaur, "The European Community's Policy of Implementation of Environmental Directives," 14 *Fordham Int. L.J.* 455, 468 (1991) (noting that directives are widely used, particularly in environmental protection, but advocating greater use of regulations).

137 See R. Wägenbaur, "The European Community's Policy on Implementation of Environmental Directives." By way of comparison, EPA alone has about 19,000 employees.

138 Article 5 of the EC Treaty (old Article 3(b)); see, e.g., U. Collier, J. Golub, and A. Kreher eds., *Subsidiarity and Shared Responsibility: New Challenges for EU Environmental Policy* (Baden-Baden: Nomos, 1998); Bermann, "Taking Subsidiarity Seriously"; R. Dehousse, "Does Subsidiarity Really Matter?" (EUI Working Paper LAW No. 92/32); N. Emiliou, "Subsidiarity: An Effective Barrier Against 'the Enterprises of Ambition'?" 17 *Eur. L. Rev.* 383 (1992); *Subsidiarity: The Challenge of Change* (Proceedings of the Jacques Delors Colloquium, European Institute of Public Administration, Maastricht, 1991).

more difficult, for some states may not enforce those regulations as effectively as others. Moreover, the demand for "subsidiarity" itself means that Member States will continue to write their own risk regulations, sometimes simply adding them to those of the EU, as EU administrators search for some kind of a "touchstone" that will identify, subject matter by subject matter, which regulations ought to be the concern of which level of government (a "touchstone," by the way, that may not exist).[139]

If "subsidiarity" refers to the political desire for local control, then "flexibility" and "legislative and administrative simplification" reflect the economic side of the coin. The early 1990s were characterized by a growing concern that elaborate and detailed EU rules imposed prohibitive burdens on national administration and industry alike, thus weakening national competitiveness and growth. In September 1994, the European Commission set up a Group of Independent Experts to analyze this problem. Within a year, the Group released a landmark report, generally referred to as the "Molitor Report" (alluding to the chairman of the Group, Bernard Molitor, a former economic advisor to the German government), which suggests that national competitiveness, employment, and growth would be better served by a more flexible approach to EU legislation and regulation. Broadly framed, goal-oriented EU prescriptions would leave greater scope for national variety and discretion in implementation, and would encourage increased use of new instruments to further social policy objectives.[140] Recent EU legislation and proposals in the area of environmental policy (for example, the 1996 Directive on integrated pollution prevention and control (IPPC), the air quality control Directive of the same year, and the proposal for a water policy framework) indicate that the ideas launched in the Molitor Report are indeed finding application in practice. The IPPC Directive, for instance, creates substantial scope for national, or regional, discretion. It stipulates that industrial exploitation permits, awarded by local authorities, shall contain emission limit values for pollutants. However, it continues that "emission limit values may be supplemented *or replaced*" (emphasis added)[141] by equivalent parameters or technical

[139] See, e.g., Lord Mackenzie-Stuart, "Assessment of the Views Expressed and Introduction to a Panel Discussion," in *Subsidiarity: The Challenge of Change*.

[140] Report of the Group of Independent Experts on Legislative and Administrative Simplification, COM (95) 288 final/2 (21 June 1995).

[141] Council Directive 96/61/EC of 24 September 1996 concerning integrated pollution prevention and control, OJ L 257/26 (1996).

measures. Member States, in other words, may adopt alternative regulatory techniques to control pollution. Moreover, the directive provides that, as a rule, emission limits are fixed at the level of the individual installation. The task of fixing emission limits is thereby delegated to local authorities. This is quite a change from former approaches, such as the one followed in the 1976 Directive on aquatic pollution,[142] which provided that at least for a select number of pollutants, the Council should establish limit values (discharge standards), which would apply throughout the European Union.[143]

## BREAKING THE POTENTIAL EUROPEAN VICIOUS CIRCLE

This, then, is the European predicament. On the one hand, our analysis revealed a likely future of increased EU high regulation, issued by a central regulatory body. The European Commission, which already fulfills a number of regulatory functions, is possibly the best placed and qualified to become the central EU risk regulatory authority. On the other hand, there are a number of countervailing tendencies in the EU that might complicate, or compromise, the further development of a central risk authority. The first is the growing insistence on the democratic legitimacy of EU decision-making processes, which are presently perceived as overly technocratic. The second is the strong political demand for increased local control, expressed as a demand for "subsidiarity" or "flexibility." How can the EU reconcile this tension between centralizing and decentralizing forces? We cannot answer this question, but we can list, in summary fashion, a few of the ways the United States has tried to deal with somewhat similar problems.

The first set of solutions tackles the legitimacy deficit of regulations prepared (and in certain instances adopted) by technocratic bureaucracies such as the EPA or, in Europe, the Commission.

1 The US has developed an elaborate "notice and comment" rulemaking system, whereby local communities, interest groups and states have an opportunity to see the rules federal administrators are considering and comment upon them before the administrators adopt the rules. The core

[142] Council Directive 76/464/EEC of 4 May 1976 on pollution caused by certain dangerous substances discharged into the aquatic environment of the Community, OJ L 129/23 (1976).

[143] See Krämer, *Focus on European Environmental Law*, 231.

idea is to bring interested groups into the process before the administrators are "frozen" into position. A similar openness to national, regional, and specific interests, integrated early on in the decisionmaking process, might strengthen the democratic legitimacy of EU regulations. There are, at present, a number of avenues for input to EU risk-regulatory decisionmaking. However, compared to the open and quite egalitarian consultation process in the US, the EU style of interest consultation appears less accessible, more "layered" or "staged," and more institutionalized (and thus more in keeping with the stronger corporatist traditions in Europe). The Member States' position on legislative proposals, for instance, is provided by the Committee of Permanent Representatives (COREPER), which prepares the respective Member States' positions on Commission proposals before they reach the Council.[144] Obviously, the Council members, representatives of the Member State governments, also have a keen eye for the national interest. In the case of Commission decisionmaking on issues affecting risk regulation, the national viewpoint usually is championed by Member States' representatives who make up the committees which the Commission is bound to consult.[145] As to regional, sectional, and public interests, there are formal as well as informal channels for influence. Formally, regional and sectional interests (covering employer and worker interests) are represented by the Committee of the Regions (CoR) and the Economic and Social Committee (ECOSOC), two advisory bodies that issue (non-binding) opinions on the work of Commission and Council.[146] Public and private interest groups (such as industrial associations, environmental and consumer groups) are more dependent on informal consultation and lobbying to get their viewpoints across. Many interest groups (particularly environmental and consumer interest groups) feel that they are not adequately represented in the "formal" channels for influence, and that the informal ones are insufficient or ineffective.[147] EU institutions are aware of the desire for

[144] See, e.g., Kirchner, *Decision Making in the European Community*, 75–80.

[145] See, e.g., A. Bücher, C. Joerges, J. Neyer, and S. Slacke, "Social Regulation through European Committees: An Interdisciplinary Agenda and Two Fields of Research," in R. Pedler and G. Schäfer eds., *Shaping European Law and Policy: The Role of Committees and Comitology in the Political Process* (Maastricht Institute of Public Administration, 1996), 33–60.

[146] Articles 7, 257 to 265 of the EC Treaty (old Articles 4, 193 to 198c). See, e.g., McCormick, *The European Union*, 191–93.

[147] Cf. House of Lords Select Committee on the European Communities, *Community Environmental Law*, 13–15.

increased and more open participation;[148] the Commission, for example, issued a Communication on dialogue with special interest groups, which confirms its commitment to participation, and adds some structure and clarification to informal consultation processes.[149] Still, various interest groups insist that it will take more than a non-binding commitment to move towards a more participatory form of decisionmaking.[150] The US "notice and comment" procedures may serve both as an example and a warning, illustrating that greater openness can lead to more informed decisionmaking, but also run the risks of excessive formality and delay and of undue administrative responsiveness to the specific, often narrow, viewpoints represented in an interest-representation model of decisionmaking.

2 Even in cases where an agency's decision is within its statutory authority, federal judges in the United States will sometimes (but rarely) directly examine the substantive merits of an administrative action to see if it is "arbitrary, capricious, an abuse of discretion,"[151] or (much more frequently) engage in a "hard look" at the justifications offered by an agency for its decision and the extent of support in the record for such justifications, a technique that in practice may sometimes approximate review of the substantive merits.[152] Just how closely the American judges ought to review the substantive merits is a highly debatable matter.

In Europe, regulatory and administrative decisions could traditionally count on a high level of deference from the judiciary, which only exercised a marginal form of review. However, the times may be changing. Growing discontent with costly regulation, changing ideas about access to administrative justice, and the emergence of new layers of regulatory and administrative authority (such as authority exercised by EU bodies), may gradually shift the balance in favor of tighter judicial review. With some trepidation perhaps, the European Court of Justice has started to formulate some general principles for EU regulatory decisionmaking (proportionality, reliance on scientific evidence, review, etc).[153] At least

[148] See, e.g., M. Shapiro, "Codification of Administrative Law: The US and the Union," 2(1) *Eur. L.J.* 40 (1996).

[149] Commission Communication on an open and structured dialogue between the Commission and special interest groups (SEC/92/2272/FINAL).

[150] House of Lords Select Committee on the European Communities, *Community Environmental Law*, 13–15.

[151] 5 U.S.C. § 706(2) (A).

[152] See Breyer et al., *Administrative Law and Regulatory Policy*, 345–414.

[153] See above, pp. 317–19.

one EU commentator has predicted that, in the coming years, the Court will subject regulatory measures adopted by EU institutions to an ever closer scrutiny, examining not only whether decisions are procedurally correct, but also whether they are substantively sound.[154] If judicial involvement in EU risk decisionmaking does indeed increase, American experience might help decide whether such involvement, on balance, would help or hurt.

3 Suggestions have been made in America to give the President greater discretionary authority over risk-related budgets. Congress might, for example, allow him considerable discretionary authority to transfer resources from one risk-related area to another, insisting only that he demonstrate, after the event, that the transfer saved significantly more lives. Since the implementation of EU health, safety, and environmental policies practically takes place at the national or regional level, it is difficult to envisage a similar approach, whereby an international authority – say, the European Council – reallocates national funds, in the European context. Particularly in light of previously mentioned decentralization and subsidiarity concerns, this approach would probably be considered an excessive encroachment on national authority. Alternatively, one might try to find ways that the EU could encourage private firms to spend funds on the environment or health which would make evident that those expenditures are more efficient alternatives to regulation that (at greater expense) seeks to eradicate tiny risks.[155] Council Regulation 1836/93, which encourages European industries to implement a voluntary eco-management and audit scheme, in order to improve the industry's environmental performance above the level prescribed in EU regulation, is an attempt in this direction.[156]

[154] See, e.g., Shapiro, "Codification of Administrative Law," 42–43; M. Shapiro, "The Giving Reasons Requirement in European Community Law," 1992 *U. Chi. L.F.* 179–220.

[155] See, e.g., R. Stewart, "Environmental Law in the United States and the European Community: Spillovers, Cooperation, Rivalry, Institutions," 1992 *U. Chi. L.F.* 41, 75–79 (discussing alternatives to "command-and-control" regulation); E. Steyger, "European Community Law and the Self-Regulatory Capacity of Society," 31 *J. Common Market Studies* 171 (1993) (exploring ways to mediate the tension between increasing efforts at harmonization by direct EC regulation and increasing awareness of the benefits of self-regulation as an aspect of "subsidiarity").

[156] Council Regulation (EEC) No. 1836/93 of 29 June 1993 allowing voluntary participation by companies in the industrial sector in a Community eco-management and audit scheme OJ L 168/1 (1993).

The second set of solutions aims to deal with the problems of inconsistency and incoherence that can easily emerge in the wake of fragmentation or decentralization of regulatory decisionmaking. As transpired from our synopsis of the arguments developed in *Breaking the Vicious Circle*, the American example does not offer ready-made solutions: regulatory inconsistencies among different risk-regulatory programs, both within the federal government as well as between federal and state governments, frequently crop up in US risk policies. Here are some considerations that might benefit both US and EU regulators.

1 It seems likely that, both in the United States and in Europe, the development of a coherent approach to risk regulation, i.e., a system for deciding how to deal with individual risks, would help win public acceptability at the local, as well as the national, level. The "cost of service ratemaking" system in the US, which we discussed earlier in the text,[157] could serve as a blueprint for central risk regulators, who might develop a similar rough and ready system for evaluating risks and suggesting what regulators might do about those risks. Such a system would *not* consist of rules, but of standards, examples, instructions, methods; it would use comparisons, not valuations of human life, to suggest what might be appropriate.[158] The central regulators could make the system available to local regulators, or local governments interested in regulating local enterprises.

   In recent years, the European Union has made a few inroads in this direction. For example, in a Commission directive and regulation, the Commission has laid down uniform principles for the risk assessment and evaluation of chemical substances.[159] Admittedly, these documents hardly constitute an overarching framework for the development of risk strategies: they only pertain to risks from chemical substances, and focus on science-based testing protocols rather than the more policy-oriented aspects of risk evaluation, comparison and, ultimately, decisionmaking.

157 See p. 303 above.

158 Cf. C. Sunstein, "Health–Health Tradeoffs," 63 *U. Chi. L. Rev.* 1533–71 (1996).

159 See Commission Directive 93/67/EEC of 20 July 1993 laying down the principles for assessment of risks to man and the environment of substances notified in accordance with Council Directive 67/548/EEC, OJ L 227/9 (1993); Commission Regulation (EC) No. 1488/94 of 28 June 1994 laying down the principles for the assessment of risks to man and the environment of existing substances in accordance with Council Regulation (EEC) No. 793/93, OJ L 161/3 (1994).

Nonetheless, they may constitute valuable building blocks in the establishment of an overall EU risk-management strategy. The growing body of literature on the maturing of European administrative law, on the need for guidelines and standards for EU as well as national administrative decisionmaking, the pros and cons of codification of administrative law, and the rising interest in "proceduralized" styles of lawmaking and regulation (i.e., rules that emphasize the "how to" of decisionmaking), suggest a willingness further to explore this avenue.[160]

2 The European Environment Agency gathers and disseminates various kinds of environment-related information. Might it, among other things, devise a method for measuring the cost per life saved (or life-year or quality of life) of the regulatory measures applied locally by Member States? If so, one would have a very rough comparative measure of national effectiveness, thereby encouraging Member States with high costs per life saved to look for explanations, and perhaps leading a Member State to explore a different, more integrated and systematic "life saving" approach.

3 Recently, the American Congress has been trying to find ways to make federal regulation more responsive to local interests. Among other things, it has responded to complaints that national law too often imposes requirements upon states ("unfunded mandates") that they find costly to meet, by modifying congressional rules so that they permit any individual legislator to require Congress to consider local costs explicitly before voting on the legislation, and by requiring agencies to consider the costs and benefits of major regulatory rules, including an examination of geographically disparate economic impacts of a rule and the state and

[160] See, e.g., C. Harlow, "Codification of EC Administrative Procedures? Fitting the Foot to the Shoe or the Shoe to the Foot," 2(1) *Eur. L.J.* 3–6 (1996); K. König, "Neue Verwaltung oder Verwaltungsmodernisierung: Verwaltungspolitik in der 90er Jahren," 48(9) *Die Öffentliche Verwaltung* 351 (1995); P. Swan, "Droits écologiques procéduraux et démocratie déliberative," 35 *Revue Interdisciplinaire d'Etudes Juridiques* 8 (1995); W. Hoffmann-Riem, "Ökologisch orientiertes Verwaltungsverfahrensrecht – Vorklärungen," 119 *Archiv des öffentlichen Rechts* 621 (1994); K. Ladeur, "Zur Prozeduralisierung des Vorsorgebegriffs durch Risikovergleich und Prioritätensetzung," *Jahrbuch des Umwelt- und Technikrechts* 297, 318 (1994); J. Schwarze, "Tendances vers un droit administratif commun en Europe," 29(2) *Revue trimestriel de Droit européen* 235–45 (1993); G. Teubner, *Law as an Autopoietic System* (Eng. translation, Blackwell, 1993), 67; H. Simon, "Rationality as Process and as Product of Thought," 68(2) *Am. Econ. Rev.* 1, 9 (1978). See also Esty and Gerardin, "Environmental Protection and International Competitiveness," 35–39.

local resources needed and available to implement a rule. The procedures include a requirement of consultation with state and local officials.[161] Congress also has considered requiring administrators to take account, through formal statements, of such matters as local impact, costs and benefits, and risk analysis.

Similar issues are being debated in the EU.[162] During the 1992 Edinburgh summit, the European Council established that Community decisions should be assessed for conformity with the principles of subsidiarity and proportionality.[163] In other words, it promoted the ideas of both a "federal impact assessment" and a form of "cost-effectiveness" assessment. A few years later, the need for quality assessment of Community legislation was reiterated in the Molitor Report, which furthermore proposed that, when drafting a new piece of legislation, the Commission must ensure that a study is carried out on its incorporation into Member States' national legislation.[164] Such information, we believe, may prove extremely valuable: it can help the Commission to anticipate variation in national implementation, to spot potential for regulatory inconsistencies resulting from national variation, and to consult and coordinate with national authorities in order to achieve greater coherence and consistency of Community policies. The Commission itself has responded with an extensive set of guidelines to improve the quality of legislative drafts, generally reflecting the same ideas as those launched in Edinburgh, and in the Molitor Report.[165] In the years to come, it will be very interesting to monitor whether legislative preparation and drafting guidelines indeed improve the quality of Community legal documents, and whether this higher quality in turn reduces regulatory inconsistencies and national implementation gaps.

Summarizing, the US and EU, albeit following different routes, apparently look for similar solutions to improve regulatory efficiency: increased transparency, some degree of participation in decisionmaking, judicial

[161] See Breyer et al., *Administrative Law and Regulatory Policy*, 117–18 (discussion of 1995 Unfunded Mandate Reform Act).

[162] See, e.g., Ogus, "Quality Control for European Regulation," 325–38.

[163] Cf. the "Interinstitutional Declaration on democracy, transparency, and subsidiarity with annexed thereto the Interinstitutional Agreement of 25 October 1992," *EC Bulletin* 10/1993, 125.

[164] Report of the Group of Independent Experts on Legislative and Administrative Simplification, COM (95) 288 final/2 (21 June 1995).

[165] See, e.g., C. Timmermans, "How Can One Improve the Quality of Community Legislation?" 34 *Common Market L. Rev.* 1241–47, 1255–57 (1997).

review, and procedural quality standards for regulatory activity. The only options that presently seem foreclosed to the EU are those that involve powers or resources its institutions do not yet possess, such as the power to reallocate funds between nationally implemented regulatory programs. On the other hand, the younger EU institutions, such as the agencies established in the early 1990s, are probably more flexible and adaptable to change than their more established US counterparts, which might facilitate the road towards regulatory reform in Europe.

## Risk regulation: a global perspective

The example of the European Union clearly illustrates that the regulation of small risks is no longer necessarily devised and implemented within the confines of one nation: as the Union develops, risk regulation slowly but steadily is drawn into European decisionmaking processes. Considering the EU's "roots" as a customs union primarily designed to facilitate trade between the Member States, the question arises whether other international trade agreements – such as NAFTA and the GATT/WTO – may equally entail an internationalization of risk regulation. To be sure, many of the EU's features are unique; no other supranational structure boasts the same level of institutional sophistication, and no other group of supranational institutions enjoys the same breadth of competency as the Council, the Commission, the European Parliament, and the Court of Justice.[166] Nevertheless, we can think of a number of reasons why GATT/WTO and NAFTA – both more modest in their objectives and institutional set-up than the EU – can equally interfere with domestic regulation of small risks. Furthermore, while the positive development of international risk regulation under the auspices of GATT/WTO and NAFTA is still largely a thing of the future, it is by no means farfetched.

GATT/WTO rules may affect domestic risk regulation because such regulation might constitute an inadmissible barrier to international trade. The mechanism in Article XX(b) of the GATT, for example, resembles the one laid down in Articles 28 and 30 of the EC Treaty:[167] national measures that have the effect of restricting international trade are admissible only if (1) they do not constitute a means of arbitrary or unjustifiable discrimination

[166] See, e.g., F. Abbott, "Integration Without Institutions: The NAFTA Mutation of the EC Model and the Future of the GATT Regime," 40 *Am. J. Comp. L.* 917, 918 (1992).
[167] Old Articles 30 and 36.

between countries, or a disguised restriction on international trade, and (2) they are "necessary" to protect human, animal, or plant life or health. Although GATT panels have traditionally afforded governments large discretion in the pursuit of domestic health, safety, and environmental policies,[168] the requirement of necessity provides at least the formal basis for international review of regulatory measures. Moreover, the history of GATT/WTO reveals that it shares yet another aspect with the European Union: albeit at a slower pace, GATT/WTO is gradually evolving from a shallow to a deeper form of economic integration, one that will increasingly confront regulatory policy issues in areas including consumer, health, and environmental protection.[169] Deepening integration is visible in the proliferation of international agreements that supplement the GATT framework, such as the Agreement on Technical Barriers to Trade (TBT Agreement), and, most importantly for risk regulation, the Agreement on Sanitary and Phytosanitary Measures (SPS Agreement).

The latter Agreement confirms the Members' right, implied in Article XX(b) GATT, to pursue their own health policy. However, the conditions are more tightly defined than the standard of necessity in Article XX(b).[170] Roughly summarized, Members' sanitary and phytosanitary measures must be supported by scientific evidence (if available) and preceded by a risk assessment (Articles 2, 3 and 5 SPS). The Agreement furthermore paves the way for a modest amount of positive integration: it stipulates that, in order to achieve harmonization of sanitary and phytosanitary standards, Member States are to base national measures on standards, guidelines, or recommendations developed by international organizations (Article 3(1) SPS), in particular the Codex Alimentarius Commission, the International Office for Epizootics, and the organizations established within the framework of the International Plant Protection Convention (Article 3(4) SPS). National measures that conform to international standards are presumed to be in conformity with the SPS Agreement (Article 3(2) SPS), whereas those that aim for a level of protection higher than that foreseen by international standards, guidelines, or recommendations need to be justified scientifically or

[168] See, e.g., J. Cromer, "Sanitary and Phytosanitary Measures: What They Could Mean for Health and Safety Regulations under GATT," 36 *Harv. Int. L.J.* 560 (1995).

[169] See, e.g., Esty, "Revitalizing Environmental Federalism," 645.

[170] See, e.g., Y. Shin, "An Analysis of the WTO Agreement on the Application of Sanitary and Phytosanitary Measures and its Implementation in Korea," 32(1) *J. World Trade* 85–100 (1998); Cromer, "Sanitary and Phytosanitary Measures," 561–62.

on the basis of a risk assessment (Article 3(3) SPS).[171] Thus, standards issued by the aforementioned international organizations – which prior to the SPS Agreement were of an entirely voluntary nature – obtain quasi-regulatory status, while more stringent national standards might be condemned for lack of scientific justification and/or risk assessment.

The ramifications of these arrangements for national risk regulation are obvious. Already, WTO Dispute Settlement Bodies (DSBs) have declared a number of health measures – notably the EU restrictions on specified beef hormones and Australian quarantine requirements relating to the importation of fresh and frozen salmon[172] – incompatible with GATT rules, and more cases are pending.[173]

Regarding dispute settlement, it should be noted that settlement mechanisms have undergone substantial change as a result of the Uruguay Round. Prior to the entry into force of the Dispute Settlement Understanding (DSU), which took place on 1 January 1995, the procedures for settling conflicts between GATT Members were diplomatic and conciliatory in nature, with Member States negotiating through the intermediary of working groups or panels to arrive at a politically acceptable, rather than a legally accurate, compromise.[174] Trade conflicts under the GATT/WTO, in turn, receive a much more "judicialized" treatment. Dispute settlement panels no longer seek a political compromise, but draft recommendations that are based on a legal analysis of the case. Dispute settlement decisions, issued in the form of Reports, have obtained quasi-automatic validity, and an appeals procedure has been established.[175] Reports are made available on

[171] Article 3(3) is unclearly formulated and has already given rise to different interpretations. In the appeal of the *European Communities – Measures Affecting Meat/Livestock and Meat Products (Hormones)* Case (WT/DS26/AB/R and WT/DS48/AB/R), the WTO Appellate Body for dispute settlement ruled that, practically, the distinction between "scientific justification" and "risk assessment" has very little effect.

[172] *Ibid.*; *Australia – Measures Affecting Importation of Salmon* (WT/DS18/R).

[173] See, e.g., *Japan – Measures Affecting Agricultural Products* (WT/DS76/1); *European Communities – Measures Affecting Imports of Wood of Conifers from Canada* (WT/DS137/1); *European Communities – Measures Affecting the Prohibition of Asbestos and Asbestos Products* (WT/DS135); and *United States – Measures Affecting Imports of Poultry Products* (WT/DS100/1).

[174] See T. Cottier, "Dispute Settlement in the World Trade Organization: Characteristics and Structural Implications for the European Union," 35 *Common Market L. Rev.* 334–35 (1998).

[175] See F. Abbott, *Law and Policy of Regional Integration: The NAFTA and Western Hemispheric Integration in the World Trade Organization* (Boston: Martinus Nijhoff, 1995), 102.

the Internet, which guarantees greater transparency of the decisionmaking process. Furthermore, Reports rendered by WTO Dispute Settlement Bodies do have some bite to them, since non-compliance with decisions allows other GATT/WTO Members to suspend their obligations vis-à-vis the infringing country.[176]

NAFTA, which creates a free trade area between Canada, the United States, and Mexico, was tailored along similar lines as the GATT/WTO, and from its inception contained a set of sanitary and phytosanitary provisions. NAFTA requirements may therefore influence US, Mexican, or Canadian risk regulation. It should be mentioned that the NAFTA sanitary and phytosanitary requirements place a slightly stronger emphasis on the Parties' right independently to determine the appropriate level of national health protection, and that a conscious effort was made to draft the NAFTA SPS requirements broadly enough to avoid overt interference with national health policies.[177] Still, the NAFTA provisions do call for respect of scientific principles and reliance on risk assessment, requirements that could potentially be used to scrutinize the legality of national risk measures. Moreover, if the NAFTA framework follows the EU and GATT/WTO example and gradually moves towards deeper integration, as some commentators have already predicted, the SPS requirements might be imbued with more specific meaning.[178] NAFTA also establishes dispute settlement mechanisms, similar to the ones followed under the GATT/WTO.

If we accept the hypothesis that increasing global economic interdependence will result in the partial internationalization of risk regulation, a second question presents itself, namely, whether this internationalization will further or obstruct rational risk regulation. Not surprisingly, we predict that compliance with international trade agreements will have some beneficial, and some negative effects on domestic risk regulation. On the positive side, we distinguish the following aspects:

1 *Pooling of resources and expertise.* International agreements usually lead to a flurry of institutional activity: in the wake of both GATT/WTO and NAFTA, a host of commissions, committees, working groups, intergovernmental fora, and other organizational marvels sprang to life. Such organizations may provide valuable platforms for sharing resources and

[176] See, e.g., Cottier, "Dispute Settlement in the WTO," 334–46.
[177] See, e.g., Article 754 of the NAFTA; Abbott, "Integration Without Institutions," 938–39.
[178] *Ibid.*, 930–46.

expertise. This may substantially reduce the costs of information for each country, and thus allow the production of better, more reliable scientific data. Recalling that the first part of this chapter identified scientific uncertainty as one of the factors propelling the vicious circle, better information may increase both the quality of risk decisions and, hence, the prestige of risk decisionmakers, which in turn may lead to better risk regulation.

2 *International standards for rational regulatory behavior.* International prescriptions (for example, the SPS requirements in GATT/WTO and NAFTA that regulatory measures that are more stringent than corresponding international standards, recommendations, or guidelines be based on a risk assessment) may prove a useful check against emotive decisionmaking, one of the most frequent causes of tunnel vision. When confronting public pressure for disproportionately costly safety or health measures – or for symbolic measures that would not result in real risk reduction – regulatory and administrative authorities can now argue that, in addition to being scientifically and/or economically unsound, such action would be in breach of the country's obligations under GATT/WTO or NAFTA. Conversely, in countries with relatively unsophisticated or unaccountable bureaucracies, international standards may help to structure and systematize regulatory decisionmaking.

On the other hand, internationalization brings its own set of potential problems, including:

1 *Loss of administrative discretion.* The creation of international standards and new institutions may reduce administrative discretion. Adherence to international agreements adds to the list of watchdogs of regulatory administration: in addition to the legislature and the public, regulatory agencies' actions are monitored and can be challenged by foreign governments, as well as various international institutions in charge of implementation and compliance control. As a result, agencies may lose some of their flexibility in decisionmaking, flexibility that they might need to structure efficient risk tradeoffs, or to follow experimental, but promising new risk strategies. Finally, there is only so much legitimizing, justifying and substantiating a regulatory agency can do before it loses track of the ultimate goal of its activities: ensuring a high level of health and environmental protection for the public. In other words, too much pressure for procedural correctness, exerted on too many different levels (the public, special interest groups, parliamentary oversight committees,

neighboring exporting states, international treaty compliance committees, dispute resolution bodies, etc.) may divert regulatory attention away from the intrinsic quality of proposed risk management measures, or may even threaten to paralyze regulatory activity altogether.

2 *A shifting balance between judicial and administrative authority for risk regulation.* To effectuate harmonization of product standards, which is in turn conducive to international trade flows, international organizations are to a greater extent dependent on the mechanisms of negative integration than regional or national bodies. With the exception of the EU, international associations simply do not have the political authority to promulgate uniformly applicable health, safety, and environmental standards for products circulating within the borders of a liberalized or free trade area. To a certain extent, GATT/WTO and NAFTA fill in this gap by referring to the work of international standardization bodies (the Codex Alimentarius Commission, the International Office for Epizootics, etc.), and establishing a presumption that standards set by these bodies conform to treaty requirements. This may encourage voluntary positive harmonization by states. However, this route to harmonization is not as forceful as the adoption of internationally valid, mandatory product standards (or, at the very least, the adoption of uniform essential requirements for products) which takes place, for example, within the European Union. Hence, liberalization efforts will mainly be enforced through general treaty stipulations of the type that "there should be no arbitrary discrimination between products from different countries," and "national regulatory measures should not constitute disguised restrictions to trade." Unjustifiable barriers to trade will often be revealed through conflict, and resolved through a judicial or quasi-judicial mechanism rather than a directly political one.

The upshot is that court-like bodies (for instance, the WTO Dispute Settlement Bodies) will play an important role in evaluating, sanctioning, or condemning risk regulation, an activity for which, as we have discussed, they are perhaps not optimally equipped. They may decide to defer to the wisdom of regulatory and administrative agencies, but then again, they may not, which would entail a further reduction of administrative discretion and, in the long run, prestige.[179] In fact, the European

[179] See S. Croley and J. Jackson, "WTO Dispute Procedures, Standard of Review, and Deference to National Governments," 90 *Am. J. Int. L.* 206–11 (1996).

Communities – Measures Concerning Meat and Meat Products (Hormones) report, issued by the Dispute Settlement Appellate Body of the WTO in January 1998,[180] suggests that judicial review of national regulatory measures might become more penetrating than GATT/WTO Members had anticipated. The background to the dispute is the following: The EU prohibits imports of beef that has been treated with hormones, on the stated grounds of possible risks to health. A number of the hormones falling under the EU restrictions are legally used in Canada and the US. The latter countries claim that the EU's concerns about health risks associated with the use of these hormones have no foundation in fact; scientific evidence, they argue, does not bear out the allegation that the hormones jeopardize human health. The suggested motive for the restriction is protection of European farmers. The WTO panel examined the scientific evidence submitted by both parties, as well as evidence supplied by a group of independent experts appointed by the panel itself. The majority of evidence supported the US and Canada's case, and this was a crucial factor in the panel's decision that the EU restrictions on beef hormones constituted an illegal trade barrier.

One of the issues raised by the EU during the appeal was that the WTO panel (which saw the case in first instance) had paid insufficient deference to the decision of EU regulatory bodies to pursue a restrictive, precautionary policy. The EU referred to the "reasonableness–deference standard" that is traditionally used in GATT and GATT/WTO anti-dumping cases. According to this standard, the WTO panel should not conduct a *de novo* review of the evidence, but rather should constrain itself to assessing whether, on the basis of the facts before it, the national authority could reasonably have arrived at the decision it took. The panel does not have to arrive at the same decision as the one embraced by the national authority. It does not even have to agree with the decision; as long as it believes the national authority's decision is a reasonable one, it should defer to administrative discretion.[181]

The Appellate Body, however, dismissed the high level of deference

[180] WT/DS26/AB/R and WT/DS48/AB/R.

[181] See, e.g., Croley and Jackson, "WTO Dispute Procedures," 193–213. See generally, G. Richardson and H. Genn, *Administrative Law and Government Action. The Courts and Alternative Mechanisms of Review* (Oxford: Clarendon Press, 1994), 13–104; D. J. Galligan, *Discretionary Powers. A Legal Study of Official Discretion* (Oxford: Clarendon Press, 1986).

proposed by the EU. Instead, it stated that the appropriate standard for judicial review could be inferred from Article 11 of the WTO Dispute Settlement Understanding. Article 11 states that a panel should make an objective assessment of the matter before it. The Appellate Body continued that this objective assessment of "the matter" should be interpreted to cover an objective assessment of the facts of the case, including the scientific facts. It concluded that the panel's review and critical evaluation of scientific evidence submitted by the parties and by the independent experts fell within the scope of "objective assessment of the matter." In other words, the panel did not need to defer to the assessment made by the EU authorities, but instead could make and rely on its own evaluation of the facts. Although the Appellate Body formally stated that the standard of review to be applied by panels for these cases is situated "somewhere between" deference and *de novo* review, it is difficult to see how the standard developed in the Beef Hormones case differs from *de novo* review. Having determined that the panel had applied the proper "objective assessment" legal standard, the Appellate Body did not itself undertake *de novo* review of the panel's decision on the merits. Deciding that the panel's assessment of the facts of the particular case was not unreasonable, the Appellate Body in the end dismissed the EU's claim. The logic followed in the Beef Hormones case apparently reduces to the following rule of thumb: as long as a WTO panel's interpretation of scientific evidence is plausible, it may set aside any regulatory measure based on a different interpretation. It is improbable that this was an outcome intended by the drafters of the DSU, and future dispute settlements will show whether this trend will be continued or abandoned.

3 *New coordination problems.* The last problem for discussion is also the most speculative one, since it may only manifest itself if international trade agreements indeed move towards the predicted deeper level of integration, organizing risk regulation on an international scale. Internationalization of risk regulation may foster coordination and consistency in risk policies between countries, but may simultaneously lead to new problems in cross-sectoral coordination. To date, there is no centralized, international regulatory or supervisory body for the coherent development of international risk strategies. Rather, a wide range of different committees, working groups, and agencies touch upon subsets of risk issues, which may at times overlap. Under the auspices of the WTO, for example, we find a Committee on the Environment, a

Committee dealing with Technical Barriers to Trade, an SPS Committee, and so on. Unless coordination between these different bodies is managed very dexterously, the scattering of organizations with some responsibility for international risk regulation may result in inconsistent policymaking.

## Conclusions

This chapter does not aspire to firm conclusions. Its object has been to summarize the argument of *Breaking the Vicious Circle*, to suggest why that work may be relevant to European experience, to note special European problems, to highlight certain aspects of American experience that may be relevant to those problems, and to provoke discussion about that experience, and briefly to review how similar issues may arise in the context of international free trade regimes other than the EU. Europeans may find ways to adapt some of that experience to help them with risk-regulatory problems. If so, Americans can then learn from that European experience. Continued dialogue and sharing of experience is, we believe, of great value on both sides of the Atlantic, for we have both common problems and common goals. This sharing of experiences becomes particularly crucial when we start seriously to consider the international dimension of risk regulation, a dimension that will only gain in importance as the trends towards growing economic interdependence and globalization gradually unfold.

# 11

# SCIENCE AND INTERNATIONAL ENVIRONMENTAL POLICY: THE INTERGOVERNMENTAL PANEL ON CLIMATE CHANGE

JOHN HOUGHTON

POLLUTION DUE to human activities on a *local* scale, of air, water, or land, has been around for a very long time. What is relatively new and what is giving rise to much current environmental concern is the existence of human activities which lead to pollution on the *global* scale – pollution emitted by one person locally that has global effects. One example is the release of small quantities of chemicals containing chlorine, such as chlorofluorocarbons (CFCs), that cause damage of global extent to the ozone layer in the stratosphere. Another example relates to emissions of "greenhouse gases" (GHG) such as carbon dioxide that spread through the whole atmosphere and result in climate change with its potential deleterious effects. The existence of global environmental problems requires solutions that are organized on a global scale. Scientists and policymakers worldwide have to respond to this imperative and find appropriate ways of meeting the challenge. In this chapter I address in particular the issue of human-induced climate change and describe the role which scientists have played in assisting in the determination of policy.

## Formation of the Intergovernmental Panel on Climate Change

During the 1980s it began to be recognized that the increasing use of fossil fuels was resulting in a substantial increase in the concentrations in the atmosphere of the GHG, carbon dioxide and methane. Estimates were made that the carbon dioxide concentration could double before the end of the twenty-first century.[1] The possibility of serious consequences for the

[1] A comprehensive account of global warming and climate change can be found in John Houghton, *Global Warming: the Complete Briefing* (2nd edn., Cambridge University Press, 1997).

world's climate was increasingly raised by scientists and those with environmental concern. In 1988 an international conference was staged in Toronto which for the first time pressed for specific international action to mitigate climate change. It was in that year too that world leaders began to speak out about it; for instance, Mrs Thatcher expressed her concern in a speech to the Royal Society of London that was widely publicized.

It was therefore timely that in 1988 a new scientific body, the Intergovernmental Panel on Climate Change (IPCC), was set up to address the issue jointly by the World Meteorological Organization (WMO) and the United Nations Environment Programme (UNEP). Bert Bolin from Sweden, a scientist with a distinguished record of contributions to the science of climate, agreed to chair the IPCC. Three Working Groups were established, WGI to address the science of anthropogenic climate change, WGII to address the impacts of climate change, and WGIII to address the policy options. I was appointed chairman of WGI and I will illustrate the work of the IPCC particularly from my experience of that Working Group.

In its structure the IPCC followed closely the structure of the Assessment Panels of the Montreal Protocol which had been set up in 1987 by UNEP and WMO to address the problem of the depletion of stratospheric ozone by CFCs and related chlorine-containing chemicals. Through the negotiation of the Protocol, with its arrangements for inputs from scientists and other experts, methods had begun to be developed in the international community through which global pollution problems could be addressed. Although the problem addressed by the Montreal Protocol was a more limited one than that of global climate change, especially in the range and size of the human activities that contribute to it, it was appropriate that the IPCC should build on this experience in addressing climate change issues. The development within the IPCC of ways to involve large numbers of scientists and of formal procedures for peer review in turn influenced the ongoing work of the Assessment Panels of the Montreal Protocol.

## The IPCC 1990 Report

It was agreed at the first meeting of the IPCC that a new assessment of the whole issue of anthropogenic climate change should be prepared. There had, of course, been assessments of the climate change issue before, notably one published in 1986[2] organized under the auspices of the Scientific Committee on Problems of the Environment (SCOPE) of the International Council of Scientific Unions (ICSU), again under the chairmanship of Bert Bolin. The IPCC saw its task as updating previous assessments but with a difference. Previous assessments had involved relatively few of the world's leading climate scientists. Because of the global nature of the issue that brought with it a large measure of international concern, the IPCC's ambition from the start was to involve as many representatives as possible from the world scientific community in the new assessment.

To assist in the preparation of the WGI report, a small Technical Support Unit was set up within the part of the UK Meteorological Office at Bracknell which was concerned with climate research. The IPCC's first scientific assessment of the relation between greenhouse gas emissions and climate change was issued in 1990.[3] The report comprised eleven chapters totalling over 300 pages dealing with different components of the scientific issue together with a Policymakers' Summary and an Executive Summary. Twelve international workshops were held to address these different components. In all, 170 scientists from twenty-five countries contributed to the report either through participation in the workshops or through written contributions. A further 200 scientists were involved in the peer review of the draft report. The thorough peer review assisted in achieving a high degree of consensus amongst the authors and reviewers regarding the report's conclusions.

The Policymakers' Summary (twenty pages) together with its Executive Summary (two pages) was based on the conclusions presented in the chapters and was prepared particularly to present to those without a strong background in science a clear statement of the status of scientific knowledge at the time and the associated uncertainties. In preparing the first draft of the Policymakers' Summary, the lead authors of the chapters were first involved; it was then sent out for the same wide peer review as the main report. A revised draft of the Summary was then discussed line by line at a Plenary Meeting of the Working Group attended by government delegates from thirty-five countries together with lead authors from the chapters, and the final wording agreed at that meeting. A flavour of the style and content

[2] Bert Bolin, Bo Doos, Jill Jager, and Richard Warrick eds., *SCOPE 29, the Greenhouse Effect, Climatic Change and Ecosystems* (John Wiley, 1986).

[3] J. T. Houghton, G. J. Jenkins, and J. J. Ephraums eds., *Climate Change, the IPCC Scientific Assessment* (Cambridge University Press, 1990).

of the report is given by the first few paragraphs of the Executive Summary which read as follows:

> We are certain of the following:
>
> there is a natural greenhouse effect which already keeps the Earth warmer than it would otherwise be.
>
> emissions resulting from human activities are substantially increasing the atmospheric concentrations of the greenhouse gases: carbon dioxide, methane, chlorofluorocarbons (CFCs) and nitrous oxide. These increases will enhance the greenhouse effect, resulting on average in an additional warming of the Earth's surface. The main greenhouse gas, water vapour, will increase in response to global warming and further enhance it.
>
> We calculate with confidence that:
>
> some gases are potentially more effective than others at changing climate, and their relative effectiveness can be estimated. Carbon dioxide has been responsible for over half the enhanced greenhouse effect in the past, and is likely to remain so in the future.
>
> atmospheric concentrations of the long-lived gases (carbon dioxide, nitrous oxide and the CFCs) adjust only slowly to changes in emissions. Continued emissions of these gases at present rates would commit us to increased concentrations for centuries ahead. The longer emissions continue to increase at present day rates, the greater reductions would have to be for concentrations to stabilise at a given level.
>
> the long-lived gases would require immediate reductions in emissions from human activities of over 60% to stabilise their concentrations at today's levels; methane would require a 15–20% reduction.
>
> Based on current model results, we predict:
>
> under the IPCC Business-as-Usual (Scenario A) emissions of greenhouse gases, a rate of increase of global mean temperature during the next century of about 0.3°C per decade (with an uncertainty range of 0.2°C to 0.5°C per decade); this is greater than that seen over the past 10, 000 years. This will result in a likely increase in global mean temperature of about 1°C above the present value by 2025 and 3°C before the end of the next century. The rise will not be steady because of the influence of other factors.

Later sections of the Summary addressed the scientific uncertainties and the question of the degree to which anthropogenic climate change had been observed in the climate record.

Over the period of the preparation of the IPCC report, a significant change occurred in the attitudes of the scientists involved. To begin with there was a strong feeling, particularly amongst some scientists, that the scientific uncertainty was too large for any useful statement to be made regarding future climate change. However, gradually we all realized our responsibility to articulate carefully and honestly the knowledge which is available, distinguishing clearly between what could be said with a good degree of certainty and the areas where the uncertainly is large. This responsibility seemed all the more important because many individuals not possessing much expert scientific knowledge were making forecasts of future climate change – often of an extreme kind. Also, we increasingly recognized that there was enough certainty in the science to provide meaningful information regarding the likely future provided that the uncertainty, including the significant uncertainty range regarding predicted global warming under a Business-As-Usual Scenario presented in the 1990 Report and its Executive Summary, was also fully explained.

## Ownership by scientists and by governments

Many of the world's leading scientists involved with the understanding of climate and climate change contributed to the report. Inevitably they came mostly from developed countries. However, a significant number of contributors from developing countries were also involved. That so many of the world's scientists contributed or were involved in the review process meant that there was a genuine feeling of ownership of the report by the world scientific community.

The IPCC process led to a significant degree of consensus. It is sometimes pointed out that 'consensus' amongst scientists is not necessarily a sign of scientific health; argument and disagreement are seen to be more usual building blocks of scientific advance. But the "consensus" achieved by the IPCC is not complete agreement about everything. It is agreement particularly about what we know and what we do not know – distinguishing clearly those matters about which there is reasonable certainty from those where there remains much uncertainty and where there continues to be lively debate and disagreement. It is this limited "consensus" which is reflected in the Executive Summary of the 1990 IPCC Report which has been widely acclaimed for the clarity and crispness of its presentation.

It was clear from an early stage that not only was the scientific content of the assessment important but also the way in which it was presented. Scientists left to themselves do not always recognize what is relevant to policymakers or present their material with the maximum clarity. Further, the presentation of a scientific document can appear to a policymaker to convey a political message even though none was intended, for instance through the selection of the particular material employed.

It has therefore been helpful in the presentation of the science of climate change to involve policymakers themselves or their representatives in the formulation of the summaries of the reports. For instance, they were full participants in the government review process and in the Working Group Plenary Meeting which agreed the wording of the report. The report was greatly improved in its relevance and clarity through their participation. In addition the large number of governments which had a part in the process felt ownership of the report.

The IPCC was therefore able to provide to the Earth Summit at Rio de Janeiro in 1992 a clear assessment of the science of climate change that was owned both by the world scientific community and by governments. These characteristics were essential to providing governments with the confidence to formulate and to sign the Framework Convention on Climate Change at that 1992 Conference and to take appropriate action. They have continued to be essential in the generation of subsequent reports which have provided input to the ongoing work of the FCCC, for instance to the Kyoto Protocol of 1997.

## The science–policy interface

The work of the IPCC illustrates the following five important features which I believe should characterize the scientific assessments that form an input to policymaking:

1 The first has already been mentioned, namely, the separation of what is known with reasonable certainty from what is unknown and very uncertain. All statements from scientists that have policy implications should make this distinction and should describe and quantify the uncertainty as fully as possible.

2 It has been important for its continued credibility that the IPCC has confined itself in its reports and statements to scientific information and has avoided making judgments or giving advice about policy. Often in the past these areas have been confused. The scientific information must, of course, be comprehensive and must include input from all relevant scientific disciplines including the social sciences. But in the formulation and presentation of policy options or in making policy judgments the scientific input must be clearly distinguished from the policy judgments and decisions. The importance in environmental decisionmaking of this separation of scientific and other expert assessment from policy judgment is argued in a recent report of the Royal Commission on Environmental Pollution in the UK.[4]

3 All parts of the assessment process need to be completely open and transparent. IPCC documents including early drafts and review comments have been freely and widely available – adding much to the credibility of the process and its conclusions.

4 The purpose of an assessment is to take account of all scientific data and all genuine scientific opinion and to elucidate and articulate the best scientific interpretation and conclusions from the information available. Scientific assessments must not start with preconceived assumptions and no compromises must be made to meet any personal or political agendas. A thorough and wide peer review process helps to guarantee the honesty and comprehensiveness of the process.

5 The scientific information must be integrated in a thoroughly balanced way. The amount of data available concerning climate and climate change is very large and it is easy to select data that fits in with a wide range of preconceived ideas or assumptions. However, by involving so many scientists from the complete range of relevant disciplines it has been possible to develop a balanced integration of the information in a way that has commanded general acceptance.

## IPCC's work in science applications and in social sciences

Working Groups II and III of the IPCC have been concerned with the impacts of climate change and with adaptation to and mitigation of

[4] A full discussion of the inputs to the environmental policy determination and the process of decisionmaking is given in the Twenty-first Report of the UK Royal Commission on Environmental Pollution, 'Setting Environmental Standards' (The Stationery Office, London, 1998).

climate change, respectively. Consideration of these has involved not only natural scientists but also experts from many areas of social science, especially economics. As with WGI, the aim of the other Working Groups has been to involve scientists with a wide range of expertise and from as many countries as possible. This has been less easy in the social sciences than in the natural sciences where, especially in a subject like the science of climate, there has been a long tradition of scientists working together across national boundaries. However, through the stimulation of the IPCC a substantial international community of social scientists has been brought together to address the variety of problems exposed by the climate change issue.

In this area as in natural science the IPCC has stressed the importance of separating the scientific analysis from policy judgments. But it is clearly more difficult when dealing with economic or political analysis to make this separation convincing. Because of this some have argued that the IPCC should not become engaged in analysis in these social science areas. The IPCC has consistently refused to accept that argument, believing that a great deal of useful technical supporting work needs to be done in providing analyses of some of the economic or political options which might be taken up in response to the impact of climate change. Further, it is a great advantage if this work is pursued outside government agencies or other political institutions. Such analyses are essential input for international negotiations regarding the options and essential preparation for decision-making.

## The 1992, 1994, and 1995 IPCC Reports

As soon as the 1990 Report was complete, the IPCC began work on further reports. In 1992, in time for the Earth Summit, a report was produced updating what was known about GHGs,[5] their sources and sinks, and about observations and modeling of climate change. In addition the 1992 Report developed various emission scenarios for GHG emissions over the next century based on a variety of assumptions regarding factors such as world population, economic growth, availability of fossil fuels, etc.

[5] J. T. Houghton, B. A. Callander, and S. K. Varney eds., *Climate Change 1992: the Supplementary Report to the IPCC Assessment* (Cambridge University Press, 1992).

The 1994 Report updated the information and analysis regarding the radiative forcing of the various GHGs.[6] Of particular importance was the new work carried out on the profiles of emissions of carbon dioxide and other GHGs which would lead to the stabilization of these gases in the atmosphere at different levels of concentration.

By 1995, when the IPCC produced its second comprehensive assessment,[7] five years after the first assessment in 1990, the community of scientists involved with the IPCC had become substantially greater. More scientists from more countries were involved both in the report's preparation (about 480 scientists from more than twenty-five countries) and in its review (over 500 from forty countries). The participants at the Plenary Meeting of WGI that approved the Summary for Policymakers included 177 delegates from ninety-six countries, representatives from fourteen non-governmental organizations, and twenty-eight lead authors. Regarding climate change over the next century and its likely impacts, the messages of the 1995 Report were essentially the same as those of the 1990 Report. Some further detail had emerged during the five years in between, especially regarding the likely contribution to climate change from atmospheric aerosols –the small dust particles that are present in the atmosphere as a result of industrial activity. Also, there was more confidence amongst scientists that the historical increase in global average temperatures that has occurred since wide-scale industrialization might be the result of anthropogenic change. The WGI Plenary Meeting debated for a considerable time how to express this somewhat greater scientific confidence in the interpretation of the recent climate record – although still surrounded by much uncertainty. A sentence carefully crafted by the meeting was unanimously agreed by the delegates: "the balance of evidence suggests a discernible human influence on global climate."

[6] J. T. Houghton, L. G. Meira Filho, J. Bruce, Hoesung Lee, B. A. Callander, E. Haites, N. Harris, and K. Maskell eds., *Climate Change 1994: Radiative Forcing of Climate Change and an Evaluation of the IPCC IS92 Scenarios* (Cambridge University Press, 1996).

[7] J. T. Houghton, L. G. Meira Filho, N. Harris, A. Kattenberg, and K. Maskell eds., *Climate Change 1995: The Science of Climate Change* (Cambridge University Press, 1996); R. T. Watson, M. C. Zinowera, and R. H. Moss eds., *Climate Change 1995: Impacts, Adaptation and Mitigation of Climate Change* (Cambridge University Press, 1996); J. Bruce, Hoesung Lee, and E. Haites eds., *Climate Change 1995: Economic and Social Dimensions of Climate Change* (Cambridge University Press, 1996).

## Attacks on the IPCC

The IPCC and its work have been attacked from two fronts, on the one hand by those who argue that the projections of global warming and its consequences have been grossly overplayed and that there is no need for any action, and on the other hand by those who believe that possible serious consequences of global warming have been ignored and that there is urgent need for much more drastic action. Both these points of view have been bolstered by appeals to aspects of the scientific data available and their interpretation.

Most of the controversy regarding these extreme positions has been exposed in the media, which in general is much more interested in extreme views than in the more balanced approach adopted by the IPCC. Particular points that can be made about the controversy and the attacks that have been directed at the IPCC are as follows.

Amongst the scientists who have contributed to the IPCC there is a wide range of views – the uncertainty ranges associated with the IPCC projections of future climate change illustrate this range.

All scientists are, of course, interested in genuine scientific debate, the existence of which is fundamental to scientific advance. Contrary to some of the allegations that have been made, the IPCC has not tried to inhibit debate or to minimize the uncertainties that exist.

From the wide range of scientific data that exist it is relatively easy to select data to support any preconceived conclusion or position. The best place to pursue debate and discussion about the data is in the scientific literature with its discipline of honesty and integrity and tradition of careful peer review. It is regrettable, therefore, that most of those who have challenged the scientific conclusions of the IPCC reports have chosen to pursue that challenge in the media rather than in the scientific literature where a more scientifically useful debate could be conducted.

The number of scientists who have taken the extreme positions mentioned above and who have also contributed significantly to climate science is very few compared with the hundreds who have contributed to the IPCC process.

Some vicious attacks in the media have been made not so much on the science but on the integrity of the IPCC process and some of the scientists involved in it.[8] That these attacks possess no real foundation is illustrated by the fact that they have received no formal support from any of the delegates to the IPCC even from those countries strongly opposed to any action concerning climate change.

## The FCCC and the IPCC

The United Nations Framework Convention on Climate Change (FCCC), signed by over 160 countries at the Earth Summit in Rio de Janeiro in June 1992, sets the context in which international discussion regarding appropriate action can be pursued. The development of the Convention's agenda clearly requires continuous scientific and technical input. The Conference of the Parties (COP) to the FCCC has set up a Subsidiary Body for Science and Technological Advice (SUBSTA) to organize this input. The IPCC is working closely with SUBSTA through a Joint Working Group (JWG) to ensure that IPCC assessments are geared to provide the detailed scientific and technical input required.

The objective of the FCCC is contained in Article 2. It recognizes the need to prevent continued change of the climate and therefore to stabilize the causes of climate change. It reads as follows:

> The ultimate objective of this Convention and any related legal instruments that the Conference of the Parties may adopt is to achieve, in accordance with the relevant provisions of the Convention, stabilization of greenhouse gas concentrations in the atmosphere at a level that would prevent dangerous anthropogenic interference with the climate system. Such a level should be achieved within a time frame sufficient to allow ecosystems to adapt naturally to climate change, to ensure that food production is not threatened and to enable economic development to proceed in a sustainable manner.

The IPCC has been at pains to explain that what constitutes 'dangerous' is a policy, not a scientific decision. But the need to make such policy decisions immediately raises many scientific and technical questions. For instance, what carbon dioxide emission profiles will lead to stabilization of atmospheric concentration and by when? What effect will current proposed emission limitations by developed countries have on atmospheric concentrations? What technologies, policies, and measures might be available for

[8] See, for instance, Susan K. Avery et al. (the Executive Committee of the AMS), "Open Letter to Ben Santer," *Bull Am. Met.Soc.* 1962–67 (1996).

mitigating climate change? How vulnerable are different regions of the world to possible climate change? To assist in answering these questions the IPCC has produced a series of Technical Papers addressing the detail of some of the issues involved.

An issue which has been highlighted by the third session of the COP at Kyoto in 1997 is that of the contributions which are made by deforestation, afforestation, reforestation, and changes in land use to the sources or sinks of greenhouse gases, especially of carbon dioxide. This is an area where what is meant by different human activities (e.g. de-, af-, or reforestation) requires very careful definition, where there is much scientific uncertainty, and where there are many possibilities for the propagation of perverse incentives. The IPCC is already very involved in this area through its work on the development of detailed guidelines[9] for the production of national inventories of greenhouse gases which include both sources and sinks. It is the IPCC Guidelines to which the Kyoto Protocol refers. The IPCC is beginning to develop further advice for the FCCC on the interpretation of the Protocol and the use of the Guidelines.

## The future work of the IPCC

Preparation is now starting for a third comprehensive assessment report to be completed in 2001 which will take into account the large growth in research in both the natural sciences and the social sciences in topics related to climate change, its impacts, and its mitigation. Guidelines for this assessment and for future IPCC work are:

- to continue with an open, transparent, rigorous assessment process involving as many in the world scientific community as possible.
- to ensure the relevance of the assessment to the policy needs of the FCCC.
- to seek contributions from those in industry, business, and commerce increasingly so as to stimulate the active participation of the industrial sector in the action required for adaptation to and mitigation of deleterious climate change. For instance, a report recently completed on "Aviation and the Global Atmosphere" has been prepared in cooperation with the International Civil Aviation Organization (ICAO)

[9] IPCC Guidelines for National Greenhouse Gas Inventories (IPCC Secretariat, World Meteorological Organization, Geneva).

and with substantial participation from all aspects of the aviation industry.

to integrate the scientific, technical, and economic analyses in ways that illuminate as clearly as possible the various policy options.

It is a little more than ten years since there was wide realization of the potential danger of anthropogenic climate change to the world community and it became a significant political issue. During this relatively short time substantial progress has been made. The world's scientists have carefully articulated what is known about the likely climate change (together with the nature of the substantial uncertainty regarding it) and the governments of the world have signed up to the FCCC and agreed the first steps towards mitigation measures. Further progress will be dependent on there being full understanding of the issues by all sections of the community in all countries. It is, for instance, important that the general public are adequately informed about all aspects of the environmental problems under assessment so that, so far as is possible, they too can be part of the decisionmaking process. More could be done through the media and otherwise to bring this about.

Of particular importance is that the world industrial sector – which after all is the engine of change – should be adequately informed and made aware of environmental issues. As with scientists and governments, industry also needs to feel ownership of the expert assessments. I have mentioned the encouragement felt by the IPCC through the industrial involvement in its latest report on Aviation and the Global Atmosphere. It is encouraging too to see the way in which leading industrialists are beginning to see matters of environmental concern as presenting opportunities rather than threats. For instance, in a speech on global climate change, John Browne, the Chief Executive of BP, said, "No single company or country can solve the problem of climate change. It would be foolish and arrogant to pretend otherwise. But I hope we can make a difference – not least to the tone of the debate – by showing what is possible through constructive action."[10]

## The IPCC in the context of other global issues

The question is often asked as to whether the IPCC provides a pattern or a model for supplying the means for scientists from all disciplines to give

[10] From a speech in Berlin, 30 September 1997.

input to policy determination in other areas of concern. The elements which we have mentioned which have been critical to the success of the IPCC have been those of: (1) ensuring the widest possible participation by experts from all relevant disciplines; (2) ensuring a clear separation between scientific assessment and policy determination; and (3) through the close involvement of the expert community, of governments and, more recently, of relevant industry, ensuring wide ownership not only by the community of experts but also by those who have a stake in the policy process. Although anthropogenic climate change is perhaps the largest and most complex problem concerned with the global environment that we face, it is not unique. Models similar to that of the IPCC with its essential elements could be applied elsewhere.

Climate change is, of course, not the only global issue facing the planet. Because of the commonality between them, other problems such as population growth, resource overuse, and poverty need to be considered alongside climate change and other environmental problems, including biodiversity loss, deforestation, and desertification. The development of the work of the IPCC has demonstrated the enormous capacity for the international community to work together towards the common aims of care for humanity and care for the environment and provides encouragement in the belief that problems as complex as that of climate change are capable of solution.

# Part V

## INTERNATIONAL ENVIRONMENTAL LAW AND SUSTAINABLE DEVELOPMENT

# 12

# ENVIRONMENTAL PROTECTION IN THE TWENTY-FIRST CENTURY: SUSTAINABLE DEVELOPMENT AND INTERNATIONAL LAW

PHILIPPE SANDS

THIS CHAPTER addresses some of the key issues facing the international community as it seeks further to develop and apply rules of international law for the protection of the environment. A decade or so ago a paper on this topic would probably have begun with a discussion as to whether the subject of international environmental law even existed: there were no treatises or journals specifically on the subject, only a very limited number of law school courses were being taught, and most treatises on general international law made no mention of the environment (with little risk of being criticized for incompleteness).

Today the situation is very different, as the environment comes to occupy a more central position in the international legal order. Within the past couple of years the International Court of Justice has confirmed the "obligations of States to respect and protect the natural environment"[1] and expressed the opinion that their "general obligation . . . to ensure that activities within their jurisdiction or control respect the environment of other States or of areas beyond national control is now part of the corpus of international law relating to the environment."[2] This latter obligation, it is now clear, is applicable at all times and to all activities.[3]

These are expressions of a general obligation. They will have to be further

1 *Request for an Examination of the Situation in Accordance with Paragraph 63 of the Court's Judgment of 20 December 1974 in the Nuclear Tests (New Zealand v. France) Case*, Order of 22 September 1995, ICJ Reports 1995, 306, para. 64.

2 *Legality of the Threat or Use of Nuclear Weapons*, 8 July 1996, Advisory Opinion, ICJ Reports 1996, 226 at 241.

3 *Ibid.*, para. 33.

elaborated in the context of particular objectives and cases. In this regard, account will have to be taken of the international community's expressed commitment, at the 1992 UN Conference on Environment and Development ("UNCED"), to treat environment and development in an integrated manner and to cooperate "in the further development of international law in the field of sustainable development."[4] There therefore exist two principal challenges. The first is to develop the content of the rules of international environmental law, recognizing what Professor Philip Allott identified as the need to reconcile the inherent and fundamental interdependence of the world environment with the sovereign world of independent states.[5] The second challenge is to define the relationship between international environmental law and other areas of international law, particularly in the economic and social domain. It is appropriate to recall, in this regard, that the Brundtland Report considered that "international law is being rapidly outdistanced by the accelerating pace and expanding scale of impacts on the ecological basis of development."[6] These two challenges raise issues about the nature of international society and the structure of the international legal order.

There is no novelty in environmental issues, even if they have become more complex. International legal efforts to protect the environment go back at least as far as the 1880s when a dispute was submitted to international arbitration as a consequence of United States efforts to prevent British vessels from exploiting fur seals in international waters of the Behring Sea. Although that international arbitral tribunal did not find in

[4] See Rio Declaration on Environment and Development, Principle 27; Report of the UN Conference on Environment and Development ("UNCED Report"), A/CONF.151/26/Rev.1 (vol. II), 3; 31 *I.L.M.* 874 (1992). As an international legal concept "sustainable development" remains in an early stage of development. Thus, although references to "sustainable development" and international law abound in Agenda 21, none of the formulations apparently follows that of Principle 27 ("international law in the field of sustainable development"), and there remain occasional references to "international environmental law" (Agenda 21, para. 39.2). Whether the variable terminology arises by accident or design is unclear. Anecdotal evidence suggests that the head of the Brazilian delegation persuaded Working Group III of UNCED's Preparatory Committee to replace every reference in Agenda 21 to "international environmental law" to "international law in the field of sustainable development" (the diplomat, Pedro Motta Pinto Coelho, apparently remarked that this change would "keep you lawyers busy well into the 21st century"): see P. Sand, "UNCED and the Development of International Environmental Law," 3 *Ybk. I.E.L.* 3 at 17 (1992).

[5] P. Allott, *Eunomia: New Order for a New World* (Oxford, 1990), para. 17.52.

[6] Brundtland Commission, *Our Common Future* (Oxford, 1987), 4.

favor of the unilateral US approach to conservation (early shades of current issues in the GATT/WTO context), it did adopt Regulations for the "proper protection and preservation" of fur seals. These Regulations have served as an important precedent for the subsequent development of international environmental law, reflecting a recognition that environmental problems transcend national boundaries and can require action under international law.[7]

In this chapter I consider the prospects for that law within the framework of "sustainable development," including whether the integration of environmental law into sustainable development law will tend to make environmental objectives more or less easily attainable. The first part briefly introduces the historic development of this emerging area of international law, including the institutional arrangements, and the traditional legal order within which environmental challenges fall to be addressed. It then summarizes the general principles and basic rules of international environmental law, as well as the principal legal techniques which exist for implementing them. The second part addresses the impact of UNCED on international law by reference to six key issues: (1) risk assessment and decisionmaking in the face of scientific uncertainty; (2) subsidiarity and federalism: the proper level for lawmaking and decision-taking; (3) international institutional reform, including lawmaking processes; (4) the role of non-state actors; (5) the relationship between – and the integration of – different subject matters in international law (especially by reference to trade and environment); and (6) enhancing compliance with international environmental law. By way of conclusion I assess future challenges and likely developments by reference to the principal themes of this book: regulation in multi-jurisdictional contexts, the use of economic analysis and economic incentive systems, and the relationship of economic methodology and normative economic theory to international environmental law.

## International environmental law: history, principles, rules, and techniques

The relationship between environmental protection and international law has been transformed in recent years. International environmental issues are now a central concern of the UN, GATT, and other international

[7] *Great Britain* v. *United States*, 1 Moore's International Arbitration Awards 755 (1893).

institutions, and of all governments. Scientific and political concern about global and regional environmental issues is indicated by a sharp increase in the number of international agreements relating to the protection of the environment. At any given time negotiations are in progress for many different instruments in different fora, making it virtually impossible for all but the most highly resourced states to maintain effective, and consistent, negotiating positions.

Despite impressive achievements, there is reason to doubt the impact of this body of law on actual governmental and human behavior. Limited implementation and enforcement suggests that international environmental law remains in its formative stages. Lawmaking is decentralized, with legislative initiatives being developed in literally dozens of different intergovernmental organizations at the global, regional, and sub-regional level. Coordination between the various initiatives is inadequate, leading to measures which are often duplicative and sometimes even inconsistent. Moreover, the lawmaking process tends to be reactive and somewhat *ad hoc* in nature, often vulnerable to the vagaries of political, economic, and scientific events and findings.

This section summarizes international environmental law as it currently stands – the general principles, the basic rules, and the emerging legal techniques for their implementation and enforcement.[8] Although no single international legal instrument establishes binding rules or principles of global application, the pattern of state behavior has given rise to an emerging set of guiding principles and minimum standards of acceptable behavior in relation to particular environmental resources. These principles and standards are summarized in the following sections.

## PRINCIPLES OF GENERAL APPLICATION

To begin with, a number of general principles and rules of international environmental law have emerged, or are emerging.[9] These are reflected in

[8] For a more comprehensive treatment see A. Boyle and P. Birnie, *International Law and the Environment* (Oxford, 1992) and P. Sands, *Principles of International Environmental Law* (Manchester, 1995).

[9] On the distinction between "principles" and rules, see R. Dworkin: "principles and rules point to particular decisions about legal obligations in particular circumstances, but they differ in the character of the direction they give. Rules are applicable in an all-or-nothing fashion . . . [A principle] states a reason that argues in one direction, but does not necessitate a particular decision . . . All that is meant, when we say that a particular principle is

treaties, binding acts of international organizations, state practice, and soft law commitments. They are general in the sense that they are potentially applicable to all members of the international community across the range of activities which they carry out or allow.

### *Sovereignty over natural resources and the responsibility not to cause damage to the environment of other states or to areas beyond national jurisdiction*

The rules of international environmental law have developed in pursuit of two principles which pull in opposing directions: that states have sovereign rights over their natural resources, and that states must not cause damage to the environment.[10] These objectives are reflected in Principle 21 of the Stockholm Declaration and Principle 2 of the Rio Declaration and, as indicated above, have been endorsed by the International Court of Justice as forming "part of the corpus of international law relating to the environment [and] provide the foundation of international environmental law."[11]

The first element (sovereignty) reflects the pre-eminent position of states as primary members of the international legal community. It is, however, tempered by the second element (environmental protection), which places limits on the exercise of sovereign rights. Saying that Principle 21/Principle 2 reflects customary international law is not the critical issue however. Principle 21 and Principle 2 indicate the need to address other questions, including: What is environmental damage? What is the extent of environmental damage which is prohibited (any damage, or just damage which is serious or significant)? What is the standard of care applicable to the obligation (absolute, strict, or fault)? What are the consequences of a violation (including appropriate reparation)? And what is the extent of any liability (including measure of damages)? A further and pervasive question is the issue of risk: to what extent and in what circumstances does the obligation to prevent environmental damage extend to preventing a risk of such damage? In international environmental instruments this question is addressed by the precautionary principle. Its adequacy and its application are considered further below and in the following section.

a principle of our law, is that the principle is one which officials must take into account, if it is relevant, as a consideration inclining in one way or another," *Taking Rights Seriously* (Harvard University Press, 1977), 24, 26.

10 See Sands, *Principles*, at 186–94.

11 Note 2 above.

### *Good neighborliness and international cooperation*

The principle of "good neighborliness," as enunciated in Article 74 of the UN Charter for social, economic, and commercial matters, has been extended to environmental matters by the numerous international rules promoting international environmental cooperation.[12] It applies particularly where activities carried out in one state might have adverse effects on the environment of another state or in areas beyond national jurisdiction. In general terms, the obligation includes commitments to implement treaty objectives, or to improve relations outside specific treaty arrangements. In specific terms the obligation can require information-sharing, notification, consultation, or participation rights in certain decisions, the conducting of environmental impact assessments, and cooperative emergency procedures, particularly where activities might be ultrahazardous. The construction of nuclear power plants on borders is an example where cooperative obligations are particularly well developed.

### *Sustainable development*

This principle requires states to ensure that they develop and use their natural resources in a manner which is sustainable.[13] Although the ideas underlying the concept of "sustainable development" have a long history in international law, the term has only recently begun to be used in international agreements. What "sustainable development" means in practice remains unclear. Where it has been used it appears to refer to at least four separate but related objectives: First, it refers to a commitment to preserve natural resources for the benefit of present and future generations. Second, sustainable development refers to appropriate standards for the exploitation of natural resources based upon harvests or use (examples include use which is "sustainable," "prudent," or "rational," or "wise" or "appropriate"). Third, yet other agreements require an "equitable" use of natural resources, suggesting that the use by any state must take account of the needs of other states and people. And a fourth category of agreements require that environmental considerations be integrated into economic and other develop-

[12] Sands, *Principles*, 197–98.

[13] *Ibid.*, 198–208. Also P. Sands, "International Law in the Field of Sustainable Development," 1994 *British Ybk. Int. L.*, 303–81.

ment plans, programs, and projects, and that development needs are taken into account in applying environmental objectives.

### *Common but differentiated responsibility*

This principle has emerged from the application of the broader principle of equity in general international law, and from the recognition that the special needs of, *inter alia*, developing countries must be taken into account in the development, application, and interpretation of rules of international environmental law.[14] The principle is reflected in a handful of international environmental agreements and is applicable in the Climate Change Convention which requires Parties to protect the climate system "on the basis of equity and in accordance with their common but differentiated responsibilities and respective capabilities."[15] The principle contains two important elements. The first expresses the common responsibility of states to protect certain environmental resources. The second relates to the need to take account of differing circumstances, particularly in relation to each state's contribution to the creation of a particular environmental problem and its ability to respond to, prevent, reduce, and control the threat. In practical terms the application of the principle of common but differentiated responsibility has certain important consequences. It entitles, or possibly requires, all concerned states to participate in international response measures aimed at addressing environmental problems. And it leads to the adoption and implementation of environmental standards which impose different commitments for states.

### *Precautionary principle*

The precautionary principle emerged in international legal instruments in the mid-1980s, though it had previously been relied upon in some domestic legal systems.[16] It aims to provide guidance to states and the international community in the development of international environmental law and policy in the face of scientific uncertainty. Although potentially the most radical and far-reaching of environmental principles, its meaning and

[14] Sands, *Principles*, 217–20.

[15] *1992 UN Framework Convention on Climate Change*, 31 *I.L.M.* 849 (1992), Art. 3(1).

[16] Sands, *Principles*, 208–13.

effect are unclear and remain mired in controversy. Some of its supporters invoke it to justify pre-emptive international legal measures to address potentially catastrophic environmental threats such as ozone depletion or climate change. Opponents, on the other hand, have decried the principle for allowing overregulation of a range of human activities. The core of this emerging legal principle, which has now been endorsed in a number of agreements, is reflected in Principle 15 of the Rio Declaration, which provides, *inter alia*, that "[w]here there are threats of serious or irreversible damage, lack of full scientific certainty shall not be used as a reason for postponing cost-effective measures to prevent environmental degradation." Its application by the ICJ and WTO dispute settlement bodies is addressed below.

### *Polluter-pays principle*

The polluter-pays principle refers to the requirement that the costs of pollution be borne by the person or persons responsible for causing the pollution and the consequential costs.[17] It is of particular significance as an effort to apply an economic approach to environmental regulation with the goal of cost externalization. Its precise practical consequences, however, remain open to question, since international practice is limited. Nevertheless, it has attracted broad support, for example in Principle 14 of the Rio Declaration, OECD Council Recommendations, the EC Treaty and related instruments, and the 1992 Agreement establishing the European Economic Area.

## STANDARDS

Beyond these principles of general application, international standards have been adopted regionally and globally to address an ever-wider range of matters. These standards have generally been adopted through separate conventions to address the protection of particular resources. The most important resources have been flora and fauna, water quality, air quality, hazardous substances, and waste. The difficulty with an approach which regulates on a sector-by-sector basis is that it tends to transfer harm from one environmental medium to another, or to substitute one form of harm for another. Thus, the prohibition on the dumping of radioactive wastes at

[17] *Ibid.*, 213–17.

sea may result in harm to land-based resources resulting from long-term storage. Efforts to address this problem have led to the emergence of the concept of integrated pollution control, which requires states and other actors to consider and minimize the impact of activities on all environmental resources at each stage of the processes which contribute to that activity. Another difficulty is that the fragmentation of instruments and approaches inhibits the development of systemic, ecosystem-based approaches to resource conservation and sustainable use.

Within the various areas, the scope and specificity of international regulation is remarkably uneven. In relation to *flora and fauna*[18] – the subject of the earliest international standards – there are now widely accepted global rules which seek to protect or conserve wetlands, [19] trade in endangered species,[20] and the conservation of biodiversity generally.[21] Fisheries and forests remain subject to only the most limited global rules, and regional efforts at conservation remain patchy and often ineffective. Successful efforts at conservation remain the exception rather than the rule: notable examples include the 1982 decision by the International Whaling Commission to adopt a moratorium on commercial whaling, which has contributed to a recovery in stocks. International law to prevent pollution of *oceans and seas*[22] is relatively well developed at the global and regional levels. The 1982 UN Convention on the Law of the Sea, for example,[23] establishes a comprehensive framework to address marine pollution from various sources, and other global agreements limit or prohibit dumping of waste at sea.[24] However, no global agreement regulates pollution from land-based sources, which is particularly significant since this accounts for more than 70 percent of the total. Regional instruments are reasonably well developed, if not actually applied, particularly in relation to the UNEP Regional Seas Program.

As to *freshwater resources*,[25] many individual rivers and river systems are subject to special rules governing their use and the maintenance of the quality of their waters. Noteworthy examples include the Rhine in Europe,

[18] *Ibid.*, chapter 10.

[19] 1971 Convention on Wetlands of International Importance, Ramsar, 996 U.N.T.S. 245.

[20] 1973 Convention on International Trade in Endangered Species, 993 U.N.T.S. 243.

[21] 1992 Convention on Biological Diversity, 31 *I.L.M.* 822 (1992).

[22] Sands, *Principles*, chapter 8.

[23] 21 *I.L.M.* 1261 (1982).

[24] See Sands, *Principles*, 308–18.

[25] *Ibid.*, chapter 9.

the Zambezi in Africa, and the River Plate in South America, each of which has been subject to treaty protection for many years. In 1997 the United Nations adopted a global convention on the non-navigational uses of international watercourses, which establishes general obligations intended to prevent pollution or over-use. However, its provisions remain general and do not incorporate some of the more recent techniques relating to risk assessment or economic instruments.

International law for the protection of the *atmosphere*[26] is subject to increasing attention, with global rules now in place for ozone depletion and climate change. These two sets of rules do seek to apply non-traditional approaches, including rudimentary efforts at risk assessment and the use of economic approaches (see below). In Europe and North America, however, there are regional rules governing transboundary air pollution, for example sulfur dioxide and volatile organic compounds, but not elsewhere. As regards *waste management*,[27] international rules are limited to regulating or prohibiting trade in certain wastes and their disposal at sea or elsewhere. The management of hazardous substances other than waste, including chemicals and pesticides, is emerging as an important new area, with trade restrictions being used to encourage participation in the new rules and compliance.

## LEGAL TECHNIQUES

The different legal techniques used to implement environmental principles and standards at the regional and global level remain fairly rudimentary. Apart from the widespread reliance upon prohibitions and statutory regulations – typically referred to as "command and control" – there is growing support for and recourse to innovative techniques which have originally been developed at the national level.

For example, a growing number of regional or subject-specific agreements include provisions on *environmental impact assessment.*[28] Moreover, there is now recognition of the role of *environmental information techniques:*[29] improving the informational base upon which decisions are made, influencing the behavior of consumers and other actors, and ensuring full

26 *Ibid.*, chapter 7.
27 *Ibid.*, chapter 12.
28 *Ibid.*, chapter 15.
29 *Ibid.*, chapter 16.

participation of citizens in decisionmaking processes. A growing number of treaties impose *liability*[30] upon a state or, as is more frequently the case, directly on the private actor engaged in the activity which causes environmental harm (including civil liability rules at the national level). Finally, the limited effectiveness of traditional "command-and-control" regulatory approaches has given rise to a degree of support for increasing reliance upon *economic and fiscal measures*[31] to protect the environment. Recent agreements and other international acts, including the Rio Declaration, encourage the use of such measures and there are some signs that the growing interdependence of international economic and environmental law may provide a framework for their increased use. This aspect is considered in further detail below. In the meantime, environmental issues have progressively permeated regional and global trade and economic cooperation arrangements: the GATT, EC, and the North American Free Trade Agreement have each had to address the situation where one state unilaterally adopts environmental protection measures which have the effect of limiting or prohibiting trade. Further, an increasing number of agreements rely on trade prohibitions, both to encourage participation in the regime (by prohibiting trade in certain substances or goods with those outside the regime) and to promote compliance.[32]

The use of *financial resources*[33] provided by the public sector to encourage environmentally beneficial activities and projects has become an increasingly important topic in international environmental law. It entails two essential aspects: first, ensuring that the multilateral development and lending institutions incorporate environmental considerations into their activities; and second, ensuring the availability of international public sector funds to assist poorer countries in meeting the costs associated with increasingly stringent international environmental protection requirements. With regard to the former, all the multilateral development banks

30 *Ibid.*, chapter 17.

31 *Ibid.*, 130–4.

32 The 1987 Montreal Protocol and its 1990 Amendments (30 *I.L.M.* 537 (1991)), for example, use trade prohibitions and restrictions to limit production and consumption by non-parties, by prohibiting the import of controlled substances from any state which is not a party to the Protocol; providing for the eventual prohibition on the import from any non-party state of products containing controlled substances; and providing for the possible prohibition on the import from any non-party state of products produced with, but not containing, controlled substances.

33 Sands, *Principles*, chapter 19, at 727–42.

have recognized the need to address and integrate environmental concerns into their policymaking, and to varying degrees have adopted measures to achieve that objective. With regard to the latter, the most significant development in recent years has been the linkage made between the provision of financial resources by developed countries and the fulfillment of treaty commitments by developing countries. The 1990 Montreal Protocol amendment was the first agreement to make the fulfillment by developing countries of their obligations dependent upon the provision of finance by developed countries, and led to the establishment of a Multilateral Fund to meet certain incremental costs which arose under the Convention. This has now been followed by the adoption of similar arrangements under the Climate Change and Biodiversity Conventions and the establishment of the Global Environment Facility to provide grants or concessional loans to developing countries on an additional basis to enable them to implement programs that protect the global commons.

## CONCLUSIONS

The UNCED process, including the convention negotiations, presented significant challenges to international law and institutions. These arose from the large increase in the number of states participating in the negotiation processes, and from the broad range of interests which they brought to the negotiating table. Although the "Cold War" came to an end during preparations for UNCED, other conflicts emerged, largely between developed and amongst developing countries, but also amongst developed countries and amongst developing countries. These conflicts have revolved around the interplay between environmental measures, economic competition, and international trade and investment flows; the developing countries' insistence on their right to develop economically; and disagreements about how the burden of taking action to deal with common environmental concerns should be borne. Several broad conclusions can be drawn on the state of international environmental law.

The central role of international law and institutions in addressing these challenges and differences has been confirmed. At this point, there is no indication that the traditional approach to public international law is considered by states to be inadequate and in need of radical overhaul. Thus, although it has been suggested that the pursuit of "international law in the field of sustainable development" might lead to radical transformation in international relations,[34] the UNCED process indicated that States are not prepared to set in motion a radical transformation of the international legal order. International law in the field of sustainable development points to a body of principles and rules drawn from traditional approaches, evolutionary rather than revolutionary.

## Critical issues for international environmental law after UNCED

It is against this general background that one asks: What are the prospects for and challenges to international environmental law? In this part I address the six key issues which are cross-cutting and which formed the subject of much of the discussion at the La Pietra Symposium. These issues are: (1) risk assessment; (2) subsidiarity and federalism; (3) international institutional reform; (4) the role of non-state actors; (5) the relationship between and the integration of different subject matters in international law (especially by reference to trade and environment); and (6) enhancing compliance.

### RISK ASSESSMENT

In what circumstances is it necessary or appropriate for a law to be adopted or a decision taken under international law in order to respond to an actual or potential threat to an internationally valued environmental resource? The development of international law has been notoriously *ad hoc*: treaties and conventions are adopted on the basis of a range of socio-political, economic, and institutional considerations, of which environmental threat is but one among many.[35] Similar considerations apply to international decisions which need to be taken under treaties or other international laws: the establishment of an international scientific panel charged with the task of identifying on the basis of a broad consensus the need for future international environmental actions, such as the Intergovernmental Panel on Climate Change described by Sir John Houghton,[36] has been the exception rather than the rule.

Nevertheless, in recent years there has been more of a concerted effort to

[34] A. Kiss and S. Doumbe-Bille, "La Conférence des Nations Unies sur l'Environnement et le Développement," *Annuaire Français de Droit International* 823, at 841 (1992).

[35] See Sands, *Principles*, 136–37.

[36] See chapter 11.

ensure that international norms are developed and decisions taken on the basis of appropriate scientific information. Multilateral environmental agreements invariably exhort parties to take decisions on the basis of best available scientific information. A number of such agreements establish scientific bodies, for example to "provide timely information and advice on scientific and technological matters."[37] And, as mentioned above, the precautionary approach has emerged as a principle to assist in decisionmaking where serious environmental harm is threatened and where there exists scientific uncertainty. Nevertheless, recent developments indicate that there exists no *regle de base* for dealing with risk in the face of scientific uncertainty: each international body (or court) is left to develop its own practice on the basis of the rules which it is called upon to apply. Two recent examples serve to illustrate the difficulties that lie ahead. Both the International Court of Justice and the Appellate Body of the World Trade Organization have adopted decisions which throw some light on the circumstances in which a state (or regional economic integration organization such as the European Community) may be entitled to take preventive or precautionary measures to protect the environment or human health in the face of uncertainty.

In the case concerning the *Gabcíkovo–Nagymaros Project* the International Court had to determine whether Hungary was entitled unilaterally to suspend work on its part of a project to construct a barrage and hydroelectric generating station on the Danube in which it had been jointly engaged with Czechoslovakia.[38] Invoking the precautionary principle, Hungary argued that the project was likely to cause significant or irreversible damage to drinking water supplies and biodiversity over the long term, and that in those circumstances its unilateral suspension of the project was justified as "necessary" under the law of state responsibility. Slovakia considered that there was no scientific evidence to justify Hungary's assessment of the risk. The Court concluded that for Hungary to be able to justify its suspension of works in 1989 it had to satsify the requirements outlined in Draft Article 33 of the International Law Commission's 1980 Draft Articles on the International Responsibility of States.[39] These requirements

[37] 1992 Climate Change Convention, 31 *I.L.M.* 849 (1992), Art. 9 (establishing Subsidiary Body for Scientific and Technological Advice).

[38] *Case Concerning the Gabcíkovo–Nagymaros Project*, 25 September 1997, ICJ Reports 1997, 7.

[39] *Yearbook of the International Law Commission*, 1980, vol. II, Part 2, p. 34. The Draft Articles have not yet been adopted and are being revised by the ILC.

included that the suspension "must have been occasioned by an 'essential interest' of [Hungary]" and that "that interest must have been threatened by a 'grave and imminent peril.'"[40] The Court had no difficulty in concluding that "the concerns expressed by Hungary for its natural environment in the region affected by the Gabcíkovo–Nagymaros Project related to an 'essential interest' of that State";[41] obvious as this conclusion may now seem, this did constitute the first time an international tribunal had made such a pronouncement. However, the Court went on to conclude that Hungary had not proved that "a real, 'grave' and 'imminent' 'peril' existed in 1989 and that the measures taken by Hungary were the only possible response to it."[42] It is the Court's reasoning as to what constitutes a "real, 'grave' and 'imminent' 'peril'" that is of interest for present purposes.

The Court noted that the "verification of the existence, in 1989, of the 'peril' invoked by Hungary [and] of its 'grave and imminent' nature" were "complex processes," even in the context of the "'uncertainties' as to the ecological impact of putting in place the Gabcíkovo–Nagymaros barrage system" which Hungary had pointed to. The Court said:

> serious though these uncertainties might have been they could not, alone, establish the objective existence of a "peril" in the sense of a component element of a state of necessity. The word "peril" certainly evokes the idea of "risk"; that is precisely what distinguishes "peril" from material damage. But a state of necessity could not exist without a "peril" duly established at the relevant point in time; the mere apprehension of a possible "peril" could not suffice in that respect. It could moreover hardly be otherwise, when the "peril" constituting the state of necessity has at the same time to be "grave" and "imminent". "Imminence" is synonymous with "immediacy" or "proximity" and goes far beyond the concept of "possibility" . . . That does not exclude, in the view of the Court, that a "peril" appearing in the long term might be held to be "imminent" *as soon as it is established*, at the relevant point in time, *that the realization of that peril*, however far off it might be, *is not* thereby *any less certain and inevitable.*[43]

As to the Nagymaros (upstream) part of the Project, the Court concluded on the facts that "[t]he peril invoked by Hungary had . . . already materialized to a large extent for a number of years, so that it could not, in 1989,

[40] Judgment, para. 52.

[41] *Ibid.*, para. 53.

[42] *Ibid.*, para. 54.

[43] *Ibid.* (italics added).

represent a peril arising entirely out of the project."[44] As to the Gabcíkovo (downstream) part of the Project, the Court concluded that "[h]owever 'grave' it might have been, it would accordingly have been difficult, in the light of what is said above, to see the alleged peril as sufficiently certain and therefore 'imminent' in 1989."[45] Hungary's claim to invoke environmental necessity to justify its unilateral suspension of project work therefore failed.

The Court appears to be concluding that a state of environmental necessity can only be invoked under the general international law of state responsibility if there is a sufficient degree of certainty and inevitability that the peril *will* occur, that is to say that the fact that the peril will arise much later in time is not itself a bar. And the Court does not indicate what degree of certainty or inevitability will be "sufficient." It is notable, however, that the Court did not in express terms provide for the possibility that necessity could be invoked where any degree of uncertainty (or lack of inevitability) existed, and it pointedly did not refer at this stage to the precautionary principle as such, to which both Hungary and Slovakia had indicated their attachment (albeit with no agreement as to its meaning or effect). Of course when the International Law Commission prepared its Draft Articles in 1980 the precautionary principle (or approach) had not yet hit the international stage. By 1989 it was only emerging as an international principle. This may be why the Court, elsewhere in its judgment, was at pains to point out that what "might have been a correct application of the law in 1989 or 1992 could be a miscarriage of justice if prescribed in 1997"[46] and that new norms of environmental law had emerged and had to be taken into consideration in respect of old and new projects.[47] It cannot therefore be excluded that in some future case the

[44] *Ibid.*, para. 55; the Court also concluded that Hungary had means available to it, other than the suspension and abandonment of the works, to respond to any peril.

[45] *Ibid.*, para. 56. This conclusion was said to have been reached on the basis of the material made available to it by the parties. Rather curiously, however, the Court had earlier said that: "Both Parties have placed on record an impressive amount of scientific material aimed at reinforcing their respective arguments. The Court has given most careful attention to this material, in which the Parties have developed their opposing views as to the ecological consequences of the Project. It concludes, however, that, as will be shown below, it is not necessary in order to respond to the questions put to it in the Special Agreement for it to determine which of those points of view is scientifically better founded": *ibid.*, para. 54.

[46] *Ibid.*, para. 134.

[47] *Ibid.*, para. 140; the Court said: "Owing to new scientific insights and to a growing awareness of the risks for mankind – for present and future generations – of pursuit of such interventions at an unconsidered and unabated pace, new norms and standards have been

Court (or another international tribunal) would read into the ILC's Draft Articles (or the Articles as they may soon be adopted) scope for precautionary action in the face of scientific uncertainty where the potential environmental risks over the short or long term are substantial. In the meantime, however, it would appear that the general rule in international law (to the extent at least that it is reflected in the law of state responsibility) as at 1989 was that any degree of uncertainty precluded decisive preventive action of the type taken by Hungary. There was, in other words, little scope for arguments based upon risk assessment where such assessment indicates uncertainty. It is important to note that here the issue is presented in the context of an asserted breach of a clear treaty obligation, which may invite a more restrictive approach than would be followed in other contexts, for example where the required conduct arises under a more general international obligation.

In contrast to the approach of the International Court one may consider the practice of the Appellate Body of the World Trade Organization in the Beef Hormones case.[48] Here the Appellate Body was faced with the application of a rule of risk assessment adopted in the specific context of WTO law. The United States had challenged a unilateral ban imposed by the European Community on the importation of American beef produced with the use of artificial hormones. The European Community considered that the beef constituted a threat to the health of European citizens and the environment; the United States countered that the European Community had no adequate scientific basis upon which to reach that conclusion, since it had failed to carry out the risk assessment required by Articles 5.1 and 5.2 of the SPS Agreement.[49] In interpreting Article 5.1 the WTO Appellate

developed, set forth in a great number of instruments during the last two decades. Such new norms have to be taken into consideration, and such new standards given proper weight, not only when States contemplate new activities but also when continuing with activities begun in the past."

[48] EC Measures Concerning Meat and Meat Products (Hormones), report of 16 January 1998, AB–1997–4, WT/DS 26/AB/R ("Report").

[49] Article 5.1 of the SPS Agreement provides: "Members shall ensure that their sanitary or phytosanitary measures are based on an assessment, as appropriate to the circumstances, of the risks to human, animal or plant life or health, taking into account risk assessment techniques developed by the relevant international organizations."

Article 5.2 of the SPS Agreement provides: "In the assessment of risks, Members shall take into account available scientific evidence; relevant processes and production methods; relevant inspection, sampling and testing methods; prevalence of specific diseases or pests; existence of pest- or disease-free areas; relevant ecological and environmental conditions; and quarantine or other treatment."

Body concluded that it "does not insist that a Member that adopts a sanitary measure shall have carried out its own risk assessment. It only requires that the SPS measures be 'based on an assessment, as appropriate for the circumstances.'"[50] The Appellate Body found that Article 5.1 "requires that the results of the risk assessment must sufficiently warrant – that is to say, reasonably support – the SPS measure at stake. The requirement that an SPS measure be 'based on' a risk assessment is a substantive requirement that there be a rational relationship between the measure and the risk assessment."[51] Significantly, the Appellate Body went on to state:

> We do not believe that a risk assessment has to come to a monolithic conclusion that coincides with the scientific conclusion or view implicit in the SPS measure. The risk assessment could set out both the prevailing view representing the "mainstream" of scientific opinion, as well as the opinions of scientists taking a divergent view. Article 5.1 does not require that the risk assessment must necessarily embody only the view of a majority of the relevant scientific community. In some cases, the very existence of divergent views presented by qualified scientists who have investigated the particular issue at hand may indicate a state of scientific uncertainty. Sometimes the divergence may indicate a roughly equal balance of scientific opinion, which may itself be a form of scientific uncertainty. In most cases, responsible and representative governments tend to base their legislative and administrative measures on "mainstream" scientific opinion. In other cases, equally responsible and representative governments may act in good faith on the basis of what, at a given time, may be a divergent opinion coming from qualified and respected sources. By itself, this does not necessarily signal the absence of a reasonable relationship between the SPS measure and the risk assessment, especially where the risk involved is life-threatening in character and is perceived to constitute a clear and imminent threat to public health and safety. Determination of the presence or absence of that relationship can only be done on a case-to-case basis, after account is taken of all considerations rationally bearing upon the issue of potential adverse health effects.[52]

On the basis of the documentation made available to the panel the Appellate Body concluded that no risk assessment that reasonably supported or warranted the import prohibition embodied in the EC Directives had been provided to the panel.[53] Accordingly the Appellate Body confirmed the panel's conclusion that the EC import prohibition was not based

[50] Report, para. 190

[51] Report, para. 193.

[52] Report, para. 194.

[53] Report, para. 208.

on a risk assessment within the meaning of Articles 5.1 and 5.2 of the *SPS Agreement* and was therefore inconsistent with the requirements of Article 5.1. Nevertheless, and unlike the International Court, the Appellate Body appears to have recognized the possibility that a WTO Member may unilaterally prohibit the importation of a product on sanitary and phytosanitary grounds even where there is a degree of uncertainty as to whether the product would be harmful to human health: "we do not believe that a risk assessment has to come to a monolithic conclusion that coincides with the scientific conclusion or view implicit in the SPS measure." What is required is that the risk assessment must "reasonably support or warrant" the import prohibition. And the Appellate Body's approach does not exclude the possibility that a risk assessment could be relied upon even if it indicated a degree of uncertainty.

The decisions of these two international bodies indicate the absence of a common approach to the issue of risk assessment, although the different treaty contexts in which the two issues arise are of course significant. One might well ask: is it appropriate that the international community should have one rule of risk assessment in relation to the environmental and human health risks associated with the construction of a large barrage, and another rule of risk assessment in relation to the potential threats posed to the environment and human health by the production of beef using artificial hormones? It may be that the answer to that question is yes, but if so such an answer ought to be justified on the basis of some coherent approach to decisionmaking in the context of uncertainty, rather than the vagaries determining the forum (and applicable law) in which an issue arises or the rules which that body then applies. The fragmented nature of international environmental law will only be reinforced by developments such as these.

## SUBSIDIARITY AND FEDERALISM: THE PROPER LEVEL FOR LAWMAKING AND DECISION-TAKING

A second issue which arises is this: at what level of decisionmaking is it most appropriate for international environmental norms to be set? This is a question addressed by Professor Revesz in chapter 1. For the international lawyer this means asking oneself when an international (as opposed to a national) rule will be justified, and where it is justified whether the rule should be adopted at a bilateral, regional, or global level. The kind of analytical framework proposed by Revesz has barely been addressed in relation to international conventional instruments; the differences which he identifies between the United States and the European Union are even greater in relation to global arrangements.[54]

There is as yet no generalized rule of international law or guideline which indicates the circumstances in which an international environmental convention should be adopted or a normative decision taken. There is in international environmental law no equivalent to Article 3b of the Treaty establishing the European Community (as amended by the Treaty on European Union), which provides that "the Community shall take action, in accordance with the principle of subsidiarity, only if and so far as the objectives of the proposed action cannot be sufficiently achieved by the member States and can therefore, by reason of the scale or effects of the proposed action, be better achieved by the Community."[55] The development of international environmental law, principally by treaty-making at the three levels (bilateral, regional, global), has tended to react to events or incidents or the availability of scientific evidence, rather than anticipate general or particular environmental threats and put in place an anticipatory legal framework.[56] It can hardly be said that the *acquis* of international environmental law reflects the results of any sort of prior determination by the international community (or parts of it) of the environmental and related objectives of proposed action by reference to its intended scale or effects. The closest the international community has now come is in Principle 11 of the Rio Declaration on Environment and Development: "States shall enact effective environmental legislation. Environmental standards, management objectives and priorities should reflect the environment and developmental context to which they apply. Standards applied by some countries may be inappropriate and of unwarranted economic and social cost to other countries, in particular developing countries." These themes are broadly taken up in Agenda 21, which commits the international community to setting "priorities for future law-making on sustainable development at the global, regional or sub-regional level" by taking into account the need to enhance the efficacy of international law, particularly by inte-

[54] See chapter 1, at pp. 69–73.

[55] It will be recalled that this provision finds its origins in the 1986 amendments to the Treaty establishing the European Economic Community, at which time the principle of subsidiarity was limited only to the environmental field: see old Article 130r of the EEC Treaty.

[56] See Sands, *Principles*, 25–6.

grating environment and development, and ensuring that new laws and international standards must take into account the different situations and capabilities of countries.[57] As discussed in the first part of this chapter, over the past three decades global rules have been adopted in relation to a broad range of different subject matters. Originally focusing on flora and fauna and cultural heritage, it is only more recently that attention has turned to environmental issues with a clear and direct transboundary impact. In particular, ozone depletion and climate change have recently been the subject of global rules, recognizing that the source of emissions of substances that deplete the ozone layer is of no ecological relevance in the context of the global resource to be protected (although it will be relevant in a socio-economic and political sense). Clearly there are other areas in which inter-connections between different regions require a globalized approach: oceans and other atmospheric issues are examples. In other areas, however, resources may have only a bilateral or regional connection: a case in point would be watercourses, and in this context one is bound to wonder whether a recently adopted global convention is likely to attract sufficient adherence to come into force.[58] Even if the 1997 Convention does come into force, its substantive provisions are so general – and open to creative interpretation and application – that one is bound to ask whether they can have any real impacts upon the environment or utilization of a shared resource. The procedural rules – for example to consult – are much firmer, of course.

Another area which has been the subject of global attention is biodiversity conservation, even if damage to resources in one area does not necessarily have immediate impacts on other areas. The 1992 Biodiversity Convention has now been used as a vehicle to address the global regulation of biotechnology, a technological development which apparently does have implications of potentially global concern and which requires global attention. In general, then, it might be said that in practice international efforts at environmental protection more or less adopt the approach within the European Community context, namely that where the scale or effects of proposed measures cannot be achieved at the national or regional level alone, then global action is required. However, as in the European Community a range of policy considerations meld to determine whether to adopt environmental

[57] Agenda 21, Report of the UN Conference on Environment and Development, A/CONF.151/26/Rev.1 (vol. I), para. 39.2(b) and (d).

[58] See 1997 UN Convention on Non-navigational Uses of International Watercourses, 36 *I.L.M.* 700 (1997).

legislation at a centralized (international) or decentralized (national) level. In this regard, it is fanciful to suggest that economic considerations play any real role in political decisionmaking as to *whether* an international instruments needs to be adopted, or whether national legislation alone can be sufficient. Accordingly, the type of analysis proposed by Professor van den Bergh, premised on the belief that "economic theory teaches that decentralization is the first-best solution,"[59] misses the point of much international legislation, namely that it is as much about consciousness-raising and process developments as it is about achieving short- or medium-term substantive outcomes.

International policy and practice reflect a presumption against international rules unless it can be shown that international environmental objectives can best (or perhaps only) be served by an international rule, or unless economic (competitiveness) arguments militate in favor of an economically more level playing field. Nevertheless, for the reasons indicated by Professor Ferejohn in relation to developments favoring centralization at the national level, a range of societal objectives – including those of a non-economic nature – are increasingly in favor of pushing environmental regulation to the international level.[60] But even after that has been determined, the development of the new international environmental rule must take into account the needs of different countries and communities, integrating other social and economic concerns into the lawmaking process. These factors point to a system of international norms premised upon differentiated standards, in which the conventional rules might establish an environmental floor below which designated countries may not fall, but above which they may rise (subject to the consequences of other rules of international law, for example in the trade field). To the extent that harmonization of environmental norms is a goal, therefore, it is limited by the ability to accommodate differences between countries with different values (particularly as to the importance of environmental protection, including the extent to which it might limit or alter development paths), ecological and geographical conditions, economic capacities, and historic contributions to the problems that are being addressed. It is most unlikely that standards could be the same. Developmental needs mean that they will almost certainly not be the same.

The area in which differentiated standards will arise most directly is in

[59] See chapter 2, p. 94.
[60] See chapter 3, p. 103.

the international trade field. WTO bodies are now grappling with the question of when a state may unilaterally apply its own more stringent environmental standards (1) to prevent the import of goods which do not meet those standards and (2) to activities carried on in areas outside its jurisdiction. The distinction between these two situations reflects the distinction between regulation of products on the one hand, and regulation of processes on the other. It is evident that a state will have an interest in limiting the introduction of products which it considers are likely to cause harm to health or the environment within its own territory. A state may have a different interest where it is concerned with the impact on the environment of a *process*, since that process is not necessarily likely to harm its own environment, but may offend against its values or indirectly cause harm to its environment or damage the health of its population. Of course, developments in our understanding of impacts are indicating that environmental spillovers can less and less be limited to a particular region or territory. In this regard, there is a growing temptation to permit states to extend their powers of regulation, whether prescriptive or enforcement, to activities relating to processes outside their territory. But even where the effort is to regulate the introduction of a particular product – as for example in the case of beef hormones – it can be seen that it is notoriously difficult to reach agreement between different communities as to the appropriate standards to be applied in seeking to protect human health and the environment, and even the methodology of risk assessment to be carried out. Surely the principal concern of the international community is to accommodate, as best it can, competing interests, and avoid the imposition by one community of its value system on another. Ultimately this means that international law, whether of an environmental or trade character, must establish minimum standards. In this regard the recent decision of the WTO Appellate Body in the Shrimp–Turtle case is of prime importance.[61]

The US had prohibited the importation of shrimp from certain Asian countries on the grounds that the shrimp were being harvested in a manner which threatened sea turtles, which were internationally recognized as an endangered species, and which did not meet the standards applied domestically by the United States to its shrimp producers. The WTO Appellate Body ruled that the sea turtles at issue "constitute 'exhaustible natural resources' for purposes of Article XX(g) of the GATT 1994," that the US

[61] United States – Import Prohibition of Certain Shrimp and Shrimp Products, AB–1998–4, WT/DS58/AB/R, 12 October 1998.

measure was "a measure 'relating to' the conservation of an exhaustible natural resource within the meaning of Article XX(g) of the GATT 1994," and that the US measure was "a measure made effective in conjunction with the restrictions on domestic harvesting of shrimp, as required by Article XX(g)."[62] Accordingly the US measures were "provisionally justified" under Article XX(g) of GATT 1994.[63] Of great significance here is the fact that the Appellate Body recognized the legitimacy of one state (the United States) acting to conserve resources located outside its territory, even in the territory of a third state:

> The sea turtle species here at stake, i.e., covered by Section 609, are all known to occur in waters over which the United States exercises jurisdiction. Of course, it is not claimed that *all* populations of these species migrate to, or traverse, at one time or another, waters subject to United States jurisdiction. Neither the appellant nor any of the appellees claims any rights of exclusive ownership over the sea turtles, at least not while they are swimming freely in their natural habitat – the oceans. We do not pass upon the question of whether there is an implied jurisdictional limitation in Article XX(g), and if so, the nature or extent of that limitation. We note only that in the specific circumstances of the case before us, there is a sufficient nexus between the migratory and endangered marine populations involved and the United States for purposes of Article XX(g).[64]

This is more than a nod towards unilateralism. However, the US measures were found to be inconsistent with the chapeau of Article XX and did not qualify for exemption thereunder: they had been "applied in a manner that constitute[d] a means of arbitrary or unjustifiable discrimination between countries where the same conditions prevail or a disguised restriction on international trade."[65] Specifically, the US measures had treated similar

[62] *Ibid.*, paras. 134, 142, 145. Article XX of the GATT 1994 (entitled General Exceptions) provides, in relevant part:

> "Subject to the requirement that such measures are not applied in a manner which would constitute a means of arbitrary or unjustifiable discrimination between countries where the same conditions prevail, or a disguised restriction on international trade, nothing in this Agreement shall be construed to prevent the adoption or enforcement by any contracting party of measures: . . .
>
> (b) necessary to protect human, animal or plant life or health; . . .
>
> (g) relating to the conservation of exhaustible natural resources if such measures are made effective in conjunction with restrictions on domestic production or consumption.

[63] *Ibid.*, para. 147.

[64] *Ibid.*, para. 133 (footnote omitted).

[65] *Ibid.*, para. 186.

countries in a discriminatory manner and "*without* taking into consideration different conditions which may occur in the territories of those other Members."[66] Moreover, the US had failed "to engage the appellees, as well as other Members exporting shrimp to the United States, in serious, across-the-board negotiations with the objective of concluding bilateral or multilateral agreements for the protection and conservation of sea turtles, before enforcing the import prohibition against the shrimp exports of those other Members."[67] This last point indicates the conditions under which unilateralism might be permitted, establishing the requirement that previous efforts be made to achieve the environmental objectives by agreement.

This then raises the question of whether such an agreement is more properly concluded at the regional or global level. As environmental issues are increasingly seen to have global consequences there has been a real (as well as relative) increase in the number of global instruments (admittedly from a low starting point). This has occurred in particular where there has existed a sufficient consensus on scientific data, on national interests, and on the need for a global approach. The agreements on ozone, climate change, and biodiversity have been supported by a balance of developed and developing countries from the various regions. In other sectors, however, the global approach has failed, as illustrated by the failed efforts of the OECD countries to push their agenda for a global forest convention. In that case the necessary consensus did not exist, either on the environmental need for such an instrument or the basic principles upon which it might be elaborated. The developing countries essentially took the view that the developed countries should put their own houses (forests) in order before calling on developing countries to address the issue.

It has also been suggested that global conventions reduce the scope and extent of environmental and economic commitments which might be achieved, as states compromise in an effort to achieve universality of participation amongst 180 or more states. This is the case, for example, in relation to the Biodiversity Convention, which at the final hurdle failed to adopt a list of endangered or specially protected species as a large number of countries had wanted. Regional agreements may, therefore, be more appropriate where countries in a region require particular action or measures, or where the history of a group of countries suggests that they will need to adopt their

[66] *Ibid.*, para. 164 (italics added).
[67] *Ibid.*, para. 166.

own measures before calling on the rest of the world to join in. Moreover, regional agreements will only be possible, for example, in relation to forest protection where no global consensus exists on the need for action.

## INTERNATIONAL INSTITUTIONAL REFORM, INCLUDING LAWMAKING PROCESSES

Even where the international community has determined that environmental and scientific considerations require international action, and that a regional or global convention or other decision is required, the forum within which the legislative initiative is to be taken has to be decided. It is now apparent that the international apparatus for the making of international environmental law is in need of complete overhaul. Beyond improvements in risk assessment policy and the refinement of an internationalized subsidiarity principle, one of the primary means for enhancing international environmental law is institutional reform. This is needed to avoid duplication in lawmaking, to assist in filling the many gaps in the existing law, to improve participation (in particular of developing countries), and to achieve a proper balance and relationship between regional and global initiatives. Three observations can be made.

First, it is clear to all involved in the field that the world finds itself with a fragmented institutional structure which is ill-equipped to meet future environmental needs. There has been at once an over-proliferation of institutions (in the form of a multiplicity of treaty-based secretariats) and an absence of an appropriately effective and sufficiently financed central institution. There are literally dozens of multilateral environmental agreements, each with their own secretariat and approaches. Often these bodies will not connect in a systematic way, and rules may pull in opposite directions. Does it make sense for there to be separate secretariats dealing with trade in endangered species, biodiversity, migratory species, and wetlands? Would it not make more sense for these secretariats to be integrated into a single body with overarching competence and particular jurisdiction in relation to parties to particular agreements? UNCED made something of a start by identifying problems, but has failed to take any of the decisions necessary to put in place an effective institutional infrastructure. No developments since UNCED have improved the situation, with the consequence that other organizations – the World Bank and the WTO, for example – make the running on aspects of international environmental policy. To the extent that these issues are part of a generic problem of international law and institutions, the fiftieth anniversary efforts of the United Nations in 1995 provided an opportunity to put in effect real reforms. That opportunity has been missed.

Second, environmental considerations have shifted from being issues addressed exclusively by a small or limited number of international organizations with specialized environmental objectives. It is now clear that the environment is a matter of concern for virtually all the organizations established in the period after the Second World War to address matters of international security and economic well-being, as well as the newer institutions. Environmental issues now have a central role at the main economic institutions, such as the WTO and the World Bank, as well as in the UN system more generally. In this way, environmental concerns have increasingly become integrated into the mainstream international legal order. However, that integration has led to overlapping jurisdictions, turf wars, and a fragmented and decentralized structure which hardly promotes efficient decisionmaking or law development and enforcement. In consequence, the general principles and rules often fall to be determined by adjudicatory bodies charged with identifying norms of general application and then applying them.

A third factor for change – addressed in the following section – is that non-state actors, including environmental organizations and corporations, have become central players in the international legal process relating to environmental issues.

These observations combine around a central focal theme: international environmental concerns are forcing important structural changes in the traditional institutional arrangements of the international legal order. Most international organizations are being asked to deal with issues which did not exist when they were established, and to recognize that environmental considerations transcend the sectoral and fragmented institutional structure born of the 1940s and 1950s. The United Nations Charter, adopted in 1945, makes no mention of the environment. When the World Bank was created it could hardly be imagined that the organization would be called upon to integrate environmental factors into the design and implementation of its activities. Moreover, as discussed below, although they continue to play a central role, states are increasingly acting in partnership with new actors in the processes associated with developing and applying principles and rules of international law, including international organizations and a wide range of different non-governmental actors.

A number of reforms are needed to address these issues (all dependent upon requisite political will). First, there is a need for a lead institution to identify key environmental needs and push the environmental agenda. UNEP should be strengthened and upgraded to full UN agency status to meet this task, or it should be abolished altogether. Its current half-way position in which it is underresourced (and located in Nairobi) means that it is ill-equipped to carry out the tasks with which it has been entrusted to play the sort of leadership role the 1972 Stockholm Conference envisaged. Second, the performance of the Commission on Sustainable Development (CSD) needs to be critically examined, and if found to be wanting measures should be taken to institute effective reform or abolish the body altogether. The CSD was created in 1992 at the UN Conference on Environment and Development, to follow up on the Conference and to "enhance cooperation and rationalise the inter-governmental capacity for the integration of environment and development and to examine progress in the implementation of Agenda 21 at the national, regional and international levels."[68] It meets annually at the UN in New York, and is assisted by a secretariat. Thus far the CSD has been little more than a talking shop which has made little, if any, real contribution to the development of the environmental agenda or to the integration of environment and development. Whilst it may have contributed to consciousness-raising generally, the international community is well past that stage and needs action. To the extent that action is reflected in the development or application of law, the CSD's contribution has been virtually non-existent, notwithstanding the commitment of its secretariat. Third, there is an urgent need for rationalization of the institutions (conferences of the parties, secretariats, etc.) established under the hundreds of international environmental agreements. It is an absurdity on substantive environmental (and economic) grounds for each treaty to have its own institutions. One could easily envisage the secretariats of, say, the Biodiversity Convention and CITES, or the Climate Change and Ozone Conventions, being merged. Expertise would be shared, costs minimized – it is difficult to see what the downside would be (save for the disappearance of a large number of political/bureaucratic fiefdoms). Similarly, treaty institutions existing at the global level should be brought into a closer relationship with those at the regional level. This is especially the case for the marine environment, where UNEP-sponsored regional institutions exist

[68] Agenda 21, para. 38.11.

outside the new Law of the Sea institutions and frequently duplicate functions. For example, other than the global obligations under the 1972 London Convention, the dumping of wastes at sea is regulated by at least six regional agreements which adopt different, and in some instances inconsistent, requirements.[69]

Beyond the need for institutional reform, there is also a pressing need to rethink lawmaking in areas where knowledge and needs are fast-moving. It has also become readily apparent that traditional international lawmaking procedures are ill-equipped to deal with environmental issues. These frequently require a global and rapid response. General principles and obligations provide no solution to issues which require detailed technical standards, as efforts to address ozone depletion, climate change, and marine pollution from land-based sources have demonstrated. Treaties take time to be negotiated and do not enter into force until they have been ratified and, frequently, became subject to national implementing measures. These limitations become all the more significant in the face of global environmental issues requiring a global response from 180 or more states. The evolution of customary norms will be even slower. Moreover, by its nature custom cannot provide the specificity needed to address complex issues.

In this context it is inevitable that environmental norms will increasingly be adopted through acts of international organizations, including decisions of the conferences of the parties to international environmental agreements. The attraction of this approach is that it allows new rules or technical standards to be adopted on the basis of a majority of states party to a treaty, in which those opposing have the opportunity (in most but not all cases) positively to opt out of the new obligations. This approach is tried and tested in relation to ozone depletion and the marine environment.[70] Coupled with institutional reforms outlined above, it would streamline lawmaking, and allow for a more integrated, inter-sectoral approach to lawmaking.

The disadvantage to the approach, at least from the perspective of states if not the environment, is that it calls for a transfer of sovereignty to the international community. Increased use of this approach would mean that

[69] See Sands, *Principles*, 308–17.

[70] See, for example, the procedure for adopting Adjustments to the 1987 Montreal Protocol: Sands, *Principles*, 116; and the adoption under the 1972 London Convention of a moratorium on the disposal at sea of radioactive waste: *ibid.*, 116 and 312–13.

participation in an international agreement would expose states to majority decisionmaking. Provided that states retain the ability to opt out in specified circumstances – as indicated above in relation to the moratorium on disposal at sea of radioactive wastes, or in relation to whaling[71] – the risks should be acceptable.

## THE ROLE OF NON-STATE ACTORS

The contribution of non-state actors is now felt at each level of the legal process and constitutional structure: in the development of legislation as well as its implementation and enforcement. A proper and more formalized arrangement for their participation needs to be developed. This has become an issue before a number of fora. At the WTO, environmental groups have sought to persuade Dispute Settlement Panels to allow them to file *amicus* briefs in the absence of rules to that effect. Even in the rather closed and traditionally intergovernmental system of the WTO there appears to be some movement. In October 1998 the Appellate Body overturned a ruling by a WTO panel that "accepting non-requested information from non-governmental sources is incompatible with the [WTO Dispute Settlement Understanding],"[72] thereby opening up the possibility for the filing of such briefs. Political commitment for this new approach is now evident at the highest levels. In June 1998 President Clinton had called for the WTO to open its doors to the scrutiny and participation of the public. He proposed that "all hearings by the WTO be open to the public, and all briefs by the parties be made publicly available" and, noting that there was no mechanism for private citizens to provide input into WTO trade disputes, he called for the WTO to "provide the opportunity for stakeholders to convey their views, such as the ability to file 'amicus briefs', to help inform the panels in their deliberations."[73]

As part of the process of reform, it is apparent that the progressive development of international environmental law will require the fuller participation of all states in international lawmaking and an enhanced participation of the new actors (NGOs, corporations, etc.). UNCED reflected a broad acceptance of this need. For states, the critical issue will be to ensure the full

[71] *Ibid.*, 116.

[72] United States – Import Prohibition of Certain Shrimp and Shrimp Products, at para. 110.

[73] Statement of President Clinton on the occasion of the fiftieth anniversary of the GATT/WTO, 18 May 1998, *http://www.wto.org/wto/anniv/clinton.htm.*

and effective participation of developing countries in legal initiatives, especially at the regional and global level. The Climate Change and Biodiversity negotiations illustrated the tremendous human and financial strains imposed by complex international negotiations, and it will be critical to the successful implementation of these and other agreements that developing countries are provided with means to participate fully and effectively. This will mean enhanced training and development of necessary skills, including international legal expertise, appropriate structuring and scheduling of negotiations, and the provision of financial resources to allow for participation in international lawmaking efforts. The important role played by international organizations and NGOs in the lawmaking process is reflected by their extensive participation in recent negotiations (particularly climate change and ozone), by the extent to which they have, in their observer capacity, been able to influence text, and by their ability to introduce into the international legislative process non-state views. That participation needs to be formalized, encouraged and enhanced in each aspect of the international legal process to ensure that intergovernmental activities are broadly supported by those they are most likely to affect.

## THE RELATIONSHIP BETWEEN AND THE INTEGRATION OF DIFFERENT SUBJECT MATTERS IN INTERNATIONAL LAW

Until relatively recently environmental protection has been a subject lying on the periphery of international law. As international environmental regulation has increasingly placed limits on the permissibility of certain activities and touched upon vital economic interests, more attention has been placed on the need to ensure greater integration of environmental considerations in mainstream policy- and lawmaking. As indicated above, this was one of the great themes of UNCED, and is reflected in particular in Principle 4 of the Rio Declaration.[74] Similarly, the 1992 amendments introduced into the EC Treaty by the Maastricht Treaty on European Union require that environmental protection requirements be "integrated into the definition and implementation of other Community policies" (amended Article 130r(2)).

[74] Principle 4 provides: "In order to achieve sustainable development, environmental protection shall constitute an integral part of the development process and cannot be considered in isolation from it."

An integrated approach to environment and development has important consequences, most notably that environmental considerations will increasingly become a feature of economic policy, and vice versa. This is necessary if environmental regulations are to be effective: whether one likes it or not, economic discourse remains a primary motivating force in the development of international law and policy. Steady changes have taken place since the mid-1980s which suggest that economic concerns are increasingly being subjected to environmental integration. Important milestones since the mid-1980s include the amendment of the 1957 EEC Treaty to include a Title on the Environment; the establishment of an Environment Department at the World Bank and its implementation of formal environmental impact requirements; the convergence of trade with environment at the GATT; the elaboration of language on sustainable development in the Articles of Agreement of the EBRD;[75] and the development of national and international case law in areas such as competition, subsidy, and intellectual property law.[76]

These piecemeal developments need to be subjected to a more coherent approach to the integration of environmental considerations. The true battleground for the future of international environmental law is likely to be in the fields of trade, financial resources, and intellectual property. How is integration to be achieved where international law traditionally provides for different treaties to address different subject matters?

Article 30 of the 1969 Vienna Convention on the Law of Treaties establishes basic rules to determine which treaty obligation is to apply where two or more treaties are adopted at different times but have an overlapping subject matter and are in conflict.[77] This is a rule of application which imposes hierarchy. By way of example, in the case of a conflict between a treaty obligation establishing a prohibition on restrictions on trade (the 1994 GATT/WTO) and a treaty obligation establishing certain restrictions on trade (for example restrictions on trade in hazardous wastes established

[75] Article 2(1)(vii) of the Articles of Agreement of the EBRD states that one of the functions of the Bank is "to promote in the full range of its activities environmentally sound and sustainable development": 29 *I.L.M.* 1077 (1991).

[76] See Sands, *Principles*, chapter 18.

[77] Assuming that two agreements do address the same subject matter, and the parties to the earlier treaty are also parties to the later treaty, then only those provisions of the earlier treaty which are compatible with the later treaty will apply (Art. 30(3) and (4)(a)). But where one state is not a party to the later treaty, then it is the earlier treaty which will govern their relations (Art. 30(4)(b)).

by the 1989 Basle Convention on Transboundary Movement of Hazardous Wastes), then, as between parties to both, the latter – the 1989 Convention – will prevail. But where both are party to the former and only one is party to the latter then the former will apply, as a matter of treaty law. Of course the Vienna Convention does not define the words "same subject matter", which presumably will be left to the parties to a dispute to fight over. But, taking the Beef Hormones case, a treaty obligation to apply the precautionary principle (for example under a new Protocol on Biosafety) would clearly relate to the same subject matter – risk assessment – as Article 5.1 of the SPS Agreement and if later in time and binding *qua* treaty law could override Article 5.1 of the SPS Agreement. Presumably where two treaty rules do not address the same subject matter no dispute is likely to arise as to which prevails.

There is no equivalent rule governing the relationship between different norms of customary (as opposed to treaty) law, although in practice conflict is less likely to arise. In these circumstances the "later in time" rule would generally apply. Even less straightforward is the relationship between a treaty obligation and an obligation arising under customary law relating to the same subject matter: for example, what is the relationship between Article XX(b) and (g) of GATT 1994 and customary rules of international environmental law? Specifically, are the former to be construed and applied in accordance with the precautionary principle as a customary obligation which has arisen later in time? The Vienna Convention includes no rule of *application* to govern this relationship. Rather, this is to be dealt with as a matter of *interpretation* under Articles 31 and 32 of the Vienna Convention.[78] Of particular relevance is Article 31(3), which provides that in the process of interpretation there shall be taken into account, together with the context, subsequent agreement regarding interpretation, subsequent practice, and – in its paragraph (c) – "any relevant rules of international law applicable in the relations between the parties." Article 31(3)(c) reflects a "principle of integration,"[79]

[78] Article 31(1) provides that a treaty is to be interpreted "in good faith in accordance with the ordinary meaning to be given to [its] terms . . . in their context and in the light of its object and purpose." Article 31(2) provides guidance as to contextual material. Article 32 provides for recourse to supplementary means of interpretation.

[79] Cf. Judge Weeramantry in his Separate Opinion in the *Gabcíkovo–Nagymaros Project* case, noting that the capacity of Article 31(3)(c) to address relations between treaty and custom "scarcely covers this aspect with the degree of clarity requisite to so important a matter": ICJ Reports 1997, at 114.

emphasizing the "unity of international law" and the sense in which rules should not be considered in isolation from general international law.[80] Article 31(3)(c) appears to be the only available instrument of international law for achieving an integrated approach to competing norms. It is therefore of great potential significance in contributing to "sustainable development." How it works in practice is very much an open question, since it appears to have been expressly relied upon only very occasionally in judicial practice, and has attracted little academic comment.

There appears to be a general reluctance to refer to Article 31(3)(c), even when clear opportunities present themselves. For example, the 1991 and 1994 GATT panels concerned with the Mexico/US dispute over tuna fishing felt no need to refer to the techniques for integrating norms of international law which arise outside the GATT into the GATT. The 1994 panel looked at various international environmental agreements, and in so doing referred to Article 31(3)(a) and (b) of the 1969 Vienna Convention but – conspicuously – not 31(3)(c).[81] The failure may reflect a fear that reference to 31(3)(c) might have opened up the self-contained GATT system to the unwelcome influence of external sources, first environment, then labor, and perhaps ultimately human rights.[82] How might the conclusions of those panels have differed if they had taken into account other rules of international environmental law, in application of Article 31(3)(c)? The panels might have considered whether there were any relevant rules of international law which were applicable in relations between the parties, including principles, such as the precautionary principle and the obligation to prevent transboundary environmental harm. If they had identified such rules, they would then have applied them to the facts of a particular case. One can imagine, for example, that the 1994 panel would have indicated that if the dolphins which were being sought to be protected by the United States legislation were internationally recognized as an endangered species (which they were not and still are not), its conclusion might have been different. Such a difference could have been accommodated by construing Article XX of the GATT in accordance with these other rules of international law. If this approach were to be taken, it would tend to enhance the

[80] See J. Combacau and S. Sur, *Droit International Public* (2d edn., Paris, 1995), at 177.

[81] Panel Report on United States Restrictions on Imports of Tuna, 33 *I.L.M.* 839, at para. 5.19.

[82] See J. Cameron, "Introduction," in J. Cameron, P. Demaret, and D. Geradin, *Trade and the Environment: The Search for Balance* (London, 1994), 16.

value and authority of the principles and substantive rules which I have identified in the first part of this chapter.

The debate persists, although there has been some movement in recent decisions of the WTO's new Appellate Body.[83] In its very first decision, also concerning the interpretation of Article XX(g) of GATT 1994, the WTO Appellate Body found that the panel below had failed to apply the basic principles of interpretation reflected in the general rule of interpretation found in Article 31(1) of the 1969 Vienna Convention. According to the Appellate Body this rule had attained the status of a rule of customary or general international law. It was to be applied by reason of Article 3(2) of the WTO Dispute Settlement Understanding,[84] a provision which, according to the Appellate Body, reflected "a measure of the recognition that the General Agreement is not to be read in clinical isolation from public international law."[85] Although the Appellate Body did not invoke Article 31(3)(c), there can be little doubt that this *dicta* indicates a step in that direction. Even more recently, in the Shrimp–Turtle case, the WTO Appellate Body took express account of general international environmental law, although it did not feel the need to refer to Article 31(3)(c).[86]

How might Article 31(3)(c) be developed into an operationally useful tool? Its terms establish a number of parameters. The first point is that for a customary norm to be taken into account in interpreting a treaty it must be "relevant" and it must be "applicable." Assuming these hurdles to have been jumped, then two further points must be considered. The first is that a customary norm is to be *interpreted* by a conventional norm, not applied instead of it (as is the case for Article 30 and successive treaties). In other

[83] On the role of the WTO and the environment see generally the contributions by Professors Roessler, Petersmann, and Barrett, chapters 4, 5, and 6.

[84] Final Act Embodying the Results of the Uruguay Round of Multilateral Trade Negotiations, 15 April 1994, 33 *I.L.M.* 1140, Annex 2: Understanding on Rules and Procedures Governing the Settlement of Disputes 33 *I.L.M.* 1226. Article 3(2) provides: "The dispute settlement system of the WTO is a central element in providing security and predictability to the multilateral trading system. The Members recognize that it serves to preserve the rights and obligations of Members under the covered agreements, and to clarify the existing provisions of those agreements in accordance with customary rules of interpretation of public international law. Recommendations and rulings of the DSB cannot add to or diminish the rights and obligations provided in the covered agreements."

[85] Report of the Appellate Body in United States – Standards for Reformulated and Conventional Gasoline, 35 *I.L.M.* 603 (1996), at 621.

[86] See note 72 above.

words, under Article 31(3)(c) the treaty being interpreted retains a primary role. The customary norm has a secondary role, in the sense that there can be no question of the customary norm displacing the treaty norm, either partly or wholly. The second point is that there "shall be taken into account" the customary norm. This means that in interpreting the customary norm an adjudicatory body is not entitled to exercise discretion. It must "take account" of the customary norm. The words "take account" are nowhere generally defined in international law. The practice described above indicates a range of different approaches and results. Ordinary usage suggests that the formulation is stronger than "take into consideration" but weaker than "apply." Beyond this, what might it mean, and when could it be said that an international tribunal has failed properly to apply Article 31(3)(c)?

One example which springs to mind is the case of *Balmer-Schafroth* v. *Switzerland*, at the European Court of Human Rights.[87] The Court was faced with an application by a group of individuals claiming that Switzerland had violated, *inter alia*, Article 6 of the European Convention on Human Rights,[88] by failing to provide them with access to a "tribunal" within the meaning of that provision to challenge the decision by the Swiss Federal Council to extend the operating license of the Mühleberg nuclear power plant. The applicants believed that the power plant had serious and irremediable construction defects, that it did not satisfy current safety standards, and that its condition entailed a greater than usual risk of accident and damage to them. The applicants also alleged that the procedure followed by the Swiss Federal Council had not been fair. The European Commission found by sixteen votes to twelve that there had been a violation of Article 6. However, by twelve votes to eight the Court overturned the ruling, finding that the applicants had not established "a direct link between the operating conditions of the power station . . . and their right to protection of their physical integrity, as they failed to show that the operation of Mühleberg power station exposed them personally to a danger that was not only serious but also specific and, above all, imminent." It followed from this that

> neither the dangers nor the remedies were established with a degree of probability that made the outcome of the proceedings directly decisive within the meaning of the Court's case-law for the right [under Article 6] relied on by

[87] Judgment of 26 August 1997.

[88] Article 6(1) provides: "In the determination of his civil rights and obligations . . ., everyone is entitled to a fair . . . hearing . . . by [a] . . . tribunal . . ."

the applicants. In the Court's view, the connection between the Federal Council's decision and the right invoked by the applicants was too tenuous and remote.[89]

The majority may have taken a different view if they had had recourse to the body of rules of international environmental law which had developed outside the context of the European Convention. No account had been taken of these rules, a point made forcefully in the principal Dissenting Opinion of Judge Pettiti. Asking whether a local population first had to be irradiated before being entitled to exercise a remedy, he criticized the majority judgment for ignoring "the whole trend of international institutions and public international law towards protecting persons and heritage" as reflected in numerous international instruments, including the Rio agreements, and the precautionary principle and the principle of conservation of the common heritage.

This approach which I am suggesting – and which the European Court did not take – is broadly consistent with that of many municipal courts which, in interpreting domestic legislation, assume that the municipal legislature adopts laws intended to be consistent with international obligations.[90] It is also broadly consistent with that recent international judicial practice which has sought to weave the various strands of international law into a coherent whole.[91] And it is an approach which would tend to unify rather than fragment the international legal order. If, then, environmental considerations are to be given further effect – in particular by appropriate integration into other norms – it is likely that Article 31(3)(c) will be used more frequently.

## IMPROVING IMPLEMENTATION AND ENFORCEMENT

Ensuring compliance by states and other members of the international community with their international environmental obligations has become a matter of increasing concern in international relations in recent years. This is evident from the attention which the issue of compliance received

89 Para. 40.

90 See, for example, the approach of the English Court of Appeal in *Salomon* v. *Commissioners of Customs and Excise* [1967] 2 Q.B. 116 C.A., at 141.

91 See, for example, the effort by the International Court of Justice to meld humanitarian law, human rights law, environmental law, and law governing the use of force into a systematic structure: Advisory Opinion on the *Legality of the Threat or Use of Nuclear Weapons*, ICJ Reports 1996, 226.

during the preparations for UNCED, and in the negotiation and implementation of recent environmental agreements, for example in relation to ozone depletion and climate change. The response to those concerns has resulted in several initiatives to develop further existing mechanisms for implementation, enforcement, and dispute settlement, including the decision in July 1993 by the International Court of Justice to establish a Chamber for Environmental Matters.

At least three reasons underlie the increased attention being paid to compliance with international environmental obligations. First, the nature and extent of international environmental obligations has been transformed in recent years as states take on more environmental commitments which are increasingly stringent and with which they must comply. Second, the growing demands and needs of states and those subject to their jurisdiction for access to natural resources, coupled with a finite, and perhaps even shrinking, available resource base, provide the conditions for increasing conflict over access to natural resources. And third, as international environmental obligations increasingly address fundamental economic interests and needs, states which do not comply with their environmental obligations are perceived to gain unfair, and perhaps unlawful, economic advantage from their environmentally harmful activities in relation to those states which are complying with their obligations. Non-compliance is important because it limits the overall effectiveness of treaties and agreements, undermines international legal commitments, and can lead to conflict between states and instability in the international order. It is widely accepted that the subject requires greater attention and in respect of this existing international legal arrangements and mechanisms may not be adequate.

Addressing compliance will require a comprehensive effort to develop rules and institutional arrangements at three levels: for implementation, enforcement, and dispute settlement. First, with regard to implementation, the provision of technical, financial, and other assistance to states, particularly developing states, points to the growing "internationalization" of the domestic legal process, and an awareness that international environmental law will not achieve its objectives if it does not also take account of the need to and techniques available for improving domestic implementation of international environmental obligations.[92]

[92] See generally J. Cameron, J. Werksman, and P. Roderick eds., *Improving Compliance with International Environmental Law* (Earthscan, 1996).

Second, with regard to enforcement, states remain unwilling, for a variety of reasons, to bring international claims to enforce environmental rights and obligations, and this will further reinforce the supplementary role of international organizations and, to a lesser extent, non-governmental actors in the international enforcement process. Broadening the category of persons formally entitled to identify violations and take measures to remedy them is a process which is underway and which should be further encouraged if states and other members of the international community are to be subjected to the sorts of pressures that will lead them to improve compliance with their obligations. This might be done, for example, by giving non-state actors a formal role in the non-compliance procedure established under the Montreal Protocol. If states are unwilling to give these actors the right to initiate proceedings, they could at the very least give them the right to intervene as third parties or with *amicus* briefs.

And third, as the dispute between Hungary and Slovakia over the Gabcíkovo–Nagymaros dam has shown, the availability of a broad range of mechanisms for dispute settlement, including the compulsory jurisdiction of certain regional and sectoral courts and other international bodies, suggests an important and growing role for independent international adjudication. Whilst I remain skeptical about the need to establish a specialized International Environment Court,[93] there is clearly a need to enhance the ability of existing and new international courts to address environmental issues (in particular the new International Tribunal for the Law of the Sea, the WTO Appellate Body, and the Permanent Court of Arbitration). In this regard, recent progress may be seen in the efforts of the WTO Appellate Body to draw upon general international environmental law.

Finally, Principle 10 of the Rio Declaration and recent developments in the EC reflect the recognition that ensuring effective access to judicial and administrative proceedings, including redress and remedies, is appropriately a matter for consideration by the international community. The decision of the World Bank and other development banks to establish administrative review bodies is as innovative and welcome as the recent refusal of the European Court of Justice to accept that individuals and associations have *locus standi* to challenge the legality of acts of the EC

[93] See P. Sands, "International Environmental Litigation and its Future," 32 *U. Richmond L.R.* 1–23 (1998).

Commission which are alleged to affect the environment is unwelcome (and contrary to international policy if not law).[94]

## Conclusions

It is apparent from the broad review set out in this chapter that environmentally sustainable development is now part of the lexicon of international law. The basic issue now is not whether it is part of the law, but how it is to be applied and developed in a practical manner, and in specific cases. These questions arise both in a legislative and a judicial context. Recent case law from the International Court of Justice and the Appellate Body of the WTO indicates the difficulties faced by judges in applying normative elements of "sustainable development."[95]

The application of "sustainable development" itself raises broader issues. I have indicated the extent to which different bodies are now faced with the need to develop a more sophisticated approach to risk assessment and decisionmaking in the face of scientific uncertainty, seeking to apply one of the basic principles of "sustainable development," namely the precautionary principle. There is clearly a need for greater policy coordination on the approach which international bodies should take to this question, as indicated by the current debate on whether, and if so to what extent, commercial growing of genetically modified seeds should be permitted. The differences of approach – even between Europe and the United States – suggest that there may not be room for a single approach, that risk taking and risk assessment must be determined in the specific cultural and societal context in which they are being applied. To that extent, "globalization" remains something of a misnomer. This of course raises the related question concerning the proper level for decisionmaking in the areas of economic and environmental relations: is it to be sub-national, national, regional, or global, or a combination of these different levels? This issue is not peculiar to international lawmaking and development, but applies equally within single states (the United States) and economic agglomerations of states (the European Union). However, it is clear that much greater thought will have to be given to the appropriateness of different levels of

[94] Case T-585/93 *Stichting Greenpeace Council and Others* v. *EC Commission*, 10 *J. Env. L.* 331 (1998).

[95] See P. Sands, "International Courts and the Application of the Concept of 'sustainable development'," 1998 *Ybk. UN* 389–405.

decisionmaking in the fields of environment and sustainable development, and the factors which should be taken into account in determining the right level. This, in turn, raises issues about the current arrangements for international legislative efforts in this field, and the need to avoid duplicative or even incompatible or inconsistent efforts at law-development.

Overarching each of these issues is an even bigger question, and one which is central to the law of sustainable development: how are the different areas of international law (trade, human rights, environment, and so on) to intersect and interrelate? As described in this chapter, the techniques of international law designed to achieve an integrated approach are rudimentary, to say the least. The prospects for a more integrated approach are scarcely assisted by the fragmentary and disunified arrangements the international community has put in place to ensure compliance and resolve disputes.

Each of these matters suggests that the law of sustainable development is still finding its feet. The international community, such as it exists, has at its disposal a system of international law which can hardly be expected, at this time at least, to master the complex societal, technical, and cultural matters which will have to be balanced in the quest to attain "sustainable development." The fact that they are now being addressed holistically for the first time as a result of the emergence of "sustainable development" indicates the contribution the term might make to the development of international law. But it has to be recognized that these are still early days, and we cannot expect too much from a legal system and its institutional structures which remain basic, certainly as compared to arrangements within certain – but by no means all – national jurisdictions.

# 13

## MARKETS AND SUSTAINABILITY

GEOFFREY HEAL

### Introduction

PROVIDING A definition is a good way to start talking about sustainability. There is no simple, operational, and generally agreed definition that we can lift from the literature, so let me suggest one. Sustainability is doing things that we can safely continue indefinitely: doing things that can be continued over long periods without unacceptable consequences, or without unacceptable risks of unacceptable consequences. This seems to capture much of what is implicit in general discussion, although it is perhaps more focused than the legal principles traced by Sands.[1] Most people think of current fisheries policies as unsustainable: clearly they are so according to this definition. Energy policies, involving the emission of greenhouse gases, imply an unacceptable risk of climate change, and are unsustainable both in common parlance and by this definition. So are

[1] The definition that I offer is close to the definition in J. P. Holdren, G. C. Daily, and P. R. Ehrlich, "The Meaning of Sustainability: Biogeophysical Aspects," in M. Munasinghe and W. Shearer eds., *Defining and Measuring Sustainability: Biogeophysical Aspects* (World Bank, Washington D.C., 1995), and is the one used in G. M. Heal, *Valuing the Future: Economic Theory and Sustainability* (Columbia University Press, 1998). The Brundtland Report defines sustainable development as "development that meets the needs of the present without compromising the ability of future generations to meet their own needs." While eloquent, this is very thin on operational content. See World Commission on Environment and Development, *Our Common Future* (Oxford University Press, 1987). Sands suggests that, as used legally, sustainability involves four components. One is a commitment to preserve natural resources for the benefit of present and future generations. A second refers to "prudent," "rational," "wise," or "appropriate" use of natural resources. A third is an equitable use of resources, and a fourth implies that the environmental objectives are integrated into development plans, and vice versa. See chapter by Philippe Sands (Chapter 12).

important aspects of agricultural policies, those that result in loss of soil fertility, or in massive run-offs of nutrients into rivers, lakes, and ground waters.[2]

Given a working definition, a natural next step from an economic perspective is to ask: Do existing institutions lead us to make sustainable choices? This question is clearly rhetorical: the examples cited above show that the answer is "no." Two more sets of questions follow immediately from this: Why not? And: What can we do about this?

I think we can group the answers to "Why not?" under three general headings. The first heading is that we do not recognize the great value of many environmental systems: we are not conscious of the importance of natural ecosystems to modern societies. The second – and this is related to the first heading – is that the economic incentives are wrong. Finally, we place too little value on the future, and many of the benefits from environmental conservation, from sustainable economic and social organization, are far into the future. I argue here that changes in the economic and legal framework, changes that in some cases are already under way, can make a significant contribution to the first two problems here. The third is more complex: better use of markets can certainly help, but a complete solution will require more far-reaching changes.

## The importance of nature

How important is nature to modern societies? Because of our technological sophistication, we can easily come to see ourselves as remote from and independent of nature. This attitude is wrong and dangerous, and contributes very directly to the environmental problems that we face. Natural ecosystems provide critical infrastructure for all human societies. Societies derive a wide array of important economic and life-support benefits from biodiversity and the natural ecosystems in which it exists.[3] Biologists use the term "ecosystem services" to refer to these benefits. Ecosystem services are the conditions and processes through which natural ecosystems, and the species that are a part of them, sustain and fulfill human life. These services yield ecosystem goods, such as seafood, wild game, forage, timber, biomass

[2] For more detail, see P. M. Vitousek et al. "Human Domination of Earth's Ecosystems," 277 *Science* 494–99 (25 July 1997).

[3] This discussion draws heavily on, and at some points quotes, G. D. Daily, *Nature's Services: Societal Dependence on Natural Ecosystems* (Washington: Islan Press, 1997).

fuels, natural fibers, many pharmaceuticals, industrial products, and their precursors. The harvest and trade of these goods represent an important and familiar part of the economy. Natural ecosystems also perform less-appreciated but critical life-support services, upon which the well-being of all societies depends. Daily[4] lists these as:

purification of air and water
mitigation of droughts and floods
generation and preservation of soils and renewal of their fertility
detoxification and decomposition of wastes
pollination of crops and natural vegetation
dispersal of seeds
cycling and movement of nutrients
control of the vast majority of potential agricultural pests
maintenance of biodiversity
protection of coastal shores from erosion by waves
protection from the sun's harmful ultraviolet rays
stabilization of the climate
moderation of weather extremes and their impacts
provision of aesthetic beauty and intellectual stimulation that lift the human spirit.

This array of services is generated by a complex interplay of biological, geological, and chemical cycles driven by solar energy and operating across a wide range of spatial and temporal scales. Soil fertility, for instance, is a product both of bacteria, whose fleeting lives may take place in a space smaller than the period at the end of this sentence, as well as of the aeonic, planet-wide cycles of major chemical elements such as carbon and nitrogen. Pest control is created by both natural enemies (e.g., birds; bats; parasitic wasps, ladybugs, spiders, and other predacious arthropods; fungi; viruses) and by climate patterns generated globally. The stratospheric ozone layer that shields Earth's surface from ultraviolet radiation was originally produced primarily by the photosynthetic activities of blue-green algae and by photochemical reactions occurring high in the atmosphere.[5] Ecosystem services operate on such a grand scale and in such intricate and

[4] *Ibid.*

[5] These examples are taken verbatim from Daily, *Nature's Services*, which contains many others.

little-explored ways that most could not be replaced by technology.[6] Above I listed fourteen important ecosystem services. Some of these could be replaced in part by synthetic alternatives, but for the great majority not even a partial replacement is currently possible. We have no substitutes for many critical services provided by the natural world: we are therefore very dependent on nature but alarmingly unaware of this and fail to capture this dependence in our economic decisions.

## Incentives and markets

What does it mean to say that the economic incentives with respect to resource maintenance and use are wrong? A preliminary estimate of the economic value of the services provided to humans by ecological systems and the national capital stocks which produce them is in the range of \$16–54 trillion annually, compared to a global gross national product of \$18 trillion annually.[7] Most of these services are not captured in markets or conventional economic accounts. Accordingly, economic incentives to maintain these services and the stock of national capital are often absent or inadequate. In many cases the costs of maintaining these services will fall on one group and the benefits will accrue to others. There are often no market or other institutional mechanisms to charge the beneficiaries in order to reimburse and provide incentives to those in a position to maintain the services in question.

A concrete case will make the point. Consider conservation of Amazonian rain forests. This has some costs and some benefits. I believe, as do most people who have thought carefully about this, that the benefits greatly outweigh the costs. The costs are borne by people who live in and around the forest: they are opportunity costs, costs of not being able to use the land for cash crops or for ranching, and of not being able to sell the timber. Some of the benefits, on the other hand, accrue to everyone: to you, to me, to all humans, because they are in the form of carbon sequestration and biodiversity support. Others accrue to people in Brazil, but not to those in the forest region: these are benefits from stream and flood control, regional climate control, ecotourism, and many others. So in essence one

[6] For more details see Daily, *Nature's Services.*

[7] R. Costanza et al., "The Value of the World's Ecosystem Services and National Capital," 389 *Nature* 253 (1997).

set of people pays the bill and another set eats the meal. This is obviously not a stable situation: the bill payers will drop out. We can only expect the forest to be conserved if some of the benefits from conservation accrue to the bill payers. The essence of this rain forest example could be replicated many times.

How can we change institutions to avoid this problem? Four examples will provide much of the groundwork for arguments about how more effective use of markets can realign incentives and at the same time lead to a more realistic appreciation of the value of natural ecosystems.

## GROWING CARBON AND THE KYOTO PROTOCOL

The Kyoto Protocol provides an interesting example of how markets might provide powerful incentives for environmental conservation.[8] The Protocol contains provisions for carbon sequestration credits: countries that remove carbon from the atmosphere, for example by growing trees, will receive credits for this in the form of tradable greenhouse gas emission permits. No one knows what exactly the value of these permits will be. Preliminary economic calculations[9] suggest that their value could be in the range $10 to $50 per ton of carbon or equivalent. What would this mean for the economics of conserving tropical forests? Again, we do not know for sure, but we can do some rough calculations. Growing moist tropical forests remove carbon from the air at a rate in the range of 7 to 20 tons per hectare per year, possibly more.[10] Taking these two ranges of numbers together, we see that growing forests could be remunerated by carbon sequestration credits at a rate of $70 to $1,000 per hectare per year. This is a lot of money: ranches in Costa Rica, for example, make profits of at most $100 to $125 per hectare per year. Reforesting has a one-off cost of planting the seedlings, which can be as high as $900 per hectare.[11] Even with this initial cost, it seems possible that if the world as a whole were to pay for carbon sequestration, just one of the many services of tropical forests, it could change radically the economics of forest conservation. On a very small scale, some of this is already hap-

[8] For further discussions of the Kyoto Protocol see the chapters by Stewart and Chichilnisky (chapters 7 and 9).

[9] Conducted by the Program on Information and Resources at Columbia University using a modified version of the OECD's GREEN computer model of the global economy.

[10] Personal communication, Steve Pacala, Ecology Department, Princeton.

[11] Personal communication, Daniel Botkin.

pening through the schemes for joint implementation encouraged by the Global Environment Facility and the World Bank.

Analytically this example demonstrates the following point: the sequestration of carbon by forests is a global public good. By stabilizing the climate it benefits all of humankind. Typically it is difficult for the providers of such a service to appropriate all or even a significant part of the benefits, so that it is underprovided, as we noted above. A combination of a tradable permit system for greenhouse gas emissions plus a regime of giving permits for sequestration may allow providers of sequestration services to capture the full economic value of what they provide.[12]

## WATERSHEDS

Another example of how new institutional arrangements to charge beneficiaries can provide the resources and incentives needed to maintain national services is already up and operating. Ninety percent of New York's water comes from a watershed in the Catskill Mountains. Until recently purification processes carried out by roots and micro-organisms in the soil as the water percolates through, together with filtration and sedimentation occurring during this flow, were sufficient to cleanse the water to US Environmental Protection Agency standards. Recently sewage, fertilizer, and pesticides in the soil reduced the efficacy of this process, to the point where New York's water no longer met EPA standards. The city was faced with a choice: restore the integrity of the Catskill ecosystems, or else build a filtration plant at a capital cost of $6–8 billion, plus running costs of the order of $300 million annually. In other words, New York had to invest in environmental conservation or in treatment facilities.

Which was more attractive? Investment in conservation in this case meant buying land in and around the watershed so that its use could be restricted, and subsidizing the construction of better sewage treatment plants. The total cost of measures of this type needed to restore the watershed is expected to be in the range of $1–1.5 billion. So investing $1–1.5 billion in conservation could save an investment of $6–8 billion in treatment facilities, giving an internal rate of return of between 90 percent and

[12] The assertion that markets give appropriate incentives for providing public goods is a surprising one to most economists in view of the free-rider problem. For a detailed analysis, see G. Chichilnisky and G. M. Heal eds., *Environmental Markets* (Columbia University Press, 1998).

170 percent.[13] This return is an order of magnitude higher than is normally available, particularly on relatively riskless investments. These calculations are conservative, as they consider only one watershed service, although watersheds, which are typically forested, often provide other important services.

In 1997 New York City floated an environmental bond issue, and will use the proceeds to restore the functioning of the watershed ecosystems responsible for water purification. The savings produced by using a conservation strategy rather than "end of pipe" technological controls will more than meet the interest and capital costs of the bonds. An alternative means of financing the conservation measures would have been market techniques for securitization of assets. Securitization involves issuing tradable contracts in the form of securities that entitle the owners to a fraction of the benefits from a venture. In this case, the securities would entitle their owners to a fraction of the cost savings resulting from watershed restoration: they would be "watershed securities." In exchange for the securities, investors would contribute the capital needed for restoration. In effect they would invest in the restoration and receive in return a share of the benefits. Securitization is already used in securitizing the savings from increased energy efficiency in buildings. Under many securitization arrangements, owners are contractually entitled to a specified fraction of the savings. Typically these contracts are tradable, issued to the providers of capital, and can be sold by them, even before the savings are realized. This is a way of making investment in saving energy attractive to the investing public and institutions: it does not imply any transfer of ownership of the underlying asset. The US Department of Energy has a standard protocol for estimating the savings from enhanced building energy efficiency and several financial agencies are willing to accept these estimates of energy savings as collateral for loans.

Thus, in the New York watershed case, the city could have opened a "watershed savings account" into which it paid a fraction of the costs avoided by not having to build and run a filtration plant, which would pay investors for the use of their capital. The purpose of securitization is to make it possible to finance projects such as New York's watershed restoration without using the credit of the City itself, an important issue in devel-

[13] The discussion of the New York watershed case is taken from G. Chichilnisky and G. M. Heal, "Economic Returns from the Biosphere," 391 *Nature* 629–30 (12 February 1998).

oping countries whose metropolitan areas often do not have credit ratings comparable to New York's.

One could take the introduction of market forces a step further. Imagine a corporation managing the restoration of New York's watershed. It has the right to sell to New York City some of the benefits of the services of the ecosystem by providing water meeting EPA standards. Ownership of this right would enable it to raise capital from capital markets, to be used for meeting the costs of conserving the watershed. Of course some regulation would be needed: for example, the corporation would be a natural monopoly so that it would be appropriate to regulate its prices. It would also be reasonable to place some restrictions on the modifications that it could make to the natural ecosystems in the watershed area.

Analytically, what is the general point illustrated by this example? It is that water is a good for which individuals or municipalities are willing to pay. They are willing to pay for quality as well as quantity, and this in effect puts a potential price on the water management and purification services provided by a watershed. The demand for high quality water generates an indirect demand, what economists call a derived demand, for watersheds. In this case there is a possible replacement for the ecosystems services provided by the watershed: this is the filtration plant. The cost of this alternative – in the New York case $8 billion plus – puts an upper limit on what it would make sense to spend on restoring the watershed, looking at it only from the water management and purification perspective. Of course, the watershed may have many other values to society: in this case, the Catskills are a much-valued recreational area, and society has a substantial willingness-to-pay for this in addition to the watershed services.

## ECOTOURISM

Another powerful example comes from South Africa, in the form of the Conservation Corporation, or Conscorp.[14] This imaginative venture has capitalized on the demand for ecotourism and hunting: this demand is such

[14] This website is *http://www.world-travel-net.co.uk/conscorp*. For more discussion see *http://economics.iucn.org*. A paper on the IUCN website by Terry Anderson, "Enviro-Capitalists: Why and How to Preserve Their Habitat," provided most of the material on Conscorp used here. The exact address is *http://economics.iucn.org/96–01-14.pdf*. Also of interest is Michael 't sas-Rolfes, "The Use of Auctions as an Incentive Measure for Wildlife Conservation", *http://economics.iucn.org/96-03-16.pdf*.

that land yielding $25 per hectare annually for ranching and $70 per hectare for cropping can yield between $200 and $300 per hectare as part of a reserve managed for tourism or hunting. Conscorp contracts with landowners to incorporate their land in its reserves: it does not buy the land outright. Landowners have to maintain their land in accordance with tightly specified regulations and to stock it with specified animals. Conscorp manages the business part of the operation, bringing tourists and hunters, building facilities and providing guides and vehicles. To date they have restored several hundred thousand hectares of farmland to their original ecosystems. An interesting detail is that the presence of lions will add about 30 percent to the revenues from an area, so that the incentive to restock with lions is great. Supporting lions, at the top of the food chain, requires maintenance of most of the rest of the chain beneath them: what the lions eat, what the lion's food eats, and so on. There is a strong economic incentive to do a thorough job of restoration. This is in fact clear from the very explicit rules used by Conscorp, whose Articles of Association for a specific reserve state that its aims are "to promote and conserve endemic wildlife within the confines of the area; to establish the Reserve as a sanctuary in perpetuity for endemic wildlife and habitat so as to ensure sustainable resource utilization; to endeavor to increase the area of the Reserve; and to maximize the long term economic and ecological value of the properties." Landowners even agree not to keep any domestic animals, dogs and cats included. An interesting quote from a South African writer captures some of what is happening in this movement:

> The interesting thing is that untold hundreds of thousands of hectares and morgen that even a few years ago were scrub grazing for a mixture of game and cattle have now been entirely allocated to game. Why? Economics, as always. Game pays its own way, eats nearly anything, is more resistant to disease and predators and generally produces a higher and better use for the land. Even the old enemies become assets to the farmer who switches from cattle to game. One friend of mine used to lose as many as thirty calves a season to leopards. Now those same leopards are worth a cool $3,000 to $4,000 to sport hunters, not a bad trade-off for animals that caused a liability of well over ten grand and had to be poisoned! Tell me, is that bad for leopards?[15]

Similar developments are occurring in Kenya. The land there is less productive and the country has less infrastructure, so that numbers are all

[15] P. H. Capstick, cited by Anderson, "Enviro-Capitalists."

lower. But they tell the same story in terms of incentives: in the Laikipia region of Kenya ecotourism can bring $5 to $30 per hectare per year, compared with less than $2 per hectare per year for traditional livestock husbandry.[16]

## PROSPECTING FOR PHARMACEUTICALS

Bioprospecting is another activity that can yield cash for conservation. Bioprospecting means seeking for leads in the development of new drugs, or new chemicals for use in agriculture, by looking at biological resources. As a matter of fact, over 60 percent by value of prescription drugs in the US are or were initially derived from plants and insects, so this is a reasonable place to start looking. The key point is that certain plants and animals are known to produce substances that are highly active pharmacologically. Plants that live in insect-infested areas produce substances that are poisonous to insects, and these have been used as the basis for insecticides. Some snakes produce venom that paralyzes parts of the nervous system, and others produce venom that reduces blood pressure. Other insects produce anti-coagulants. All of these have been adapted for medical use. Observations of this type have led most major drug companies to pursue bioprospecting as a way of finding new pharmacologically active substances to serve as a basis for drug development. Typically they have sought these compounds in the tropics, in areas where there is extensive inter-species competition. They have been willing to pay quite substantial sums for access to these regions, and have made deals with host countries that involve giving hosts a royalty on the products that might eventually be based on this prospecting. Such royalties could be large relative to the incomes of the countries concerned. Preliminary calculations have suggested that in some of the world's biodiversity hotspots, the right to bioprospect may be worth as much as $9,000 per hectare, equal to about a century of ranching income.[17]

Here the economic point is recognizing the value of the knowledge that can be derived from natural systems, controlling access to the systems in order to lay the foundation for contracts between hosts and bioprospectors

[16] D. I. Rubenstein, "Science and the Pursuit of a Sustainable World," 3 *Ecol. Applications* 585–87 (1993).

[17] See G. C. Rausser and A. A. Small, "Valuing Research Leads: Bioprospecting and the Conservation of Genetic Resources," paper presented at the Conference on Managing Human-Dominated Ecosystems at the Missouri Botanical Gardens, March 1998.

that grant access, and then establishing intellectual property rights in the knowledge gained from the prospecting. The property rights are needed to ensure that some of the value ultimately created by that knowledge returns to the host.

These examples – carbon sequestration and the Kyoto Protocol, the New York watershed, Conscorp and bioprospecting – make two points. One is that, with the right institutional structures and property rights in place, the market can be used to attach an economic value to certain natural assets and the ecosystem services that they provide. The second is that, if this is done, the incentive problem can be corrected. If the market will yield a higher return through conservation than through any other use, then entrepreneurs will find a way to conserve. Of course, I have cited particular examples: they do not imply that all valuable natural capital can be conserved this way. What they do suggest is that we should look more into the potential of this approach. This approach is completely consistent with the Convention on Biological Diversity, which states (in Article 11) that "Each Contracting Party shall, as far as possible and appropriate, adopt economically sound measures that act as incentives for the conservation and sustainable use of biological diversity." For example, preliminary estimates suggest that up to 10 percent of the land area of the US, and a comparable or greater area worldwide, could be economically conserved on the grounds of watershed protection.[18] I am not aware of comparable studies for ecotourism, but this has certainly become a major industry in several regions of the world, including Central America and East and Southern Africa. Some countries in these regions are now earning about one third of their foreign exchange from ecotourism.

A final observation: the different ways of obtaining a return from ecosystem conservation described in the examples above are not mutually exclusive. A forest could obtain returns from carbon sequestration, bioprospecting, managing a watershed, and ecotourism. In fact, the region of the Mata Atlantica (Brazilian coastal rain forest) inland from Rio de Janeiro is in a position to do exactly this. It contains the watershed for Rio, supports

[18] These numbers come from "A Business Plan for Ecosystem Services: Extending the New York City Watershed Model to Other Geographic Regions and Other Ecosystem Services," paper presented by W. V. Reid of World Resources Institute at the Conference on Managing Human-Dominated Ecosystems at the Missouri Botanical Gardens, March 1998. In this paper, Reid begins to explore the scope for generalizing the New York case to other regions.

a wide range of endemic species, sequesters carbon, and acts as a magnet for tourists. Currently the region obtains a financial return only on the last of these activities. Institutional initiatives that could generate an economic return for the first three activities as well could enhance incentives for ecosystem conservation.

## Valuing the future

Valuing the future is critical to sustainability. Environmental assets provide flows of services over long periods of time. New York's Catskills watershed has purified water and controlled stream flow for hundreds if not thousands of years, and if left intact will continue to do so for at least as long again. Insects have pollinated flowers for much, much longer, and could continue as long again if not driven to extinction by pesticides.[19] No human systems have such lifespans. Physical assets produced by humans last perhaps ten, perhaps fifty, years: at best their lifespans are measured in decades rather than centuries or millennia. Knowledge and culture are the only assets we produce that can rival natural assets in their durability: Shakespeare thrives at half a millennium, and Plato and Pythagorus at several millennia. Because of the totally different time scales of the capital assets that humans and nature produce, the techniques that we use for valuing capital assets really cannot be applied to natural assets. We value the capital that we produce by cost-benefit analysis, taking as its benefits the present discounted value of the flow of services that it produces. By discounting at rates in the range of 5 to 10 percent, as is common in many contexts, we in effect choose an implicit time horizon, a date beyond which nothing matters. This is in the region of twenty to thirty years. At a 5 percent discount rate, one dollar twenty years hence has a present value of 22 cents and at 10 percent its value is 5 cents. When we apply this kind of calculation to environmental assets, we are cutting out most of the contributions that they will make to human societies: we are taking account of twenty years of the contributions of assets that could contribute, at no extra cost, for twenty decades or perhaps twenty centuries. Clearly we are undervaluing them grossly.

[19] See G. P. Nabhan and S. L. Buchmann, "Services Provided by Pollinators," chapter 8 of Daily, *Nature's Services.*

## DISCOUNTING

Discounting has always been a source of controversy between economists and those from other disciplines interested in the environment. After all, if you discount at 5 percent over 100 years, then you are giving a future dollar a present equivalent of only two-thirds of a cent. It is hard for a non-economist to reconcile this with taking the future at all seriously. Perhaps less well known is the fact that discounting has also been a source of controversy within the economics profession. Frank Ramsey, the first person to think seriously about dynamic economics and author of a seminal 1926 article on long-run planning, commented that discounting "is ethically indefensible and arises merely from the weakness of the imagination."[20] His contemporary Roy Harrod added that it is a "polite expression for rapacity and the conquest of reason by passion."[21] These are strong words, from people who clearly believed that they were right.

Why has discounting been controversial in economics, and why has the controversy been particularly acute in the environmental area? The key point about the environmental area is that it often forces one to consider long time horizons. In the climate change area, a century is the minimum time horizon that makes sense. Probably it is too short. The same is true about species extinction and biodiversity loss and disposal of nuclear waste. Scientific processes relating to the environment naturally unfold over this type of horizon. Such time horizons are completely outside the normal range in economic decisionmaking. Corporations and governments normally look at most decades ahead, rather than centuries. The longest "normal" time horizons in economics are those for infrastructure investments such as power stations, where thirty years is a possible horizon. Five to fifteen years is much more common as a planning horizon, and is still longer than the average. Horizons of this type are not long enough to raise one of the issues central to long-term environmental problems, namely equity between generations. For five to fifteen years in the context of business plans, the efficient use of money is the central issue. For a century or more, when considering the planet's life-support systems, equity and "sustainability" naturally come to the center of the stage (although efficient use of capital does not leave the stage). Thus, normal intertemporal economic

[20] F. Ramsey, "A Mathematical Theory of Saving," 38 *Economic Journal* 543 (1928).

[21] R. Harrod, *Towards a Dynamic Economics* (London: Macmillan, 1948).

problems and long-term environmental problems have quite different time scales and involve different issues. It is natural that the methodology for one does not fit the other perfectly.

In resolving long-term environmental issues, we want to achieve two aims: one is to strike a fair balance between the present and the future, and the other is to use our limited economic resources, including societal capital, efficiently. What is involved in efficient use of capital? Efficient use of capital requires that the rates of return on all types of capital and durable goods and equipment (including durable natural systems) are the same. Establishing markets in all such goods, or in their services, will meet this condition. Capital will flow towards investments in activities where it is relatively more productive, in terms of market value of goods and services, until the return on capital, and its cost, is equal for all investments. We need a cost for capital to make sure we do not waste it: however green your values, you certainly want to use society's capital as productively as possible. However, establishing a market price for the use of capital and discounting the future are two quite different matters. The first does not imply the second.[22]

How do we strike a proper balance between present and future? This is a harder question to answer: in the end, this is a matter of ethical judgment, the same category of judgment as we make when we say that a particular distribution of income is acceptable, or is too unequal. This does not mean that it is just a matter of opinion, and that all opinions are equally good. There are some basic principles that we can establish, and these can provide valuable guides. But in the end, there is no purely scientific definition of a "proper" balance between present and future. The controversy within economics over discounting arises from disagreements about what is a proper balance, plus perhaps some confusion of the issues of intergenerational equity and efficient use of capital and a lack of clarity on how they interact.

What about adopting a more future-friendly decisionmaking algorithm than exponential discounting? There are approaches to valuing income streams over long time periods that give more weight to the future than the standard practice, and that are just as compelling and logical, indeed from many perspectives even more so.[23] In fact, empirical studies seem to suggest

[22] See, e.g,. P. S. Dasgupta and G. M. Heal, *Economic Theory and Exhaustible Resources* (Cambridge University Press, 1979), chapter 7.

[23] They are discussed at length in Heal, *Valuing the Future.* An interesting possibility is to be found in G. Chichilnisky, "An Axiomatic Approach to Sustainable Development," 13(2) *Social Choice and Welfare* 219–48 (1996).

that individuals do not follow the standard model when making choices over time. It appears that most individuals use discount rates that are lower, the longer the time horizon that they consider.[24] Most of the alternatives are consistent with the competitive market, in the sense that they imply intertemporal price sequences that reflect maximizing behavior, producing socially optimal outcomes. However, maximizing behavior and the associated social optimum may not mean maximizing the present value of profits: it may mean maximizing the long-run level of profits or some combination of this objective and the present value of profits. Intuitively this makes sense: fishing fleets are clearly seeking to maximize short-run profits to the detriment of long-run profits – paying more attention to the latter would lead to quite different behavior that would be more consistent with the longer run welfare of society. Unfortunately it is not clear what it would take to change such behavior patterns throughout most of society. Some points are clear, however. Certain types of institutions, in particular NGOs (non-governmental organizations), make it their business to lobby for future-oriented decisions, and to try to tip the scales in that direction. In the UK, for example, the National Trust has as its primary purpose the purchase of land and properties of outstanding environmental or historical importance, to be held in trust for the future. The Nature Conservancy in the US has a similar role vis-à-vis the environment. More should be done, but these institutions indicate a potential mechanism for promoting and implementing future-oriented decisions even in a society where most decisions involve short time horizons.

## LIQUIDITY CONSTRAINTS AND CAPITAL MARKETS

Existing financial markets can in some cases be useful in conservation, without any changes, by providing current liquidity for investments in

[24] This pattern may reflect a tendency by people to respond to proportional rather than absolute changes in distance in time. Postponing a reward by one year from the first to the second year, and by one year from the twentieth to the twenty-first, are both one-year postponements, but one matters a lot and the other does not. One is a doubling and the other a 5 percent change. If it is the percentage change that matters and not the number of years, then people discount according to the logarithm of time, thus: $e^{-0.1 \log t}$ for a 10 percent discount rate. This leads to a far higher relative value in the future. For example, discounting logarithmically gives almost 14,000 times more weight, in terms of net present value, to a benefit provided 100 years in the future than discounting exponentially.

ecosystem conservation that provide returns over a long term. Suppose that a developing country has valuable environmental assets, such as forests, and can derive some income from these, for example by carbon sequestration or bioprospecting. But suppose in addition that this country is very poor, and is in a state of economic and financial crisis, in desperate need of income. The country faces a steady stream of income continuing into the future from its environmental assets, but has an acute need for income now. It would gladly trade future income for present income, but the inability to do so might lead it to choose the strategy of selling forests as timber, which gives lots of cash now and none in the future, rather that conserving them, which gives less cash now but more in total. Here financial markets can help: one of their main purposes is to move income over time, and let people and institutions spend now in anticipation of future income. This is exactly what a mortgage does: lets the borrowers consume in excess of income now in exchange for consuming less than income in the future.

In a situation such as the one we have described, financial institutions or markets could readily provide current income against the security of repayment from future environmental income. To put flesh on these bones, consider the case of Costa Rica and Merck. Costa Rica's InBio signed an agreement with Merck under which it provides Merck with specimens to be tested for pharmaceutical potential, in exchange for a one-time payment and a royalty on any drug eventually produced. The right to a royalty is a right to a part of the profits of specified Merck products. This right could eventually produce huge payments, but these may be twenty or more years in the future: it can take fifteen years to take a drug from conception to market. Costa Rica has here a right to an uncertain future income. Some or all of this right could, however, be sold for cash now: it constitutes a form of security deriving its value from profits on certain Merck products. If Costa Rica were to suffer from an acute cash crisis, this ability to convert the agreement into cash now would enable it to bring future income forward and avoid pressure to liquidate environmental assets because of cash constraints.

The use of financial markets to anticipate income does not change fundamentally the way we value the future relative to the present. It allows us to avoid situations where current income shortages might force us into short-sighted choices, which we will subsequently regret. A current income crisis can push the value of the future into insignificance relative to the present. The ability to anticipate future income can avoid this trap.

## Conclusions

What can we conclude about market forces and sustainability? Which services of the environment are amenable to management by the market? One clear prerequisite is that the ecosystem to be conserved must provide goods or services to which a commercial value can be attached. Watersheds, for example, satisfy this criterion: drinkable water is becoming increasingly scarce, and indeed the availability of such water is one of the main constraints on health improvements in many poorer countries.

Commercial value of an ecosystem service is necessary but not sufficient for privatization: some of that value has to be appropriable by the producer. A critical issue in deciding whether ecosystem services can be privatized is the extent to which they are public goods. Pure public goods are challenging to privatize: they are goods which if provided for one are provided for all. It is hard, though often not impossible, to exclude from benefiting from their provision those who do not contribute to their costs, so that their providers cannot appropriate all of their returns. Water quality is a public good, in the sense that if it is improved for one user of a watershed, then it is improved for all. But the consumption of water itself is excludable, so the watershed case involves bundling a public with a private good. Ecotourism is also a hybrid: the existence of stable populations of flora and fauna is a public good from which everyone benefits to some degree. But this is not what Conscorp and its competitors are selling: they are selling room-nights in game lodges, meals, the services of guides, and many other accouterments of up-market tourism. These are private goods. So in both of these cases conservation conserves a public good (water quality, stream flow, wildlife), but the incentive to do this comes from the resulting enhanced ability to sell an associated private good. The presence of a public good means that the market incentives to conserve are less strong than required for overall economic efficiency, but by capturing some of the value of that good the market improves on the pre-existing situation. The same is true of bioprospecting, although in this case there is the additional interesting point that the final product, knowledge, has many of the features of a public good, and so has to be protected by intellectual property rights regimes.

Carbon sequestration is different. Here the market is paying for a pure public good. Nonetheless, the market can be used to help produce this public good in a cost-effective manner through national legislation or an international agreement that limits the extent to which the atmosphere can be used for disposing of residuals such as carbon dioxide and creating a limited stock of use rights that can be allocated to private owners and traded. The use of such techniques to address problems such as sulfur dioxide emissions or greenhouse gases is discussed further in other contributions to this book.[25] In this case the conditions for overall economic efficiency depend on the initial distribution of use rights, leading to an interesting connection between efficiency and distribution.[26]

To summarize: to date, markets have not performed notably well in conserving our planet's environment. Indeed, they have done quite the opposite. But this poor record is not intrinsic in markets. They can be reoriented in a positive direction, in which case their potential for good is immense. Markets need legal infrastructure, as we see from the role of the Securities and Exchange Commission in financial markets in the US, from the legislative and administrative measures taken in the US to establish an emissions trading system to reduce sulfur dioxide emissions, and from the shortcomings of markets without legal infrastructure in Russia. Lawyers and legal scholars with an environmental bent should be focusing on how to play a similar enabling role more broadly. Markets may not be able to do the entire job of maintaining ecosystem services and the stock of natural capital. Direct regulation will be needed as well. But redeployment and restructuring of markets and the development of new forms of property rights can go a long way towards promoting ecosystem conservation in an economically and socially efficient manner.

25 See the chapters by Stewart, Rehbinder, and Chichilnisky.

26 See Chichilnisky and Heal, *Environmental Markets.*

# INDEX